NATO ASI Series

Advanced Science Institutes Series

A series presenting the results of activities sponsored by the NATO Science Committee, which aims at the dissemination of advanced scientific and technological knowledge, with a view to strengthening links between scientific communities.

The Series is published by an international board of publishers in conjunction with the NATO Scientific Affairs Division

A Life Sciences B Physics	Plenum Publishing Corporation London and New York
C Mathematical and Physical Sciences D Behavioural and Social Sciences E Applied Sciences	Kluwer Academic Publishers Dordrecht, Boston and London
F Computer and Systems Sciences G Ecological Sciences H Cell Biology I Global Environmental Change	Springer-Verlag Berlin Heidelberg New York London Paris Tokyo Hong Kong Barcelona Budapest

NATO-PCO DATABASE

The electronic index to the NATO ASI Series provides full bibliographical references (with keywords and/or abstracts) to more than 30000 contributions from international scientists published in all sections of the NATO ASI Series. Access to the NATO-PCO DATABASE compiled by the NATO Publication Coordination Office is possible in two ways:

- via online FILE 128 (NATO-PCO DATABASE) hosted by ESRIN, Via Galileo Galilei, I-00044 Frascati, Italy.
- via CD-ROM "NATO-PCO DATABASE" with user-friendly retrieval software in English, French and German (© WTV GmbH and DATAWARE Technologies Inc. 1989).

The CD-ROM can be ordered through any member of the Board of Publishers or through NATO-PCO, Overijse, Belgium.

The ASI Series Books Published as a Result of Activities of the Special Programme on ADVANCED EDUCATIONAL TECHNOLOGY

This book contains the proceedings of a NATO Advanced Research Workshop held within the activities of the NATO Special Programme on Advanced Educational Technology, running from 1988 to 1993 under the auspices of the NATO Science Committee.

The books published so far as a result of the activities of the Special Programme are:

Vol. F 67: Designing Hypermedia for Learning. Edited by D. H. Jonassen and H. Mandl. 1990.

Vol. F 76: Multimedia Interface Design in Education. Edited by A. D. N. Edwards and S. Holland. 1992.

Vol. F 78: Integrating Advanced Technology into Technology Education. Edited by M. Hacker, A. Gordon, and M. de Vries. 1991.

Vol. F 80: Intelligent Tutoring Systems for Foreign Language Learning. The Bridge to International Communication. Edited by M. L Swartz and M. Yazdani. 1992.

Vol. F 81: Cognitive Tools for Learning. Edited by P.A.M. Kommers, D.H. Jonassen, and J.T. Mayes. 1992.

Vol. F 84: Computer-Based Learning Environments and Problem Solving. Edited by E. De Corte, M. C. Linn, H. Mandl, and L. Verschaffel. 1992.

Vol. F 85: Adaptive Learning Environments. Foundations and Frontiers. Edited by M. Jones and P. H. Winne. 1992.

Vol. F 86: Intelligent Learning Environments and Knowledge Acquisition in Physics. Edited by A. Tiberghien and H. Mandl. 1992.

Vol. F 87: Cognitive Modelling and Interactive Environments in Language Learning. Edited by F. L. Engel, D. G. Bouwhuis, T. Bösser, and G. d'Ydewalle. 1992.

Vol. F 89: Mathematical Problem Solving and New Information Technologies. Edited by J. P. Ponte, J. F. Matos, J. M. Matos, and D. Fernandes. 1992.

Vol. F 90: Collaborative Learning Through Computer Conferencing. Edited by A. R. Kaye. 1992.

Vol. F 91: New Directions for Intelligent Tutoring Systems. Edited by E. Costa. 1992.

Vol. F 92: Hypermedia Courseware: Structures of Communication and Intelligent Help. Edited by A. Oliveira. 1992.

Vol. F 93: Interactive Multimedia Learning Environments. Human Factors and Technical Considerations on Design Issues. Edited by M. Giardina. 1992.

Vol. F 95: Comprehensive System Design: A New Educational Technology. Edited by C. M. Reigeluth, B. H. Banathy, and J. R. Olson. 1993.

Vol. F 96: New Directions in Educational Technology. Edited by E. Scanlon and T. O'Shea. 1992.

Vol. F 97: Advanced Models of Cognition for Medical Training and Practice. Edited by D. A. Evans and V. L. Patel. 1992.

Vol. F 104: Instructional Models in Computer-Based Learning Environments. Edited by S. Dijkstra, H. P. M. Krammer, and J. J. G. van Merriënboer. 1992.

Vol. F 105: Designing Environments for Constructive Learning. Edited by T. M. Duffy, J. Lowyck, and D. H. Jonassen. 1993.

Designing Environments for Constructive Learning

Edited by

Thomas M. Duffy

Instructional Systems Technology
Indiana University
Bloomington, IN 47405, USA

Joost Lowyck

Instructional Psychology and Technology
Catholic University of Leuven
B-3000 Leuven, Belgium

David H. Jonassen

Instructional Technology
University of Colorado
Denver, CO 80217-3364, USA

With the assistance of

Thomas M. Welsh
Indiana University, Bloomington

Springer-Verlag
Berlin Heidelberg New York London Paris Tokyo
Hong Kong Barcelona Budapest
Published in cooperation with NATO Scientific Affairs Division

Proceedings of the NATO Advanced Research Workshop on The Design of Constructivist Learning Environments: Implications for Instructional Design and the Use of Technology, held at the Catholic University Leuven, Belgium, May 14–18, 1991

CR Subject Classification (1991): K.3

ISBN-13: 978-3-642-78071-4 e-ISBN-13: 978-3-642-78069-1
DOI: 10.1007/ 978-3-642-78069-1

Softcover reprint of the hardcover 1st edition 1993

Typesetting: Camera ready by authors
45/3140 - 5 4 3 2 1 0 - Printed on acid-free paper

Preface

The idea for this book grew out of a NATO Advanced Research Workshop held at the Catholic University at Leuven, Belgium. We are grateful to NATO for support in conducting this workshop and for support in the preparation of this book. We are particularly grateful for their emphasis on designing the workshop to build collegiality. They suggested that we hold the meeting in a small town and that we organize evening activities to keep the group together and to promote informal and extended discussions. What sage advice. The excitement grew over the three days as we shared understandings and enriched our perspectives. Indeed, there was even a proclaimed "near" conversion to a constructivist perspective from one colleague trained in traditional instructional design methods. While we report this as a bit of a humorous anecdote, it most clearly reflects the sense of excitement that developed.

We would also like to thank the staff at the Catholic University for their great support during the workshop. Their efforts and their good cheer were important components in the success of the meeting. In particular we would like to thank Jan Elen, Catherine Vermunicht and Jef Van den Branden.

Finally we would like to thank the personnel at Indiana University for their help in assembling this book. Deborah Shaw prepared the index. We thank her for the skill and speed with which she was able to work. Tom Welsh took the lead in assembling, copy editing, and formatting the chapters. We may never have gotten this book out without his very competent support.

November 1992

T.M. Duffy
J. Lowyck
D.H. Jonassen

Table of Contents

Part II: Design Issues

Introduction

Education! A critical topic in virtually all the nations of the world. What do children need to know in a world where information is growing at such a tremendous rate? How do we help them become lifelong learners so that they can avoid having their understanding become outmoded in a few years?

The traditional approach to schooling has reflected a view of knowledge as entities existing independent of the learner or any context. Since knowledge exists independently, understanding can be objective, absolute, and unconditional. Cognition, in this view, is regarded as the rule based manipulation of symbols via processes that will ultimately be describable through the language of mathematics and logic.

We are now beginning to see a change in the basic epistemology of schooling. A constructivist epistemology argues that knowledge is not acquired as a collection of abstract entities but rather is constructed in the context of the environment in which it is encountered. Context is integral to understanding; meaning arises from context and context is an integral part of that meaning. People construct knowledge socially, through collaboration and discussion. It is this social process that results in shared meaning and understanding.

The chapters in this book explore the implications of a constructivist view for the design of learning environments and for the role of technology in that design. An examination of these chapters makes it clear that constructivism is not a unified point of view. There seems to be general agreement as to the importance of the authenticity of the learning task and the context in which the student works. There is also general agreement on the importance of collaborative learning as a means of developing a richer understanding through considering alternative perspectives.

Perhaps the greatest difference across the chapters arises from focusing on constructivism as a learning theory or as a set of instructional strategies. As a learning theory, the focus of constructivism is on how we understand and what it means to understand. It is a lens through which we see the world: all learning is seen from a constructivist perspective. For even the most basic learning task, meaning is constructed and understanding occurs in context. There is no restriction on the instructional strategies that can be used. If drill and practice is the most efficient strategy for developing the particular ability and understanding, then that is the instructional strategy that should be used. The critical issue is that the drill and practice occur in a context of a larger problem so that the learner sees the learning activity as a means of developing a skill that is needed. The criterion for success is the ability of the learner to use that skill in the larger context. That is, the learning that occurs through drill and practice or through reading and discussion is seen as a means to an end – a tool. The Cognition and TechnologyGroup at Vanderbilt makes this point, in particular, in considering strategies for using the Jasper series. It is also a focus of the Honebein, Duffy, and Fishman chapter.

Some authors tend to focus on constructivism as a set of instructional strategies rather than as a learning theory. The instructional design prescription may read something like, "if the goal is a rich understanding and if the problem domain is ill-structured, then constructivist learning strategies should be applied." This prescription is part of a repertoire of instructional strategies that is used when the goal and the conditions are appropriate. It is from this instructional strategy perspective that *Jonassen, Mayes, and McAleese* argue that constructivist learning is only for advanced knowledge acquisition and for ill-structured problems. Our goal is to move toward the integration of theory and practice and we hope the reader finds this book to be a step in that direction.

In Part I, *Constructivist Learning Environments,* the authors focus on learning environments that they have designed. What is clear throughout these presentations is that a constructivist learning environment calls for a view of the classroom – the student and teacher activities – that is quite different from what we typically see. The authors use the environment they describe as a context or point of reference for discussing their theoretical views of constructivism and their views of the implications of those views for instructional design and practice.

The first two chapters examine the instructional application of media and computer based tools. *The Cognition and Technology Group at Vanderbilt* focus on the Jasper series they developed for use in mathematics classrooms but which is now being extended to other content areas. Three different models for using the Jasper series are described and critiqued. Seven instructional design principles are presented. In contrast to this content based system, *McMahon and O'Neill,* in Chapter 2, describe a content-free tool designed in HyperCard, known as *Bubble Dialogue,* which is based on a Vygotskian perspective. *Bubble Dialogue* is designed to facilitate the making of meaning by promoting a dialogue in which both internal thoughts and speech are represented in the exchange. McMahon and O'Neill discuss both the instructional design prescriptions and the theoretical principles underlying the design of constructivist learning environments.

Abbott shifts the scale of the learning environment considerably with his discussion of *Education 2000* in Chapter 3. Rather than an application for use in a classroom, they are focusing on the restructuring of an entire school district. Interestingly, both the approach to the design process (the learning process for the community) and the new design of the school system, reflect a constructivist perspective. The community was given ownership of the restructuring effort, and the formal committee served as resources and as guides. The goal in the design of the schools is to develop life-long learners, and Abbott sees a constructivist environment as the most effective way to achieve this goal.

In the next three chapters, the authors focus on one or two critical characteristics in their design of learning environments. In Chapter 4, *Honebein, Duffy, and Fishman* discuss the authenticity and complexity of the learning environment from a constructivist perspective. They present instructional principles for realizing these design goals and describe two learning environments in which they feel these goals are reached. One environment is a computer environment to support developing research skills in environmental sociology and the other is a classroom environment for developing educational research skills. In Chapter 5, *De Corte, Verschaffel, Schrooten, Olivie´, and Vansina* discuss the problem of balancing the exploratory goals of learning with the need to provide direction so that content and skill based instructional goals will be achieved. They discuss the problems in the open exploration approach that have characterized many of the uses of Logo. They further describe the design of a Logo tool kit, to be used with elementary school children, which provides a balance between guidance/structure and open exploration. In Chapter 6, *Jones, Knuth, and Duffy* describe their work in teacher education in which they apply constructivist principles in the design of *Strategic Teaching Frameworks (STF)*. *STF* includes two components: a teleconferencing strategy and a computer-based hypermedia system.

The final chapter in this Part, Chapter 7, brings a research focus to the design and evaluation of a constructivist learning environment. *Pontecorvo* describes her research with school children using computers in a literacy curriculum. The dialogue promoted both by the computer tasks as well as in the basic use of the computers is the focus of her analysis. She sees this research as reflecting a learning theory based approach to schooling.

In Part II, *Design Issues,* the authors focus on the implications of constructivism for the practice of instructional design. *Knuth and Cunningham*, in Chapter 8, set the stage for the discussion in this section by presenting what they call an extreme constructivist position. The position is based on the work of Maturana which emphasizes that living systems are informationally closed and thus to understand learning we need to focus on the interactions within the learning system (the individual), not on the structure of the environment. What we call learning they suggest is really the system's response to perturbations. They describe three computer-based tools that can facilitate learning from this perspective.

The next three chapters examine the instructional design model and process and discuss the implications of cognitive theories in general and constructivism in particular for both the model of instructional design and instructional design practice. In Chapter 9, *Winn* discusses the three primary activities in traditional instructional design and questions the underlying assumption from a constructivist perspective as well as from other perspectives. The activities and the underlying assumptions he questions are: instructional analysis and the assumption of reductionism; selection of methods and the assumption of determinism; and evaluation and the assumption of replicability. Winn examines what instructional design might look like under a constructivist framework that does not make these assumptions.

Lowyck and Elen take a broad view of cognitive theories and examine the implications of these theories for the practice of instructional design in Chapter 10. They discuss the dimensions along which cognitive theories impact instructional design models by examining five views of the relationship. They examine in detail how a "mild constructivist approach" leads to a reconceptualization of the instructional design process. Then, in Chapter 11, *Jonassen, Mayes, and McAleese* take a more prescriptive approach. They present principles for the design of a constructivist learning environment for university level instruction. They discuss each principle and describe technology based support that could help in implementing this design principle.

Chapters 12 and 13 focus on the design and use of computer tools in a constructivist environment. *Zucchermaglio* distinguishes between three kinds of software applications: closed technologies, open technologies, and technologies for doing. She argues, consistent with Winn's proposal, that we need to develop principles for the design of open technologies which support the constructive activities of students – a cognitive ergonomics of educational technology is required. *Allen and Hoffman* discuss the application of a particular open technology. *SemNet* is a tool for representing and analyzing semantic networks. Allen and Hoffman argue that the strength of *SemNet,* from a constructivist framework, is in the learning that occurs while constructing a semantic network of a content domain. *SemNet* emphasizes the types of links between concepts rather than the concepts themselves. Thus, in using the system, the user must think about relationships between concepts and be prepared to defend the proposed relationships. Of particular pedagogical importance for Allen and Hoffman is the balance between leaner generated link types and system provided link types (i.e., to what degree does the instructional designer let the learner specify the types of relationships that are possible?). The issue is one of the degree to which the learner or the system should constrain the learning environment, a problem already raised by De Corte et al.

In Chapter 14, *Simons* focuses on issues involved in developing self-regulated learners. The discussion includes a consideration of what it means to learn, what he means by constructive learning, and what the practical issues are in implementing a constructive learning approach to develop self-regulated learners. In Chapter 15, *Prenzel and Mandl* tackle the particularly vexing problem for constructivism of the nature of transfer. They criticize the vagueness in most constructivist discussion of the learning process and the problems that this poses for considering the process of transfer.

In the final chapter, Chapter 16, we once again return to a research agenda. *Entwistle, Entwistle, and Tait* report their research and other work on the factors that influence student learning in the university classroom. Their analysis leads to a "conceptual map" of the components of the learning environment which have been shown to influence the nature of, or level of, understanding that develops. In particular, their research indicates that the type of teaching, the nature of the assessment, and the student's preferred way of learning all dramatically impact student learning and what it means to "understand" in the learning environment.

Part I

Constructivist Learning Environments

1 Designing Learning Environments That Support Thinking: The Jasper Series as a Case Study[1]

Cognition and Technology Group at Vanderbilt[2]

Vanderbilt University, Nashville, Tennessee, USA

Most instructional design efforts involve a minimum of four components; namely, a specification of (a) the goals to be met, (b) materials to be used, (c) teaching strategies to be employed and (d) items and procedures for assessment. These components seem to be important for any domain of instruction imaginable. Specific curricula involve specific values for each of the four components of instruction. Thus, curriculum designers often specify in great detail the goals, materials, teaching procedures and assessments. The strength of such well-specified efforts is that they make a complete curriculum package that is relatively easy to implement and evaluate. There is also a potential problem with such efforts. The more complete the specification of the values for each instructional component, the less inclined teachers may be to map into the unique features of particular students and communities.

During the past several years, we have been experimenting with an approach that provides some specific tools for instruction yet also leaves room for a great deal of flexibility. Our approach is based on a specific theoretical framework and set of goals, but it also allows considerable room for a variety of assumptions about content, pedagogy and assessment. The basis of the approach is to begin by creating semantically rich "anchors" that illustrate important problem solving situations (e.g., Cognition and Technology Group at Vanderbilt, 1990). These anchors create a "macrocontext" that provides a common ground for experts in various areas, as well as teachers and students from diverse backgrounds, to communicate in ways that build collective understanding (Bransford, Sherwood, Hasselbring, Kinzer, & Williams, 1990; CTGV, 1991b). Macrocontexts are semantically rich environments that can be used to integrate concepts across the curriculum and in which meaningful, authentic problems can be posed. Our macrocontexts are also designed to facilitate experimentation by researchers so that the implications of choosing specific instructional options can be studied. In short, we have not

---

[1]Preparation of this paper was supported in part by National Science Foundation Instructional Materials Grant MDR 9050191 and by the James S. McDonnell Foundation. However, neither should be held responsible for the contents of this paper.

[2]Members of the Cognition and Technology Group at Vanderbilt who contributed to this paper are Linda Barron, John Bransford, Olin Campbell, Ben Ferron, Laura Goin, Elizabeth Goldman, Susan Goldman, Ted Hasselbring, Allison Heath, Charles Kinzer, James Pellegrino, Kirsten Rewey, Robert Sherwood, Nancy Vye, Susan Warren, Susan Williams.

attempted to provide a finished curriculum in the sense described above. Instead, we are attempting to provide anchors that serve as contexts for (1) collaborative inquiry in classrooms, and (2) research on learning.

At the heart of our approach is (perhaps) a fundamental departure from more traditional instructional design conceptions of the nature of knowledge, the teaching-learning process, and the implications of these for the design of instruction. We contrast our view with one that holds that knowledge is an identifiable entity with some absolute truth value. The goal of instruction is met if students acquire this knowledge, usually as transmitted by whatever teaching mechanisms are in place (e.g., a teacher, a tutoring machine, etc.). Under this view of knowledge, the transmittal process is optimized if the knowledge can be specified and an ideal acquisition sequence identified. All that remains is for this sequence to be delivered in as "teacher-proof" a fashion as possible. In many cases, systematic instructional design seems to have been a response to the pragmatic reality of instructors with no teaching knowledge or expertise.

An alternative conception, one that our group and many other constructivists adhere to, represents a blend of ecological psychology (e.g., Gibson, 1977) and constructivism. On the ecological side, we believe that there is structure in the world, both the physical world and the epistemological world, that places constraints on knowing. On the constructivist side, we believe that there are sufficient degrees of freedom in the structure of physical and epistemological worlds to allow people to construct their own personal theories of their environments, of what is "known" or believed by others about those environments, and of themselves.

So how do people come to agree on events or find ways to settle differences? Here we join others (e.g., Vygotsky, 1978) in emphasizing the social nature of cognition. The constraints on constructed knowledge come largely from the community of which one is a member. In the absence of any community, we suppose that it would be possible for an individual to have an idiosyncratic view of the world - but then because there is no community the idiosyncrasy is irrelevant. As soon as there are two views, one of two things must occur: the idiosyncratic views must be brought into harmony or the individuals involved must "agree to disagree." In other words, the individual is free to build his or her own interpretation of the world, so long as that interpretation is coherent with the general zeitgeist. Knowledge is a dialect process, the essence of which is that individuals have opportunities to test their constructed ideas on others, persuade others of the virtue of their thinking and be persuaded.

By continually negotiating the meaning of observations, data, hypotheses and so forth, groups of individuals construct systems that are largely consistent with one another. One of our major goals in instruction is to encourage students to develop socially acceptable systems for exploring their ideas and their differences in opinion. For example, we want to help them appreciate rules of "good argumentation" and to continually look for appropriate ways to test their ideas. But we also want them to realize that these ideas of "goodness" (good theory, good science, good debate, etc.) are subject to change over time.

We will illustrate our (evolving) approach to instruction by discussing our Jasper Woodbury problem solving series. The Jasper series consists of a set of specially designed video-based adventures that provide a motivating and realistic context for problem posing, problem solving and reasoning. The series allows students, teachers and others to integrate knowledge from a variety of areas such as mathematics, science, history and literature (e.g., CTGV, 1991b).

To use the terminology of James Gibson (1977), the Jasper adventures and extra materials to accompany them are designed to provide "affordances" for teaching and learning. Gibson noted that different features of the environment afford classes of activities for particular organisms such as "walk-onable," "climbable," "swim-able," and so forth. But the mere existence of these affordances does not guarantee that "afforded" activities will occur. Occurrence depends on how the organism perceives and reacts with the environment.

Our Jasper adventures afford activities such as generating sub-goals, identifying relevant information, cooperating with others in order to plan and solve complex problems, discussing the advantages and disadvantages of possible solutions, comparing perspectives by pointing out and explaining interesting events. The degree to which these affordances are realized depends on the teaching model that one adopts in the context of Jasper. This means that the Jasper series can be used to test a number of different assumptions about teaching, learning and transfer.

In the next section we describe key characteristics of the Jasper series and the nature of the activities afforded by it. Although several aspects of the Jasper series have been described elsewhere, a summary of this information is re-provided below so that readers will not have to search for other publications (e.g., CTGV, 1990, 1991a, b; VanHaneghan, Barron, Young, Williams, Vye, & Bransford, in press). We then discuss how the realization of the activities afforded by the Jasper adventures depends on the model of teaching governing classroom activity. These models can vary on a number of dimensions including assumptions about feedback, teachers' roles, students' roles, and content sequencing. After discussing some possible teaching models, we consider issues of assessment that need to be explored.

An Overview of the Jasper Series

As noted above, the Jasper series consists of a set of specially designed video-based adventures that provide a motivating and realistic context for problem solving and reasoning. The Jasper adventures are designed to afford powerful skills of problem generation or problem posing (e.g., Brown & Walters, 1983; Silver, 1990) and identification of relevant information. These affordances contrast with those of traditional math problem solving materials, i.e., math story problems. The latter typically focus primarily on procedural or computational aspects of problem solving and rarely do students have to identify problem goals or discriminate among relevant and irrelevant data. In addition, because many students dislike word problems, they frequently are not emphasized in school (see Porter, 1989). As a result, students often do quite poorly in real world situations where math problem solving skills learned in school might be useful (see for discussion, Charles & Silver, 1988; Schoenfeld, 1989).

Description and an Example Adventure

Each video in the Jasper series has a main story that is 14 to 18 minutes in length. The "end" of each video features one of the characters stating the problem that has to be solved; it is posed as a challenge and the students have to generate relevant sub-problems in order to generate the solution. The problem to be solved is very complex but all the data needed to solve it are provided in the video as a natural part of the story. Each Jasper adventure also includes a conclusion that students can watch after they have solved the problem themselves.

The Jasper adventures are organized into pairs; both members of each pair involve similar types of problems (i.e., trip planning for the first pair, using statistical data to develop a business plan in the second pair; making arguments about data gathered from meaningful uses of geometry in the third). There are also many links in each video that allow students and teachers to extend their explorations across the curricula. For example, the first four episodes provide strong links to river travel, flight, entrepreneurship, and recycling, respectively.

The first episode of the pair of trip planning videos, "Journey to Cedar Creek," has been described elsewhere (e.g. CTGV, 1990,1991a). Here, we will describe the second episode, "Rescue at Boone's Meadow." This episode opens with a view of Larry Peterson flying his ultralight airplane. We soon learn that Larry also teaches others to fly and we see him with one of his pupils, Emily Johnson. Through a series of lessons, Larry introduces Emily (and the viewers) to a variety of information about his ultralight such as fuel capacity, speed, payload limits, how the shape of the wing produces lift and so forth. Emily learns her lessons well and soon flies solo. To celebrate, she and Larry join Jasper Woodbury at a local restaurant.

At the restaurant, we learn that Jasper plans to take his annual fishing trip. He drives to Hilda's (where she has her house and runs a gas station) and then hikes approximately 15 miles into the woods to Boone's Meadow. The conversation reveals other information such as the fact that Larry flew his ultralight to see Hilda last week and set it down in the field beside her house. At the end of the restaurant scene both Larry and Emily weigh themselves.

As the adventure proceeds we see Jasper on his fishing trip. As he is eating his catch he hears a shot and goes out to investigate. He finds a wounded eagle and uses his CB radio to call for help. Hilda answers Jasper's call and relays the message to Emily, the student pilot we met earlier. Emily consults with Doc Ramirez, the veterinarian, who supplies additional information about eagles, distances, etc. His map reveals that there are no roads between Cumberland City (where Larry and Emily are located) and Boone's Meadow (the location of Jasper and the Eagle). The doctor has another patient to attend to but emphasizes to Emily that time is of the essence in rescuing the eagle.

The adventure ends with a shot of Emily beginning to pose the problem that confronts her: "What's the fastest way to rescue the eagle and how long will that take?" This is the challenge that is presented to the students. It is at this point that students move from the passive, television-like viewing to an active generation mode. They must solve Emily's problem; to do so they have to generate the kinds of sub-goals that she must consider in order to make the decision about the fastest way to rescue the eagle. All the data needed to solve the problem were presented in the video and students go back and search for the information they need.

The problem looks deceptively simple; in reality there are numerous possible solutions but each involves defining and then testing a route against payload, range, and landing constraints. For example, the video includes data that are necessary to construct a map that shows the locations and distances of key spots such as Cumberland City, Hilda's, and Boone's Meadow. Using the map, students need to decide on a route, vehicle for each leg of the route, and the character that will actually carry out the rescue operation. For any route, the feasibility has to be evaluated by checking whether range, payload, and landing requirements are met on each leg of any route. To calculate the range of the ultralight, students must consider fuel capacity and rate of consumption along with distance, which means they need to search for information about size of the gas tank on the ultralight, miles per gallon, etc. Information in the video showed that the range could be extended by carrying an extra gallon of gas in a cargo box. But the weight of the fuel affects payload. Overall, there are a number of possible and feasible routes, with some being faster than others. In order to adequately explore and discuss the possibilities, students generally need three or four class periods. Even college students find the Jasper problems challenging (e.g., see Goldman, Vye, Williams, Rewey, Pellegrino, & CTGV, 1991; VanHaneghan et al, in press).

Analogs and Extensions of the Basic Challenge

In addition to the major problem for each Jasper adventure, we are designing print and additional video materials that present analog and extension problems. The purpose of these materials is to help students develop flexible knowledge representations plus help them begin to make connections between the Jasper adventures and the thinking and planning that took place in many historical and contemporary events.

Analog problems are formed by altering one or more of the parameters of the problem. For example, after students have solved Emily's rescue problem, which took place on a calm day, they can be asked to reconsider whether her solution would work if there were a 6 mile per hour headwind while she flew from Cumberland City to Boone's Meadow (it wouldn't). Similarly, students can be asked to imagine that Emily used a different ultralight that had different fuel consumption, speed, etc. We are also designing an analog "adventure maker" that allows students to create their own analog adventures given specific constraints. For example, students might be asked to choose among a set of values that would allow Emily to rescue the eagle if she were using an ultralight with a 4-gallon rather than 5-gallon fuel tank.

Extension problems are designed to help students see how the planning involved in the Jasper adventures relates to historical and current events. An excellent extension problem for "Rescue at Boone's Meadow" involves a consideration of the planning that Charles Lindbergh had to do in order to prepare for his flight from New York to Paris. Another involves the planning needed for the first trip to the moon. We are currently experimenting with a format that enables us to create extension videos that contain enough data for students to engage in problem posing. That is, instead of questions being posed in the extension videos, we want the students to learn to pose relevant problems for themselves.

The Jasper series is optimally used in a videodisc format, although it is available on videotape. The disc format facilitates the search for information and sub-goal generation required of the students. The random access, search, and freeze-frame capabilities inherent in videodiscs make this format preferable to the videotape format and we strongly encourage schools to use videodiscs.

In addition, the Jasper series includes specially designed multi-media publishing software that allows students and teachers to research various topics (e.g., about principles of flight or about endangered species) and use this knowledge to create multi-media products for teaching others. This software is designed to work in conjunction with the videodisc version of the Jasper adventures (see for more details CTGV, 1991a). The software requires that computers be used in conjunction with the videodisc format of the Jasper adventures and the analogs and extensions. Note, however, that implementation of the Jasper series does not require computers; all that is required is a videodisc player with remote control or bar code reader capabilities.

Theoretical Framework Underlying the Jasper Series

There is an explicit theoretical rationale for the Jasper adventures, analogs and extensions. The rationale is consistent with ideas and goals expressed by researchers and educators who are attempting to enhance the quality of learning (e.g., American Association for the Advancement of Science, 1989; NTCM, 1989; Resnick & Klopfer, 1989). They have emphasized the need to rethink the goals of education and the assumptions about learning that underlie many curricula and teaching practices. These two topics and implications for learning materials are discussed below.

Assumptions About Goals

One way to define the goals of our Jasper series could have been "to improve test scores in mathematics." We did not define our goals in this way because, like many others, we have serious concerns about what is measured (and equally important, what is not measured) on typical tests. We agree with the following statement by Resnick and Resnick (in press):

> ...the very idea of using test technology as it has developed over the past century may be fundamentally inimical to the real goals of educational reform." (p. 1, preprint)

Our concern with most existing tests stems, in part, from the fact that some of the test items (e.g. arbitrary word problems) do not seem very authentic. Nevertheless, our primary concern is not so much with what is tested as with what is not tested. Tests serve to define the goals of one's instruction (e.g., Fredericksen & Collins, 1989). We believe that instructional goals for mathematics and science need to be quite different from the ones illustrated by typical test items that focus primarily on component skills such as computation with whole numbers and fractions, the ability to identify concepts such as "area" versus "perimeter," and so forth (Goldman, Pellegrino & Bransford, in press). These component skills are important, to be sure. But we want to help students develop them in the context of meaningful problem posing and problem solving activities rather than as isolated "targets" of instruction. If our primary goal were to improve test scores on existing tests, we would have developed instructional units that are quite different from the Jasper series as it currently exists.

The goals for learning that underlie our development of the Jasper series emphasize the importance of helping students – all students – learn to become independent thinkers and learners rather than simply become able to perform basic computations and retrieve simple knowledge facts (e.g., Bransford, Sherwood, Vye, & Rieser, 1986; Bransford, Goldman & Vye, in press; Scardamalia & Bereiter, 1991; Resnick, 1987; Resnick & Klopfer, 1989; Schoenfeld, 1987, 1989). An especially important consideration is that students must learn to identify and define issues and problems on their own rather than simply respond to problems that others have posed (e.g., Brown & Walters, 1983; Bransford & Stein, 1984). Research conducted by our group indicates that sixth grade students at the 8th and 9th stanines of mathematical achievement can solve basic word problems that are provided to them but do extremely poorly when faced with situations (e.g., solving the "Rescue at Boone's Meadow" problem that was described above) that require them to generate the relevant sub-problems and figure out what data are needed to satisfy the subgoals that they generate on their own (e.g., CTGV, 1990; Goldman et al., 1991; Van Haneghan et al., in press). The theme of generative learning and problem solving is explored in more depth in the discussion below.

Assumptions About Learning

Our assumptions about learning are consistent with a class of theories called constructive theories. As Scardamalia and Bereiter (1991) argue, constructive theory by itself provides few specific guidelines for instruction. When one's goal is to help students become independent learners and problem solvers in specific areas, more guidelines become available (e.g., Bransford & Vye 1989; Clement, 1982; Minstrell, 1989; Resnick & Klopfer, 1989; Schoenfeld, 1989). Several aspects of our version of constructive learning theory are discussed below.

Generative Learning: A number of theorists emphasize the importance of helping students engage in generative rather than passive learning activities. In physics, for example, many students bring a number of preconceptions to learning, some of which are misconceptions (e.g., Clement, 1982; Minstrell, 1989). For students to overcome their misconceptions, it is not sufficient to simply memorize how a scientist represents and explains various phenomena. Instead, students need to engage in argumentation and reflection as they try to use and then refine their existing knowledge as they attempt to make sense of alternate points of view.

In the mathematics domain, efforts to reform the nature of mathematics curricula also stress that mathematics classrooms need to shift from an emphasis on the teacher imparting knowledge to one in which students attempt to use their current skills and knowledge to approach problems to be solved (e.g., Charles & Silver, 1988; NCTM, 1989; Schoenfeld, 1985, 1989; Yackel, Cobb, Wood, Wheatley, & Merkel, 1990). Even the ability to learn effectively from worked-out examples involves the construction of links to other aspects of one's knowledge (e.g., Chi, Bassok, Lewis, & Glaser, 1989). As Resnick and Resnick (in press) note, in order for concepts and principles to be learned effectively "... they must be used generatively – that is, they have to be called upon over and over again as ways to link, interpret and explain new information" (p. 4). Silver (1990) discusses several types of materials that might encourage such activities including worked examples that involve active construction, open-ended problems, and problems in which concepts and procedures are connected.

Findings from a number of studies suggest that knowledge that is not acquired and used generatively tends to become what Whitehead (1929) called "inert knowledge" – knowledge that is not used spontaneously even though it is relevant (e.g., Bransford et al., 1986; Gick & Holyoak, 1980, 1983; Scardamalia & Bereiter, 1985). Data indicate that knowledge is less likely to remain inert when it is acquired in a problem solving mode rather than in a factual-knowledge mode (Adams, Kasserman, Yearwood, Perfetto, Bransford, & Franks, 1988; Lockhart, Lamon, & Gick, 1988).

Anchored Instruction: In addition to our focus on the generative aspects of learning, our Jasper series is based on a theoretical framework that emphasizes the importance of anchoring or situating instruction in meaningful problem solving contexts that allow one to simulate in the classroom some of the advantages of apprenticeship learning (e.g. Brown, Collins, & Duguid, 1989; CTGV, 1990, 1991a). A major goal of this approach is to create shared environments that permit sustained exploration by students and teachers and enable them to understand the kinds of problems and opportunities that experts in various areas encounter and the knowledge that these experts use as tools.

Theorists such as Dewey (1933), Schwab (1960) and Hanson (1970) emphasize that experts in an area have been immersed in phenomena and are familiar with how they have been thinking about them. When introduced to new theories, concepts, and principles that are relevant to their areas of interest, the experts can experience the changes in their own thinking that these ideas afford. For novices, however, the introduction of concepts and theories often seem like the mere introduction of new facts or mechanical procedures to be memorized. Because the novices have not been immersed in the phenomena being investigated, they are unable to experience the effects of the new information on their own noticing and understanding. Novices especially need help in moving from a general goal to the generation and definition of distinct sub-goals necessary to achieve the overall goal.

Cooperative Learning and Generativity: Our Jasper adventures are also designed with an eye toward their use in cooperative learning settings. A number of theorists argue that cooperative learning and cooperative problem solving groups enhance opportunities for generative learning. In cooperative groups, students have the opportunity to form communities of inquiry that allow them to discuss and explain and hence learn with understanding (e.g., NCTM, 1989; Palincsar & Brown, 1984, 1989; Vygotsky, 1978).

We are also aware of potential disadvantages of cooperative learning groups. For example, Salomon & Globerson (1989) discuss many pitfalls in the implementation of groups in classrooms. In addition, some groups work more effectively than others and members experience differential benefits of group work (Cosden, Goldman, & Hine, 1990; Goldman, Cosden, & Hine, 1987; Hine, Goldman, & Cosden, 1990). Pilot data suggest this is true for

Jasper as well (CTGV, in progress). Even when a group does well in solving a problem, measures of subsequent, individual problem solving indicate that some individuals do not learn well from the group interactions (e.g., Williams & Sternberg, 1988). For example, in some groups one individual may dominate and solve the problem while the rest listen, watch, or engage in off-task activities (like daydreaming). For the listeners, the learning is as passive as it is when the teacher lectures. In other groups, members may too easily get off track and generate wrong information. Data from the generative learning literature show quite clearly that self-generated information is better remembered than passively received information irrespective of whether the information is right or wrong. This means that self generated errors cause more subsequent interference than passively received wrong information (e.g., Bransford, Franks, Vye & Sherwood, 1989; Perfetto, Yearwood, Franks, & Bransford, 1987). As we discuss in more detail later, one of our instructional goals is to help teachers provide scaffolds (degrees of structure) that help initially less-skilled groups begin to explore ideas without going too far astray yet, eventually, help them become generative learners who are self-directed rather than teacher-directed.

The Importance of Learning Materials

In general, different types of materials are differentially effective for helping students engage in particular kinds of learning activities (Jenkins, 1979). Some problems may lend themselves to protracted problem posing and formulation whereas other problems may structure the situation completely, leaving little to do but "add up the numbers." Earlier we noted the specific contrast between the types of activities the Jasper series affords and those afforded by traditional math problem solving materials. Traditional word problems provide the goal and only those numbers needed to solve the problem. Thus, they afford computational selection. In contrast, the Jasper series affords students opportunities to create problem structure as they solve the problem, potentially leading to more opportunities for group interactions that support generative learning.

As noted earlier, the types of learning activities that we want our materials to support are consistent with recommendations suggested by the National Council of Teachers of Mathematics (NCTM) Commission on Standards for School Mathematics (1989). The NCTM's suggestions for changes in classroom activities include more emphasis on complex, open-ended problem solving, communication and reasoning; more connections from mathematics to other subjects and to the world outside the classroom; more uses of calculators and powerful computer-based tools such as spreadsheets and graphing programs for exploring relationships (as opposed to having students spend an inordinate amount of time calculating by hand). In proposing a more generative approach to mathematics learning, the NTCM states:

> ...(t)he mathematics curriculum should engage students in some problems that demand extended effort to solve. Some might be group projects that require students to use available technology and to engage in cooperative problem solving and discussion. For grades 5-8 an important criterion of problems is that they be interesting to students. (p. 75)

Design Principles for the Jasper Series

Our assumptions about goals, about learning, and about learning materials are encapsulated in the seven design principles shown in Table 1. The design principles guide the construction of the Jasper adventures, analogs, and extensions. These design principles mutually influence one another and operate as a Gestalt rather than as a set of independent features of the materials. For example, the narrative format (principle 2), the generative design of the stories (principle 3) and the fact that the adventures include embedded data (principle 4) makes it possible for students to learn to generate sub-goals, find relevant information, and engage in reasoned decision making. The complexity of the problems (principle 5) helps students deal with this important aspect of problem solving and the use of video (principle 1) helps make the complexity manageable. The video format also makes it easier to embed the kinds of information that provide opportunities for links across the curricula (principle 7). The video is also important because it makes complex mathematics problem solving accessible to students having difficulties with reading. The pairs of related adventures (principle 6) afford discussions about transfer. These design principles are described in more detail elsewhere (CTGV, 1991a).

Similar sets of design principles are applicable in many curricular domains, including science and literacy (CTGV, 1990, in press(a); McLarty, Goodman, Risko, Kinzer, Vye, Rowe, & Carson, 1990). For example, the Sherlock project used the movie "The Young Sherlock Holmes" as a macrocontext for reading and writing activities that focused on setting and character, vocabulary, and plot development (e.g., Bransford, Vye, Kinzer, & Risko, 1990). Gains in student performance were significantly greater than a comparison group that engaged in similar activities but in the absence of the macrocontext (Risko, Kinzer, Goodman, McLarty, Dupree, & Martin, 1989).

Contrasting Models for Teaching with Jasper

As we indicated earlier, affordances do not guarantee actions. Critical to student learning activities with Jasper is the model of teaching at work in the classroom. There are at least three important dimensions of these instructional models that define the assumptions teachers have about learning in the classroom context. The first dimension deals with assumptions about the sequencing of content and tasks in the curriculum. At one end of this dimension is the extreme reductionist view that all components of a skill must be mastered before the components can be

	Design principle		Hypothesized Benefits
1.	Video-based format	A.	More motivating
		B.	Easier to search
		C.	Supports complex comprehension
		D.	Especially helpful for poor readers yet it can also support learning
2.	Narrative with realistic problems (rather than a lecture on video)	A.	Easier to remember
		B.	More engaging
		C.	Primes students to notice the relevance mathematics and reasoning for everyday events
3.	Generative format (i.e. the stories end & students must generate the problems to be solved)	A.	Motivating to determine the ending
		B.	Teaches students to find and define problems to be solved
		C.	Provides enhanced opportunities for reasoning
4.	Embedded data design (i.e. all the data needed to solve the problems are in the video)	A.	Permits reasoned decision making
		B.	Motivating to find
		C.	Puts students on an "even keel" with respect to relevant knowledge
		D.	Clarifies how relevance of data depends on specific goals
5.	Problem Complexity (i.e. each adventure involves a problem of at least 14 steps)	A.	Overcomes the tendency to try for a few minutes & then give up
		B.	Introduces levels of complexity characteristic of real problems
		C.	Helps students deal with complexity
		D.	Develops confidence in abilities
6.	Pairs of Related Adventures	A.	Provides extra practice on core schema
		B.	Helps clarify what can be transferred and what cannot
		C.	Illustrates analogical thinking
7.	Links Across the Curriculum	A.	Helps extend mathematical thinking to other areas (e.g. history, science)
		B.	Encourages the integration of knowledge
		C.	Supports information finding

Table 1: Seven design principles underlying the Jasper Adventure Series

assembled into the skill they comprise. At the other end is the view that components are meaningless unless students understand them in the context of the "composed" skill.

A second dimension deals with assumptions about the value of making errors and floundering with a task. At one end of this dimension is the assumption that errorless learning is ideal; at the other, that important lessons of learning occur only when students make errors or reach impasses and are then helped to correct their initial misconceptions (Borasi, 1987, in press; Clement, 1982; Minstrell, 1989; Schank, & Jona, 1991; VanLehn, 1990). A third dimension deals with assumptions about the teacher's role in the learning process; the dimension runs from authoritative provider of knowledge to a resource who may sometimes be consulted by the students and at other times might even become the student whom others teach.

In laying out these dimensions we have knowingly provided the extremes. Points along these dimensions may be actualized in different combinations by different teachers and by the same teacher in different situations. The values along these dimensions define particular instructional models. We discuss three such models below, although many others are possible. These three provide contrasting cases of capitalizing on the affordances of the Jasper series and are thus illustrative of the importance of the instructional model in determining classroom learning activities.

Example Model 1: Basics First, Immediate Feedback, Direct Instruction

One model of instruction that many people have suggested to us is what we call the "basics first" model. People who recommend this model feel that the Jasper adventures provide an excellent application for practicing one's skills. However, they assume that Jasper should be used only after students acquire all the necessary sub-skills and sub-concepts. Thus, if an adventure involves decimals, measurement, time and so forth, proponents of the "basics first" model argue that each of these areas should be taught prior to working on a Jasper adventure.

In many existing curricula, basic concepts and skills are taught in workbook or computer-based drill-and-practice environments that present the materials in an out-of-context format. Teaching usually follows a direct instruction model wherein teachers (or the authors of the materials) explain the concepts and demonstrate how to do the problems that exemplify the particular sub-skill. A particular sub-skill is considered acquired when the student can supply correct answers to the problems. Students practice doing these problems until accurate performance is demonstrated.

Feedback typically focuses on correctness of the answer - a product orientation. Students complete their workbook exercises, they are "corrected," and information about number correct is provided. Computerized drill and practice software makes possible immediate feedback, sometimes with the correct response provided. Although it is possible to implement quite sophisticated feedback via computers, most drill and practice software pays little attention to how the student arrived at the answer or to what the answer indicates regarding the student's representation of the task (e.g,. Hasselbring, Goin & Bransford, 1988).

The role of the teacher is to provide knowledge to the students–knowledge such as how to do the problems and what constitutes correct answers. In classrooms operating under this type of model, virtually all questions are initiated by the teacher and are directed at the whole class or at one student; responses are directed at the teacher. This pattern of interaction means there is little peer interaction over the subject matter.

Overall, the "basics first" teaching model is one in which students are shown how to do problems exemplifying particular sub-skills; these problems are then practiced until the student accurately answers them and then the next subskill is introduced in the same way. If the Jasper series were used in classrooms operating under this model of instruction, few of the generative activities uniquely afforded by the Jasper adventures would be realized. Because they see their role as one of providing students with knowledge, teachers operating under this model would tend to structure the solution for students and "walk them through it," occasionally asking them to supply the "facts" needed to solve the problem.

On the three dimensions of content sequencing, feedback and the role of the teacher, the decontextualized "basics first" model of teaching stands in direct contrast to the anchored instruction approach that we described earlier in this paper and elsewhere (e.g. CTGV, 1991; see also Brown, et al., 1989). By helping students understand the nature of real-world problems that are inherently interesting and important, a major goal of anchored instruction is to help students understand why it is important to learn various sub-skills and when they are useful. Our argument for the importance of this contextualized approach to learning is as follows: When instruction is separated from occasions of usage, the knowledge acquired tends to remain inert and therefore is not used spontaneously for meaningful problem solving (e.g., Bransford, Franks, et al., 1989; Simon, 1980; Whitehead, 1929). A related argument is that the "basics first" model does not provide students with enough opportunities to find and formulate problems on their own. A third argument involves the danger that "basics first" curricula often lead to misconceptions about the nature of mathematics. When mathematics is discussed by practicing mathematicians, it becomes clear that it is a science of order and pattern finding that is much more interesting and creative than the mere computation of numbers (e.g. see NCTM, 1989; Schoenfeld, 1985, 1989).

There is some evidence that the "basics first" model is particularly ubiquitous in the education of students who are at-risk of school failure, a situation that further estranges these students from meaningful mathematics instruction: "as schools serving [at-risk] children focus their resources on increasing the use of well-known methods for drilling the basics, they decrease the opportunities for those children to participate in the higher level activities that are needed to excel in mathematics and science" (Cole & Griffin, 1987). Thus, rather than helping the educational attainment of at-risk students, the "basics first" teaching model may actually exacerbate the problem (Vye, Sharp, McCabe, & Bransford, in press).

In criticizing the example of a "basics first" teaching model, we are not dismissing the importance of developing proficiency in subskills. In fact, we have devoted considerable attention to understanding how fluent arithmetic skills are arrived at and how this process might be enhanced (e.g., Bransford, Goin, Hasselbring, Kinzer, Sherwood & Williams, 1988; Goldman, Pellegrino, & Mertz, 1988; Goldman, Mertz, & Pellegrino, 1989; Hasselbring, et al., 1988). In the context of the Jasper software, we are in the process of developing "Curriculum Links" that use the Jasper episode as an anchor for developing fluency for basic concepts and procedures, such as figuring out elapsed time, fuel consumption per unit time, and cost per unit.

Unlike the "basics first" model, we advocate the use of basic exercises in conjunction with work on Jasper. Data we have collected indicate that problem solving experiences are extremely important. For example, even when students become quite good at subskills, they often remain poor at assembling the subskills for purposes of solving problems unless they have had the opportunity to explore complex problem environments (e.g., Hasselbring, Sherwood, Bransford, Fleenor, Griffith, & Goin, 1988; Van Haneghan, et al., in press). Similarly, the opportunity to watch students explore problems such as Jasper helps teachers identify and correct important misconceptions involving both concepts and procedures (e.g., Goldman, et al., 1991). In addition, the opportunity for students to work in groups and eventually to define and research their own issues related to the Jasper adventures helps reinforce the idea that the teacher is not the sole proprietor of all knowledge. Because it is very difficult for anyone to know everything about a Jasper adventure (including immediate answers to "what if" questions such as "What if the ultralight went 20 miles per hour rather than 30?"), students get the opportunity to see models of their fellow students and teachers as learners and information finders. Such models are not apparent when the major classroom activity is to memorize concept definitions and engage in computational drills.

Example Model 2: Structured Problem Solving

A second model of instruction that has been suggested to us focuses on the need to help students minimize errors and feelings of confusion. We call this the "Structured Problem Solving" model. It differs from the "basics first" model in that the introduction of complex problems is not delayed until the "basics" have been mastered; rather, the complex is introduced in parallel or slightly asynchronously with the more basic. Thus, this model capitalizes on the potentially motivating features of having students see complex situations in which their "subskills" might be used.

An important feature of the "structured problem solving" model is the attempt to eliminate errors and feelings of confusion on the part of the students. Thus, instead of beginning instruction by having students attempt to generate the kinds of sub-goals that must be considered and to then figure out how to evaluate options (e.g. in order to help Emily find the fastest way to rescue the eagle), the teacher prepares a set of worksheets that specify possible rescue plans and guide students through the processes of evaluating these plans. The greater the degree of guidance, the higher the probability that the students will not make errors.

Table 2 includes examples of some structured exercises that can guide students through a set of possible solutions to "Rescue at Boone's Meadow." In the full set of exercises, eight possible routes are provided; some are not feasible, others are feasible but require a lengthy amount of time. Students consult the episode (either the video or a storyboard form of it) to fill in the data that are left out of the route description. On the basis of the data, they make decisions regarding feasibility and comparative speed of one route versus another (e.g., the time it takes for Emily to fly from CC-B-H and back to CC compared to Larry's flying CC-H-B-H and driving back to CC from Hilda's - see Table 2). The errors that these materials eliminate are those involved in constructing the routes and determining the factors that need to be considered in evaluating each route.

We are currently using structured exercises such as these in an experiment designed to compare their effects to a situation in which students have to generate the routes and the factors that need to be evaluated (see Model 3, below). We suspect that the "structured problem solving" (Model 2) will lead to excellent mastery of the solution to the specific Boone's Meadow problem. Nevertheless, our observations of classes of students using these worksheets makes clear the fact that, even when students sit in groups (with one worksheet per group), the interactions among them are minimal and are confined to fact-finding and computation. Not surprisingly, we see no evidence of sub-goal generation and of the kinds of monitoring that in less structured situations are necessary to keep discussions on track.

Overall, the strong point of the "structured problem solving" model is that students only work on correct plans; the tradeoff is that they do not engage in problem generation and monitoring. We noted earlier that an important part of everyday problem solving is the ability to generate the sub-goals necessary to achieve one's objectives. Based on assumptions about "transfer appropriate processing" (e.g., Morris, Bransford and Franks, 1979; Bransford, Franks, Morris & Stein, 1979), we believe that the best way to develop such abilities is to allow students to engage in generative learning activities. A model for teaching that emphasizes generation is discussed next.

Plan1: Emily thinks that the quickest way to rescue the eagle would be for Larry to fly from Cumberland City to Boone's Meadow and back the same way. Will this plan work and if so, how long will it take?

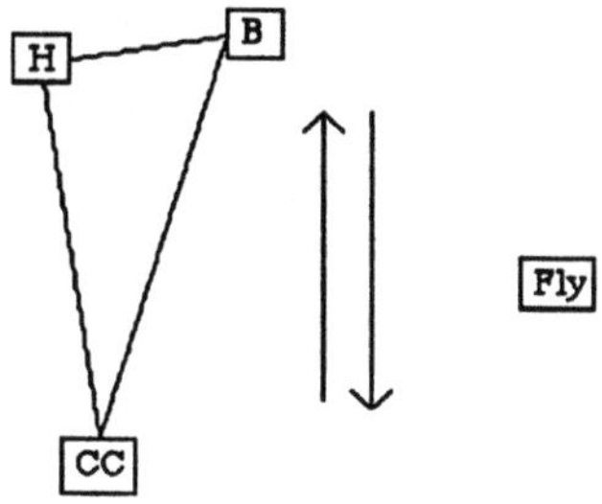

KEY: CC = Cumberland City; B = Boone's Meadow; H = Hilda's

Is there enough landing area at Boone's Meadow?

Emily first wanted to figure out if Larry would have enough space to land at Boone's Meadow. The vet said that most planes need about ____________ feet of runway, and that Boone's Meadow was half of that distance. That meant that the runway at Boone's Meadow was ________ feet long.

Emily remembered that Larry had told her that the ultralight needed __________ yards of runway to land. Changing this to feet she found that the ultralight needed __________ feet to land.

Can the ultralight land at Boone's Meadow?

YES NO (circle one)

DO YOUR CALCULATIONS IN THE SPACE BELOW

Will the plane have enough gas?

Next Emily wanted to figure out if the plane would have enough gas to fly the route. To answer this question she first had to figure out how far the plane could fly on 1 tank full of gas.

Emily knew that the plane could fly _________ miles on 2 gallons of gas. With this she calculated that the plane could fly _________ miles on 1 gallon of gas. Emily also knew that the gas tank held ________ gallons of gas. From this information, Emily calculated that the plane could fly ___________ miles on a full tank of gas.

To decide if the plane would have enough gas to fly the route, Emily next had to determine how far the plane would have to travel. She knew that the distance between Cumberland City and Boone's Meadow was _____________ miles. She calculated that the total distance to Boone's Meadow and back to Cumberland City would be __________ miles.

Can the plane travel from Cumberland City to Boone's Meadow and back the same way without running out of gas?

YES NO (circle one)

DO YOUR CALCULATIONS IN THE SPACE BELOW

Table 2: Example of Structured Exercises for Rescue at Boone's Meadow

Example Model 3: The "Guided Generation" Model

Our third example is the one we think is the most powerful teaching model; it emphasizes the importance of generative activities on the part of students. Meaningful generation most frequently occurs in relatively complex situations where the sub-goals necessary for solution are not pre-specified, so this teaching model attempts to make maximum use of the affordances present in the Jasper series. Teachers sometimes provide guidance and often adopt the role of learner–especially when students are allowed to explore issues that are suggested by the Jasper adventures (e.g., what do spoilers on the wing of a plane do? When did eagles become endangered?). Teachers will probably not know the answers but can attempt to help students learn how to find out for themselves.

The use of cooperative groups helps make the generative teaching model feasible. Initial data from several ongoing studies (Rewey, 1990) indicate that students are much more likely to solve the Jasper problems when working in groups than when working alone, and that they like working in groups on the Jasper problems. In groups, there is a higher probability of generating more of the possible solution space and of monitoring errors. In addition, the widely-held belief that a great way to learn is to teach suggests that, when a student has to explain an idea to another student, the explainer's (as well as the explainee's) understanding should increase.

Of course, it should come as no surprise that some groups of students work together much better than others (e.g., see Cosden et al., 1990; Hine et al., 1990; Salomon & Globerson, 1989). It takes time to establish the kind of "community of inquiry" that we and others envision (e.g., Lipman, 1985; Scardamalia & Bereiter, 1991). It is in this context that theorists such as Vygotsky (1978) become especially helpful. In his developmental theory, Vygotsky (1978) emphasized the importance of social support for learning provided by parents, peers, and others. He defined the "zone of proximal development" as the region wherein students could exceed performance levels they could reach on their own *with the right kind of help or scaffolding*. The challenge in guiding instruction is to find those zones of development and to create situations in the classroom that facilitate opportunities for scaffolding to occur.

In our work on Jasper, experienced teachers are helping us find ways to provide levels of support for students depending on the latters' skills and knowledge. Thus, as we stated in the introduction to this chapter, we have not attempted to construct a pre-specified curriculum that we train teachers to administer. Instead, our goal is to collaborate with teachers by providing them with some powerful tools and then learning from them.

In our research, we are beginning to explore the effects of various types of scaffolds. For example, many teachers begin each Jasper exploration by asking students to summarize the story and then try to recall relevant data. Students often erroneously remember specific facts and events. This provides the opportunity for important lessons about the constructive nature of memory; students can compare memories, search the disc and eventually check for accuracy.

With respect to problem solving we find that at least for their first Jasper adventure all of our teachers supply some degree of structure that helps students begin to generate sub-goals and plans for reaching them. Nevertheless, it is rare to find the degree of structuring shown in Table 2 (see Model 2, above). The structuring that our experienced teachers provide is much less restrictive than the structure discussed under Model 2.

Teachers are also helping us find and study ways to adapt the complex Jasper adventures to the needs of students with different degrees of preparation. For example, imagine that students do not yet know how to multiply decimals. There are ways to help them solve the Jasper problems using other means (e.g.instead of dealing with 1.5 hours, students can deal with 60 minutes and 30 minutes and then combine them). In other cases, teachers have helped us see that options can be built into the Jasper adventures that let students take simpler versus more complex routes.

A particularly interesting example of teacher-provided support was shown to us by Nancy Johnson, a teacher who taught "Rescue at Boone's Meadow" to first graders. She did not expect these students to deal with the entire problem. Nevertheless, by handing out a map and manipulatives that represented a standard for distance, Johnson was able to help the students figure out the time and distance to rescue the eagle given a particular route. One group of students was even able to determine that the pilot would have to take more gasoline.

Our plan is to continue to work with teachers in order to collect "scaffolding" or "guidance" information that will be included in our Jasper teaching materials and, in some cases, in the design of Jasper analog problems that will be available on video. Scaffolds should be most important early in the Jasper series. The ultimate goal of our instruction is to remove as many scaffolds as possible and let students solo on their own.

Scaffolds and Problem Complexity

The issue of creating scaffolds for problem solving is related to our earlier discussion of the Jasper design principle of "complexity". We noted that our Jasper adventures are purposely complex in order to reflect the complexity of real-world problems. We also noted that this is a cause for concern when one's goal is to work with students who may not begin instruction with strong backgrounds (e.g., Dick, 1991). Clearly, one could make "baby Jaspers", and some of our analog problems do in fact decrease the complexity of the basic adventure and the math skills needed to solve it. Nevertheless, as much as possible, we want to let students see the nature of the problems that, eventually, they might confront in everyday life. Our Jasper adventures are designed to be complex yet ultimately manageable.

One reason for letting students see realistic levels of complexity is that the experience of dealing only with simple problems can lead to misconceptions about the nature of problem solving and explanation. Schoenfeld (1985) notes that many college students feel that problems that are not solvable in 5 minutes or less are not solvable by them. Similarly, Spiro and colleagues (1991) document a number of misconceptions that stem from oversimplified teaching materials. Real apprenticeships provide a contrast to the oversimplified materials used in many curricula (e.g., see Brown et al., 1989). Students in apprenticeships get to see the finished products even though they may be unable to create them on their own. This gives them a clear goal and helps them understand why they need to learn new skills.

The idea of building an understanding of the need for further learning is very important for the Jasper series. The adventures are designed to create "teachable moments" that can lead to the meaningful acquisition of new knowledge. Proponents of problem-based instruction in medical education provide a similar emphasis on the importance of helping students see the need to learn new information (e.g., Barrow, 1985; Williams, 1991). Once these insights about need occur, we believe that it can be beneficial to then let students find environments (e.g. drill and practice programs) that can help them master specific types of information more efficiently. In short, we have no problem with Model 1 above as long as it is used in conjunction with experiences that provide a foundation for meaningful learning. Purists in the constructivist tradition may disagree, so this is an area that would benefit from research.

Extra Demands on Teachers

The idea of designing experiences that provide the opportunity for a wide variety of "teachable moments" that arise from student interests and questions places a heavy demand on teachers. It is impossible to know everything that could possibly be relevant to our Jasper series (e.g., principles of flight, the history of what has happened to the eagle population, etc.). An important aspect of teaching with Jasper according to Model 3 is that teachers need to stop being purveyors of knowledge and become learners along with the students. We are experimenting with uses of telecommunications that can provide students and teachers with access to resources that will enable them to find relevant information relatively efficiently (CTGV, 1991b). Without this kind of support for teachers, there is a natural tendency for teachers to over-rely on pre-packaged, workbook-type approaches such as those discussed as Models 1 and 2.

Issues of Assessment

We close our discussion of instructional design and the Jasper series by briefly discussing issues of assessment. Different approaches to assessment have important implications for the conclusions one draws about instructional design, and vice versa (Goldman, Pellegrino, & Bransford, in press).

As an illustration, consider the goal of assessing the benefits of Models 2 and 3 that were discussed earlier. To do so, one might show "Rescue at Boone's Meadow" to fifth and sixth grade students who are then randomly assigned to one of two conditions: (1) A highly structured "model 2" condition with workbook-like exercises such as those in Table 2 versus (2) a generative condition that provides some general guidelines for how to approach the problem and then lets students attempt to solve the problem by working in groups.

It seems clear that, for many types of assessments, Model 2 might well seem superior to or at least as good as Model 3. In particular, because students who work under Model 2 are led through a variety of different rescue routes, one would expect them to do well on a mastery test that asked them to re-solve the problem. They should also do well on a highly analogous problem where the routes are pre-specified and their task is to evaluate which is fastest.

The goal of Model 3 is to facilitate generative problem finding as well as problem solving. The kinds of assessments relevant to the generative emphasis in Model 3 are ones that present students with new problems that require them to generate sub-goals, determine the information relevant to solving them, and then proceed to a solution. Model 3 also emphasizes the importance of helping students find issues that interest them that they then research, and of beginning to spontaneously notice connections between events outside of Jasper and the problems they solved in the Jasper series. Assessments of changes in these types of activities are tricky yet possible. For example, portfolio assessments can be used to illustrate changes in students' research and writing on topics related to the Jasper adventures. In addition, we are in the process of finding events in magazines, newspapers and other sources that can be used to ask students to discuss the questions that they might ask about these areas. As an illustration, imagine that students who are taught with Models 2 & 3 are later given a paragraph about Christopher Columbus and asked to state questions about it that they would like to think about. We suspect that students who work with Jasper under Model 3 will be more likely to ask about issues such as the kind of planning that Columbus did before embarking on his trip.

Data being collected on our Jasper adventures is relevant to problem generation as well as problem solving and suggests that, for teachers who teach in a manner consistent with Model 3, there is marked improvement in their students' abilities to generate the classes of sub-problems that need to be considered in order to solve complex problems (e.g., Pellegrino, Heath, & Warren, with the Cognition and Technology Group at Vanderbilt, 1991). An example of a written problem that asks students to generate what they would need to plan for a solution is illustrated in Figure 1. Our data also suggest that interview tests on transfer problems that

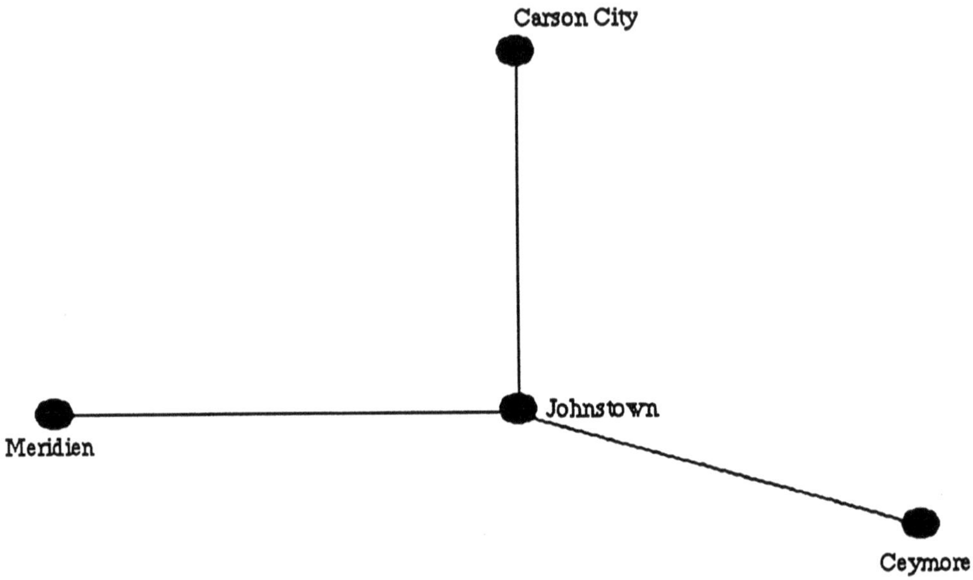

Jill lives in Carson City. She wants to drive her car from her house to a friend's house in Meridien. As shown on the map, Jill can take the road from Carson City to Johnstown and Johnstown to Meridien. Her car is filled with gasoline and ready to go. There is a gas station in Carson City, Ceymore, and Meridien, but there is not one in Johnstown. Jill plans to leave on her trip at 8:00 in the morning.

The Challenge: What does Jill need to think about to figure out how long it will take her to make the trip?

Figure 1: Written Problem Generation: An Example

require generation as well as problem solving show a strong superiority for Jasper students compared to controls (e.g. Goldman, et al., 1991; Van Haneghan, et al., in press).

Furthermore, reports from our implementation sites indicate that, when faced with complex real-world problems, students often spontaneously say "oh this is a Jasper problem." They then seem to have much more of a tolerance for the initial feelings of confusion that complex problems generate; hence they are more likely to persevere.

It is important to note that the control conditions used in the studies reported above involve students who engaged in problem solving activities that are not Jasper related. We are just beginning the kinds of studies that assess the effects of different types of instruction (e.g., Models 1, 2, 3) within the context of Jasper. And we are just beginning to develop assessments of "noticing connections" and of the ability to engage in independent research and communicate one's findings to others in the class. Furthermore, many of our previous studies have looked at the effects of working with only one Jasper. Longitudinal studies are needed to truly assess the degree to which various types of instruction can promote independent thinking and learning. As data from these kinds of studies become available, we should be in a better position to begin to understand different approaches to instructional design and their long-term effects.

Summary and Conclusions

We began by noting that our approach to instructional design has not been to create a prepackaged curriculum that specifies goals, teaching strategies, materials and assessments. Instead, we have designed video-based "anchors" or "cases" that depict realistic problem settings that have face validity. Our goal has been to put these cases into the hands of experienced teachers and researchers in the hopes that they will provide a common ground for further inquiry and research.

We used our Jasper Woodbury problem solving series as an illustration of one set of anchors or cases. The design principles underlying our Jasper series (see Table 1) provide a set of features that afford, but do not dictate, particular types of teaching and learning activities. In designing our Jasper adventures, we have been particularly sensitive to goals for instruction that emphasize the importance of helping students become independent learners who engage in generative problem finding as well as problem solving (e.g. Bransford,et al., in press; Resnick, 1987; Resnick & Klopfer, 1989; Scardamalia & Bereiter, 1991; Schank, 1991). Unlike many existing sets of materials (e.g., traditional word problems), the Jasper adventures afford generative learning activities and, because of their complexity, provide an environment that is especially conducive to group work.

Despite the affordances of our Jasper series, we noted that different models of instruction utilize these affordances to different degrees. After discussing three dimensions of instructional models, we discussed three possible models for teaching with Jasper. The Jasper adventures provide a context for studying these teaching models in more detail.

We ended our discussion by noting that any attempt to determine the relative effectiveness of teaching models must deal with issues of assessment. It seems clear that many types of assessment will be insensitive to the different teaching models we discussed. In other cases, one model may look superior to another on one set of tests but not another (e.g., Morris, et al., 1979). This possibility highlights the need to motivate one's assessments from a theoretical perspective and to design tests that are sensitive to that perspective (Goldman, et al., in press).

Current work by members of our group is paying special attention to the generative aspects of problem generation as well as problem solving. Our initial data indicate clear benefits for problem generation, but we also indicated that much more work is needed – especially longitudinal work that follows students over time units such as a semester, a year, or longer.

We are hopeful that others will be motivated to design their own sets of instructional studies so that issues of instructional design can be explored in more detail.[3]

References

Adams, L., Kasserman, J., Yearwood, A., Perfetto, G., Bransford, J., & Franks, J. (1988). The effects of facts versus problem-oriented acquisition. *Memory & Cognition, 16,* 167-175.

American Association for the Advancement of Science (1989). *Science for all Americans.* A project 2061 report on literacy goals in science, mathematics, and technology. Washington, DC: Author.

Barrow, H. S. (1985). *How to design a problem-based curriculum for the preclinical years.* New York: Springer-Verlag

Borasi, R. (1987, November). Exploring mathematics through the analysis of errors. *For the learning of mathematics,* 7(3), 1-8.

Borasi, R. (in press). *Learning mathematics through inquiry: A study of practice.* Portsmouth, NH: Heinmann Educational Books.

Bransford, J. D., Franks, J. J., Morris, C. D., & Stein, B. S. (1979). Some general constraints on learning and research. In L. S. Cermak and F. I. M. Craik (Eds.), *Levels of processing and human memory.* Hillsdale, NJ: Erlbaum.

Bransford, J. D., Franks, J. J., & Vye, N. J. & Sherwood, R. D. (1989). New approaches to instruction: Because wisdom can't be told. In S. Vosniadou & A. Ortony (Eds.), *Similarity and analogical reasoning.* New York: Cambridge University Press.

Bransford, J.D., Goin, L.I., Hasselbring, T.S., Kinzer, C.K., Sherwood, R.D., & Williams, S.M., (1988). Learning with technology: Theoretical and empirical perspectives. *Peabody Journal of Education, 64*(1) 5-26.

Bransford, J. D., Goldman, S. R., & Vye, N. J. (in press). Making a difference in peoples' abilities to think: Reflections on a decade of work and some hopes for the future. In L. Okagaki & R. J. Sternberg (Eds.), *Directors of development: Influences on children.* Hillsdale, NJ: Erlbaum.

Bransford, J. D., Sherwood, R., Vye, N., & Rieser, J. (1986). Teaching thinking & problem solving: Research foundations. *American Psychologist, 41*(10), 1078-1089.

Bransford, J., Sherwood, R., Hasselbring, T., Kinzer, C., & Williams, S. (1990). Anchored instruction: Why we need it and how technology can help. In D. Nix & R. Spiro (Eds.), *Cognition, education, and multimedia: Explorations in high technology.* Hillsdale, NJ: Erlbaum.

Bransford, J. D., & Stein, B. S. (1984). *The IDEAL problem solver.* New York: W. H. Freeman & Co.

[3] Information on how to obtain the Jasper Adventures may be obtained by contacting the authors at the Learning Technology Center, Vanderbilt University.

Bransford, J.D. & Vye, N. J. (1989). A perspective on cognitive research and its implications for instruction. In L. Resnick & L. E. Klopfer (Eds.), *Toward the thinking curriculum: Current cognitive research..* Alexandria, VA: ASCD.

Bransford, J.D., Vye, N., Kinzer, C., Risko, V. 1990). Teaching thinking and content knowledge: Toward an integrated approach. In. B. Jones & L. Idol (Eds.), *Teaching thinking*. Hillsdale, NJ: Erlbaum.

Brown, J. S. Collins, A., & Duguid, P. (1989). Situated cognition and the culture of learning. *Educational Researcher, 17*, 32-41.

Brown, S. I. & Walters, M. I. (1983). *The art of problem posing*. Hillsdale, NJ: Erlbaum.

Charles R., & Silver, E. A., (Eds. (1988). *The teaching and assessing of mathematical problem solving*. Hillsdale, NJ: Erlbaum & National Council for Teachers of Mathematics.

Chi, M. T., Bassok, M., Lewis, P. J., & Glaser, R. (1989). Self-explanations: How students study and use examples in learning to solve problems. *Cognitive Science, 13*, 145-182.

Clement, J. (1982). Algebra word problem solutions: Thought processes underlying a common misconception. *Journal of Research in Mathematics Education, 13*, 16-30.

Cognition and Technology Group at Vanderbilt (in press(a)). Anchored instruction and science education. In R. Duschl & R. Hamilton (Eds.), *Philosophy of science, cognitive psychology and educational theory and practice*. NY: SUNY Press.

Cognition and Technology Group at Vanderbilt. (in press(b)). Anchored instruction approach to cognitive skills acquisition and intelligent tutoring. In W. Regian &V. J. Shute (Eds.), *Cognitive approaches to automated instruction*. Hillsdale, NJ: Erlbaum.

Cognition and Technology Group at Vanderbilt. (1990). Anchored instruction and its relationship to situated cognition, *Educational Researcher, 19*(3), 2-10.

Cognition and Technology Group at Vanderbilt. (1991a). Technology and the design of generative learning environments, *Educational Technology, 31*(5), 34-40.

Cognition and Technology Group at Vanderbilt. (1991b). *Video environments for connecting mathematics, science, and other disciplines*. Paper presented at the Wingspread Conference on Integrated Science and Mathematics Teaching and Learning. Racine, WI.

Cole, M., & Griffin, P. (1987). *Contextual factors in education*. Madison, WI: Wisconsin Center for Education Research.

Cosden, M. A., Goldman, S. R., & Hine, M. S. (1990). Learning handicapped students' interactions during a microcomputer-based writing activity. *Journal of Special Education Technology, 10*, 220-232.

Dewey, J. (1933). *How we think: Restatement of the relation of reflective thinking to the educative process*. Boston: Heath.

Dick, W. (1991). An instructional designer's view of constructivism. *Educational Technology, 31*(5), 41-44.

Frederiksen, J. R., & Collins, A. (1989). A systems approach to educational testing. *Educational Researcher, 18*, 27-32.

Gibson, J. J. (1977). The theory of affordance. In R. Shaw & J. Bransford, (Eds.), *Perceiving, acting, and knowing*. Hillsdale, NJ: Erlbaum.

Gick, M. L. & Holyoak, K. J. (1980). Analogical problem solving. *Cognitive Psychology, 12*, 306-365.

Gick, M. L. & Holyoak, K. J. (1983). Analogical problem solving. *Cognitive Psychology, 15*, 1-38.

Goldman, S. R., Cosden, M. A., & Hine, M. S. (1987, April). *Writing groups: A context for interactive communication among learning disabled children.* Poster presented at the meetings of the Society for Research in Child Development. Baltimore, MD.

Goldman, S. R., Mertz, D. L., & Pellegrino, J. W. (1989). Individual differences in extended practice functions and solution strategies for basic addition facts. *Journal of Educational Psychology, 81*, 481-496.

Goldman, S. R., Pellegrino, J. W., & Bransford, J. (in press). Assessing programs that invite thinking. In H. O'Neill & E. Baker (Eds.), *Technology assessment.* Hillsdale, NJ: Erlbaum.

Goldman, S. R., Pellegrino, J. W., & Mertz, D. L. (1988). Extended practice of basic addition facts: Strategy changes in learning disabled students. *Cognition & Instruction, 5*, 223-265.

Goldman, S. R., Vye, N. J., Williams, S. M., Rewey, K., Pellegrino, J. W., & the Cognition and Technology Group at Vanderbilt (1991, April). *Solution space analyses of the Jasper problems and students attempts to solve them.* Paper presented at the American Educational Research Association. Chicago, IL.

Hanson, N. R. (1970). A picture theory of theory meaning. In R. G. Colodny (Ed.), *The nature and function of scientific theories*. Pittsburgh: University of Pittsburgh Press.

Hasselbring, T., Goin, L., & Bransford, J. D., (1988). Developing math automaticity in learning handicapped children: The role of computerized drill and practice. *Focus on Exceptional Children, 20*(6).

Hasselbring, T., Sherwood, R., Bransford, J., & Fleenor, K., Griffith, D., Goin, L., (1988). An evaluation of a level-one instructional videodisc program. *Journal of Educational Technology Systems, 16*(2), 151-169.

Hine, M. S., Goldman, S. R., & Cosden, M. A. (1990). Error monitoring by learning handicapped students. *Journal of Special Education, 23*, 407-422.

Jenkins, J. J. (1979). Four points to remember: A tetrahedral model and memory experiments. In L. S. Cermak & F. I. M. Craik (Eds.), *Levels and processing in human memory.* Hillsdale, NJ: Erlbaum.

Lipman, M. (1985). Thinking skills fostered by Philosophy for Children. In J. Segal, S. Chipman, & R. Glaser (Eds.), *Thinking and learning skills: Relating instruction to basic research.* Hillsdale, NJ: Erlbaum.

Lockhart, R.S., Lamon, M., & Gick, M.L. (1988). Conceptual transfer in simple insight problems. *Memory & Cognition, 16*, 36-44.

McLarty, K., Goodman, J., Risko, V., Kinzer, C. K., Vye, N., Rowe, D., & Carson, J. (1990), Implementing anchored instruction: Guiding principles for curriculum development. In J. Zutell & S. McCormick (Eds.), *Literacy theory and research: Analyses from multiple paradigms.* Chicago, IL: National Reading Conference.

Minstrell, J. A. (1989). Teaching science for understanding. In L. B. Resnick & L. E. Klopfer (Eds.), *Toward the thinking curriculum: Current cognitive research.* Alexandria, VA: ASCD.

Morris, C. D., Bransford, J. D., & Franks, J. J. (1979). Levels of processing versus transfer appropriate processing. *Journal of Verbal Learning and Verbal Behavior, 16*, 519-533.

National Council of Teachers of Mathematics. (1989). *Curriculum and evaluation standards for school mathematics.* Reston, VA: Author.

Porter, A. (1989). A curriculum out of Balance: The case of elementary school mathematics. *Educational Researcher, 18* (5), 9-15.

Palinscar, A. S., & Brown, A. L. (1984). Reciprocal teaching of comprehension-fostering and comprehension monitoring activities. *Cognition and Instruction, 1*, 117-175.

Palinscar, A. S., & Brown, A. L. (1989). Instruction for self-regulated reading. In L. B. Resnick & L. E. Klopfer (Eds.), *Toward the thinking curriculum: Current cognitive research.* Alexandria, VA: ASCD.

Perfetto, G., Yearwood, A., Franks, J., & Bransford, J. (1987). The effects of generation on memory access. *Bulletin of the Psychonomics Society, 25*(3), 151-154.

Pellegrino, J. W., Heath, A., & Warren, S., with the Cognition and Technology Group at Vanderbilt (1991). Collaboration at a distance: A Jasper implementation experiment in nine states. *Paper presented at the annual meeting of the American Educational Research Association*, Chicago, IL.

Porter, A. (1989). A curriculum out of balance: The case of elementary school mathematics. *Educational Researcher, 18* (5), 9-15.

Resnick, L. (1987). *Education and learning to think.* Washington, DC: National Academy Press.

Resnick, L. B. & Klopfer, L. E. (Eds.), (1989). *Toward the thinking curriculum: Current cognitive research.* Alexandria, VA: ASCD.

Resnick, L. B., & Resnick, D. P. (in press). Assessing the thinking curriculum: New tools for educational reform. In. C. O'Connor & B. Gifford (Eds.), *New approaches to testing: Rethinking aptitude, achievement and assessment.* New York: National Committee on Testing and Public Policy.

Rewey, K. L. (1990). *Scripted cooperation and anchored instruction: Interactive tools for improving mathematics problem solving.* Unpublished Manuscript, Texas Christian University, Fort Worth, Texas.

Risko, V. J., Kinzer, C. K., Goodman, J., McLarty K., Dupree, A., & Martin, H. (1989). *Effects of macrocontext on reading comprehension, composition of stories, and vocabulary development.* Paper presented at the meeting of the American Research Association, San Francisco, CA.

Salomon, G. & Globerson, T. (1989). When teams do not function the way they ought to. *International Journal of Educational Research, 13*, 89-99.

Scardamalia, M., & Bereiter, C. (1991). Higher levels of agency for children in knowledge building: A challenge for the design of new knowledge media. *Journal of the Learning Sciences, 1*(1), 37-68.

Scardamalia, M. & Bereiter, C. (1985). Fostering the development of self-regulation in children's knowledge processing. In S. F. Chipman, J. W. Segal, & R. Glaser (Eds.), *Thinking and learning skills: Research and open questions (Vol. 2).* Hillsdale, NJ: Erlbaum.

Schank, R. C., & Jona, M. Y. (1991). Empowering the student: New perspectives on the design of teaching systems. *Journal of the Learning Sciences, 1*(1), 7-36.

Schoenfeld, A. (1985). *Mathematical problem solving*. Orlando, FL: Academic Press.

Schoenfeld, A. H. (1988). Problem solving in context(s).In R. I. Charles, & E. A. Silver (Eds.), *The teaching and assessing of mathematical problem solving (Vol. 3.).* Hillsdale, NJ: Erlbaum & National Council for Teachers of Mathematics.

Schoenfeld, A. H. (1989). Teaching mathematical thinking and problem solving. In L. B. Resnick & L. E. Klopfer (Eds.), *Toward the thinking curriculum: Current cognitive research.* Alexandria, VA: ASCD.

Schwab, J.J. (1960). What do scientists do? *Behavioral Science, 5*, 1-27.

Silver, E. A. (1990, April). *Discussant: Reflections on directions of mathematics curriculum reform from the cognitive and social sciences.* Invited Address at the American Educational Research Association meetings, Boston, MA.

Simon, H. A. (1980). Problem solving and education. In D. T. Tuma & R. Reif (Eds.), *Problem solving and education: Issues in teaching and research.* Hillsdale, NJ: Erlbaum.

Spiro, R. J., Feltovich, P. L., Jacobson, M. J., & Coulson, R. L. (1991). Cognitive flexibility, constructivism, and hypertext: Random access instruction for advanced knowledge acquisition in ill-structured domains. *Educational Technology, 31*(5), 24-33.

Van Haneghan, J., Barron, L., Young, M., Williams, S., Vye, N., & Bransford, J. (in press). The Jasper series: An experiment with new ways to enhance mathematical thinking. In D. Halpern (Ed.), *Concerning: The development of thinking skills in the sciences and mathematics.* Hillsdale, NJ: Erlbaum.

VanLehn, K. (1990). *Mind bugs: The origins of procedural misconceptions.* Cambridge, MA: The MIT Press.

VanLehn, K., & Brown, J. S. (1980). Planning nets: A representation for formalizing analogies and semantic models for procedural skills. In R. E. Snow, P. A. Federico, & W. E. Montague (Eds.), Vol 2: *Cognitive process analyses of learning and problem-solving*. Hillsdale, NJ: Erlbaum.

Vye, N. J., Sharp, D. M., McCabe, K., & Bransford, J. D. (in press). Discussion: Exploring a reasoning-based program for teaching arithmetic. In B. Means (Ed.), *Models for teaching advanced skills to disadvantaged students.* San Francisco, CA: Jossey-Bass, Inc.

Vygotsky, L. S. (1978). *Mind in society.* Cambridge, Mass: Harvard University Press.

Whitehead, A. N. (1929). *The aims of education.* New York: MacMillan.

Williams, S. M. (1991). *Case-based approaches to instruction in medicine and law.* Unpublished manuscript, Vanderbilt University, Nashville, TN.

Williams, W. M., & Sternberg, R. J. (1988). Group intelligence: Why some groups are better than others. *Intelligence, 12*, 351-377.

Yackel, E., Cobb, P., Wood, T., Wheatley, G., & Merkel, G. (1990). The importance of social interaction in children's construction of mathematical knowledge. *Teaching and learning mathematics in the 1990s. 1990 yearbook of the national council of teachers of mathematics.* Reston, VA: NCTM.

2 Computer-Mediated Zones of Engagement in Learning

Harry McMahon and William O'Neill

Language Development and Hypermedia Research Group, Faculty of Education,
University of Ulster, Northern Ireland

Even the most casual observer of any activity that could be vaguely described as learning could not but be impressed with the social dynamics of the activity. The complex and intense interactions between teachers and pupils have defied any simple categorization but, however it is described, education cannot fail to be seen as entailing a special form of discussion; teachers and learners engage in a form of dialogue which is highly context bound, in that it relates at the very least to the social environment of classrooms, with all that that entails.

The same kind of generalization can be made about our own learning experiences, and the dialogue that that entails, as the authors engage in research and development. Whether we like it or not (in fact, we like it very much) our research is also context bound and the direction it has taken and the products which have flowed from it reflect that context. The tool for learning which has led us to think more deeply about the zones of engagement which are generated as pupils and teachers work together on computers was born three years ago. Back then we were engaged as usual in the business of educating trainee teachers, working with school teachers on the use of computers in the development of literacy, monitoring new technologies for possible instructional applications, looking out for opportunities to contribute to the amelioration of the strife torn atmosphere of Northern Ireland, raising children, walking dogs and generally enjoying life. It was the confluence of all this "busyness" that produced a set of circumstances which led us to develop the generic computer-based tool for learning which has come to be known as "bubble dialogue" and to conceptualize the associated zones of engagement in learning that are the subject of this paper.

The Genesis of Bubble Dialogue

Ginny "Speaks" and "Thinks"

In September 1988, Harry acquired his first Macintosh and, landscape artist that he is, immediately began to explore the drawing tools in HyperCard. A Christmas present of a book on HyperTalk, the scripting language which gives HyperCard its power as a development tool, and exposure to Amanda Goodenough's delightful Californian cat, Inigo, led Harry to embark on the creation of an animated adventure story for children about his dog, Ginny. As was the case with Inigo, Ginny's adventure was entirely pictorial. She explored her neighborhood, recognizable to children in local schools, and encountered characters in a textless world. It was

Bill's criticism of Harry's picture story that made us take the first step towards the creation of bubble dialogue. According to Bill, Ginny did not belong to the children: the characters and the plot were Harry's, not theirs. The children had no sense of ownership. Harry's response was to provide Ginny and the other characters in the story with empty thought and speech bubbles as in a comic strip: he reasoned that the children could get closer to ownership of the characters displayed on the screen if they paused the action at critical moments in the story and made the characters speak and think about the situation they were in.

We hardly knew it at the time, but we were launched on a research and development path that has produced some very interesting results. This was not a case of instructional designers formally deciding what their goals were and systematically setting out to achieve them -- it was more a case of educators talking and thinking about the fun they were having with a new toy (actually a new tool), like children and teachers talking and thinking about what you can do with a pencil. If we had played the formal role of designer and not been our context-bound selves, the outcomes would probably have been very different.

Orla Takes a Skip and a Jump Towards Literacy

As life and luck would have it, at the same time Bill's six year old daughter, Orla, was using HyperCard to produce a picture story featuring her own creations, a sister and brother called Kim and Pat. Although Orla had embued her characters with much vitality -- they were richly illustrated, oozing with personality and interest -- her associated writing, in contrast, was rather pedestrian, simply relating a sequence of events. As Bill saw it, Orla was a specific case illustrating the generality that awareness of those aspects of language required for literacy does not develop spontaneously from spoken language. Faced by the task of writing rather than talking about Kim's and Pat's adventure, she was caught within the narrative form, unable to convey the richness of her knowledge of the characters she had created.

It was at this stage we made a breakthrough. We gave Ginny's speech and thought bubbles to Orla's characters, Kim and Pat. The results were, to us at least, astonishing. Orla's characters suddenly came to life as she made them speak and think. They thought about the possible consequences before they went through the door. They took account of what each other might be thinking as they bargained for leadership. They exhibited a richness of experience and an inner life that told us volumes about Orla. We knew immediately that we were onto something special that had to be tried out in a classroom.

The Derry Girls Reveal Their Hidden Selves

An invitation to help out in a history project on the 17th century Siege of Derry, being undertaken by a class of thirteen year olds in a Londonderry school, was taken up and the notion of creating bubble dialogue was introduced to a group of five girls. They liked the idea and a visit to the city walls with a video camera, with the children acting both as role players and camera crew, allowed several role play scenes (defending and attacking soldiers, starving citizens, modern day meetings between locals and tourists) to be captured on video for later transfer into HyperCard.

More by design than by accident, the scenes were captured on a section of the city walls where the work of a contemporary sculptor was installed. A Janus-like statue in iron depicts two anonymous life size figures fused together, arms stretched out as in a crucifix, back to back, one looking out over the Catholic Bogside, the other into the walled city. At the right moment Harry wondered aloud, "I wonder what the statues would say if they could speak?", only to be answered by a thirteen year old's joke: "My arms are killing me!".

But the children liked the idea of making the statues speak for themselves and on the following day, after creating firstly an hilarious bubble dialogue between a starving citizen and an about-to-be-eaten mouse and then an imaginary but historically consistent exchange between two defending (Williamite) soldiers deciding whether or not to fire a cannon at the advancing King James, they moved on to make the statues talk. After considerable discussion the children decided that the statues were old, that one was a Williamite and the other a Jacobite, and that they were looking back to their past. The following text emerged over a period of about thirty minutes, each sentence being committed to the screen after considerable discussion among the five. It was a matter of great concern as to which statue, soon dubbed the "Protestant" and the "Catholic" rather than the academically respectable Williamite or Jacobite, should next be made to say or to think what, and why. The outcome was, to put it mildly, startling -- to both the typist/observer (Harry) and the children's teacher:

Two statues stand back to back on Derry's walls; all of a sudden, one of them speaks.

Jacobite says: When I was a young boy life was hard. We hadn't got half as much as you had and we still don't. You've got a swimming pool and we've got nothing. Your toilets are twice the size of ours.

Note: Here, and throughout, Harry typed in what the girls wanted the statues to say without questioning it or giving any sign of approval or disapproval. He had no idea why the children were making the statues talk about toilets and swimming pools. He just typed the sentences in as if they were perfectly normal things for statues to be talking about.

Jacobite thinks: Its not fair. You and your stupid swimming pool. You're no better than us.

Williamite says: Our ancestors fought hard for what we've got. We shouldn't have to suffer for what happened years ago.

Williamite thinks: The Protestants are the better race. History can prove that.

Jacobite says: We are the rightful religion because Catholic was the original religion in Ireland. The Protestant religion is only a recent thing.

Williamite says: The only reason there had to be a new religion was because the old one was wrong.

Jacobite thinks: The original religion wasn't good enough for you and your private swimming pool.

Jacobite says: It wasn't wrong; it just didn't suit you and your fancy ways.

Williamite says: Let's not go over this all over again. Anyway, my arms are killing me.

Jacobite thinks: My arms are killing me too, but I'm not going to let a Protestant get the better of me.

Note: The irony of the pun on the word "arms" was lost on the children but not the adults who have since read this dialogue script.

The emerging text seemed to us and to the teacher to have captured the reality of the pub and soap-box rhetoric of the Ulster conflict as well as, and perhaps better than, any practiced journalist or playwright might. The teacher's first startled reaction was momentarily to feel ashamed that something so starkly reflective of simple sectarian thinking, albeit of both views of the conflict, could have emerged in her classroom. Her next was to wonder how parents would react if they knew that their offspring could produce such writing. Then she asserted that this kind of writing could never have emerged in her classroom by any other method. And finally she claimed that she had a chance now to debate an issue on the basis of the children's own "controversial" writing rather then on material of her own making, artificially introduced. Her immediate request to us was to turn the statues to face one another. Her hypothesis -- the new face-to-face dialogue would be interestingly different and through class debate about the differences her goal of cross-community empathy and reconciliation could thereby be advanced.

Harry's question to the teacher was "Why did the Catholic statue complain about not having proper sized toilets or a swimming pool?" The answer was simple but significant on a number of dimensions -- the children had been on an "Education for Mutual Understanding" visit two weeks earlier to a school on the other side of the community divide. What had been designed as an opportunity to promote reconciliation had in fact served to reinforce attitudes associated with privation and discrimination. What was also significant was that the children had made the statues speak for themselves in the context of their recent experience and in so doing had brought their hitherto private world into the public domain.

These two early experiences with children's creation of bubble dialogue convinced us of the need to explore the technique in depth in at least two contexts. Orla's use pointed us towards the exploitation of the technique in the development of literacy. The Derry girls made it clear that we needed to explore its use as a tool for learning in curriculum contexts where the expression of empathy with historical or contemporary figures, real or imagined, might enhance learning. Since then, the bubble dialogue tool has gone through several iterations of design and trial in realistic settings and many new applications have emerged as it has been used by people around the world.

Some Features of the Bubble Dialogue Tool

As it now stands, bubble dialogue combines elements of role play, dialogue creation and a process we have called reflexive dialogue analysis. Users play out the parts of characters on the computer screen, creating and reflecting upon dialogue in the characters private domain (their thoughts or "inner speech") as well as in the public domain (their public speech). Students using it engage actively with their own ideas and those of others, including those of their teacher. Initially, through the creation of bubble dialogue in a context, and then, through reflection about that dialogue, they have the opportunity to express personal (perhaps naive) views of the world, to contemplate multiple perspectives in both public and private domains and to accommodate their own thinking to contrary views. By sensitive selection of the roles and the topics of bubble dialogue, the teacher can ensure that learning takes place embedded in realistic contexts relevant to everyday life. These characteristics make the tool compatible with constructivist views of the nature of the learning process. (Cunningham, 1991)

The power of the tool and its attraction to users lies in its versatility -- in principle, it is possible to create bubble dialogue between any characters in any context. In practice, users make use of a stack called BubbleMaker to create characters or choose them from a graphics library, paste them into the comic strip framework, write a prologue which sets the dialogue in a context, and allocate an opener, a first speech and/or thought, to one of the characters. With these steps completed any number of copies of the customized stack can be created for students to "fill" with dialogue. (McMahon and O'Neill, 1991)

Each page of a bubble dialogue stack contains four icons, representing a speech bubble and a think bubble per character. Clicking on one of these icons brings up an empty speech or think bubble for the chosen character. We have found that both children and adults readily engage with the characters, debating what they should be made to say and think and often competing with one another to enter text into the empty bubbles. Typically, as the dialogue is created, users show every sign of being thrown forward by the emerging dialogue in much the same way as one finds oneself thrown forward in animated discussion.

Creation and Review Modes

One of the important features we have incorporated in the tool is the distinction between creation and review modes. In creation mode, (see Figure 1), the only movement possible is forward -- to the next chosen empty speech or think bubble. In addition, during creation of dialogue a turn-taking protocol makes sure that users cannot make either character have an extended conversation with himself or herself. Once a character has had one speech, and optionally one thought, the user's only course of action is to transfer attention to what the other character is going to be made to say or think.

In contrast, in review mode, which can be switched into at any stage, users can move backwards and forwards through the dialogue at will, adding notes, editing the text of the dialogue, adding thoughts or speech where they did not previously exist, or extending the dialogue beyond its "ending". Use of the tool in review mode has proven to be very powerful, encouraging reflexivity in the users. Sometimes we allow students to review their own dialogues and add comments in the notes field about "what's happening" or comments on the motives and feelings of the characters. At other times we have asked students to add thoughts to a dialogue which had previously been created in speech only by their peers. Alternatively or additionally, teachers and researchers may also annotate the dialogues in any manner they see fit, adding field notes, commentary on the dialogue from the teachers point of view, questions for the students to consider as they review their work, and so on.

Figure 1. The tool in creation mode

Figure 2. The tool in review mode

At any time, getting access by a reserved key stroke, the teacher can set or reset a number of options: unlock or lock existing text so that it can or cannot be edited, allow or disallow the choice of new think or say bubbles, change the names of the characters, allow or disallow lookbacks, change text size. This facility allows the teacher to present the tool in a wide variety of modes. Finally, we think it is very important that users have access to a printout of the dialogue. Clicking on the printer icon produces a comic strip version of the dialogue which they can have to keep. The icon just above this produces an annotated script like the one presented above. We have found these scripts ideal for further analysis, by the students themselves, or by the teacher or researcher. Another feature of the bubble dialogue tool is an archive which is created continuously. This can be the repository of such information as the users editing of the content of speech and thought bubbles created by themselves or others, or the sequence in which they add notes during the review process.

Possible Instructional Strategies

In bubble dialogue, the subject of discourse is largely determined by the choice of characters and the prologues and openers which guide the users in a particular direction. However, the interactions which take place on and off screen also depend on the number of pupils, the role played by the teacher and the method of allocation of screen roles to teacher and pupils. The various arrangements which are possible amount to different instructional strategies. There are many possibilities; some examples of how the tool can be used in education will serve to illustrate the range. Readers will be able to think of modalities more relevant to their own working environment.

Teacher and Pupil -- One on One

Probably the most direct approach to using bubble dialogue is for the teacher to focus her time and attention on one particular learner. This strategy involves the teacher sitting down at the keyboard with a single pupil and playing one character on the screen while the pupil plays the other. For example, a pupil thought to be misunderstanding a key concept could be asked to play the role of an expert on the screen and the teacher could play the role of a novice interrogating the expert at an appropriate level of cognitive demand. Evidence of the pupil's learning deficit accumulates on the screen and in the off-screen dialogue about what is happening on the screen.

One Pupil Playing Both Roles

A strategy worth exploring after pupils have gained some experience of the tool is to have a single pupil play both roles. This was the arrangement when Orla first revealed the power of the technique as a device for making children break out of strictly narrative prose. The topic of conversation on the screen could be anything from a dialogue between two historical characters, or two characters in a novel or play, to a recollected or imagined exchange between a bully and a victim in the school yard. Whatever the subject, there is no escaping the fact that the teacher still has to be involved at some stage to discuss the authenticity of the historical dialogue or to share the problem of how to talk oneself out of being seen as a "natural victim" in the eyes of the school bully.

Two Pupils -- One on One

A third instructional strategy involves each of a pair of pupils being allocated one of the two characters. For example, if the subject of study in a social studies class is sex role stereotyping in the work place, mixed pairs of pupils could use the tool to create bubble dialogue between male and female characters whose opening dialogue is sexist in tone. The pupils work with the tool in two stages, one in which allocation of character to user is on a same sex basis, each user entering dialogue for the character of the same sex, and then the reverse. The teacher intent on reducing sex role stereotyping then debates the two scripted dialogues with the pupils. Why are they the same? Why are they different? What was it like to play the role of someone of the opposite sex?

Two or More Pupils Sharing Both Roles

In another approach to allocation of roles, the pupils could be grouped in single sex and/or mixed sex groups and asked to collaborate in the analysis of a previously "canned" dialogue, entered in speech only by the teacher, between two characters from a television soap. The task allocated to groups, to jointly decide and enter on the screen what each of the characters must have been thinking as the dialogue developed, is then followed up by a full class debate on the dialogue in which the teacher makes sure that the class explores notions of power relationships, privacy, self esteem, peer pressure, and so on, and their implications for interpersonal behavior .

Teacher and Pupils: One on Several

A fifth strategy is for the teacher to play one character while a group of pupils collaboratively play the other. Take, for example, the situation where a physics teacher, working with the class on the physics of circular motion, has encountered the popular misconception that astronauts float around inside space ships because they are outside the field of gravity of the earth. She has done her best to correct the misconception, but wants to make sure that several particular pupils have the chance to show that they really understand the role that gravity plays in determining the orbits of space ships and their contents. The characters on the screen are Cheri, a sixteen year old visitor to Cape Kennedy, and John Glenn. The opener has Cheri saying "All the books say that you are weightless up there; and they say that because there is no gravity outside the earth's atmosphere". The teacher plays the part of Cheri in speech only while the pupils do their best to collaboratively create the speech and thought of John Glenn as he explains what being "weightless" really means. In the process the teacher, listening carefully to what the pupils have to say to each other about the unfolding bubble dialogue between Cheri and John, makes sure that the pupils have to show that they can counter all the popular but spurious arguments that they have used themselves, plus perhaps a few extra ones that she throws in for good measure. The group then debates the resulting scripted dialogues with the teacher, who in the discussion reveals what she thinks Cheri would have been thinking and John Glenn should have been thinking and saying as he tried to get Cheri to understand what goes on inside a space ship.

The Theoretical Frame

We have outlined five possible instructional strategies which can be used with bubble dialogue. Our experience of using these strategies, and various refinements of them, suggests that they have features in common which arise from the projective nature of bubble dialogue and from the special characteristics of the social contexts in which it is used in creative and review modes. In this section we explore the theoretical frame in which our work is grounded and in the next we make use of the idea of zones of engagement in learning to look more closely at what we think is happening when people use bubble dialogue.

Interpsychological and Intrapsychological Functioning

One of the most fundamental assumptions that has guided our work is the view of Vygotsky that the mind is continually engaged in a process of social formation. In his view, the cultural and historical dimensions of the social world of which we are part have a major influence on learning. Not only do they inform and sustain what we consider to be our individual worlds, they also ensure that our individuality is itself derivative and secondary, developing out of and underpinned by social interaction. In the classroom, much of the influence on our actions is highly context bound, relating to the social dynamics of the particular situation that we find ourselves in. Recognizing the importance of this pervasive societal dimension of the educative process, Vygotsky sought to define those areas of social engagement which specifically concern the development of the higher mental processing which are fundamental to institutional education. His research brought him to the conclusion that intellectual development takes place between people before internalization takes place; essentially we learn in dialogue between each other: "Any function in the child's cultural development appears twice, or on two planes. First it appears on the social plane and then it appears on the psychological plane. First it appears between people as an interpsychological category, and then within the child as an intrapsychological category." (Vygotsky, 1981, p. 163). For Vygotsky, the process whereby this social learning becomes internalized was a key issue and he attempted to identify the situations when it was most likely to take place. He specified a form of dialogue between teacher and pupil in which instruction precedes development. As instruction he had in mind a form of dialogue which creates a scaffolding for the learner, one in which the learner constructs his own meaning; not in a vacuum, however, but in interaction with an adult who supports and challenges the learner, causing reflection on the process and leading to ownership of the learning by the learner. This process of internalization is seen as a constructive process, not a simple transfer from a social to a personal knowing. Vygotsky described it as taking place in the "zone of proximal development", which Wertsch succinctly describes as "the dynamic region of sensitivity in which the transition from interpsychological to intrapsychological functioning can take place." (Wertsch,1985, p.67). This zone is neither a property of the child nor of the interpsychological functioning alone but is jointly determined by the child's level of development and the form of instruction involved. The challenge to educators is to develop forms of instruction such that, to quote Wertsch, "interpsychological functioning can be structured such that it will maximize the growth of intrapsychological functioning."

The Personal Dimension

While the zone of proximal development has a social dimension, it has to be recognized that it also has a personal dimension and that much of the conversation which takes place between the learner and the teacher is invisible to one or the other, not because participants have chosen to keep things in the private domain, but because they do not share a common perception of the function of the interaction or because they are not working out of a shared conceptual base. Each of us, and not just pupils and teachers, comes to a discussion from a different ground, a different set of experiences, in which, as Lakoff and Johnson (1980, p.125) put it, "individual concepts are not defined in an isolated fashion, but rather in terms of their roles in natural kinds of experiences". Those experiences can be very different from person to person and it is part of the teachers art to find the common purpose and shared conceptual ground with each and every child.

The Private Dimension

In any exchange between discussants some aspects of the situation can be shared, and this overlap of views may exist at several levels, but some aspects remain private to both speakers. As Bruner (1987) points out, "The nature of the untold and the untellable are deeply cultural in character. ...How a culture defines privacy plays an enormous part in what people feel private about and when and how." The inner rehearsal of what has to be private and what can be public is part of an internal dialogue, private to the individual. Nevertheless, it is in public conversation, often through the power of metaphor, that life experiences are shared. Our personal knowing remains social, bound into social practices which determine what is allowed to be public in a particular context.

When does it make sense for a teacher or a pupil to make things public, to declare the inner self, if only in the intimacy of a one-on-one conversation? Wertsch, quoting Rommetveit, argues that, "Communication aims at transcendence of the private worlds of the participants." and yet our shared experience is that stripping away the layers of protection that hide our inner selves is an extremely difficult, if not impossible, thing to do. For teachers and pupils alike, aspects of knowing remain private with the effect that the misconceptions that children may have about the objects of their learning remain hidden from the teacher. Likewise, the teacher's lack of understanding of the pupil's thinking can remain hidden from the pupils. How then can we, as teachers, function in a context where the personal and private dimensions of experience and thinking can so readily get in the way of the development of shared understanding? Donaldson (1978) argues, and we agree, that teachers must help learners to turn language on itself, taking it out of its embeddedness in events, so that it allows both teachers and pupils to reflect on and reconstruct our separate and shared experience.

In summary, our theoretical position is that it is in and through our interaction with others that we make meaning. However, as much of languaging remains hidden from us, contextualized or privatized to a degree which makes it invisible to either or both parties in the exchange, we teachers must find a way to make children see and hear their own dialogue so that they can engage in the reflective, reconstructive, decontextualizing process of using language to understand dialogue. Our goal should be to develop forms of instruction, forms of scaffolding, which foster this process and so maximize internalization within the zone of proximal development. Some forms of instruction do foster these processes, but not too many of them have been featured among the products of educational software designers. We would like to suggest that bubble dialogue mirrors some of the learning processes described above and is an example of an instructional system which promotes reflection, reconstruction and decontextualization within the one of proximal development, that region of sensitivity in which the transition from social to personal knowing takes place.

Zones of Engagement

We propose to use the term "zone of engagement" to describe each of the various zones of interaction in dialogue between people (or characters standing for people) which are created as use is made of bubble dialogue. If one looks closely at the forms of interaction which occur as users make the characters "talk" and "think" about an issue in a context, zones of engagement can be seen to bind character to character, users to characters, and users to users. Even where the teacher is not a user of bubble dialogue, in the immediate sense of sitting at the keyboard driving the dialogue along by making one of the characters "speak" and "think", the users and the teacher can still be seen to share a zone of engagement. In its least complex mode of use, bubble dialogue is created by two users, each responsible for playing the part of one of the two characters on the screen. For the moment, we will take it that one of the users (on the right in Figure 3) is a teacher, the other a pupil, and that they both can see both characters (and what they have to "think" and "say") on the screen.

A complex of mediation procedures links the user's and the character's zones of engagement. Users are invariably interested in and ready to discuss the behavior of the other user's character and the way it is influenced by the behavior of their own character. For example, in the case we have illustrated in Figure 4, the pupil will be fascinated by what Character B says and thinks in relation to what she makes Character A say. But the only way the pupil can influence Character B's behavior, whom she does not directly control, is to engage in "dialogue" in either of two ways, by acting on her own character, or talking to the teacher about what he is making Character B say or think. At the same time, the teacher is fascinated by what the pupil makes her character say and think in response to his creation of Character B's public and inner speech, but he too has to work through his own character or through the user's zone of interaction. We have found that the interactions which occur in one zone trigger interactions in the other and those in turn set off yet more language activity within each zone. As we have indicated above, a turn taking protocol ensures that the two characters must take turns to "speak" and, optionally, to "think", either before or after speech. No such protocol applies to the zone of interaction binding the two users, unless it is imposed artificially by requiring the users to remain silent. While we have already experienced and observed the creation of many bubble dialogue scripts in many modalities, including the one we have just described, unravelling the complexity of the interactions in the zones of engagement is a task hardly yet addressed, yet alone completed. However, we have had enough experience to allow us to point to some of the underlying factors which we think influence the ways people use bubble dialogue and are affected by its use.

Figure 3. Zones of Engagement

Identification

In this instructional strategy, a zone of engagement binds the teacher to the student and another zone binds the two characters to each other. Each zone of engagement encompasses interpsychological and intrapsychological functioning. In the zone of engagement binding the users, the intrapsychological functioning is in the private domain, but in the character's zone of engagement the intrapsychological functioning has the special characteristic of being in the character's private domain and yet visible to the users.

Our research with 8 to 13 year olds suggests that children of this age particularly enjoy the individual responsibility of creating the speech and "thought" of one of the two characters on the screen. Many appear to identify strongly with a character in this modality, defending the character's integrity against off-screen challenge by their peers. Even where the teacher asks her pupils to share the creation of dialogue for both characters we have noticed how pupils will

Figure 4. Loci of interpsychological functioning (dotted line) and intrapsychological functioning (dashed lines)

tend to identify with one of the characters. Observation of adults also suggests that users do set out to make at least one of the characters say what they themselves would like to say.

Distancing

While users certainly identify with the characters, there is, nevertheless, a distancing effect in operation. Users do not play themselves, they play the parts of characters on the screen. The experience is something like conventional role play, but playing a character has more in common with pulling the strings of a puppet than acting a part on a stage. The user can control the character and be responsible for the character's actions without having to "become" the character. The character can be made to say and think things that the user would not want to say or have the courage to say in real life. Ideas and opinions can be explored without those ideas and opinions being ascribed to the user who is driving the character. Defense of a position taken up in the zone of engagement between the two characters, if it is needed, is not a defense of the user but of the character on the screen who can be allowed to make mistakes without loss of face or to say and think things which would normally lie outside the perceived norms of acceptable convention in a particular context.

We have found that both children and adults normally reluctant to step into roles in front of others can easily be drawn into exploring these roles in bubble dialogue and we speculate that it is this distancing effect that makes the medium a more comfortable form of role play for many people. For example, in the case of the Derry statues, the teacher was able to tolerate the statues saying what they said; it was much less likely that she would have encouraged or that the children would have readily accepted role play where the characters were people rather than statues. It was as if, for these children and their teacher, people in Northern Ireland could not be allowed to expose their private thoughts about the "Troubles", but statues could. Through the mediation of the statues, standing as they did as powerful icons for the two warring communities, the issues were brought into the public domain in a form in which they could be debated.

Slow-Thrownness

Our personal experience of the impetus which drives one along during the creation of bubble dialogue has made us note with interest Heidegger's concept of thrownness and the use made of it by Winograd and Flores in their discussion of the design of the human-computer interface. (Winograd and Flores, 1986). Thrownness describes the characteristic of real life dialogue whereby one experiences a forward push to the next element of the exchange. It is true that what one says depends on what has been said and what one surmises might be the effect of saying what one has in mind to say; but in real discussion, negotiation, argument, dialogue, (whatever one cares to call it), there is little or no time to reason it all out. The pace of debate calls out the speech and it is formed in the action of speaking; the dialogue is "thrown" forward. We think that bubble dialogue has this same characteristic of thrownness, but it has the additional advantage of being slower than real life, allowing for reflection about the dialogue in both creation and review modes. We have much anecdotal evidence from users which suggests to us that the characteristic of "slow thrownness" is important. Often, first time users of bubble dialogue will express great surprise when they discover how much time has elapsed while they have been creating a dialogue. It is as if, caught up in the dialogue on the screen, they measure time subjectively in relation to the screen dialogue ("such a dialogue would have lasted about ten minutes") and forget how much "extra" time they have put into talking with their fellow users about what the screen characters must be thinking and feeling.

Competition

An interesting effect takes place when more than one user is involved in playing a character. This is most likely to occur when there are three or more users. In this modality, users can be seen to compete to control the characters; some users will try to control both, others will concentrate on trying to control one particular character. It is as if each user has their own view of the unfolding story on the screen. As the characters are made to speak and think, each of the several users seeks to explain the character's interaction in the public domain, and the private worlds ascribed to the characters, by reference to their own unique experience. Different views thus come into conflict with each other and users are faced with the dilemma of either taking on the task of resolving the differences through a co-creation process or taking control of a character so that at least one side of the bubble dialogue is coherent (in the eyes of that user). If the latter course is taken, the user tries to own the character so that the character can be made to live sensibly in that user's world. Thus we hypothesize that the competition we have observed arises from each user's attempt to achieve coherence in the character's public discourse by taking individual control of the direction of the dialogue, and that means, as a first step, taking control of at least one character's speech and thought. The effect of this procedure may be to satisfy one or two users, but at the cost of ignoring the conflicting views of others. On one occasion, when observing a group of teachers create a cross community dialogue about mixed marriages, Harry noticed that one of the teachers withdrew from the collaborative action and said nothing. During review, his question to this "non-user" as to his feelings about what had happened brought an explosion of frustration about the inadequacy of a well meaning Protestant teacher's attempts to get into the shoes of a Catholic character on the screen. The ensuing debate on the requirements and challenges of reconciliation and the search for empathy went on for some considerable time and partial resolution came through a process of reflection, reconstruction and decontextualization long after the bubble dialogue had been created.

Co-Creation

Resolution of conflict can also come by the negotiated co-creation of "composite" characters. We have observed users setting out to make peace as soon as they come into conflict about what the characters on the screen should be made to say and think. They cooperate. They debate the issue. They explore the context. They hypothesize the effects of speech acts. They argue over what the character must be feeling and whether or not the feeling should be made public. They can be seen to compete to explain or to postulate the character's behavior, but, because the task is shared, off-screen debate has to focus on why the character should think such-and-such or be made to say so-and-so. In this way, resolution of conflict can come by the negotiated co-creation of "composite" characters. In the process, users are exposed to conflicting views of what is happening and can happen on the screen, but because the on-screen dialogue exhibits the characteristic of "slow thrownness", it is open to analysis and reflection as it is created, in a way that neither real time dialogue nor recorded dialogue can afford.

Proximal Visibility and Invisibility

These terms came into existence when we were thinking about the ways in which teachers using bubble dialogue in the classroom influence the development of children's handling of ideas. In the ordinary, everyday circumstances of the classroom, when teachers talk to children, the children do not necessarily understand what is going on. There may, on occasion, be little or no shared meaning. The old expression, "In one ear and out the other", conveys the teacher's view of the interaction with the child whose experience has not yet placed them in the position to understand what the teacher has to say in that context at that moment. Although the teacher and pupil share a zone of engagement, in that they are talking to each other, they are as if invisible to each other. As Vygotsky would have put it, they do not share a zone of proximal development. As we find ourselves expressing it, they are proximally invisible.

We think that in such circumstances bubble dialogue can mediate between the teacher and the pupil, causing them to co-create a zone of proximal development, to become cooperative, proximally visible meaning makers. We have watched the way in which children attend avidly to what the characters driven by teachers have been made to say and think. We have the feeling that, in situations where the teacher might fail to engage the child by using natural language about an issue in a context, the same teacher would not necessarily fail to catch the focused, active attention of the child where the teacher's intentions and actions in language are mediated by the interaction of bubble dialogue characters. If the two characters, driven by teacher and child, are able to maintain a meaningful interaction within the screen-based zone of engagement then the teacher and the child together achieve proximal visibility in the off-screen zone that they share. In effect, the instructional strategies made possible with bubble dialogue allow the teacher more readily to create a zone of proximal development. If children have the opportunity to compete and to cooperate with each other and with the teacher to bring coherence to the behavior of both characters as the tool is used in creative mode, then the chances of the teacher and pupil's sharing a zone of proximal development are high. Now able to reflect on the off-screen debate of the children, the teacher can take account of the children's grounded experience and their individual commitments to particular views of the world that the characters inhabit. She can also choose her contribution to the co-creation of the characters so as to cause the learners to take account of and reflect on the teacher's agenda as well as their own.

In the use of bubble dialogue there is no escaping the key role that has to be played by the teacher. Ideally, the teacher takes part in the creation process, but, if that is not possible, the use of the tool in review mode allows the teacher to contribute to later reflexive debate with the users. The teacher's answer to the rhetorical question, "I wonder what I would have said or thought if I had been that character?", can cause children to take up a new perspective on the dialogue. In all probability, they will already have experienced enough conflict of view to want to hear a fresh voice. In this way the teacher can make use of the characters created by the children as she and the children use natural dialogue to co-create a zone of proximal development where each can "see" the other, despite the fact that she was not party to the creation of the on-screen dialogue.

Looking Back

Looking back at what we have written about interpsychological and intrapsychological functioning and about the personal and private dimensions of the zone of proximal development we can see that we now face the challenge of interpreting, within that theoretical frame, our experientially derived and still context bound notions of identification, distancing, slow thrownness, competition, co- creation and proximal visibility and invisibility. Our first thoughts are that the bubble dialogue tool provides an environment which allows teachers to set up instructional strategies which assist in the development of interpsychological and intrapsychological functioning. Teaching is a form of discussion, an engagement with the learner. We believe that bubble dialogue maps onto this process. By causing learners to take up a variety of positions in dialogue and by making the public/private and personal/social dimensions of dialogue visible to scrutiny both during and after its creation, it encourages reflection on the meaning making process itself and acts as a bridge for the teacher and pupils to cross into mutual proximal visibility.

The secret in building such bridges is to achieve a balance between the degree of identification and the degree of distancing between the users and the characters. The degree of identification must be such that the users are motivated to try to make the characters behave coherently in a known (user's) world and at the same time the distancing must be such that the user feels free to explore the boundaries of that world by allowing the characters to take risks with ideas and with the conventions of what must be deemed private and public in any particular context. The competition and co-creation which occur when bubble dialogue is created by groups of users generates highly focused natural dialogue about the emerging bubble dialogue. Though bubble dialogue is slow compared to natural dialogue the level of thrownness keeps users on task for surprisingly long periods.

As they create and reflect upon bubble dialogue, whether they realize it or not, users are exploring the nature of interpsychological and intrapsychological functioning. In the process they gain access to inner worlds that are no less social for being more or less private and they have the opportunity, not often afforded learners, to draw on shared insights about inner worlds as they debate how people make meaning out of context bound dialogue. Questions about the substance and process of dialogue become the stuff of the off-screen debate. In this kind of debate, the users may expose more of themselves than they might otherwise, but we are convinced that it is not the uncovering of the inner selves of the users that is central to bubble dialogue. Rather it is the exposure to debate about the interpsychological and intrapsychological functioning of the screen characters and the social practices in which they engage that opens a window for all users, pupils as well as teachers, into the minds of others and of themselves.

Looking Forward

Meaning is created between people as they take up various positions in discourse. The extent to which they can transcend their different private worlds and create a shared social reality, no matter how fleeting, is the stuff of human interaction. We feel that the challenge for designers of computer-based learning environments is to create mediating tools which will not only respect this form of human interaction but facilitate a reflection on the whole meaning making process. The experience of creating and using the bubble dialogue tool has given us insights into the criteria which should be applied to the design of constructivist learning environments. Among the features we would expect to see in such environments are the following:

Embedded and Grounded

The learning should be embedded in relevant contexts and arise out of the concerns of the learners, fully grounded in their real and imagined experiences, thus encouraging "ownership of the learning process.

Dialogue Centered

The use of any tool to mediate meaning is essentially a language centered activity. Recognizing that learning is essentially a form of discussion, computer-based tools should build on and encourage this process.

Multimediated

Although language is central to the learning process the mediational power of other forms of representation, such as drawing, photography and music should be recognized and incorporated.

Reflexive

Not only should the computer based tools encourage expression and articulation of genuinely felt concerns but it should encourage self-awareness of the knowledge construction process itself. It is through the decontextualization of mediated sign systems that higher forms of intellectual development come about.

Just-in-Time Design

It will not be possible to provide the first of the features outlined above unless the instructional development tool can be rapidly tailored by the teacher for use with particular children in particular contexts. The tool should provide a scaffolding which structures the experience that the children have when the tool is used and allows the teacher to rapidly modify the tool for use in very particular circumstances and for very particular ends. We have sought to meet this criterion by creating a stack called BubbleMaker which the teacher can use to rapidly customize bubble dialogue to the needs of learners.

Ahead-of-Time Design

The designers of constructivist learning environments need to accept that ahead-of-time design of learning tools is also a constructive, reflexive process which is meaningless unless it is grounded in the experience of teachers and children in classrooms. Software of quality will emerge from discourse in the community of educators and educated. It once was that this discourse, the exchange of ideas about needs, prototypes and trials, was so slow that the temptation was to see it as a single exchange of formalized views. One was supposed to know and say where one was going from the outset. Object-oriented multi-media programming environments have now reached such a high level of ease of use that instructional systems designers can now contemplate a virtually continuous dialogue in classrooms. We advocate a design-through-dialogue process, a dialogue with teachers and children which exhibits a thrownness slow enough to allow the exchange to be reflexive, but fast enough to make everyone want to continue contributing to the re-specification and modification of the learning tools under development. Designers should be prepared to be context bound, in fact they should set out to bind themselves through dialogue to the communities of teachers and learners whom they serve.

References

Bruner, J. (1987). The transactional self. In Bruner, J. & Haste, H. (Eds.). *The childs construction of the world.* London: Methuen.

Cunningham, D. , (in press). Beyond educational psychology: Steps towards an education semiotic. *Education Psychology Review.*

Donaldson, M. (1978). *Childrens minds.* New York: Fontana.

Eco, U. (1984). *Semiotics and the philosophy of language.* Bloomington: Indiana University Press.

Lakoff, G. & Johnson, M. (1980). *Metaphors we live by.* Chicago: University of Chicago Press.

McMahon, H. & O'Neill, B. (1991). Bubble dialogue -- A new tool for learning and research. *Proceedings of CAL91*, University of Lancaster, (in press).

Vygotsky, L. (1962). *Thought and language*. Cambridge, Mass. : M. I. T. Press

Vygotsky, L. (1981). The genesis of higher mental functions. Quoted in Wertsch, J. V. (1985). *Vygotsky and the social formation of mind.* Cambridge, Mass. : Harvard University Press.

Wertsch, J. V. (1985). *Vygotsky and the social formation of mind.* Cambridge, Mass.: Harvard University Press.

Winograd, T. & Flores, (1984). *Understanding computers and cognition.* Norwood, New Jersey: Ablex Publishing Corporation.

3 The Creation of Effective Modern Learning Communities: Constructivism in Practice

John Abbott*

Education 2000, U.K.

The following paper is, I suspect, unusual in two ways. Firstly I am essentially a practitioner, rather than a theoretician. I have come to research late in my career... intuitively my experience, first as Principal of a large English Comprehensive School and latterly as Director of an Educational Foundation, has led me into exploring Constructivism from practice rather than theory. Secondly my current research requires me to express theory and research findings in ways which are comprehensible and, dare I say it, inspirational to lay audiences.

Re-reading this paper, after letting it rest for a while, I was conscious that it resembled - when seen as a research paper - a primitive, almost naive, art form. I was tempted to reconstruct it as a formal research paper, but realized that if I did it would lose that direct impact which has to be a feature of my work. I am confident of leaving it as it is in the hope that others beyond the research community may read it and feel that, within the ideas, there is something they can do to put constructivism into practice.

Empowering young people to see continuous learning as a means of transformation ("How do we turn present constraints into opportunities") is at the heart of my work. It has been for many years. As a teacher of geography I was always amazed at how much more rapidly young people learned from applied field work, than they did from textbooks; as a Principal I was worried by the way in which the formal structures of secondary education undermined the enthusiasm of youngsters out of good "progressive" primary schools to establish their ownership of learning.

To think about learning and how it occurs for those other than educationalists studying this as an abstract process, is difficult. Everyone "knows" about learning; everyone has their own experience to draw from, and their own favorite anecdotes. Our culture currently assigns an overriding significance to the role of the school (almost as a right of passage), and of the sub-divisions of knowledge into a set of disciplines. Earlier theories about the brain certainly produced persuasive evidence of the existence of a quality called "intelligence". The concept captured public imagination. Here was something to be measured, something which would enable people to be graded; it was easy to assume that it was indicative of certain kinds of future achievement.

---

* I wish to gratefully acknowledge R.F. Dalton for his assistance in the preparation of this chapter.

That our stereotypic views are suspect is the common stock of most reflective people; "Education is what remains after you've forgotten everything you ever learned in school". Single definitions of intelligence do no credit to the wide range of achievements that have little, if any, correlation to a general factor of intelligence. Some "school refusers" have gone on to be outstandingly successful members of society. Enormous numbers of us experience real discontinuities between what we seem to learn naturally and that which we have to learn mechanically. Increasingly people question the sub-divisions of the curriculum as being inappropriate to the structure of knowledge (and perhaps to the multi-facets of complex intelligence), and question whether such divisions, so beloved of specialists, are not counter-productive of real understanding?

So powerful are the assumptions about learning – "I'm thick and I can't learn": "School said I was a failure, but I know that was unfair": "He's a swot, not to be trusted": "She really knows what she's talking about": "You can't teach me anything" – that the basic tenet that man is a Learning Species comes as a shock to many.

> "We underrate our brains and our intelligence. Formal education has become such a complicated, self-conscious and overrated activity that learning is widely regarded as something difficult that the brain would rather not do... but reluctance to learn cannot be attributed to the brain. Learning is the brain's primary function, its constant concern, and we become restless and frustrated if there is no learning to be done. We are all capable of huge and unsuspected learning accomplishments without effort." (Smith, 1986)

After all, it is man's ability to learn that has enabled him to evolve to his current position of near master of his planet. But we sense that our learning processes are getting confused, and for many people breaking down completely. "The Crisis in our Schools" could be a headline in a paper today in America, Australia or the United Kingdom; signs are that it will soon be so also in countries as self-assured as Germany and Japan. The "Crisis" in learning is fast becoming an international phenomenon.

Young children, of pre-school age, learn extremely rapidly of their own volition; those living in stimulating and exciting homes make quite extraordinary progress by the age of five. Their "natural curiosity" seems to disappear as they move into formal schooling. Some come to terms with this and do well; too many others never recover that natural curiosity and become "restless and frustrated" not because there is no learning to do, but because they can't make a connection between their needs and a system that seems alien.

I believe that a reappraisal of how learning takes place within contemporary society is an essential first step in preparing to provide richer and more challenging learning environments which will enable ever more people to "make a connection" between their natural curiosity and the mechanisms to extend their learning in ways which are significant and meaningful.

Education 2000 is a privately funded Educational Foundation created in 1983 to carry out applied research and development. It is particularly concerned to promote those changes within pedagogic practice which enable young people to take control of their own learning so becoming equipped to be effective life-long learners. As director, I am responsible for building bridges and making partnerships which give practical demonstration to so many of the ideas that are our mainstream of thought. I have had to learn to interpret these in ways the ordinary person can comprehend. A sort of educational "Mr Fixit". My thinking revolves around such quotations as these from Peter Drucker's latest book (1989):

> "We now know how people learn. We now know that learning and teaching are not two sides of the same coin. They are different. What can be taught has to be taught and will not be learned otherwise. But what can be learned must be learned."
> "One learns a subject. One teaches a person."
> "There are more hours of pedagogy in one 30 second commercial than most teachers can pack into a month of teaching."
> "Within the next decades education will change more than it has changed since the modern school was created by the printed book over 300 years ago."
> "For today's small child the television set and the video-cassette recorder surely provide as much information as does the school - in fact probably more. But still only through the school, that is through organized, systematic, purposeful learning is this information converted into knowledge and becomes individual's possession and tool."

Finally a comment from a Conference on Industry/Educational Partnerships held in Arlington, Virginia, in November 1990.

> "Partnership in the USA has a much broader concept and philosophy than in the United Kingdom; not merely a contract between business and education but a whole way of thinking about the place of learning in the community. It is estimated that, from birth to the age of 18, children spend only 8% of their lives in school, and that they obtain only 20% of their knowledge through attendance at school. Partnerships therefore have to focus not just on the school experience but on the totality of education experience, including the influences that affect a child before the school years. The involvement of parents and the community at large, often overlooked in the United Kingdom, is essential: to achieve lasting changes and improvements in the education of young people it is suggested that both business and the education service must "reach out" to the community and form broadly based coalitions."

I have had to learn to talk about such matters without scaring the wits out of people! There is a way of doing this - "He who espouses radical ideas must always wear a dark suit."

And now I want to share some ideas with you about what learning communities could be like in the future. Do you remember the observation that, for every great technological development made in the past century, the constituent parts of this have all been around for at least 20 years before anybody realized how to line them all up. I suspect that this book is about speeding up the process of "lining up". if not, it should be.

I resigned my Headship in 1985 because I was convinced that conventional schooling was, for very many young people, actually preventing them from becoming personally involved in their own learning. Despite the efforts of my staff - and they were a good staff - it became increasingly obvious to me that many of the changes which were necessary had to be made outside the school - the school and community had to learn to come together and "develop a new act". Single institutional change was not adequate; "whole system" change was necessary.

English Education

For an international readership I need first to paint a general picture of English education - if that is ever possible! The issues are becoming increasingly matters of international concern but their resolution is entirely dependent on local circumstances... hence this detailed description of English education..

England, like so many other nations, is in educational turmoil. People are uncertain, fearful; a system which they once thought they understood is not delivering what they think they want. Certainties are becoming ever less certain; criticism is rife; bold, quick, simple solutions are sought. Teachers are blamed as a major cause of our national malaise, and then exhorted to become the leaders of our national rejuvenation. Let me give you the main bones of our skeleton.

(a) Historically British education has concentrated on quality for the few; we have done it well. Just one college at Cambridge won 26 Nobel prizes between 1945 and 1990, during which time Japan won 3. "The British invent it; the Japanese make it; the Americans sell it".

(b) Some 70% of the existing workforce left school at the earliest possible opportunity, many at the age of 14.

(c) Under the influence of eminent Victorians our highly prestigious Public Schools (which of course are private schools) concentrated on the development of character rather than intellect, and certainly on theoretical rather than applied studies.

(d) Unlike Massachusetts in its edict of 1643, compulsory education for all in England dates only from 1870. Following closely after the Factory Acts, which prevented children working in the mines and factories, its prime function appeared to many to be custodial. Schools were invested with social, ethical and academic responsibilities; parents, it seemed, need not bother about "learning" anymore.

(e) Unlike the American common High School, England developed a tripartite Secondary system in 1944. On the basis of an examination at the age of 11, 25% were deemed capable of a classical Grammar School education; the remainder went to Technical Schools and Secondary Moderns. The Grammar Schools were better staffed and equipped than the other schools.

(f) The selective system became as unpopular with middle class parents, who saw their families being split up, as it was with the Teachers' Unions. Progressively from the 1960s Comprehensive Schools replaced the tripartite system; (Margaret Thatcher as a Conservative Minister of Education actually approved more comprehensive reorganization schemes than any other Minister - Conservative or Socialist). Largely without a new philosophy, these new schools sought to include in a single institution what previously happened in three. They grew large, they needed generous staffing and their curriculum frequently resembled that which many Americans know as "The Shopping Mall High School".

(g) Freed from the need to cram children for the 11+ examination there was a flowering of exciting ideas in the Primary Schools. The Plowden Report identified the traits of the experiential learning system. At its best it created children excited by learning, inquisitive, imaginative... the "hungry student" which Ted Sizer seeks. Good teachers were needed; it was hard work but immensely rewarding. Not all teachers were up to it; their schools became sloppy - "liberal" they often claimed. Child-centred learning was seen by outsiders to be soft, lacking rigour and a major contribution to the fall in educational standards.

(h) Enormous creativity went into pockets of development in Secondary Schools - the Micro Electronics Project (MEP) did much to put British schools at the forefront of the use of computers in education in the late 1970s and early 1980s.

(i) It was a Socialist Prime Minister, Callaghan who, in 1976, first called the education service to public account by inviting the nation "to go into the Secret Garden of the curriculum". Schools belonged to the community, not to the producers, the country was told.

You need also to know something about the ownership of our schools.

(j) Our Public Schools are, of course, private. They cater for 7% of the pupils. They receive no money directly from the State and charge fees which, for a day pupil, can be at least 50% more than the State would pay for a place in one of its schools; boarding fees can be up to $20,000 per annum. The better known schools have considerable investments. To "buy into" private education is seen as a measure of financial/career success. Their catchment areas are perceptual, rather than geographic; although physically they dominate the local community, they do not belong to it.

(k) The Government Department of Education and Science saw until recently its role largely as negotiating monies from the Treasury to pass to Local Education Authorities; defining regulations for school buildings; the certification of teachers; teacher salary negotiations etc.. Central Government did not "own" a single school, nor did it define the curriculum with the exception of two subjects - Religious Education and Physical Education. It set general regulations on the structure of schools and in 1965 required all Authorities to reorganize their Secondary Schools into Comprehensives. Since 1988 regulations for the curriculum have changed dramatically.

(l) England is divided into some 120 Local Education Authorities (LEAs), varying in size from less than 200,000 (a very few) to large shire counties of a million or more and, the largest, the Inner London Education Authority. Each Authority is under local control and levies its own rate on householders; despite the fact that the greater proportion of local rates are spent on education an ever increasing proportion of education expenditure has become dependent on Central Government grants.

(m) From 1976 onwards, Central Government has become increasingly interventionist and directive. Legislation culminated in the Education Act of 1988, which set up a new National Curriculum, new examinations, and assessment at 7, 11, 14 and 16. LEA's that raised additional rates for education were penalized by a comparable reduction in Government grants. Increasing power was delegated to manage schools to Parent Governors. LEA's were required to cut back progressively on their central expenditure and allocate 85% or more of the funds directly to individual schools.

(n) Legislation to enable parents to vote to take their "Secondary" schools out of LEA control was proposed in 1988, specifically to satisfy the demands of parents who felt the overall planning of the LEA ran counter to the interests of "their" school - "opting out" - thereby gaining control of 100% of available funds. Partly as a result of Government pressure, partly from a sense of impatience with the LEAs, ever more schools are "opting out", and arrangements have now been made for Primary Schools similarly to "opt out".

Government has declared its wish for the majority of schools to opt out within 5 years. Each school becomes its own cost centre, subject to market forces. U.S. readers of Chubb and Moe ("Politics, Markets, and America's schools") should note that, as yet, this does not "open up" the supply side; it is the parents who vote on opting out, not the teachers. And in a land where education is not well regarded, and where "visions" are suspect, this is most likely to move strongly against further school-based innovation.

(o) In conclusion to this section let me add three further points:

(i) Government is currently dodging the issue of increased resources, preferring to suggest that if 120 Chief Education Officers could not run the system effectively, 4,500 Secondary Heads would all be able to do a better job with the funds saved from local central sources.

(ii) These changes reinforces the idea of the school as the unit for education - in isolation to the rest of the community, and on its own in relation to other schools.

(iii) The Policy reinforces the "split" between Primary and Secondary education.

Education in England is now high on the political agenda, but educational leadership has become tired and muted. The system is under colossal strain; directive follows directive, manual after manual, prescription chases prescription.

Is this based on any new insight into the nature of learning, or the kinds of learning that may be needed in the future? Frankly for every single insight of that nature, and they are certainly there within the subject specific requirements of the National Curriculum, there are very many more assumptions based on belief in the validity of instruction, formal discipline, basic skills and "market forces".

So, that is the background. Now to the substance.

Education 2000

The Education 2000 Trust is, I fancy, a peculiarly English phenomenon. A group of influential individuals with backgrounds in industry, commerce, education and other professions came together to express their deep concerns at the scale of change which they saw was necessary within education, change greater than the normal capacity of the system to manage. (To some they were "interfering busybodies", to others they exemplify all that is best in the determined amateurs concern for the future of his society.)

> "For too many young people education has been a passive act; they have been subject to, but not involved in, the process. The essential challenge facing education today is to ensure that youngsters become active learners, involved and committed to tasks they understand, taking an ever-increasing responsibility for their own learning, and ready for a life-time of continuous learning." (Education 2000, 1987)

The exact details of the change which they anticipated were not expressed, other than the need for a "total systems" change.

> "Our social and economic survival will depend on our ability to create a learning society, sufficiently flexible and fleet of foot to embrace and master change. It calls for fundamental changes in our school system, in the way we view learning and in the relationship between teacher and student." (Education 2000, 1987)

The Trustees summoned a week-long Conference in July 1983 and invited people from a variety of backgrounds, and varying levels of experience, to formulate a series of "Hypotheses for Education in AD2000". Utilizing the advanced technology of the time the Conference actually agreed to the text of the complete report and arranged for the near-instant publication of this through Cambridge University Press. It was a document before its time. The Media largely regarded it as unreasonably radical (it now seems old-hat). The Conference disbursed, and the ideas were set to gather dust on a shelf unless a new implementation mechanism could be developed.

I was not involved with this Conference, and knew nothing about the ideas until I read a copy of the Report. By then I'd been Headteacher of a 900-strong boys only 11-18 Comprehensive School for 10 years; I was living with all the factors I listed in my introduction.

I was particularly dismayed at the change which seemed to take place in so many young people between the ages of 11 and 16; not the change wrought by adolescence, however painful those hormones are to the young concerned. No, it was the self-inflicted wounds of the system that disturbed me. So many of those bright-eyed 11-year olds who came out of good Primary Schools, where they had been encouraged to explore and take responsibility for their own learning, were being turned-off by Secondary education.

Good English Primary Schools encourage children to want to learn, to explore relationships, to treat the world as their expanding oyster... and children become excited and motivated. They are inquisitive, the best feel a sense of personal responsibility and involvement in their work.

English Secondary Schools reflect their 19th Century origins. They are places where it is assumed that people will go "to be taught". A passive act, dominated by an earlier technology which depended upon specialists who knew the set books, and by word of mouth and the dextrous use of chalk, inculcated "learning" according to the subject posted on the outside of the classroom door.

The teacher was in charge of a process. Pupils passed through and were subject to quality control. Conformity rather than inquisitiveness; dependency rather than responsibility, were the resulting skills. In truth it created an intellectual elite that is world-renowned; but it also gave us what has been graphically called the "lumpen proletariat".

I speak with some personal experience. As a child I was all set to fail Latin for the third and final time and so forfeit my place at University. It was not that I was incapable, rather I was bored stiff by a silly teacher who spent all his time telling us about how he won the war single handed in his tank! Then I was called into the school workshops, (a very low status place), and told that I had been chosen to represent the youth of the United Kingdom at Woodcarving at an international exhibition. It meant nothing to that school (certainly it was not a rugby result!); it meant everything to my self-confidence. I went to my Latin master and said that, because I had to pass Latin in 6 weeks, I would not be attending any more of his lessons as I had to teach myself. The walls of the school shook... and still shake. But I passed Latin.

These ideas are at the heart of my thinking. Learning depends on motivation, and the ability to structure and handle information. Learning and self esteem are intricately interconnected. Young people have to be taught skills; they can, and indeed should, be encouraged to practice those skills of learning in a variety of surroundings.

The school of which I was Head was held in high regard; the English love history and my school dated from 1558 - indeed my "study" was the original temporary classroom made of oak logs cut from the forest. But I faced a staff, parents and a "feather bedded" set of employers who were fearful of change; the "status quo" was to them the way forward.

English readers will remember that Lord Bullock produced a massive report on the teaching of English in the mid-1970s. It was published weeks after I became Head. After some 760 pages he summed it all up by saying:

"If children were really to learn how to use the English language then every teacher (regardless of subject discipline) has to be a teacher of English and communications".

In other words communication skills had to be developed in every lesson, and not just for the five lessons a week of formal English. Splendid. But such cross-curriculum strategies were not for my staff.

With enormous enthusiasm, I called a staff conference on the only Saturday in the year in which there was neither a Rugby, Cricket or Hockey match; whereupon 40% of the teachers banned the conference as this was the one Saturday of the year on which they would not come to school! I asked the Parents Association to put on a special luncheon and dinner for those who did attend... I was promptly told that the Association was organized for the good of the pupils, not the staff, "and communications is not directly relevant to the outcomes of the boys' public examinations".

It was a baptism by fire, and an omen of what was to come. Not for the last time was I to reflect how badly had educationalists educated the general public about education.

Feasibility Study

In 1984 I was becoming dangerously enthusiastic for radical change. My governors suggested I should have 3 months secondment to look for models of fundamental change - I guess they thought that I would get it out of my system! Within a couple of weeks I'd found a sponsor to provide sufficient funds to do this properly, to travel widely, and to extend my study for a further 9 months. I embarked on a major Feasibility Study.

Two incidents in that rich experience influenced me greatly. The Swedish government showed me an extraordinary Project close to the Arctic Circle. Too many young, so the Swedes feared, had no clear idea of what work their parents did, neveralone what other adults did. So, at the age of 7, every child was sent to spend a day shadowing his father, and another day shadowing his mother, and two days shadowing his best friend's parents. Always one on one. So successful was this that such a shadowing had been increased to 5 days a year by the age of 10, and 15 days at the age of 16. Overawed by the sheer scale of all this I commented on how good this must be for the pupil.

"Well that's obvious" I was rebuked "but think what it does for the adults. On average we clean our shoes an extra 12 times a year. We have become used to being asked apparently naive questions which we can't answer. But, most importantly, the adults of this town are now realizing that the education of young people is too important to be hived off to a group living in a separate building. It is something for which we all have to take responsibility".

Strong stuff. Of course it is reinforced my central theme. Education can never - never could - exist in isolation from the rest of the community. Could anyone now turn this into reality?

Then the Carnegie Foundation offered to show me what they said was an exceptional School Board system. It was a town of some 50,000 people. Tired of the continuous bickering about education by various sectional interest groups, it had explored the issues in great depth. The town had set itself the task of formulating a town-wide mission statement for education. It had been an extremely difficult process. For two years they had argued. Prejudices had been aired and destroyed, noses had been broken. But eventually they got that mission statement, all within just three sentences:

"This township believes in functional literacy, that is the ability to be comfortable with all the change of a rapidly evolving, highly technological society. Comfort depends on mastering the skills of learning, and knowing that it is the individual's responsibility to develop this for a further 70 years or more after leaving school. It depends on 4 key skills. The ability to think, to communicate, to collaborate and to make decisions".

I visited a number of schools in that town. I'd never met such exciting and positive students, nor competent teachers.

"If you want high standards" said the Principal "You have to marshall all your resources, consider all the influences which the community exercises on the young. In an information rich society, school is actually becoming a decreasing component of a young person's learning experience. Alone we cannot teach communication skills or collaboration; the best training ground for that is beyond the school walls. Every adult has to be involved, and has to understand what is at stake".

We talked late into the evening. The Principal explained:

> "In practice three things have happened.
>
> Firstly school and community now work together. We are talking about the same things; we know we each have to provide learning opportunities to young people.
>
> Secondly to a man or woman my teachers are concerned to develop the autonomous learner. They use their subject specific material to develop the skills of thinking, communicating, collaborating and decision-making. Did you see how we used the computer? One to every three children. Virtually every essay is now done on a word

processor. It's not to do with keyboard skills, its to do with drafting and re-drafting, collaborative learning; its about being proud of what you do.

And thirdly we now hold back 15% of our normal staffing quota for the continuous professional development of every teacher".

I was getting close to my model for "whole system" change.

The Development of a Program

My enthusiasm was nearly extinguished when trying to promote such an idea back in England. The English - I generalize - are not too hot on theory; certainly not on educational theory , they like real examples, pictures. So I gave them these two pictures. It was the worst thing I could do! Britain has to be the home of the "not invented here" syndrome. Whatever we might say publicly we are jealous of the wealth of our ex-colonies and will never dare admit that we were following their example!

Thankfully there were still some idealists left - the Trustees of Education 2000. They were looking for a program, I was looking for a sponsor. Neither of us really knew quite where we wanted to get to. We were both agreed however on three things:

(i) That we had to demonstrate how to bring about real change in ordinary places - no green field sites for us.

(ii) That we knew it would be tough going and would take a long time.

(iii) That whatever the Trust might be able to produce by way of resources would be sufficient only to act as a catalyst on normal expenditure.

The analogy given was that of a barrel-load of cement to a builder. All the building blocks of the curriculum were in existence but they were not of uniform design; to build a wall of a new design they needed a strong, binding, matrix. Of itself the matrix - to be seen both literally in terms of resources and metaphorically as a philosophy - was insubstantial; bonded with existing structures it could be immensely powerful.

The Trustees resolved on a three-phased strategy. They would concentrate initially on a single, small, self-contained community where they ought to be able to succeed. They would follow this up at an appropriate time with several Projects in different kinds of Urban areas, and then eventually in Suburban/Rural areas.

The site selected for the first project was Letchworth, a town of 32,000 people, some forty miles north of London. It is a planned town, the pioneer of the Garden City movement of the 1890s. It has a College of Further Education, two Independent Boarding Schools taking pupils from five to 18 and, the heart of its Secondary provision, four ll to 18 Secondary Comprehensive Schools. There are also 14 Primary Schools taking pupils between the ages of five and 11.

Letchworth is, mainly, a comfortable middle-class town with, traditionally, an affinity with trendy (some say "lost") causes; vegetarianism, "natural" lifestyles (open-toed sandals), and endless Discussion Groups, Clubs and Societies. There are some rich London commuters, and several poor enclaves, mainly of Asian immigrants. Comfortable rather than radical; complacent rather than missionary.

Initially the Trust focused its attention solely on the Secondary Schools, and their relation with the community. The Primary Schools, and what I said in my introduction applies, already seemed to be concentrating reasonably effectively on pupil empowerment, so creating real problems for children transferring to Senior Schools at the age of 11.

The Secondary Schools in the town have 3,500 students and 250 teachers.

The Trust decided to raise £2.5million over five years to meet "the cost of change". This was money over and above the normal running costs of the school. At £150 per pupil per year it represented approximately an additional 10%. The money was to be allocated in the ratio of 2:2:1 to staff development costs, computer technology, and general promotional costs (mainly to do with the community). It was expected that such funds would enable the staffing of the schools to be increased by 10% for at least three years, and would provide at least one computer to every seven children in each school. The five-year program would comprise three phases - Exploration (one year), Developmental (two years), Consolidation (two years).

The Trust's program was summed up in the following statement (Education 2000, 1987):

"School-based learning in the future should have as its principal aim the development of the attitudes, the knowledge and the capabilities to support continued, life-long learning. In schools the Program should test two key hypotheses:

(a) That new approaches to the teaching/learning process are now available which are more effective than traditional teaching programs. The need for change is 3-dimensional: to shift the balance of teaching to learning; to provide a greater variety of learning experiences; to make clear the responsibility of the learner for active participation in the process and for achieving successful outcomes.

(b) That such approaches to learning would help young people to develop a range of valuable social skills - confidence, personal responsibility, enterprise and working in groups and teams - as well as in mastering the intellectual skills associated with formal, structured learning.

The Program would be based on four basic assumptions:

(i) The education of the young is the responsibility of whole communities.

(ii) Most learning takes place outside the confines of schools.

(iii) There is an untold wealth of educational opportunity within human communities.

(iv) Information Technologies have infinite possibilities.

Such a concept challenges current assumptions about the unique role of schools and their relationship to the community. It certainly challenges that conventional wisdom which assumes that learning follows directly from teaching. It also challenges the assumption that schools can "make do" with limited learning resources. Specifically, if the purpose of education is to develop the power of the autonomous learner then presumably schooling has to be concerned to wean that learner from his/her dependence on the teachers? If that is so why are the largest classes to be found in the Primary School, and the smallest in the upper years of Secondary School. Central to the Trust's thinking was the re-definition of the task of the teachers away from that of instructor to facilitator or, as I heard a speaker from industry say graphically, "No longer sages on the stage, but guides on the side!".

In the past, attempts to bring about radical change have been frustrated by:

(i) Insufficient time for all teachers to understand, accept and prepare for such change.

(ii) Insufficient resources for pupils to work independently of the teacher.

(iii) Insufficient understanding by parents in the community as to what this could mean for them.

(iv) Insufficient time for the whole process to run through before assessing its overall impact.

The Second phase of the program was the most critical. The Trust was not arguing that schools needed 10% more staffing in perpetuity (we knew that, even if that were desirable - which we doubted - it was certainly a political impossibility). Rather it was saying:

> "The instructorial model on which you teachers are working is outdated. It is 'turning off' many pupils. They no longer feel directly involved. You are taking onto your own shoulders that very responsibility for self-improvement which it is essential that the pupils develop for themselves. (Subsidiarity). The systems we are using are going against the grain - once you motivate a child it is right that he or she should be encouraged to get on at his or her own pace, and (crudely, but in practice very true) wants the teacher to get off his back and allow him/her to get on with it.
>
> But we know one of the key reasons why we teachers can't do this is that you have been starved of the very resources which the children must have ready access to if they are to be able to work by themselves effectively - books, films, audio and video-cassettes, computers, etc.. So, in addition to providing each of you with the time and support to reflect on how you can, as a team, develop your current practices, we will break the normal resource constraints and invest heavily in such equipment... which, incidentally, you must define. Finally we will, together, work to educate the community as to what they must now do to support informal learning". (Education 2000, 1987)

An offer they could hardly resist! But there was another side to the bargain.

> "In the third phase, the final two years, you must learn to carry on the idea of continuous staff development by allocating 10% of your normal teaching budget to this... in advance of writing the timetable for the students. And that timetable will have to be drawn up using only 90% of your staff. Either your class sizes will have to increase, or you'll have to find new and more imaginative ways of organizing learning, using the new rich learning environments that we have helped you to introduce and, of course,

capitalizing on the newly released potential for informal learning in the community". (Education 2000, 1987)

It would be a hard process of readjustment; considerable consultancy would be needed to institutionalize the innovation.

Implementation Issues

From the start, the Trust recognized that, while it should well be possible for schools operating on a staffing ratio of one to 16 or one to 17, to effect a more efficient use of teachers, it was a totally different question when it came to the costs of the on-going maintenance of high levels of technology, and the additional heavy demands of books and other resources.

Here the Trust anticipated it would have to make the case for increased expenditure, probably of the order of 10% per child. This would require a political decision of immense proportions. The Trust saw that this would only come if it could build a working model of what happens when all this "critical mass" is brought together, and produces outcomes so enhanced that the general public would clamour for replication (and the politicians would see increased political expenditure as being a desirable political objective).

So the Trust effectively offered the schools a deal - you show how you can reconceptualize and we will so market this to bring about the improvement in the resource base.

The idea of such a program administered by an independent Trust raised three specific issues:

(i) The Trust, starting to raise money as Britain went into recession, found it impossible to deliver all the funds when needed.

(ii) The Trust had no traditional established "locus". It had no proven authority. The work had to be in a truly federal structure, and any "contract" was entirely at a voluntary level.

(iii) The Trust had no control over the political decisions over the use of resources within State schools. As the program developed Government policy seemed frequently to be moving counter to the ideas in the Project.

Now I would like to introduce you to our "exhaust pipe" diagram (next page) – a name coined after its design, rather than before! It was produced in 1987. It is not accurate in all its detail, nor is it quite the design we would advocate for subsequent Projects. It's dated early 1987.

Chronologically it progresses from left to right. The "thickness" of the pipe relates very generally to the extent of the activity. The internal solid line suggests reasonably self-contained units of activity, while the dotted line and the arrows show how the activities start to impinge on each other, and interrelate.

Strategies for Change; the four central components

During the Exploratory Phase it had been decided that four central components should underpin the program. It was seen as essential, however, that as these components had to come together as a whole every teacher had to be involved in at least two, if not three of these so as to prevent the program becoming sectionalized.

"Exhaust Pipe" Diagram

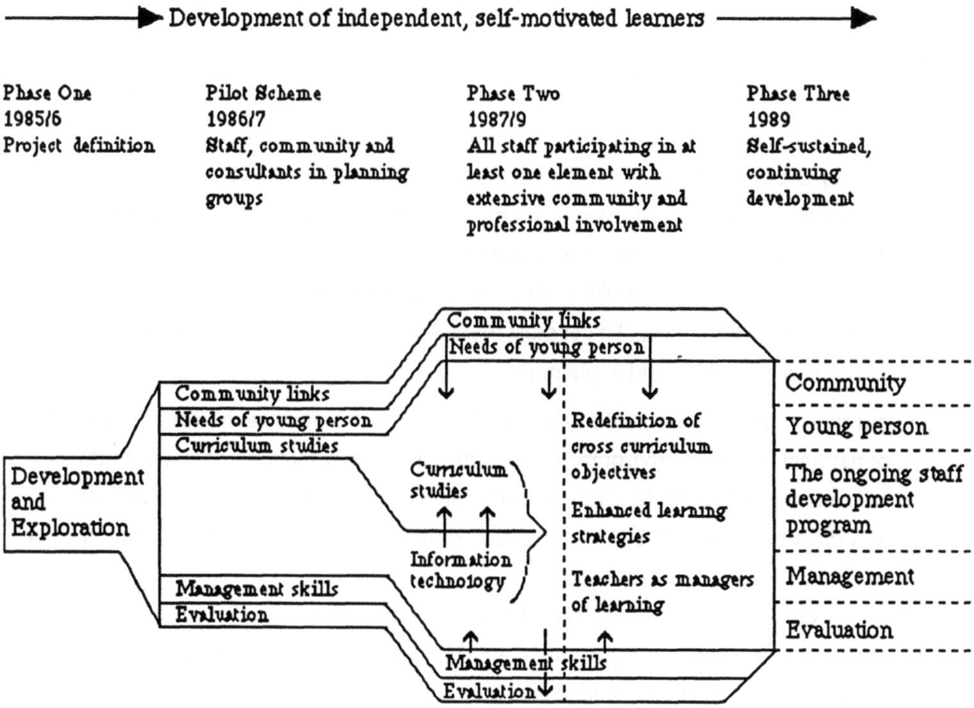

Component I: Community Links

In its earlier statement, "The Hypotheses for Education in AD2000" (1983), the Trust had highlighted the significance of the community.

"The role of the community is vital - it must be fully involved; provide leadership, ideas and finance; provide security and effect the development of relationships. Industry and commerce must participate in the "secret garden" of the curriculum and then sow the seed of communal harmony".

A few months before a Government White Paper (1984) had proposed, "That if a broad agreement about the objectives and content of the school curriculum could be explicitly formulated in partnerships between the education service and all other interested parties then:

i) It would be clear what tasks society expects our schools to accomplish. The school's performance could then be more fairly judged against the agreed expectations about these tasks;
ii) It would mean that parents, employers and the public would have a closer understanding of the purposes for which they were being asked to support the work of the schools in achieving the common aims."

Breakfast Meetings. Every fortnight, for the better part of two years, hour long breakfast meetings were held in a variety of locations within the town. Normally they were attended by some ten or twelve teachers and a similar number of community figures, drawn mainly from particular interest groups. The individuals changed each time. On a one-on-one basis people talked about the needs of education, and the town's expectations of the education service. A couple of months later teachers invited their community colleagues to shadow them for a day in schools. Not a high profile activity, not profound... but in two years it involved most of the teachers at least once. To get most involved was part of the "critical mass". Everyone had to start listening and explaining.

Secondments. Plans were made to second 15% of the teachers each year into some form of local, or national, working environment for anything between five and 15 days. In three years it was anticipated half the teachers would be involved. "To be on secondment", would cease to be a rarity to be envied, but would be the common talking point of the Common Room. More of the "critical mass".

Teachers were asked to undertake one of three lines of enquiry:

1. What does that organization expect of 16 and 18 year lds, and how does it further develop those skills over the next couple of years?
2. How does that organization plan its own professional development program for its own Senior staff, and how does that influence the rest of the organization?
3. How does that organization seek to utilize technological change to its own advantage?

Useful topics for discussion in the Teachers Room...

Study Groups. Perhaps this was the most significant area. A dozen special interest groups were defined; Employers, Council of Churches, Governors, Employeé organizations, Volunteer organizations, etc.. Each was invited to nominate 12 representatives who would agree to sit down with an equivalent number of teachers and, over a 12 month period, study what was currently happening in education, and then to produce answers to three key questions:

i) What does your "interest group" think should be the aims of Secondary education?

ii) What can you do to help the schools achieve these?

iii) What can you do, with your resources, to create informal learning opportunities outside school in which young people can gain these experiences?

This last, in particular, was a rich area for discussion. For example, it led to a much improved code of objectives for the employment of young people on a casual labour basis before they left school. It shook the local faith communities rigid as to the false assumptions they had been attempting to make about religious education within the schools. It certainly disturbed Parents Associations about the role that they would have to play in future as individuals supporting their own children's learning.

Component 2: The Needs of the Young Person

This component was at the very heart of the program. So close, I fear, that we were inclined to think it was being properly addressed - when it wasn't!

"How do young people view appropriate learning opportunities in contemporary society? What are their priorities?"

Specifically the Project stated it's aims as:

1. To establish a better understanding of the challenges and difficulties, the tasks and opportunities which face young people growing up into the 21st Century, and the influences which shape their personal and social development.
2. To bring together those working in education, youth services, social and welfare agencies, guidance and counselling services, in order to develop a co-ordinated approach to providing information and support for the young people within the community.
3. To examine the part to be played by education in the future in preparing young people to achieve adult identity in times of rapid and complex social, economic and technological change.

That was stated back in late 1985. We now know much more about these issues. I fear it was the topic which teachers were least interested in, but at the time we did not fully appreciate the reasons for this. Those reasons became clearer with time. Teachers live cheek by jowl with pupils; it is not always an easy relationship; teachers habitually survive through the control model.

"I know what is good for you; you're too immature to fully appreciate why I insist that you do it this way".

And that, quite simply, is the heart of the pedagogic issue. It's the reverse of the principle of subsidiarity. ("It is wrong for a superior body to take to itself the making of decisions which are probably within the expertise of an inferior to decide for itself"... a doctrine first annunciated by the Catholic Church and subsequently taken into the thinking of the European Commission, its implications for teachers and pupils are profound").

A group of 14 to 18 year olds from across all the schools met regularly for a year as one of the Study Groups. Although their "findings" were recorded somewhat randomly, their message was very clear.

"We want more contact with adults; we know what our parents think - we've heard it so often; we know what teachers think - you're paid to think that... but what do ordinary adults think?"

The teachers did not like the assumption that they were not ordinary people! In one instance a teacher actually sought out the pupil who he thought was party to such a statement and accused him of being a trouble-maker!

Out of an essentially well-motivated group of 24, only five said that they would make an intervention in class if they did not understand what a teacher was saying, for fear, not of the reaction of their own peer group, but because they sensed that the teacher would regard it as a criticism of himself, and therefore be antagonistic in the future to the questioner.

But a happier experience is that of a physical education teacher in his late 50's who spent three weeks in a small but fast moving high technology company. He came back a chastened man.

"Do you know", he said, "the lads who I have regarded for years as being a pain in the butt, the ones who I have seen it as being my job to cut down to size... these are just the people that this company needs, but not cut down. Do you know, I think I have actually been destroying some of the very things I should have been encouraging. I wish this had happened to me 30 years ago".

So interested has the community been in this aspect of the work that it is now offering more secondment places for the teachers than the schools can fill.

Let me return to my concern about teachers' perceptions of pupils later.

Component 3: Information and Communication Technologies

From the start the Trust was anxious to exploit the powers of the new technologies, and to take these very seriously. While it accepted that in specific instances these are a sufficient goal in their own right, in the majority of cases the Trust saw the major benefit of these technologies as the support which they could bring to the individual child as he or she sought to master their own learning by applying an ever greater range of techniques.

But there seemed to be an intractable problem. Current levels of resource were totally inadequate to provide sufficient equipment to make it possible to provide open access on demand... and demand extended right across the curriculum. Manufacturers did not see in the school market an area in which it was worth their investing research and development funds as they had no confidence that schools would ever be able to purchase their products.

We wished to break with this cycle... not for the benefit of the companies but for the benefit of the young people.

By placing a heavy emphasis on technology the Trust lays itself open to two contentious perceptions.

(1) Individual teachers can find the technology so seductive that the reasons for using the technology can become lost.

(2) For people looking at the Project from outside, it is often difficult to fully grasp the concepts involved... but it is easy to see the technologies and like them. "Education 2000 is about technology" can be the headline.

The Project opened with some finely balanced statements. One it took from a Government Report (1984).

> "The pervasiveness of information technology in particular will also require a higher level of technological knowledge and awareness among the population as a whole. It will be necessary for technological literacy to be equated with the three Rs as a desirable norm for all to achieve.
>
> It is important to ensure that students learn to use the technologies for their own purposes, for investigating and problem solving, for simulating and calculating, as well as for processing data. In this way they will gain confidence that they may control rather than be controlled by the technologies, and that their use will have a liberating, not limiting, effect upon their lives.
>
> Within education the Project adopts the view that the information technologies can be used to improve learning and to enrich and extend current curriculum practice. Ultimately, emerging technologies have the potential to transform the ways in which we learn, the ways in which we communicate and apply our knowledge and how we judge what is worth knowing. Initially their introduction to schools will be used as a catalyst for significant change in shifting the curriculum focus from teaching to learning".

That goes to the heart of the program; the empowerment of the learner.

The Project had to win the support of the teachers for the technology. A generous, and non-intimidating, approach was selected. One-third of the teachers in the first year were offered half a day per week for a term to learn how to use the technology, with one of their own colleagues having previously been trained to support this. Each was loaned a computer to have in their own home. CAD came to mean, slightly flippantly "Computer Aided Divorce", as the computer in the corner of the bedroom vied for attention. But the printers were kept in the staff Common Room. Early in the morning an ever increasing number of teachers were to be found gathered around the printer discussing with each other what they were doing. They started to talk to each other about the problems of learning.

The secret - and it remains the secret - was the combination of the equipment, the provision of time, and trust. Teachers surprised themselves with what they could do; for every extra hour provided they gave another of their own time. They looked for, and found, surprising mutual support groups amongst their colleagues. The Geographers "stole" a CAD program from the CDT teachers to create a dynamic model of geomorphic process; mathematicians developed similar programs for algebra. The religious education teacher replaced his mark book by a disc; the remedial teacher discovered whole new worlds for correlating different strategies for successfully improving children's understanding of process.

Trust (and respect); TIME... and lastly the equipment.

After a term, they were anxious to work with the pupils, and so the equipment went into the schools. Similar progress was made in years two and three. Fears expressed initially that at least one-third of the teachers would refuse ever to try and learn were completely unfounded.

A simple initial strategy to exploit word processing across all subject areas was adopted. It worked well, despite the problems resulting from intensive Government action within the curriculum, which I shall describe shortly. The pupils of that town have now been shown to have an amazingly high level of technological competence.

Staff support has been the key to this success. Recognizing immediately the scale of the opportunity, the schools pooled resources to appoint a highly skilled Information Technology Consultant to train, in each school, a half-time co-ordinator to train colleagues. Subsequently a half-time network manager was also provided within each school.

Component 4: Curriculum Studies

In the Feasibility Study I had made in 1984 looking at the nature of a curriculum for secondary education appropriate for the 21st Century, I had stated (1984):

(i) There is an overriding need to plan the curriculum as a single entity, rather than treat it as a number of separate disciplines, with clear overall objectives expressed in terms of skills, attitudes, concepts and knowledge. This planning must incorporate the school's full response to the needs of the pupils - the curricula (formal and informal) and the extra-curricula.

(ii) The curriculum needs to be seen as a continuum with a clear understanding of those skills, etc., to be learned at various stages so that the transfer between Primary and Secondary School is properly planned.

(iii) The recognition of the twin, and inseparable, aims of providing young people with a positive attitude towards, and competence within, a range of technical skills and those other skills and personal attributes which will enable them to live positive, creative, contributory lives within a modern technological society.

(iv) The need to take "the long view" of the impact of information technology on the future nature of the schools, learning skills and the practice of teachers; the use of such technology to individualize the learning process and divert more of the teachers' skills where they are uniquely applicable.

When the Project started in 1985 schools were still at the stage of being largely responsible for shaping their own curriculum. Schools were, as earlier commented, under considerable public scrutiny.

"One common theme is that they do not produce young people equipped with the range of capabilities, skills, attitudes and knowledge to sustain and expand the productive power of the economy on which the wealth of the nation depends. Pupils are not given sufficient encouragement to become responsible for their own learning. Classroom teaching can too often result in purely passive responses from pupils and essential skills such as communications and the ability to act collaboratively, are frequently ignored... pupils gain knowledge of a particular area of study, but not ways of thinking and working which are appropriate for use outside the education system."

The stance of the Project was firm.

"Any fundamental reappraisal of the curriculum which seeks to come to terms with these issues must be undertaken in partnership between education and the community that it serves, in order to dispel the mutual suspicion that seems deeply embedded in our culture" (Education 2000, 1987).

The earlier "exhaust pipe" diagram showed an early separation of the lines between information technology and curriculum studies. An initial assumption was that, with careful stimulation, intensive work within information technology would so stimulate teachers to think again about learning opportunities that this would inform their thinking about curricula issues in general, particularly following the early emphasis on word processing as a way of developing coherent strategy on the development of communication skills.

A report published in the same month as the Project started stated:

> When a group of teachers, preferably within a school, are enabled to examine their own presuppositions about their subject, work at new ideas as well as exploring open situations in an inventive way, they develop convictions about their own powers which enable them to exceed their previously acquired skills.

Our early enthusiasm for this approach was not always confirmed. Enormous energies and commitment were expended by teachers working in a variety of special groups - particularly in certain subject areas. Work within the school libraries was especially successful. With networks within each school supporting up to 100 individual computers on a network, it became possible to access library records on a word search basis almost immediately from any part of the school. Libraries subsequently reported a 300% increase in the number of non-fiction books taken out within each of two years. The use being made of CAD by the technologists, communication technology for modern linguists, and simulation exercises by a number of departments was impressive. There was, however, an emerging concern which within a couple of years led to serious questioning about whether, within such a structure, individual staff were able/willing to incorporate lessons from the different components and really open up opportunities for the young people to take increasing responsibilities for their own learning... particularly to have the opportunity to decide which of these strategies would be most appropriate and for which task. In other words, the Project might be succeeding in each component, but would it also succeed in its overall aim?

The Project had been slow in recognizing the need to invest heavily in the management skills of those staff at senior and middle levels on whom the whole program would rest if new and more flexible arrangements for structured learning were to be introduced. At an early stage the expression "fibrous management" was adopted. Traditionally British schools have operated on a strictly hierarchical system. With the appointment of co-ordinators for Information Technology, meetings across the schools, curriculum studies, the community and young people became the norm and a whole new structure for decision making was created – and it happened altogether without prior thought. It created tension, and was frustrating to those teachers attempting to develop new ideas.

One part of the program draws all these themes together: the introduction, comparatively late in the Project, of a non-simultaneous electronic conferencing system. Powered by two Digital MicroVAXs with 10 terminals in each school linked by dedicated "leased" telephone lines (and now linking progressively other schools outside the area), this system now handles an average of 650 call-ups each day, with over 1,700 of the 3,500 young people and majority of the teachers now listed as registered users. Increasingly the system is now being accessed from homes by way of modems and home computers. The software enables conversation to take place in French, German and Spanish as well as English.

Although still in it's infancy, it has been going for 18 months, it's impact is most significant. Currently there are some 50-line conferences, the most successful of which are "Helplines" operated by teachers and pupils for examination course; "Curricula Development" conferences (mainly teachers); "Story Writing" conferences; and a "Town-wide book view" system.

Developmental and Financial Problems

All does not go easily, however. Despite having a reasonably high profile - and having attracted groups of up to a dozen visitors at a time on average every four days for the past four years - the

Trustees had to terminate their funding of the Project very suddenly in mid-1989. There were three main reasons:

(i) A number of existing sponsors were so impressed with what they saw that they wanted all their future funding to go to Projects in their own geographic regions (and do note the English are not overtly given to the generosity of their sponsorship).

(ii) Government, under it's then Secretary of State, decided to seek private sector support for a totally new kind of school - a City Technology College; the scheme was not well received by industry but such was the pressure exerted by Government that most sponsors, as a defensive measure, decided that they could no longer contribute any such program.

(iii) The Trust, having under-resourced it's central core in its enthusiasm to start the Project, had to re-group and consolidate.

The timing for this could not have been more unfortunate. The Project had, in practice, been running for three years... and was aware that it would require six rather than five years to reach the stage of full "institutionalization". With very little warning the schools had to prepare to maintain at least the status quo, if not a move forward, entirely from their own budgets. And this at a time in which teachers are beginning to bear the full brunt of the implications of the National Curriculum, and tensions between Central and Local Government were fast approaching the point where a major breakdown of the earlier system was inevitable.

Outside Letchworth a further Project had already started in a town of 80,000 people with strong support from local sponsors, and four other Projects were on the point of starting in major urban areas.

Twelve difficult months followed before, in the Autumn of 1990, the Trust started again to introduce funds into the first Project in Letchworth. Now it looks likely that later this year the Project will be able to pick up, if not exactly where it was in 1989, at least not too far behind. In this, it has been totally dependent upon the goodwill - and the professional confidence - of the schools.

Evaluation

The evaluation presented a further problem. Although the Government did not contribute to the cost of the program, it did make available $300,000 for a three-year independent evaluation to be made working through the Department's own structures.

Lengthy discussions about the need for a formative, illuminative, evaluation, delayed the start of the evaluation itself, and further complications arose when the team stated and found that they had insufficient resources to evaluate all aspects of the program. To do so, it was claimed, new methods of evaluation would have to be developed to deal with something which was extremely difficult to pigeon-hole, and was, they said, more of a mission than a conventional project. "Like measuring a bucket of Scotch mist" said one; "Like studying an impressionist painting with out of focus glasses" said another. "Like looking at a wall and seeing only the matrix (cement), not the building blocks". In practice, the evaluation on which many hopes had been placed to assist in making adjustments to direction in mid-course was of only limited value and, eventually, concentrated exclusively on the impact of high levels of information technology in classroom practice.

What does all this tell us, so far?

Although the Report of the Department of Education and Science (DES)-funded Evaluation is not yet published this suggests that some two-thirds of the teachers claimed to have significantly developed their pedagogic philosophy, while one half could be shown to have changed their teaching styles. While the change in teaching styles can be shown to have been started directly as a result of the stimulation of working with the technology, it was not entirely dependent upon it... other classes where the technology was not obtrusive also showed changes in the styles adopted by teachers.

A full inspection of the Project by Her Majesty's Inspectorate (HMI) had been requested in 1988 when the program was running in its entirety but, such are the delays normal in such circumstances this was not made until a week mid-way through 1989/90 when all funding had stopped. This Report comments most favourably on staff morale and commitment; on the general levels of technological competence, on the support of the community; and notes the high level of pupil behaviour.

This report, in two key paragraphs, summarizes the expectations of the program.

> Many of the Trust's views are not new. They are shared by many other educationalists. Over a long period attempts have been made to give young people a more active role in their own learning and to make them less dependent on knowledge determined, synthesized and then delivered by a teacher. This in turn entails a re-evaluation of the role of the teacher, less obviously central to the process of education but no less critical: a role entailing management of the learning process, guidance of pupils and assessment of their progress as well as direct teaching. It does not mean abandoning the traditional role of the teacher; there will always be a place for this, but it does entail a broadening of the repertoire of teaching skills. There has also been a long-standing desire to involve the community more directly in the education of its young people. What is new in this Project is the attempt to combine these objectives in a coherent package.
>
> Previous attempts to provide a rich learning environment for pupils have relied on resource-based learning, using worksheets in a variety of audio-visual media. The computer provides a new and more powerful tool for work and learning. It makes it possible to match the learning methods and resources to the needs and learning styles of the individual pupil. With this tool, learner autonomy is more of a practical possibility than ever before. It is now feasible to work, through staff development, towards a radical change in education systems whose approach to teaching and learning has shown little change over many years.

The Report noted, however, that midway through the program the Project appeared to be still some way from achieving its main aims - that of the shift in emphasis towards pupils empowerment in learning. It is suggested that, realistically, this would probably need five to seven years to achieve, and that within that time a Project would need assurance about the provision of on-going funds, and a degree of protection from extraneous influences. All these concerns are being addressed in the subsequent projects.

To summarize, measurable and observable outcomes include:

1. evidence that two-thirds of the teachers have significantly changed their philosophy and style
2. evidence that half the teachers have significantly changed their classroom practice.
3. a marked reduction in truancy
4. a significant increase in teacher and pupil morale
5. a 300% increase in books taken out of school libraries in the past year
6. an increased awareness of the importance of education by the community at large.

Some Conclusions

Encouraging as are these outcomes, the first Project is still far from making that radical breakthrough in the way in which learning is structured, and the way schools are organized. It does, however, point the way to what is needed in the future. It particularly suggests:

(a) People do need a model to follow; to be first is an uncomfortable experience, where the wish to innovate seems always to be balanced by caution. Paradoxically others are able to see things in Letchworth that inspire them to want to go further than do the people within the town itself. To have a working model would be immensely helpful to other programs.

(b) There has to be a wholehearted commitment by all partners to the ideals, and a determination to follow the innovation through to its natural conclusions.

(c) Better networking of existing innovation, and programs, is essential; it is not easily achieved.

(d) There has to be reasonable security of funding across the programs for the work to be planned logically.

(e) Much work needs to be done in building an abstract model of what is an effective modern learning community, which would draw on research into how learning opportunities are best created, and how teachers could use these ideas.

(f) A Project needs to be given as much protection as possible from changing, external political expectations; it needs time to evolve.

(g) Parents need as much help as teachers in understanding the implications for themselves of changed learning strategies.

(h) A program concerned with "learning how to learn" has to start in the Primary Schools and work across all sections.

(i) To open up the community is not only to discover a wealth of otherwise untapped resources, it is also to uncover a range of misconceptions and negative attitudes towards schools, and learning in general, which had to be handled with the greatest delicacy.

(j) The community needs constant reminding that "what is good enough for the rich" needs to be the standard provision for all on the basis that the life of the individual is now intrinsically linked to the quality of life being lived (and the education experienced) by the whole community.

I have dwelled on the experience of the Trust's first Project, as that is it's most substantial. But in doing so I have, perhaps subconsciously, been drawing on ideas now growing in the newer Projects - of which there are now five, likely to rise shortly to seven. I have also been guilty of generalizing in my attempts to separate out what has been happening in the Project, from all the other changes which are affecting education.

In an attempt to systematize the Trust's thinking a book was published in the Autumn of 1991 "Giving Substance to a Vision" which sets out clearly what we believe to be involved in the creation of rich learning communities. In September we will be publishing another document, aimed at the general public, which should help people focus more clearly on what are the key questions about education that everyone now has to ask, and to which everyone will have to contribute answers.

A Final Footnote

I introduced myself as someone whose job it is to create the environment within which such innovation as I've sketched out can take place. The central theme is shared by all of us. To the public, however, these ideas are confusing. My introduction spoke of England as being in educational turmoil; the same is true I know of the United States; I know less of situations in other lands. If I hark back to Peter Drucker's words – "Within the next decades education will change more than it has changed since the modern school was created by the printed book over 300 years ago" – then no wonder people feel uneasy and frightened; they don't know what to do next. Many feel particularly threatened by the technology. With the skills represented in this book we ought to be able to project some most exciting strategies to exploit these technologies to support learners of all ages. We all come from democratic societies. We cannot impose our ideas on people. If we believe that we have discovered techniques which will be more effective than previous methods of learning, then we have to present these in ways which make people hungry to try them out.

I close with an extract from a Paper published by Dr Beau Jones:

Perhaps the most difficult, and the most powerful design is to assume that the community is the unit of change, as in Education 2000 (in England)... in part because individual schools cannot provide ample human and financial resources to serve the needs of the students... in part because uninvolved parents and community offer barriers to learning. But most important, it is beneficial because issues of curriculum, instruction, and assessment should be needs based and designed cohesively for a whole system as a single unit, rather than piecemeal. (in press)

References

Drucker, P.F. (1989). *The new realities: In government and politics, in economics and business, in society and world view.* New York: Harper and Row.

Education 2000. (1983). *Hypothesis for education in AD2000.* Letchworth, Hertfordshire, England: Author.

Education 2000. (1984). *Hertfordshire county council.* Letchworth, Hertfordshire, England: Author.

Education 2000. (1987). *Annual Report 1987.* Letchworth, Hertfordshire, England: Author.

Education 2000. (1988). *Annual Report 1988.* Letchworth, Hertfordshire, England: Author.

Education 2000. (1989). *Annual Report 1989.* Letchworth, Hertfordshire, England: Author.

Education 2000. (1990). *Giving substance to a vision.* Letchworth, Hertfordshire, England: Author.

Education 2000. (1991). *A nation prepared; Learners for the 21st century.* Letchworth, Hertfordshire, England: Author.

Fisher, P. (1990). *Education 2000 : Educational change with consent.* London: Cassell Educational.

Jones, B. (in press). Cognitive designs in education. In M.C. Alkin (Ed.), *Encyclopedia of educational research.* New York: Macmillan

Smith, F. (1986). *Insult to intelligence: The bureaucratic invasion of our classrooms.* New York: Arbor House.

4 Constructivism and the Design of Learning Environments: Context and Authentic Activities for Learning

Peter C. Honebein, Thomas M. Duffy, and Barry J. Fishman

Indiana University, Bloomington, Indiana, USA

Apprenticeship is one of the earliest forms of learning by doing, where a student learns a task, such as weaving, masonry, or even thinking under the tutelage of an expert. Skill and knowledge development in apprenticeship can cross several disciplines, but is always set in the context of the authentic activity of solving the larger task at hand. A skill like masonry, therefore, may require knowledge of some aspects of geology, geometry, basic mathematics, structural engineering, etc. Similarly, the development of logical thought by Plato's students was always set in the context of the larger philosophical debate and in developing rhetorical skills. Thus the larger task, the construction task, provides an organizing and unifying role and a purpose for learning.

Present day schooling is a far cry from this apprenticeship model. The introduction of mass schooling at the end of the 19th century marked the demise of the apprenticeship model in American schooling. For the first time discrete subject areas appeared. Social and professional knowledge was divided into the bite-sized chunks that we now recognize as mathematics, social studies, reading, language, science, and art. Popkewitz (1987) identifies three major forces that shaped mass schooling between 1880 and 1920 and resulted in the loss of the apprenticeship model: the efforts of the middle class to build schools that would reinforce their social values; efforts by many professions to "select, organize and evaluate" segments of the curriculum; and the rise of universities as "credentialing agents" for both people and knowledge.

Mass schooling was introduced during the Progressive Era as a means of educating the large numbers of immigrants arriving daily from Europe. As a result of these social changes, "the functions of schooling became more complex – the theological purposes of teaching were replaced more forcefully by the secular concerns of socialization and labor selection (Popkewitz, 1987, p. 3)." Rapidly advancing industrial innovations in the early 20th century, not the least of which was the assembly line, caused a similar mass-production theory of education to almost totally subsume the apprenticeship mode of schooling. There have been many theorists, Dewey for example, who have attempted to reintroduce some of the values of apprenticeship to schools. However, the tremendous bureaucratic machinery of the schools and the voices of special interests, especially those of big business and the middle class, have generally been successful in blocking those change efforts. The result is that what is taught in schools resembles "school activities" more than the activities of actual practitioners (Brown, Collins, & Duguid, 1989).

While much of learning has been relegated to the context of school activity, some styles of on-the-job training maintain linkages to the actual practice of tasks through authentic activities (Sticht & Hickey, 1988). Trade organizations still offer apprenticeships to masons, electricians and plumbers. Simulations, from flight simulators to micro-societies, provide authentic activity to learners in a safe, cost-effective environment. Lawyers, physicians, and graduate students engage in internships. And of course, our practical or "street knowledge" develops in the context of day to day functioning and survival (Sternberg & Wagner, 1987). An important element that weaves through all of these instructional methods is a functional orientation. These learning environments are full with most, if not all, of the complexity, pitfalls, mixed messages, information sources and interactions common to the actual work environment.

Constructivism

The apprenticeship model, with its emphasis on embedding learning in a larger, functional context, is a model for instruction that captures the constructivist epistemology of learning and understanding. Indeed, while there are a multitude of instructional approaches within the constructivist framework (Fosnot, 1989; Duffy & Bednar, in press; and many of the chapters in this volume), the apprenticeship model has received by far the greatest attention (e.g. Collins, Brown, & Newman, 1988). Basically, constructivism proposes that knowledge or meaning is not fixed for an object, but rather is constructed by individuals through their experience of that object in a particular context. Thus, as Brown et al. (1989) have proposed, we see understanding as indexed by experience, i.e. understanding is embedded in the experience of the individual.

"Experience" includes both the physical context in which a person works and the tasks – both cognitive and physical – that a person engages in while in that environment. That is, both the physical context for learning and the activities of the learner determine how something is understood; i.e., what is learned. And let us emphasize that it is not just the immediate context in which learning occurs (e.g. learning about photosynthesis), but the larger task or context in which the learning is situated that is essential (e.g. the contest to grow the largest tomatoes or preparing to pass a Biology test; see Bereiter, 1990). This larger task strongly influences the purpose for learning and hence what resources the learner brings to bear on the task, how those resources are organized, and what the learner attends to and does in the task environment. (Brown, Collins and Duguid, 1989; Bednar, Cunningham, Duffy, & Perry, 1991; Duffy & Jonassen, in press; Cognition and Technology Group at Vanderbilt, this volume; Spiro, this volume).

Our focus in this chapter is on the design of constructivist learning environments. As we noted, the apprenticeship model provides a good instructional model for constructivist epistemology. In this chapter we will examine what we consider to be the critical elements in the design of a constructivist learning environment: the specification of authentic activity and the stimulus or concept complexity. Within this discussion we will identify what we feel are some critical design strategies for achieving authenticity and for maintaining stimulus complexity. We will conclude the chapter by describing two learning environments that we feel reflect the real world implementation of the principles.

Authentic Activity

Authentic activity is one of the most cited features of a constructivist learning environment as reflected in the apprenticeship model. Indeed, the common quest today is for "authentic learning." Interestingly, instructional environments seem to be categorically labeled as either authentic or not as if authenticity was unique to the instruction. However, let us emphasize that authentic activity is a relative concept. An activity is authentic in relation to another activity. It is authentic to the extent that it captures the essential characteristics of that other activity. Hence it is improper to suggest that an activity is not authentic without comparing it to another activity. Within the educational framework, the authenticity of the learning activity refers to the activity of the learner in the learning environment relative to the environment in which the learning will be used. Thus, authenticity is an issue of transfer with a focus on both the physical and the psychological activity of the learner. Consider the implications of the concept of authentic activity in terms of the current debate on the adequacy of our educational systems.

We find two classes of complaints about the educational system. The first complaint is that test scores are declining and that our test scores in science and math are below those of almost every developed country in the world. The second complaint is that the students are not prepared for the real world: they do not successfully solve problems in the real world environment. Central to this failure is the inability to apply math and reading skills in solving problems.

Each of these complaints reflects a different definition of the authentic activity for which we are preparing students. As a consequence, each calls for a different redesign of the educational system. If we want our students to excel on tests, then the authentic activity is to focus on test taking behaviors. The purpose the learner brings to the task is that of passing a test. Hence, learning is focused on organizing and storing information in such a way that it can be retrieved for a test. The second author finds this behavior exemplified in the study habits of his middle school children. They study the text with a focus on the questions at the end of the chapter, the questions the teacher may have passed out, and the words in bold-face. They feel satisfied that they understand the chapter when they can answer those questions. Indeed, they are meeting the demands of the learning environment; they do "understand" as defined by the school and they are successful students. We expect them to do well on the SAT exam and to excel in university and other traditionally "academic" tasks. Their authentic context is the academic test-taking environment and the instructional approach of their school is preparing them for that environment.

The complaint that students lack real world skills suggests that a different authentic activity is needed in schools. Here the concern is not mastery on a test but rather the ability to function successfully in the environment. This includes the ability to notice when particular skills and information are called for, to be able to recall or find that information, and to be able to apply those skills and that knowledge to solve a real world problem. Here authentic activity involves not so much mastering the information in the textbook or test taking skills, but rather using the information in the textbook to solve real world problems.

What Makes an Activity Authentic?

Few would disagree that the learning environment must engage the learner in the activities of the environment that exists outside of school, whether that be on the job or in the community. Indeed, this is simply good instructional design. What the constructivist approach brings to the issue is a focus on metacognitive processes and on a holistic view of the task.

Ownership by the Learner. The development of metacognitive skills means the development of the ability to direct and monitor one's learning and performance. If learners are to function effectively in real-world environments, they must develop the metacognitive skills required to function in those authentic environments. The direct implication is that authentic learning activity requires that learners have ownership of their learning and performance. The instruction must support them in assuming responsibility for establishing and monitoring their goals and strategies.

In much of schooling, the teacher is the one who owns the task and imposes it on the students. Hence the students are performing the teacher's task. The goals are specified by the teacher and success is determined by the teacher. Of course, this characteristic is not unique to schooling. We find goals and strategies being provided for employees in many jobs. We also find many public places filled with signs telling us what we are permitted and forbidden to do. As a consequence we find many people operating mindlessly (Langer, 1989) in these environments, simply obeying or following the rules without critically evaluating the environment and hence without a clear understanding of the reason for the rules. Without assuming ownership for working or functioning in that environment, the individual will not consider alternative rules or strategies, how the strategy should be used in a particular situation, or when the rules should be broken. As Langer has described so well for so many contexts, individuals will simply accept the goals and strategies and execute them without critical evaluation.

Scardamalia and Bereiter (1991) discuss this issue of ownership in the context of Vygotsky's zone of proximal development. The zone of proximal development is the area in which the student can perform tasks successfully but only with some assistance; i.e. it is the instructional domain. Since it is instructional, the student and the teacher work together in the zone of proximal development. The question Scardamalia and Bereiter pose is: Who has ownership of the tasks in the zone of proximal development? They argue that the students must have control of their own learning. It is only with ownership that the student will have primary responsibility for noticing what is important and what must be learned to accomplish a given task and for setting and evaluating criteria for understanding. Without this ownership the student will fail to develop many of the metacognitive skills, and perhaps even the cognitive skills, essential for effective performance in the transfer environment. This is not to say that students are on their own. The teacher is there to coach and to share in evaluating their progress. However, by placing the student in control the emphasis is on self-directed learning and on the development of the metacognitive skills necessary to support it.

Project Based. The second critical feature in the design of authentic tasks is a holistic view of the task complex. Authentic activities exist as both global and local entities. Global defines the entire task, while local defines the sub-tasks. Global authentic activities might include performing a break-even analysis or designing a brochure for a business or building a deck for your home. Each of these global activities, or tasks, is comprised of a complex of local activities. For break-even analysis, local activities might include using a computer or calculator, obtaining pricing information from the finance department, and producing a report. For brochure design, client meetings, discussions with photographers, getting print estimates, and designing are all local activities.

The global task environment, including (most importantly) the purpose for undertaking the global task, gives meaning to each of the local tasks. It is therefore essential that the global activity is very closely tied to the tasks and experiences the learner will face in the transfer environment. At base, this is simply an emphasis on project based learning – the global task is the project. At the heart of the project based approach is the fact that the learning activity has a purpose that goes beyond simply demonstrating mastery of the local tasks. The purpose for a learning activity is driven by the global project context. Hence that larger context will determine the perspective that the learner brings to the specific learning task, which in turn determines the attitude taken toward the learning, what is attended to, what criteria are set for understanding and in the end, what is learned. We might think of the global task in terms of Bereiter's (1990) "contextual module." He proposes that the contextual module will determine what is brought to the learning task and what learning develops with regard to:

- procedural and declarative knowledge
- goal structures
- problem solving strategies
- affect
- self concept
- code of conduct

These factors are all to be considered in selecting or designing that global task environment in which specific learning activities occur. Typically, procedural and declarative knowledge requirements and perhaps the metacognitive requirements are the focus of any discussion of the learning task. However, Bereiter's framework also emphasizes the importance of the affective consequence of the project environment. And, as he emphasizes, we should not forget that these all interact to determine what is learned. The affect and code of conduct one brings to the task will certainly impact the problem solving strategies, goal structures, and knowledge development that occurs. We do not simply teach a code of conduct independently of the environment in which the learning occurs. Instead, it emerges from the learning/work environment we establish.

It may seem that these requirements set an impossible task for the teacher or trainer. How do we support the development of an authentic context for learning – an authentic global task environment – when so many affective and cognitive factors are involved? Of course, we seldom can achieve the full apprenticeship environment. The simple economics of instruction require environments that are less than authentic. However, perspectives such as Bereiter's provide guidance in evaluating instructional environments to determine the extent to which we have captured the cognitive and affective aspects of the transfer environment. Further, we think that there is much that can be done in instructional design to create learning environments that capture the culture of the transfer (authentic) environment. Later in the chapter, we will describe our own work in developing such learning environments.

Multiple Perspectives. The nature of the project and the student's ownership of the project are the keys to defining authentic learning environments. The metacognitive, cognitive, affective, and physical activities should all follow from these two considerations. However, we wish to bring into focus one particular cognitive activity that should be promoted in the design of most authentic learning environments: the ability to generate and evaluate alternative perspectives. A critical part of expert cognition in most authentic activities is trying to see a problem or a task from different perspectives. Consideration of those perspectives is then used to help develop and refine one's own goals and strategies.

Collaborative learning, properly implemented, is one strategy for helping to develop the skills of generating and evaluating alternative perspectives (e.g., Cunningham, in press; McMahon, Carr, & Fishman, 1992; Duffy & Jonassen, in press). Collaborative learning is used most effectively in medical training when teams of interns generate and evaluate alternative diagnoses or operating procedures. The goal is to aid the interns in considering the problem or symptoms from alternative perspectives. Thus one goal is that a future heart surgeon will have developed alternative frames of reference from which she can view a cardiac problem and these alternative frames will aid her in noticing symptoms that may suggest alternative procedures or modifications of existing procedures. Clearly we would not want a heart surgeon who views all cardiac problems from a single perspective or who always executes a fixed operating procedure.

How Do We Learn from Texts?

If authentic learning environments are a critical component of learning, then how do we ever learn to do something by reading about it in a book? We all read information that helps us to perform. As professionals we read journal articles or books (like this one) that give us perspectives we can use in solving problems quite different from anything the authors imagined. How is reading a paper about a research study an authentic activity related to conducting experiments?

Stated simply, the context is not just an external context imposed by someone else. It also includes an internal context – the frame of reference or point of application that the learner generates (envisions). The learners (or readers) bring their own framework to the task. They have real world problems that they are trying to solve and they read the text with those problems in mind. Hence the reader is cognitively problem solving in the area of application (the authentic context) while reading the text. What information is attended to, how the information is organized, and what personal knowledge is combined with the information all revolves around the problem solving activities (or those problems solving activities) – those contexts of application the reader imposes.

In essence, the more the learner is naturally embedded in the authentic use of the information and has experience in the domain to be able to determine relevance and envision the use of the information, the less we need to worry about providing an authentic learning activity. The authenticity will be self imposed.[1] For the naive learner, however, providing an authentic context is central since they do not have the experience base for generating their own context. Hence, we find the micro-society concept for schools to be a particularly exciting strategy for aiding school children in developing contexts for the societal application of their learning skills.

---

[1]Of course there may well be a conflict between the instructor's and the learner's view of authenticity. This is often the case when a professional leaves the work force to become a student and is suddenly faced with passing a multiple choice test as the goal for learning.

On the other hand, we wonder what most history teachers would see as the authentic use of history instruction. There are indeed authentic uses beyond mastery of the content (McMahon, Carr, & Fishman, 1992), but we feel relatively confident that most teachers have not considered those uses nor have they organized their learning environment to provide those alternative authentic activities.

Context

Thus far we have been concerned with the tasks engaged in by the learner. Let us turn now to the context in which those tasks occur. The concept of context has a rich history in the study of transfer. However, in this section we want to limit our focus on context to two specific issues: the management of complexity in instruction and the variation in contexts during instruction.

Complexity

A basic adage of instructional design is that the instructional sequence should progress from simple to complex (Dick and Carey, 1990). At a minimum, this has meant removing the complexities of the environment so that the learner begins learning in a greatly simplified environment, with only a small portion of the stimuli from the transfer environment represented. When this simplified environment is mastered, complexity is added. This gradual introduction of complexity continues until, if time permits, the learner is finally functioning in the "authentic" environment. This approach seems to have as a basic assumption that the new stimuli have an additive effect – understanding progresses additively as we add complexity.

We would argue for a more Gestalt view, consistent with the basic proposition that "understanding is indexed by experience." Consistent with that view, we argue that the understanding developed in a simplified stimulus environment is quite different from the understanding that develops in the full stimulus environment. Let us hasten to note at this point that when we say "understanding" our focus is on learning from authentic tasks as discussed in the last section. Hence, the emphasis is on the application of one's understanding and the ability to reflect on and defend that application. It is not simply "knowing about" something.

Spiro and his colleagues have made a similar argument for maintaining the complex stimulus environment. As Spiro, Vispoel, Schmitz, Samarapungavan, and Boerger (1987) note:

> Simplification of complex subject matter makes it easier for teachers to teach, for students to take notes and prepare for their tests, for test-givers to construct and grade tests, and for authors to write tests. The result is a massive "conspiracy of convenience [which leads to] dozens of serious errors in the concepts held by a majority of the... students... Instead of inappropriate simplification, we work with complex subject matter, acknowledging and teaching towards the complexity inherent in them... Cases and examples must be studied as

> they really occur, in their natural contexts, not as stripped down "textbook examples" that conveniently illustrate some principle (1987, pp. 180-181).

We would argue that providing realistic levels of complexity in the learning environment can actually make learning easier. To paraphrase Harel & Papert (1992): learning more can be easier than learning less. Tasks that are thought to be difficult when attempted in a decontextualized environment become intuitive when situated in a larger framework. In Harel and Papert's work, elementary school students who displayed a great dislike for fractions, tackled the task of learning about fractions with great enthusiasm when their role was changed from students to software designers. They were asked to design a computer program in LOGO (software they were already familiar with) that would teach the basics of fractions to children one year younger than themselves. In order to do this, they first had to teach themselves what was important to know about fractions. When the project was complete, the students had learned not only about fractions, but also about software design and instructional design. The children were so totally absorbed by the challenges of the design tasks, they practically "forgot" that they were also learning about fractions, a typically onerous subject for elementary school students. It really can be easier to learn more!

Spiro (see Spiro, this volume) argues that the use of the complex stimulus environment applies best to advanced knowledge acquisition in ill-structured domains. Hence his examples refer to medical training, economics, film study, and complex decision making. He argues that for beginning learners simplification may be the best approach. However, from a learner's vantage point the domain always involves advanced knowledge acquisition (after all, it is yet to be learned). In addition, we certainly expect that they will use their prior knowledge – just like advanced knowledge learners – in attempting to work in and interpret the learning environment. Furthermore, in project based learning there will be alternative paths to solution and there will almost certainly be alternative solutions (see, for example, Brown, Collins, and Duguid, 1989). Thus we see little reason to suggest different principles for the design of instruction for less advanced learners. What will almost certainly change, however, is the goal for instruction, i.e., the kind of environment in which we expect the learner to function at the end of instruction.

Limits on Complexity. Is there a limit to the amount of stimulus complexity that should be maintained? Should we place a fourth grader in a fully functional scientific laboratory? In answering these questions we must return to the notion of the "zone of proximal development." We have an end goal in terms of the environment in which we expect the learner to be able to function effectively. The end goal reflects a level of performance that the learner can now achieve only with assistance; i.e., it is in the learner's zone of proximal development. The goal of instruction is to provide the level of assistance that will eventually result in independent performance. Furthermore, given the previous discussion of authentic tasks, we expect that the learning activities will reflect authentic uses of the information domain.

We would argue that the complexity of the stimulus environment at the beginning of learning should reflect the complexity of the environment expected in the terminal performance. Rather than simplifying the environment, the goal is to aid the learner in functioning in the environment. The requirements of the constructivist view for maintaining the environmental complexity places particular burdens on the learner and on the learning advisor (teacher). However, as Perkins (in Duffy & Jonassen, in press) has argued, the potential gains from this learning environment are such that we simply must avoid the temptation to simplify the environment and instead we must search for new strategies to support the learner in working in that environment.

In answer to the question we posed, we would answer "No, the fourth grader should not be placed in a fully functioning scientific laboratory." However, she should be placed in a real laboratory where she can generate and conduct experiments with teacher present as a safety monitor and available as a consultant. That is, the laboratory should provide an environment consistent with the child's zone of proximal development.

Of course, time and cost sometimes prohibit providing the full stimulus context throughout training. Simplification is sometimes necessary for practical reasons. While we accept these realities, we would argue that the instructional designer should carefully consider the metacognitive and affective demands (effects) of the various components of the authentic task complex and work to maintain those demands in the simulation environment. Covey (in press) provides an example of the importance of and the strategy for maintaining the affective component of the stimulus environment in the teaching of ethics. Ethics is most often studied as an academic subject. While cases may be used, the "reality" of the cases is absent – they are textbook exercises. Covey argues that the emotional component of ethics has a very strong impact on what is judged ethical and not ethical. Ethics is a reflection of society. In designing his ethics course, Covey was able to use video containing interviews with an individual who had severe burns, blindness, and crippling injuries. This was not an interview years after the injury, presented as an abstract reflection on the accident. Rather, the interview begins while the individual is undergoing treatment. He insists that he be allowed to terminate treatment and die. The video and the interview bring home the agony of the pain and the deeply felt desires of the victim. The ethical issues and the logical arguments are not abstract but have to do with the real world decision making in this agonizing case. We can only believe that the understanding of ethics and ethical decision making is quite different in this learning environment than in traditional, abstracted learning environments. Covey's work clearly illustrates the potential and the importance of capturing the stimulus complex of the transfer environment. Once again, we can only emphasize the importance of seeking alternative strategies for capturing the "authentic" environment.

Variety of Contexts

It is a long standing prescription for instruction that numerous examples of a concept should be provided for study and practice. Further, the contexts in which a concept is instantiated should vary widely providing the full range of contexts in which that concept might appear (Merrill & Tennyson, 1977; Merrill, 1983). We want to reinforce, and perhaps extend both the practice and interpretation of this prescription.

One reason for raising the issue of variety of contexts is that the attempt to implement the previous design principle – providing the complex environment –frequently leads to a limitation in variety. There is often considerable depth, but little breadth. Interactive video programs, for example, often provide the complexity of the transfer environment and the decision making, but the experiences are fixed to a single scenario. For example, in an emergency room interactive video simulation we might find the learner playing the role of physician. After the patient is brought, in a variety of automatic activities unravel until, at some point, the physician (learner) must take action. Then the physician must order tests, prescribe treatments, etc., to save the patient's life. There is a potential for great realism, but since there is a single scenario, transfer to new environments may be quite limited.

The Cognition and Technology Group at Vanderbilt (this volume) have addressed this problem by providing a suite of scenarios – the Jasper Series – in which a variety of travel or transportation scenarios are provided. The same (or related) cognitive and metacognitive skills and knowledge are called for at various points within the same scenario as well as across scenarios.

Schoenfeld's (1985) approach to teaching a heuristic for solving mathematics problems illustrates the use of multiple contexts in a cognitive apprenticeship environment. Schoenfeld's goal was to aid students in learning a particular heuristic in thinking about mathematical problems. In a traditional approach we might provide examples of math problems illustrating how the principle applies. Then we would give practice with examples – perhaps with some items where the heuristic did not apply. Feedback would then outline the correct solution.

In contrast to the traditional approach, Schoenfeld asked students to bring real "mathbuster" problems to class to challenge him. He would then think out loud as he attempted to solve the problem, letting the students share in the problems and strategies as he worked toward a solution. Finally, either after solving the problem or giving up, the class would analyze Schoenfeld's problem solving strategy to identify the heuristics he used. Thus, there was a range of experience with the actual activity (albeit as a voyeur) of problem solving – not just with the steps of the heuristics. Further, there were authentic problems for Schoenfeld, not problems he had previously solved.

Before concluding this section let us briefly mention the work of Spiro and his colleagues, for they bring quite a different perspective to both the theory and the prescriptions for providing a variety of contexts. Spiro's argument, as we understand it, has two basic components. First, he argues that in any given situation an individual generates a schema or plan to guide action. The generative activity requires assembling the set of concepts and principles that are seen to apply. Second, there is a richness of meaning to a concept and the richness of one's experience determines that meaning. The concept takes on some of its meanings – and the way it might be used – from the characteristics of the particular context. Hence, the meaning is not fixed; rather, there is a rich variety of experience-based meanings.

From these two principles, one can see that learning requires a rich variety of experience with a concept to see how changes in the environment lead to changes in meaning and application. It is only through the richness of prior experience that the learner will be able to assemble the appropriate complex of concepts and strategies to guide performance in a new situation. Spiro offers particular prescriptions for providing a variety of experiences: the learner must study multiple cases and must revisit the cases with different goals and purposes. Hence, a concept is understood not only in multiple case contexts but also from multiple perspectives in the same context. For ease of reference, he refers to this instructional strategy as "criss-crossing the landscape" (Spiro, Feltovich, Jacobson, & Coulson, in press).

Constructivist Epistemology in Practice: Two Examples

This section describes the design of two learning environments: computer-based hypermedia and academic classroom instruction. Each of these environments was designed from what we believe to be a constructivist perspective. This section is intended to demonstrate the variety of ways that constructivism can influence the design of learning environments. The key elements to attend to in each example are the context and activities designed to establish a meaningful learning experience. It is also important to consider how evaluation is carried out in each of these environments.

The Lab Design Project

The Lab Design Project (LDP) (Honebein, Chen, & Brescia, 1992) is a hypermedia system designed to serve two purposes. First, it is meant to be a research tool to support the study of the sociology of biotechnology building design. Second, it is designed to support the teaching of research skills to first-year sociology graduate students. The goal of the learning component is to teach the skills students need in order to become contributing members of the research project.

The designers needed to determine how best to teach sociological research skills so that students could effectively conduct research on the sociology of a building. The designers wanted the learners to have the experience of doing research on the sociology of a building. One strategy is to take twenty students on a field trip to a biotechnology building and set them loose. That would definitely provide the richest level of context. Yet there are problems with this approach. Twenty inexperienced students running around a building would change the culture of that building, thus changing the nature of the data that would be gathered. Also, it is too expensive to take that many students into the field.

The designers began thinking of the problem in terms of a simulation. Could they simulate a building in such a way that the learners would still be able to concretely experience the activities of a sociological researcher? To investigate this, the designers began to describe the nature of the tasks of the sociological researchers. The task analysis specifically focused on the activities a culture (sociologists doing research) undertakes in daily life, relying on observation of the culture as the critical source of information (Carroll, 1990). First, the researcher would explore the building: Walk down hallways; go into labs; watch the people in the environment at work. His or her purpose is to find aspects of the building design that are questionable, or researchable. Next, the researcher would interview people in the building to get their perspective of how the building supports or inhibits their activities. Finally, the researcher would sift through a pile of papers documenting the years of communication between the funders, architects, builders, and managers of the building, looking for answers to the research questions under consideration. This analysis of the researcher in action yields an authentic task for the learner – to determine a sociological phenomena of interest in the building and explore ways to explain it.

An initial design strategy was to represent the information base in a hypermedia environment. There were several reasons for doing this. First, there is a large database of discrete chunks of information. These chunks include the images of the building, blue prints, correspondence, plans, etc. Furthermore, these chunks or nodes are all interrelated in a variety of ways, e.g., functionally, temporally, and authorship. The researcher has a goal of exploring this database, acting as a detective, looking for information to understand particular features in the design or use of the building. Finally, the researcher needs to annotate the documents, reorganize them, and collaborate with fellow researchers (as well as the mentor) during this exploration. All of these factors point to hypermedia as the ideal media for representation.

The navigational structure of the LDP hypermedia environment is designed to enable learners to explore the building as if they are actually there. In the real building, the learner would be able to walk down any hall or visit any room in any order. Exploration is never the same linear journey for all people. To accomplish this style of interaction, the navigational structure of the system takes the form of a map based upon blueprints of the actual building (see Figure 1). The learner can point to the first floor on an exterior drawing of the building, and zoom into the first floor plan. The learner can then point to a room on the first floor and zoom into a close-up of that room. At this point, the learner can "walk around" the room, viewing photographs from various perspectives as if the learner were actually in the room. The drawings and photographs are not doctored in any way to provide cues to direct the learner's attention to specific commonalties, oddities, or differences in the building design. The complexity of the actual environment is maintained so that learners are able to apply their knowledge and their own interpretation to each of the images in the system. Since there may be any of a variety of research tasks or issues, the materials cannot be "designed" to support attention to or learning about specific clues. The learner cannot be guided to the "correct" answer through the hypermedia system – it is an issue of teacher advising/consulting.

In order to model the ways that a student might use the LDP hypermedia system, the professor recorded an animated, narrated movie showing how he solved a typical problem presented by the building. The professor used a "think-aloud" strategy, allowing the students to see how he explores, what he is thinking about, what catches his attention, etc. The effectiveness of modeling is strongly supported in a number of studies (Yaeshima, Ninomiya, Ohnogi & Oda, 1982; LaNunziata, Cooper & Hill, 1985; Rivera & Smith, 1988; Baggett, 1983; Smith & Hailey, 1988). The culmination of the modeled exploration is the formulation of a research question. In this case, the professor asked, "Why are there desk lamps in some of the labs? Do some labs have poor lighting?"

Since learners cannot actually engage in interviews with building inhabitants in a hypermedia environment, the designers had to compromise on this experience. Actual interviews with inhabitants of the building, the architects who designed it, and the builders who built it were performed by the professor and his research assistants. Those interviews were transcribed and built into the hypermedia environment. While learners can not ask questions themselves, the interviews provide important data in a format consistent with the practice of sociologists. Once again, to maintain the cognitive context of the interviews, no special cues or pointers were included for the learner. A high level of complexity and "noise" was maintained in the task environment. Over 4000 pages of interview data and other documentation are included in the hypermedia system.

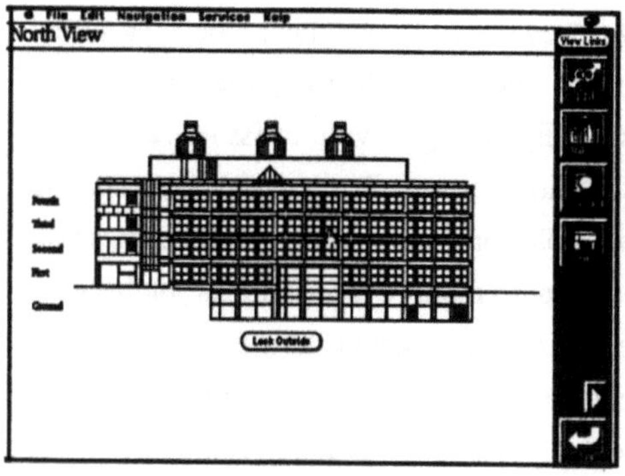

Building View. Here the learner can click on any floor to go to a floor plan graphic of that floor. In this example, the learner is clicking on the third floor.

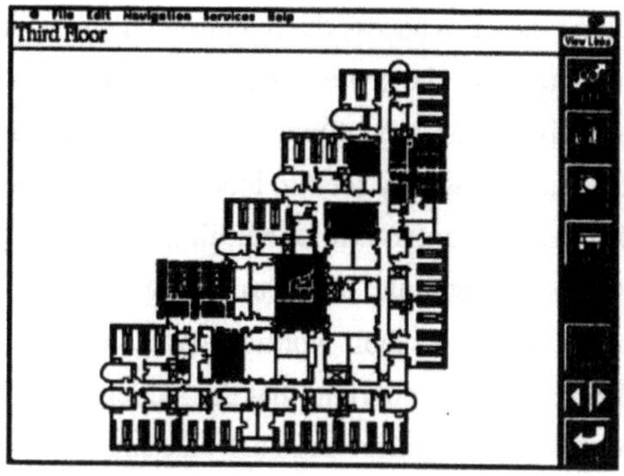

Floor View. This view shows a floor plan of the third floor. The rooms which are high-lighted can be clicked on to zoom into a closer view of that room. In this example, the learner is clicking on Lab 321.

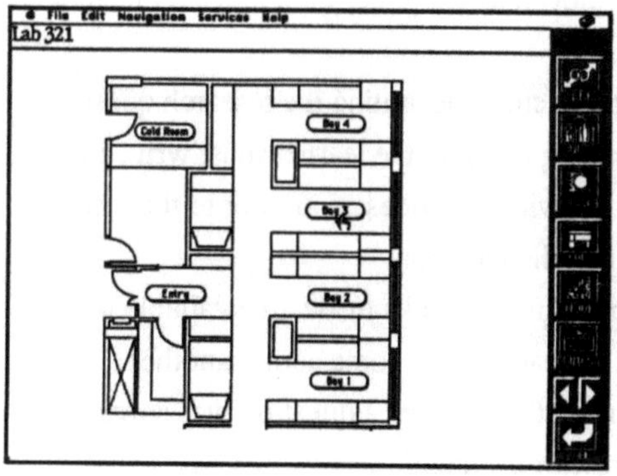

Lab (or Room) View. This view is a close-up of the floor plan for the laboratory. The buttons enable the learner to zoom into each one of the bays for greater detail. The learner is about to zoom into Bay 3.

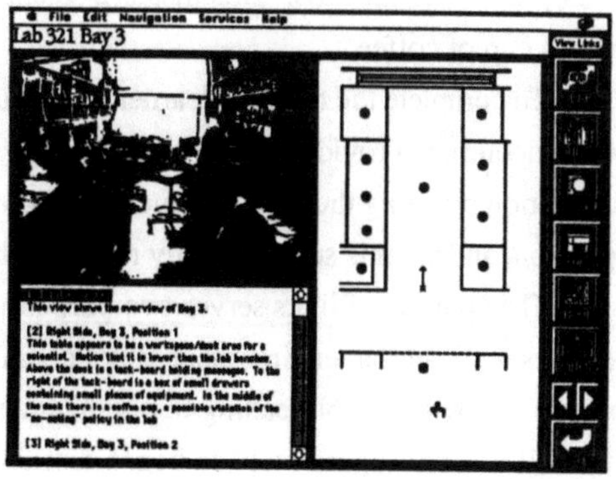

Photograph View. In this view, the learner is presented with a picture of the bay, text describing the bay, and a schematic of the bay. By clicking on the black circles in the schematic, the learner can "walk around" the bay, viewing pictures of a variety of perspectives. Notice the arrow points the position of the camera operator when the picture was taken.

Figure 1. These screen shots illustrate how the experience of "navigating" in a real building is recreated in a hypermedia environment.

Let's look briefly at how these pieces form the learning environment. In class, the professor assigns the learners a task: E.g. explore the building to determine a sociological phenomenon of interest and gather data to explain it. Learners then go to the computer lab where they can access the hypermedia environment. They view a movie that models the skills and strategies the professor uses to solve a similar task. They begin their exploration. This is an active environment with students and the professor discussing the various issues raised by the students as they seek to identify a problem. Each learner eventually discovers a phenomena that is important to him or her, illustrated by a photograph from the building that illustrates the issue. For example, one learner might wonder how the placement of the scientists' built-desk in the lab affects their working styles, and illustrate it with a photograph showing the location of the desk. It is important that the students are solving their own problems, and not the professor's. By allowing each student to determine their own object of inquiry, the task remains more interesting and relevant to them and is a sociologist's task.

The learner then attempts to find answers to his or her research question by finding and analyzing appropriate interviews and documents. One learner might learn from reading an interview stating that many scientists dislike having their desks in the lab, since there is a "no eating" policy in the labs. This means a scientist cannot sit as his or her desk and eat lunch or have a cup of coffee.

To complete the task, the learner must "link" the picture illustrating the research question to the document providing a possible answer. In making the link, the learner must write an annotation restating the research question, how the interview provides an answer to the research question, and what is sociologically relevant about the phenomenon.

The creation of links serves two purposes. First, since all links made are available to all learners, it creates an environment of collaboration. A learner may come across another person's link, and upon reading it, obtain a new perspective on how a question was solved. It's as if two colleagues met and began discussing research strategies.

The second purpose of links is evaluation. The professor has access to the links of each student and can monitor or be invited into the student's thinking as represented in the links. During the process, the professor can use this data to coach the student as necessary. When the project is complete, the professor can read the links to get a perspective on how the learner thought about the task and arrived at a solution. The professor can send comments to the student regarding the links, reinforce effective strategies or outline areas of improvement.

In summary, the LDP hypermedia environment, through simulation, provides an environment for learning that is richly detailed and situated in a meaningful context. The environment provides a level of complexity and information representative of the actual setting, the tasks and activities the students engaged in are consistent with the authentic activities of expert sociologists, and the tasks are meaningful to the learners' own research interests. Learners are able to apply and practice the same problem solving skills in accomplishing the task as if they had been in the actual environment. They are also more readily able to transfer those skills to an actual environment when they become full members of the research project.

An Introductory Course In Educational Research

Our second case is an educational research course within the Instructional Systems Technology department at Indiana University. The goal of the course is to teach graduate students how to generate, develop, conduct, and report an educational research study. As with the Lab Design Project, the goal of the course is to initiate the students into the research culture of the profession.

This class is taught from a constructivist perspective, in which it is believed that students should experience the entire process of performing an educational research project based on the authentic practices of the culture of research and researchers. This includes analyzing how an expert researcher formulates basic ideas, refining those ideas into a viable study, designing an experiment, conducting the experiment, analyzing the results, and producing a paper suitable for publication in a research journal. This task structure was derived by the professor, who is an active participant in the educational research community, reflecting upon how he conducts research.

The first day of the course, the professor lectures briefly on the goals and requirements of the course – that students prepare a publishable research paper. Students are encouraged to generate research ideas of their own, based upon their current interests in education.

Generating ideas is easy for most students. Refining a problem into a researchable issue is an enormously complex task. The student prepares multiple iterations of the "problem," each time moving closer to the specification of a researchable problem. There are two strategies for supporting this process of refinement. First there are discussions in class and in office meetings where the implications and dimensions of the problem are analyzed. The emphasis here is on analytic skills. Second, the students search the literature for relevant research that again is used to help refine the problem. Since there are an infinite number of refinements of any large problem (and students always begin with large problems), the refinement must come from the student, through the assistance of the professor. That is, the problem remains the student's.

Locating literature in the domain of interest is a new challenge for many students in the class. Multiple strategies for locating relevant literature are discussed along with the strengths and weakness of each. This includes a trip to the campus library where a research librarian demonstrates strategies for searching the ERIC computer database. Alternative strategies include searching recent issues of relevant journals and following the reference list in key, recent articles.

As students begin identifying a body of relevant research, the focus of each class meeting is on analyzing the content and relevance of individual studies. The class analyzes the paper in order to determine independent and dependent variables, the strengths and weaknesses of the paper, and how the paper contributes to refining and discussing the research problem. These studies contribute specific data to the students' research and also serve as models for the students' own nascent research proposals.

The instructor aids the learner in accomplishing the activity, not by doing the task for the learner or giving the learner the correct answers, but by providing hints and guidance that require learners to formulate their own solution to the problem. Coaching can aid both cognitive and physical activities, helping the learner to think about problems through reminders of heuristics, facts, and processes (Lesgold, LaJoie, Bunzo, & Eggan, 1991).

During class the instructor is very careful not to give "the answers" to students. Indeed, since the research is the student's own, there seldom are fixed answers but rather alternative paths to consider. The students, therefore, are encouraged to debate various points of each study with each other in order to develop and discuss the alternative perspectives. The most common interjection by the professor is, "So what? Can you explain that?" This question is used as a catalyst to get students to understand why something was in a study and what its function was.

As the course progresses, the class continues to practice activities authentic to educational research. Students form into teams where they begin shaping their ideas into a viable research study. The activity at this stage of the class is to write the introduction for the research paper. Like the research papers discussed earlier in the class, the students' papers become the central focus of class discussions. The class interaction remains similar: a group presents their introduction, then the class analyzes the argument or story being presented, the relevance of the experimental design to that story or analysis, and the viability of the study for providing the desired information. Once again, variables, complexity and meaningfulness are discussed, and the professor maintains a devil's advocate/facilitator role.

The activities progress from refining the introduction to developing and refining the method of the experiment. Class interactions maintain their discussion orientation. As teams prepare to conduct their experiments with real subjects, a midterm exam is given. However, this is not a typical exam.

For the test, students meet privately with the instructor to discuss their experiment. Students are asked to explain their experiment as if to a colleague at a conference. This is a very authentic activity for a researcher. While the instructor gets to evaluate the skills of each student individually and comment on the student's performance, the student gets the experience of verbalizing his or her research, thus helping him or her to think about it more concretely. A detailed discussion of these types of evaluation methods can be found in Cunningham (1992).

In conducting the actual research, students submit their plans to the University committee for subjects' rights, recruit subjects, administer treatments, collect data, and deal with unexpected events – such as subjects not showing up, over-scheduling subjects, etc. What is important about this activity is that no matter how prepared the students think they are, something unexpected will occur and they will have to figure a way around the problem. They experience the same types of problems that occur in real research experiments.

After collecting the data, students analyze their results and complete the results and discussion sections of their papers. Teams can hand in their papers-in-progress for the instructor to review at anytime during this process. The instructor's feedback is important in aiding the students in their writing and analysis skills.

Once the students complete their papers, the second to last activity is to present their paper. This is done in an atmosphere representative of an actual conference presentation – at the weekly colloquium session held by the Instructional Systems Technology department. The teams present their research to a group of their peers and professors, and then field questions about their research.

The final activity is another private discussion with the instructor. Like the format of the midterm, the discussion takes the format of two peers discussing a research project. In this session, the student is asked to reflect on the good and bad points of the study and asked to consider what they will change in the future to improve the study.

In summary, the strength of this class lies in its orientation to actual practice. As a part of the course, students become educational researchers. They perform the everyday activities that educational researchers perform, experience the same problems researchers face, and present their results in a forum consistent with the activities of the culture. Throughout their activities, the students are consistently supported by the instructor. The instructor acts as a facilitator rather than a giver of knowledge. Through his style of interaction, he forces students to think about what they are doing, only providing hints or possible answers as a last resort before a student breaks down in total frustration. Once again, the activities closely match real life, enabling many students to transfer the skills they learned quite easily to other research projects, such as continuations of their class experiments or their dissertations.

Conclusion

This chapter presents a number of different perspectives on the design of learning environments from a constructivist perspective. We've attempted to point out that context and authentic activities are two key design strategies which guide the creation of such environments. The focus of these strategies is on creating environments that are meaningful to learners, enabling them to successfully transfer the skills learned to tasks in the real world.

Constructivist learning focuses on skills and strategies, rather than facts and rote memorization. As students in History class, we were taught that Andrew Jackson was a President. Yet we can't remember why that fact is meaningful or applies to our lives. The more important skill to have learned would be *how* to find out who the Presidents of the United States were. That's the type of learning we see constructivism supporting.

Rarely in life do real tasks exist in a vacuum, with no distractions, interruptions or other problems to inhibit a person's performance. Our real environments are filled with stimuli – all of which impact performance. Establishing context creates learning environments that approach or simulate the complexity of the real world, thus preparing students to deal with the real world.

Merrill (in press) agrees with the constructivists (e.g. Bednar et al, 1990) that,

> "...teaching authentic tasks in context is a desirable part of the instruction" (pg. 48), yet goes on to berate constructivists for their view that context in authentic tasks cannot be simplified or broken down. So the question becomes, "Why are constructivists so hesitant to let simplification and decontextualization enter their learning environments?"

Meaningfulness of learning is one possible answer. The more context is pulled away, the less meaningful the learning. Consider some examples of present-day decontextualized education: lectures, multiple-choice tests and software "games" where children count jelly beans aided by an animated rabbit. Jonassen (1991) describes his fifth-grade daughter memorizing the names and facts of the sub-phyla of animals as an example of decontextualized learning. We remember doing that, yet we can't remember why or for what purpose.

Perhaps the examples we've outlined above contain elements that critics of constructivism might term "decontextualized." Yet the global task environment in each example provides strong linkages to real world activities that are not hidden or muted in any way. Too many contemporary educational programs either fail to recognize the value of or are unwilling to implement apprenticeship as a mode of teaching and learning. The context and authentic activities that are inherently a part of apprenticeship provide meaningful experiences for learners that help them transfer skills and knowledge to the world outside of schools or training. They are key elements of constructivism and should not be compromised in the classroom.

References

Baggett, P. (1983). *Learning a procedure from multimedia instructions: The effects of film and practice.* (Report No. TR-125-ONR). Washington, D.C.: Office of Naval Research, Psychological Sciences Div.

Bednar, A.K., Cunningham, D., Duffy, T.M., & Perry, J.D. (1991). Theory into practice: How do we link? In G. Anglin (Ed.), *Instructional technology: Past, present and future*. Denver, CO: Libraries Unlimited.

Bereiter, C. (1990). Aspects of an educational learning theory. *Review of Educational Research, 60*(4), 603-624.

Brown, J.S., Collins, A., & Duguid, P. (1989). Situated cognition and the culture of learning. *Educational Researcher, 18*, 32-42.

Carroll, J.M. (1990). *The Nurnberg Funnel: Designing minimalist instruction for practical computer skill.* Cambridge, MA: MIT Press.

Collins, A., Brown, J.S., & Newman, S.E. (1988). Cognitive apprenticeship: Teaching the craft of reading, writing, and mathematics. In L.B. Resnick (Ed.), *Cognition and instruction: Issues and agendas*. Hillsdale, NJ: Erlbaum.

Cognition and Technology Group at Vanderbilt. (in press). Technology and the design of generative learning environments. In T. Duffy & D. Jonassen (Eds.), *Constructivism and the technology of instruction: A conversation*. Hillsdale, NJ: Erlbaum.

Covey, P. (in press). A right to die? Integrating emotion in moral reasoning and learning. In J. Johnston & R. Kozma (Eds.), *Educational computing in the humanities*. Ann Arbor, MI: National Center for Research on Post Secondary Teaching and Learning.

Cunningham, D. (1992). Assessing constructions and constructing assessments: A dialog. In T. Duffy & D. Jonassen (Eds.), *Constructivism and the technology of instruction: A conversation*. Hillsdale, NJ: Erlbaum.

Dick, W., & Carey, L. (1990). *The systematic design of instruction* (3rd ed.). Glenview, IL: Scott, Foresman.

Duffy, T.M., & Bednar, A.K. (in press). Attempting to come to grips with alternative perspectives. In T. Duffy & D. Jonassen (Eds.), *Constructivism and the technology of instruction*. Hillsdale, NJ: Erlbaum.

Duffy, T.M. & Jonassen, D.H. (Eds.). (in press). *Constructivism and the technology of instruction: A conversation*. Hillsdale, NJ: Erlbaum.

Fosnot, C.T. (1989). *Enquiring teachers, enquiring learners.* New York: Teacher's College Press.

Harel, I., and Papert, S. (1992). Software design as a learning environment. In I. Harel & S. Papert (Eds.), *Constructionism* (pp. 41-84). Norwood, NJ: Ablex Publishing Corporation.

Honebein, P., Chen, P., & Brescia, W. (1992). Hypermedia and sociology: A simulation for developing research skills. *Liberal Arts Computing, 1*(1), 9-15.

Jonassen, D.H. (1991). Context is everything. *Educational Technology, 31*(6), 35-37.

LaNunziata, L.J., Cooper, J.O., & Hill, D.S. (1985). The differential effects of still illustration, motion illustration, and modeling on students' manuscript letter legibility. *Journal of Educational Research, 79*(2), 109-113.

Langer, E.J. (1989). *Mindfullness.* Reading, MA: Addison-Wesley.

Lesgold, A., LaJoie, S., Bunzo, M., Eggan, G. (1991). Sherlock: A coached practice environment for an electronics troubleshooting job. In J. Larkin, R. Chebay, and C. Scheftic (Eds.), *Computer assisted instruction and intelligent tutoring systems*. Hillsdale, NJ: Erlbaum.

McMahon, T.A, Carr, A.A., & Fishman, B.J. (1992, February). *Hypermedia and constructivism: Three approaches to enhanced learning*. Paper presented at the meeting of the Association for Educational Communications and Technology, Washington, D.C.

Merrill, M.D. (in press). Constructivism and instructional design. In T. Duffy & D. Jonassen (Eds.), *Constructivism and the technology of instruction: A conversation.* Hillsdale, NJ: Erlbaum.

Merrill, M.D. (1983). Component display theory. In C. Reigeluth (Ed.), *Instructional-Design theories and models: An overview of their current status* (pp. 279-333). Hillsdale, NJ: Lawrence Erlbaum Associates.

Merrill, M.D., & Tennyson, R.D. (1977). *Teaching concepts: An instructional design guide.* Englewood Cliffs, NJ: Educational Technology Publications.

Perkins, D.N. (in press) Technology meets constructivism: Do they make a marriage? In T. Duffy & D. Jonassen (Eds.), *Constructivism and the technology of instruction: A conversation.* Hillsdale, NJ: Lawrence Erlbaum Associates.

Popkewitz, T.S. (1987). *The formation of school subjects: The struggle for creating an American institution.* New York: The Falmer Press.

Rivera, D. & Smith, D.D. (1988). Using a demonstration strategy to teach midschool students with learning disabilities how to compute long division. *Journal of Learning Disabilities, 21*(2), 77-81.

Scardamalia, M., & Bereiter, C. (1991). Higher levels of agency for children in knowledge building: A challenge for the design of new knowledge media. *The Journal of The Learning Sciences, 1*(1), 37-68.

Schoenfeld, A.H. (1985). *Mathematical Problem Solving.* New York: Academic Press.

Smith, P.C. & Hailey, B.J. (1988). Compliance with instructions for regular breast self-examination. *Journal of Compliance in Health Care, 3*(2), 151-161.

Spiro, R.J., Feltovich, P.L., Jacobson, M.J., & Coulson, R.L. (in press). Cognitive flexibility, constructivism, and hypertext: Random access instruction for advanced knowledge acquisition in ill-structured domains. In T. Duffy & D. Jonassen (Eds.), *Constructivism and the technology of instruction: A conversation.* Hillsdale, NJ: Erlbaum.

Spiro, R.J., Vispoel, W., Schmitz, J., Samarapungavan, A., & Boerger, A. (1987). Knowledge acquisition for application: Cognitive flexibility and transfer in complex content domains. In B.C. Britton (Ed.), *Executive control processes* (pp. 177-199). Hillsdale, NJ: Erlbaum.

Sternberg, R.J., & Wagner, R.K. (1987). *Practical intelligence: Nature and origins of competence in the everyday world.* Cambridge, U.K.: Cambridge University Press.

Sticht, T.G., & Hickey, D.T. (1988). Functional context theory, literacy, and electronics training. In R. Dillon & J. Pellegrino (Eds.), *Instruction: Theoretical and applied perspectives.* New York: Praeger Publishers.

Yaeshima, K., Ninomiya, K., Ohnogi, H., & Oda, Y. (1982). Effects of exposure to a model on children's game behavior. *Japanese Psychological Review, 24*(1), 1-9.

5 A Logo-Based Tool-Kit and Computer Coach to Support the Development of General Thinking Skills

Erik De Corte*, Lieven Verschaffel*, Hilde Schrooten*, Hendrik Olivie´**, and Antoon Vansina**

*Center for Instructional Psychology and Technology (CIP&T), Catholic University, Leuven, Belgium
**Department of Computer Sciences, Catholic University, Leuven, Belgium

One of the major arguments for teaching pupils to program in Logo is the claim that this experience results in the acquisition of general thinking skills. However, research concerning this "cognitive-effects hypothesis" has shown that Logo as such does not lead to the spontaneous development of general thinking skills; this can only be obtained if Logo is embedded in a powerful teaching-learning environment aimed at the acquisition and transfer of those skills. These findings have led us to address the following research question: Is it desirable to build a part of the instructional support into the computer system? In order to study this issue, we developed a Logo-based tool-kit and computer coach that supports the acquisition of a Logo programming strategy, including planning and debugging skills. In this contribution we present the theoretical and empirical background and the design of this computer system.

Logo and Learning to Think: Past Research and Present Problem

Since the early eighties it has often been argued that learning computer programming – especially Logo – would be particularly conducive to the development of general thinking and problem-solving skills, such as planning, debugging, and problem decomposition (Papert, 1980).

However, a series of investigations about the effects of Logo programming on pupils' thinking and problem-solving capacities carried out over the first part of the past decade did not report positive results with respect to this so-called "cognitive-effects hypothesis" (De Corte & Verschaffel, 1989). For example, McCoy, Carver and Klahr (1986) examined the debugging skill of primary school children at the end of a 24-hour Logo course. The results of the post-tests showed that the pupils typically did not spontaneously trace and correct the error in their program. Instead, they adapted the original goal to the obtained wrong screen effect, or they simply quit the project and chose a new one. If the pupils were explicitly asked to debug a faulty program, they used very ineffective and cumbersome debugging strategies, such as successively checking the entire listing of the program starting with the first line. Noss (1985) reported similar sobering results for the planning skill in writing Logo programs and for the decomposition of complex programming tasks in simple parts.

Nevertheless, the so-called cognitive-effects hypothesis has not been rejected, especially because the sobering outcomes of the previous investigations have been attributed to several weaknesses of this research (De Corte, Verschaffel, & Schrooten, 1990). An important shortcoming was the poor quality of the Logo learning environments used in these prior studies. These environments were inspired by Papert's (1980) claim that computer programming skills can be acquired according to a self-discovery strategy. Learning Logo should take place in a spontaneous and natural way, analogous to how a child learns to speak. He calls this "learning without being taught" or "learning without curriculum". This conception of the teaching-learning process is based on Piaget's constructivist view which states that children build and develop their own intellectual structures through interaction with the environment, and that instruction can only follow, and not promote, that personal intellectual development. In practice, many researchers and teachers have interpreted Papert's writings as discouraging any direct intervention except in response to the child's activities and initiatives. It was hoped that the acquisition and transfer of the programming skills would somehow "happen" to the pupils, due to the unique characteristics of the Logo language (Leron, 1985).

At present this viewpoint has largely been abandoned, and most researchers now agree that the Logo learning environment should also involve direct instruction aimed at the development of problem-solving skills in programming and at their transfer to other problem situations. However, although the tendency toward providing more structure is salient, nobody denies the necessity of giving pupils ample opportunities for free exploration of Logo tasks. In other words, researchers move toward a form of guided discovery as the appropriate teaching strategy. In this respect, Leron (1985) introduced the term "quasi-Piagetian learning", which he characterized as follows: "through giving a more active role to teachers and learning materials, it is still closer to Papert's Piagetian learning than to the sort of teaching normally found in schools" (p. 32).

A series of more recent investigations, in which an attempt was made to overcome the weaknesses of the earlier work, has reported positive results both with respect to the mastery of thinking skills within the Logo environment, and to the transfer of these skills to new content domains (Carver, 1988; Clements, 1990; Lehrer, Guckenberg, & Sancilio, 1988; Littlefield, Delclos, Lever, Clayton, Bransford, & Franks, 1988; Swan, 1989; for an overview, see De Corte, et al., 1990). This was also the case in our own teaching experiment, in which a Logo environment was implemented in two sixth-grade classes for a period of one year (De Corte, Verschaffel, & Schrooten, in press). However, taken as a whole, those results strongly suggest that Logo is not in itself a genuine vehicle for thinking, but that it can be a very useful device for the acquisition of general thinking skills, if embedded in a powerful teaching-learning environment that intentionally and systematically supports the mastery and the transfer of these skills (Clark, in press).

Until now, most of this instructional support was provided by the teacher and by written materials. Taking into account the present state of the art within cognitive science on the one hand, and information technology on the other, it has become possible to build (a considerable part of) the instructional support in the Logo software itself (see also Salomon, in press; Scardamalia, Bereiter, McLean, Swallow, & Woodruff, 1989).

In this chapter we describe the initial stages of a project aimed at the construction and evaluation of a Logo-based tool-kit and computer coach that has the built-in support to foster the acquisition of planning and debugging skills. The major reason for trying to computerize part of the instruction derives from the observation that teaching thinking skills is very time-intensive. In some stages of the learning process, individualized instruction at the computer should allow a more efficient use of time as well as an overall time gain. Such built-in instruction may also be interesting in light of further research, because it makes it possible to control certain elements of the instruction, and thereby to isolate the effect of specific factors.

We will focus on the design of this new system, but first we present the Logo programming strategy, developed in our previous work, that formed the basis of the computer-based system.

A Logo Programming Strategy

In a project on "Computers and Thinking," carried out since 1986 at the Center for Instructional Psychology and Technology, we developed, implemented, and evaluated a Logo teaching-learning environment in several teaching experiments (De Corte, et al., in press).

In designing this environment we focused on a subset of four thinking skills that are considered to be sensitive to programming experience: two metacognitive skills (planning and debugging) and two heuristics (problem decomposition and construction of an external problem representation). The crucial part of the Logo environment was the teaching of a Logo programming strategy, consisting of two main phases: a planning phase, carried out independently from the computer, and an integrated coding-and-testing phase at the machine.

In the planning phase a tree-like diagram (see Figure 1) is constructed in which the complex drawing is subdivided into building blocks that are easy to program (e.g., a rectangle)[1]. This diagram also indicates the sequence in which the different parts have to be drawn on the screen. The diagram also contains the names of the "connecting links" that move a turtle from the end

[1]In this study the children were not taught how to use variables and recursion.

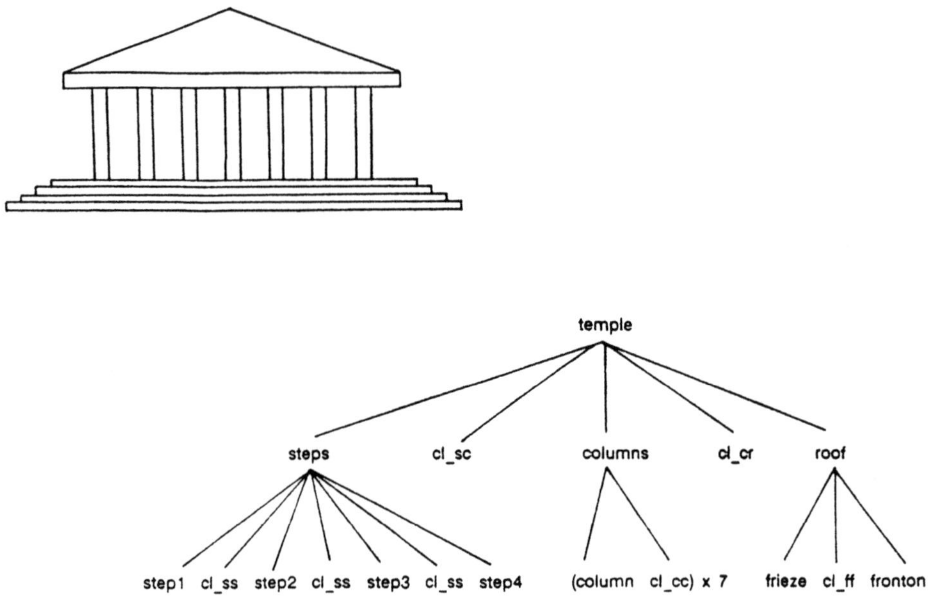

Figure 1: Tree-like diagram for the drawing of a temple

position of a previous part to the start position of the next building block[2]. Obviously, planning as a metacognitive activity takes place in this phase and also elicits the application of the two heuristics, namely problem decomposition and construction of an external representation.

Once the planning is completed, the integrated coding-and-testing phase at the machine can begin. This activity, which involves debugging, is guided by two principles, top-down programming and immediate testing and debugging. Top-down programming means that the pupils are taught to start with writing the most global procedure, called the "mother procedure", which consists of the names of all the subsequent parts from the second level of the tree-like

[2]It was agreed that the name for a connecting link between two building blocks consists of the following three parts: The characters "CL" (from Connecting Link), followed by a dash and the first characters of the previous and following block (e.g., connecting link between STEPS and COLUMNS: CL-SC).

diagram. Subsequently, each component of this procedure is specified until the lowest level of the tree-like diagram is reached[3].

The second principle consists of the immediate testing and debugging of each newly defined procedure. By calling the "mother procedure", the result appears on the screen and can instantly be evaluated. Furthermore, the error message "There is no procedure named..." indicates which procedure has to be written next[4].

To illustrate these principles, we present the interaction of a pupil with the computer. The pupil applies the strategy for drawing the temple in Figure 1. In accordance with the principle of top-down programming the pupil first defines the mother procedure (TEMPLE):

```
TO TEMPLE
STEPS CL_SC COLUMNS CL_CR ROOF
END
```

Then, following the second principle, the pupil types the name of the mother procedure (TEMPLE), resulting in the error message "THERE IS NO PROCEDURE NAMED STEPS AT LEVEL 1 OF TEMPLE". Next the STEPS procedure is defined:

```
TO STEPS
STEP1 CL_SS STEP2 CL_SS STEP3 CL_SS STEP4
END
```

As a result of the subsequent testing (TEMPLE), the error message at the bottom of the screen indicates that STEP1 is the next procedure to be written. The pupil types:

```
TO STEP1
REPEAT 2 [FD 3 RT 90 FD 155 RE 90]
END
```

When the TEMPLE procedure is executed again, the turtle draws the first step. Then the pupil writes the procedure for the connecting link between the first step and the second one (CL_SS), for example:

```
TO CL_SS
PU FD 3 RE 90 FD 5 LT 90 PD
END
```

When the TEMPLE procedure is called, the turtle draws the first step and then moves to the starting position for the second step. This process is repeated until all building blocks and

---

[3]In converting the tree-like diagram to programming code, the "depth first" method is followed. This means that at each knot in the diagram first the left branch is worked out, and then the branches more to the right. This strategy contrasts with the "breadth first" method, in which first all procedures of one level are defined, and then the procedures of the next level. We prefer the depth-first method because it permits a stepwise control of the resulting drawing.

[4]The computer does not indicate the next procedure to be written if the program contains a conditional statement.

connecting links of STEPS, and subsequently all parts of the remaining components of the mother procedure (TEMPLE) are defined.

As indicated before, the teaching of this programming strategy constituted the major component of the Logo learning environment that was used in our experiments. Starting from a moderate constructivist conception of learning, this environment was characterized by a good balance between discovery learning and personal exploration on the one hand, and systematic instruction and guidance on the other. The following instructional strategies that we used are considered in the recent literature to be effective for the instruction of general thinking skills: modelling, scaffolding, coaching, exploration, articulation, and reflection (Collins, Brown, & Newman, 1989). A series of evaluation instruments administered at the end of the Logo course showed that the pupils in the experimental classes mastered the Logo knowledge and programming skills fairly well, and that positive transfer effects were obtained for three out of the four thinking skills. For a more detailed description of the instructional system and the obtained results, we refer to De Corte, et al. (in press).

A Logo-Based Tool-Kit and Computer Coach

The Logo learning system involves three levels. The first level corresponds to the traditional Logo (turtle graphics) which enables the pupil to write Logo commands and programs for making drawings. At the second level, two additional tools that stimulate and facilitate planning and debugging activities are available. At the third level the pupil's activities are analyzed by a computer coach who gives comments and orienting help based on a comparison between the pupil's activities and the expert programming strategy described earlier. Two types of coaching differing in terms of the rigor of the diagnosis and the subsequent messages are being implemented. Before describing these three levels in greater detail, we will first mention some general and technical characteristics of the system.

The system is being developed for use on the type of computers that are becoming more and more available in Belgian primary schools, i.e. personal computers (MS-DOS) with minimally one disk-drive, with or without hard disk. EGA, VGA and Hercules graphics cards can be driven by the system. Because the software is mainly being developed for elementary school pupils, much attention has been paid to its user-friendliness. For instance, it is highly self-explanatory, menu-driven, and mouse-driven. A help-facility which outlines the program structure is available at any point. Finally, the system is designed to be useful as a prototype. It is easy to extend and modify, and it allows smooth conversions to other natural as well as programming languages.

Level 1

At level 1 the system has two major parts: an execution part and an editor. When the system is started, the execution screen appears (see Figure 2). The top part is taken by the execution window with the turtle. In the text window at the bottom of the screen, the pupil can type Logo commands that are executed immediately. Instructions containing syntactical errors are not carried out; the turtle then gives an error message. For instance, when the pupil types "FW 50" instead of "FD 50", the turtle reacts: "I don't know how to FW".

For practical reasons, we decided to limit the Logo primitives to the so-called turtle graphics: forward (FD), back (BK), right (RT), left (LT), penup (PU), pendown (PD), clearscreen (CS), and home. The system also allows the use of procedures (possibly with parameters), iteration, recursion, conditional statements, and the stop-command.

At any time, the user can consult a list of all available Logo primitives (language help). Moreover, the teacher has the possibility to suppress particular Logo primitives and concepts that pupils are not yet familiar with. To write a procedure or a program, the pupil has to switch to the editor (see Figure 3). This is done by selecting an option in the menu.

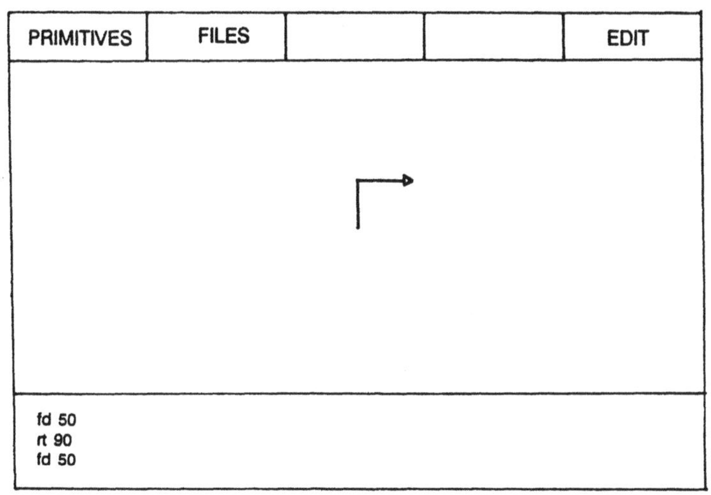

Figure 2: Execution of Logo commands in the execution part (Level 1)

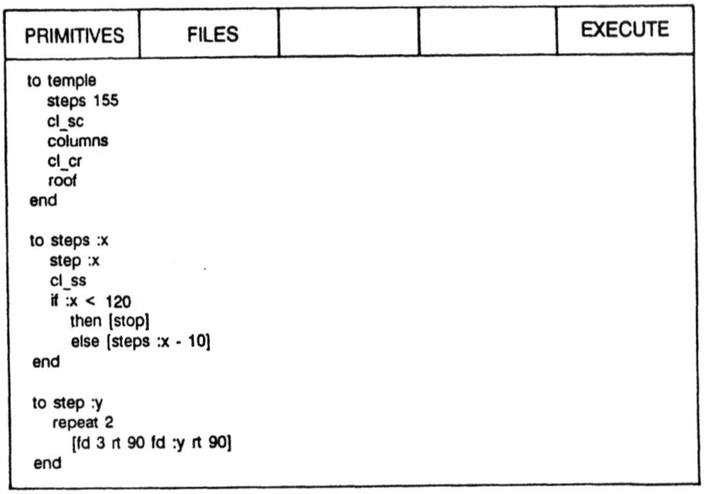

Figure 3: Writing of a Logo program for the drawing of a temple in the text editor (Level 1)

We chose a text editor because manipulations are less complicated than in a structure editor. In a text editor, the programming code is treated as text rather than as a series of instructions. The editor in our system closely resembles a word-processor. It allows the insertion and deletion of characters and has facilities for copying, moving, deleting, and tracing blocks (a block consists of one or more characters). Moreover, it is possible to copy a block of text from another program that has been saved on a disk (file management).

After finishing the program, the pupil indicates in the menu that he wants to go to the execution part. When a program is called by typing its name, the entire program is checked first. If it does not contain syntactical errors, it is executed. If not, the pupil receives an error message, and has to go back to the editor to correct the bug in his program.

The relationship between the various parts of the system at this level is represented in Figure 4. We distinguish system units, which are the central parts of the system, and facilities, which are system components that can be called from the system units. The configuration at level 1 consists of two system units, namely the executing part and the editing part, and two facilities, language help and file management. An arrow between the two parts indicates that you can switch from one part to the other.

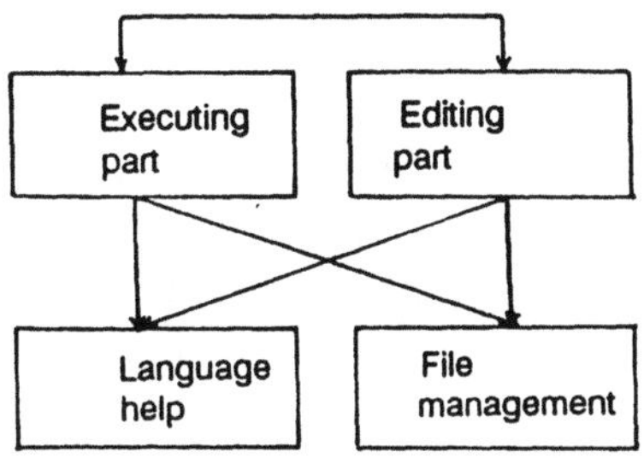

Figure 4: Relation between the various parts of the system at Level 1

Level 2

At this level Logo is supplemented with two tools that support planning and debugging activities. However, the pupil can choose whether or not he wishes to use them. The planning tool is a graphical editor that allows the construction and manipulation of a graphic representation of the structure of a program in the form of a tree-like diagram. This graphical editor has special boxes for the following Logo constructs; procedures, procedures with parameters, iteration, recursion, and conditional statements (see Figure 5). In order to keep the graphical representation at a higher level of abstraction than the code, the plan should not contain any Logo primitives (except the stop-command).

With the help of this tool the pupil can add, delete, replace, and rename parts of the tree-like diagram in an easy and flexible way. The possibility of making a tree-like diagram on the computer instead of on a piece of paper has several advantages. The first is that during the construction process, the arrangement of the tree-diagram as a whole stays clear and tidy. Our experience has shown that pupils often are rather sloppy in constructing diagrams on paper which makes it difficult to see the correct structure. Second, the plan and the corresponding program can be saved together under a common name, which prevents the plan from getting lost. Third, the constructed tree-like diagram is also available on the screen in the editor. This can stimulate pupils to use it as a reference point in coding the program. Finally, making the

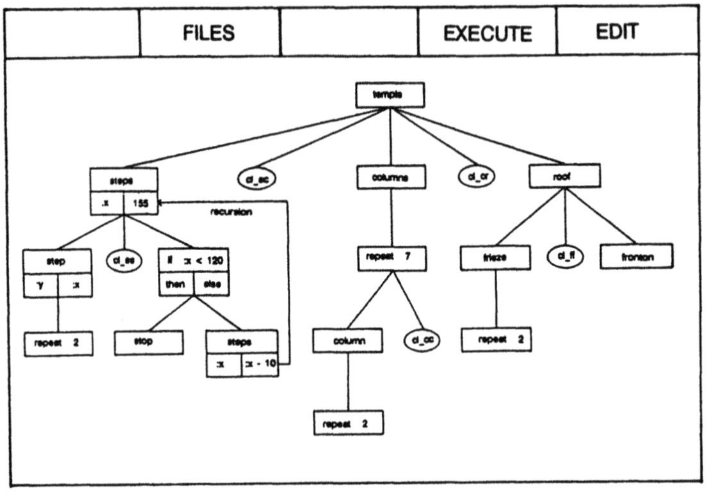

Figure 5: Construction of a tree-like diagram for the drawing of a temple with the help of the planning tool (Level 2)

tree-like diagram at the computer allows the computer coach at level 3 to analyze and possibly criticize the construction of the diagram and transpose it in Logo code.

The debugging tool has been added because in most Logo versions, it is difficult for pupils to trace a bug in their programs. This is because the code and its corresponding drawing are not available at the same time, and the execution speed is too high to see where and how an error occurs.

The debugging tool in our system enables pupils to view the code and the corresponding graphical output together on the screen; each command is highlighted as it is being executed (see Figure 6). Moreover, the execution speed can be slowed down and procedures can be carried out step-by-step (after each step the name of the actual procedure and the actual values of its parameters can be asked for).

The relationship between the various parts of the system at this level is represented in Figure 7. In comparison with level 1, this configuration contains one more central system unit (the planning tool) and one more facility (the debugging tool).

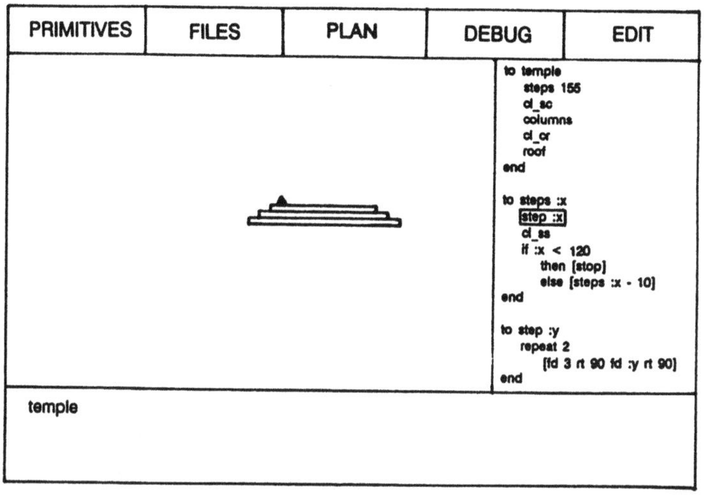

Figure 6: Tracing of the execution of a Logo program with the help of the debugging tool (Level 2)

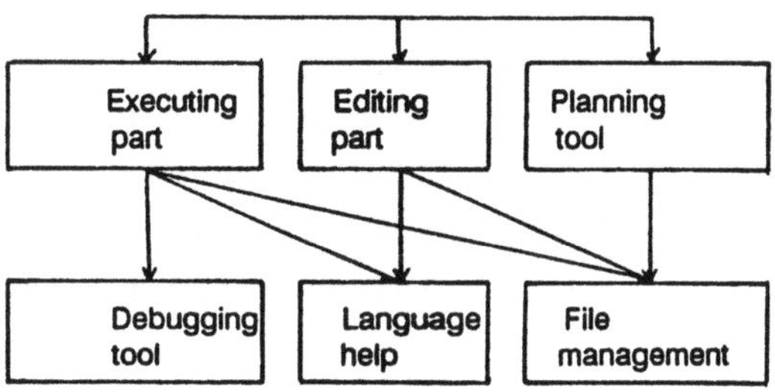

Figure 7: Relation between the various parts of the system at Level 2

Level 3

The main difference between the second and the third level is that at level 3 a coach checks the pupils' activities both in the planning phase and in the coding-and-testing phase. In both phases, the coach examines two categories of errors: syntactic and semantic errors on the one hand, and errors with respect to the programming strategy described above on the other.

In the planning phase the coach checks syntactic and semantic aspects of the pupil's input during the construction of the tree-like diagram (i.e., the names of procedures, the formal and actual parameters, the number of repeats in an iteration, and the conditions in the conditional statements). Examples of syntactical errors include the name of a procedure starting with a numerical character instead of a letter, the name of a procedure being a Logo primitive (e.g., FD, PU) or a reserved word (e.g., if, end), or the name of a formal parameter being not preceded by a colon. Examples of semantic errors include a repeat or a conditional construct that contains no statement, formal parameters that are defined but not used, or statements that are placed after the stop-command.

The coach also reacts when certain criteria for an expert tree-diagram are not fulfilled (e.g., when a procedure has too many subprocedures at the same level, when two identical procedures are defined twice, or when a procedure has a subprocedure with the same name while the pupil has not explicitly defined it as a recursive procedure by using the recursion-box). In the editor the coach reacts when the syntax of the programming code is not correct and when the semantics of the code are not in accordance with the plan.

Furthermore, the coach examines if the pupil has taken into account the two principles underlying the coding-and-testing phase, namely top-down programming and immediate testing and debugging. The principle of top-down programming means that the pupil has to start with the coding of the mother procedure; the names of the parts, as well as their sequence, have to correspond with the second level of the tree-like diagram. Moreover, the tree-like diagram has to be converted to code according to the depth-first method. The principle of immediate testing and debugging means that the pupil is asked to run the program each time a new procedure is defined. As said before, this enables the pupil to evaluate the screen effect and, if necessary, to debug the program. The execution stops when an unknown procedure is encountered. Thus, the pupil knows which procedure has to be defined next. Within this third level, we distinguish two sublevels of coaching that differ in terms of strictness.

Sublevel 1: At the first sublevel the coach gives only a warning when an error is made. The pupil has the option to ignore this warning. To illustrate this, we describe a part of the interaction between the computer coach and a pupil who is writing the "TEMPLE" procedure starting from the tree-like diagram in Figure 2. Suppose the pupil writes the following procedure for the temple:

```
TO TEMPLE
COLUMNS CL_CS STEPS CL_SR ROOF
END
```

The computer coach will then react with the following message: "This procedure is not in accordance with the tree-like diagram that you constructed." If the pupil now compares the written procedure with the tree-like diagram, he can see that the sequence of the parts in the diagram does not correspond to the sequence of the subprocedures in the TEMPLE procedure. He can solve this conflict by changing either the plan or the TEMPLE procedure. However, the pupil can also ignore this warning.

Assuming that the pupil ignores the coach's warning and continues by typing "TO COLUMNS", the coach will give the following message: "You have not yet tested your program by executing the mother procedure (TEMPLE)". Again, the pupil can choose whether he will indeed execute the TEMPLE procedure, or ignore this message and continue his coding of the COLUMNS procedure.

Sublevel 2: The error messages at sublevel 2 of the coach are binding; the pupil is not able to proceed if the fault is not corrected, or if the prescribed step from the programming strategy is not followed. To illustrate this, we consider the same example. If the pupil writes a procedure in which the subprocedures are placed in the wrong order, he receives the error message "This procedure is not in accordance with the tree-like diagram that you constructed". The pupil now has to correct the error before he can make another move. If he does not see the fault immediately, he can ask for additional help; then the coach will give the following message: "The order in which the procedures are placed is not the same as in your tree-like diagram".

If the TEMPLE procedure is corrected and the pupil wants to proceed with the coding of the next procedure, the coach will ask that he first test his program by executing the mother procedure (TEMPLE). Unless he does so, he cannot continue.

Conclusion

We have described the design of a Logo-based computer system consisting of three levels. The first level allows the pupil to acquire Logo primitives and concepts in a user-friendly way. At the following two levels the system supports the acquisition of an efficient programming strategy, involving planning and debugging skills. The second level also offers two additional tools that facilitate planning and debugging activities. At the third level a computer coach is available which provides part of the problem-solving instruction usually given by the teacher. The rigor of this coaching can be adapted to the competency and the needs of the pupil.

It is our intention to evaluate this system with 11-12 year old pupils. However, we already have some ideas for refining the system. A first refinement relates to the programming style supported by the coach. In the present system only top-down programming is supported. However, this is only one of several possible programming styles that can be equally valuable (Miller, 1982). Therefore, we plan to modify the system so that the teacher can decide to allow and support another valuable programming style as well, namely bottom-up programming.

Another refinement relates to the conversion of a plan into programming code. In the present system, the pupil has to write the programming code starting from the constructed tree-like diagram. However, given such a diagram, it is possible to let the computer generate the major part of the program automatically (Miller, 1982). We have not implemented this option in the first prototype of the system because we consider it important that, especially in the initial learning phase, the process of conversion from plan to code is transparent. This is facilitated by having the pupil himself perform the necessary actions. Later on, when a certain expertise has been achieved, the automatic generation of the code may free the programmer from a series of less interesting actions, thus allowing him to concentrate on the more exigent and creative design activities. Therefore, in a future prototype this automatic code-generation could be provided as an option for more expert programmers.

Finally, we address the following question: to what extent is this learning environment, of which a computer system is the crucial component, in line with the constructivist view of learning? In this respect, we reassert that the Piagetian conception of learning strongly influenced the developers of Logo.

It may seem as if our new system not only imposes an (expert) programming strategy on the pupil, but moreover that the built-in coach, especially at level 3.2, severely controls the learning process. This would be totally opposed to Papert's (1980) vision of the unique qualities of Logo. In his view Logo differs fundamentally from other educational applications of the computer, because it does not control the child, but on the contrary puts the child in control of his own learning. Other constructivist authors have also argued that a danger of too much guidance imposed by a (computer) learning environment is that it takes the knowledge construction and skill acquisition process out of the hands of pupils (Cobb, 1990; von Glasersfeld, 1987). It is claimed that the environment should create situations and offer tools that stimulate and help pupils to develop their own knowledge and cognitive skills.

However, we also want to reassert that early Logo research based on Papert's self-discovery philosophy has not led to the acquisition of the expected knowledge and thinking skills. As said before, these disappointing findings have led to a tendency toward more structure and guidance (Leron, 1985). In line with this prevailing conception, we have developed a system that is representative of a moderate constructivist conception of learning. It is characterized by a balance between learner-controlled activity and guidance, always taking into account the individual differences in abilities, needs and motivation of the learners. This balance permeates the entire learning environment, but becomes especially manifest in the alternation of activities in which the pupil is in control, and other activities that are guided by the teacher or the computer.

For example, the rather strict guidance of the computer coach at level 3.2 should in our view be preceded by Logo lessons in which pupils discover and discuss the value and usefulness of efficient planning and debugging strategies. Moreover, lessons in which learners work at level 3.2 should also be followed by sessions in which the pupils themselves can decide whether they still want to follow the suggestions of the coach (level 3.1), or even whether they still would like to use the available tools (level 2). In this sense learning activities in which the control and guidance is in the hands of the teacher alternate with activities in which the pupil himself guides and controls his own learning. However, overall the learner should remain in charge and take responsibility for his own learning.

References

Carver, S. (1988). Learning and transfer of debugging skills: Applying task analysis to curriculum design and assessment. In R. E. Mayer (Ed.), *Teaching and learning computer programming. Multiple research perspectives.* Hillsdale, NJ: Lawrence Erlbaum Associates.

Clark, R. E. (1992). Facilitating domain-general problem solving: Computers, cognitive processes and instruction. In E. De Corte, M. Linn, H. Mandl, & L. Verschaffel (Eds.), *Computer-based learning environments and problem solving* (NATO/ASI Series F: Computer and Systems Sciences, Vol. 84). Berlin: Springer-Verlag.

Clements, D. H. (1990). Metacomponential development in a Logo programming environment. *Journal of Educational Psychology, 82*, 141-149.

Clements, D. H. (1992). The role of social interaction in the development of higher-order thinking in Logo environments. In E. De Corte, M. Linn, H. Mandl, & L. Verschaffel (Eds.), *Computer-based learning environments and problem solving* (NATO/ASI Series F: Computer systems and sciences, Vol. 84). Berlin: Springer-Verlag.

Cobb, P. (1990). A constructivist perspective on information-processing theories of mathematical activity. *International Journal of Educational Research, 14*, 67-92.

Collins, A., Brown, J. S., & Newman, S. E. (1989). Cognitive apprenticeship: Teaching the craft of reading, writing and mathematics. In L. B. Resnick (Ed.), *Knowing, learning, and instruction. Essays in honor of Robert Glaser.* Hillsdale, NJ: Lawrence Erlbaum Associates.

De Corte, E. (1990). Towards powerful learning environments for the acquisition of problem-solving skills. *European Journal of Psychology of Education, 5*, (1), 5-19.

De Corte, E., & Verschaffel, L. (1989). Logo, a vehicle for thinking. In B. Greer & G. Mulhern (Eds.), *New directions in mathematics education*. London: Routledge.

De Corte, E., Verschaffel, L., & Schrooten, H. (1990, March). *Cognitive effects of computer-oriented learning*. Paper presented at the Seventh International conference on Technology and Education, Brussels, Belgium.

De Corte, E., Verschaffel, L., & Schrooten, H. (1992). Cognitive effects of learning to program in Logo: A one-year study with sixth graders. In E. De Corte, M. Linn, H. Mandl, & L. Verschaffel (Eds.), *Computer-based learning environments and problem solving* (NATO/ASI Series F: Computer and Systems Sciences, Vol. 84). Berlin: Springer-Verlag.

Lehrer, R., Guckenberg, R., & Sancilio, L. (1988). Influences of Logo on children's intellectual development. In R. E. Mayer (Ed.), *Teaching and learning computer programming. Multiple research perspectives*. Hillsdale, NJ: Lawrence Erlbaum Associates.

Leron, U. (1985). Logo today: Vision and reality. *The computer teacher*, 26-32.

Littlefield, F., Delclos, V. R., Lever, S., Clayton, K. N., Bransford, J. D., & Franks, J. J. (1988). Learning Logo: Method of teaching, transfer of general skills, and attitudes toward school and computers. In R. E. Mayer (Ed.), *Teaching and learning computer programming. Multiple research perspectives*. Hillsdale, NJ: Lawrence Erlbaum Associates.

McCoy Carver, S., & Klahr, D. (1986). Assessing children's Logo debugging skills with a formal model. *Journal of Educational Psychology, 76*, 1051-1058.

Miller, M. L. (1982). A structured planning and debugging environment for elementary programming. In D. Sleeman & J. S. Brown (Eds.), *Intelligent tutoring systems*. New York: Academic Press.

Noss, R. (1986). *Creating a mathematical environment through programming: A study of young children learning Logo*. Doctoral dissertation. London: Department of Mathematics, Statistics and Computing, University of London.

Papert, S. (1980). *Mindstorms. Children, computers, and powerful ideas*. New York: Basic Books.

Salomon, G. (1992). Effects with and of computers and the study of computer-based learning environments. In E. De Corte, M. Linn, H. Mandl, & L. Verschaffel (Eds.), *Computer-based learning environments and problem solving* (NATO/ASI Series F: Computer and Systems Sciences, Vol. 84). Berlin: Springer-Verlag.

Scardamalia, M., Bereiter, C., McLean, R. S., Swallow, J., & Woodruff, E. (1989). Computer-supported intentional learning environments. *Journal of Educational Computing Research, 5*, 51-68.

Swan, K. (1989). Logo programming and the teaching and learning of problem solving. *Journal of Artificial Intelligence in Education, 1* (1), 73-92.

von Glasersfeld, E. (1987). Learning as a constructive activity. In C. Janvier (Ed.), *Problems of representation in the teaching and learning of mathematics*. Hillsdale, NJ: Lawrence Erlbaum Associates.

6 Components of Constructivist Learning Environments for Professional Development

Beau Fly Jones*, Randy A. Knuth*, and Thomas M. Duffy**

*North Central Regional Educational Laboratory (NCREL), Oak Park, Illinois, USA
**Indiana University, Bloomington, Indiana, USA

The constructivist perspective, especially the emphasis on situating cognitions (Brown, Collins, & Duguid, 1989) and of helping learner's to manage cognitively complex environments (Spiro, 1988), is at the core of what we call the "Strategic Teaching Framework" (STF). STF is a conceptual framework for designing and evaluating learning environments, developed by the North Central Regional Educational Laboratory (NCREL). From this framework we are developing a wide range of professional development opportunities that incorporate in various combinations print, audio tape, video tape, computer, laserdisk, satellite broadcast, as well as other technologies. The underlying philosophy of STF is the belief that excellence in education is achieved by practitioners who are strategic in their actions. This means that they make decisions in and design instruction for their teaching/leaning contexts based on what is known about teaching and learning.

While constructivist learning environments are being increasingly developed for students of school and college age in a variety of contexts, in a critical learning context – teacher and administrator education – programs have tended to be extremely traditional in their instructional approach. In this paper we argue for the need to provide learning and professional development opportunities for teachers and administrators. We then describe two projects that are based on our Strategic Teaching Framework that represent two important components of a constructivist learning environment for educators. The first example is a computer-based system designed to support strategic teaching, learning and assessment that we presently call the "STF Hypermedia Library." The second example is a nine program videoconference and guidebook series entitled "Restructuring to Promote Learning."

Within the Strategic Teaching Framework there are seven critical dimensions that can be useful to describe teaching/learning environments. We carefully study these dimensions when developing constructivist learning components for professional development. The seven dimensions are:

1. Goals and metaphors that drive learning and instruction
2. Learner characteristics, responsibilities and values
3. Teacher characteristics, responsibilities and values
4. Tasks that define the nature and level of achievement

5. School characteristics (context) that support teaching and learning
6. Principles of sequencing
7. Principles of assessment

The Need for STF in Professional Development

Over the decades the educational system in the United States has been in a state of flux. The continual assault on the productivity of education is constant and comes from almost all sectors of the population. Colleges, businesses, parents and the government all criticize the educational system for not producing the kind of individuals who can function well after high school and beyond. Schlechty, Ingwerson, & Brooks (1988) and others argue that no longer can the educational system improve by applying the same metaphors and processes that have guided the public school system since the 1800's. The Carnegie Task Force on Teaching as a Profession echoes this viewpoint (Carnegie Forum on Education and the Economy, 1986, pp. 15-20):

> We are doing better on the old goals, often at the expense of making progress on goals that count the most. Because we have defined the problem of schools in terms of decline from earlier standards, we have unwittingly chosen to face backwards when it is essential that we face forward

In tandem with this call for changes in the educational system, there has also been dramatic growth in both the theoretical and practical understanding of learning, instruction and assessment over the past 10 years. Theories of cognition, such as the Cognitive Flexibility theory (Duffy & Jonassen, in press; Spiro, this volume) suggest that effective learning requires a more holistic approach with multiple cases and a variety of goals within a case. There must also be the potential for a flexible response. The Cognition and Technology Group at Vanderbilt University have a concept called anchored instruction (Bransford, Sherwood, Hasselbring, Kinzer, & Williams, this volume) which suggests that instructional tasks which situate the learner in an authentic context help the learner to develop rich understandings and reasonable problem solutions. Problem-based (NCTM, 1989) and collaborative learning (e.g., Cohen, 1986) approaches have also been supported by research as a means to promote learning. Research in the area of learning styles also suggests that learning is enhanced when information is available in more than one mode, for example text, audio, and video. Moreover, research into the metacognitive and affective domains points to the importance of the learner's self-determination (McCombs, 1989).

While the above discussion deals with mostly with curricular and instructional issues, assessment is also a critical aspect within the Strategic Teaching Framework. In fact, curriculum, instruction *and* assessment are treated in STF together as a unified system. Authentic (Wiggins, 1989) and performance-based (Stiggins, 1991) assessments have arisen from this viewpoint arguing that more valid measures of achievement can be obtained when tasks are integrally related to an authentic curriculum, and when standards are clearly articulated.

Within each of the school content areas, such as English (reading, writing, speaking, listening), mathematics, science, social science, and physical education, research over the past ten years has continued to explicitly define strategic learning approaches. One especially outstanding example is the notion of strategic reading. Ideas that help a learner become a "strategic reader," such as topic familiarity, reading strategies, and constructing meaning, have emerged from research in reading (Pearson & Raphael, 1990). The potential for successful learning, as is demonstrated by strategic reading, behooves practitioners to become familiar with the content-based research, and to develop practices in the classroom that utilize this knowledge.

The question is, then, how can excellent staff development opportunities be provided to educators to get this wealth of knowledge known and used? Providing in-service training for educators continues to be problematic for some schools across the United States. The number of in-service days varies widely, with some districts providing minimal opportunities for training. In particular, rural areas have difficulty obtaining quality training. Still, educators are learners in the same sense as their students are and should be given access to staff development that is based on the same principles of learning. Without professional development, especially those that provide situated learning in constructivist learning environments, educators will not have the opportunities to engage in sustained analysis of exemplary teaching, to hear expert appraisals and alternate perspectives on their own and other practice, or learn how to implement new approaches in their classrooms.

The examples described in this paper are just two of the many kinds of learning opportunities that we are designing for staff development. The first example is a "high-tech" approach that melds together text, video, audio and communications functions, designed for in-depth use by individual and groups of educators. The second example is a means for allowing widespread discussion and treatment of important educational issues.

The STF Hypermedia Library

The first learning environment described in this paper, the "STF Hypermedia Library," is an approach that makes rich learning experiences available for both in-service and pre-service teachers and administrators (Fishman & Duffy, in press).

The STF Hypermedia Library is a joint project between NCREL and Indiana University. It is being developed to help teachers implement new guidelines for curriculum, instruction, and assessment which have been established by recent research and professional organizations (e.g., see NCTM, 1989; AAAS, 1989). It is designed to serve multiple purposes in a constructivist learning environment: an information resource, a database of exemplary teaching practices and a tool to promote collaboration.

The hardware needed for the STF Hypermedia Library is a graphically based-computer system, a laserdisc player, and a television monitor. It is also planned that audio data on a CD audio format, as well as taking advantage of new compressed digital capabilities (i.e. DVI), will become a part of this environment. Information is presented to those working with the system in one of four modes: video (both motion and still), audio (voice, music), text and graphics.

In general, the STF Hypermedia Library is a video library of whole classroom sequences of instruction. It is planned to develop as many as 64 video classrooms, each accompanied by supporting auditory commentary, text and graphics materials (such as lesson plans and research articles), and a telecommunications function that allows the exchange of electronic mail between system users and experts featured in the classroom videos.

Using the STF Hypermedia Library

The STF Hypermedia Library is entered by specifying a content area (math, science, social studies, and language) and grade level (early elementary, late elementary, middle school, secondary or other). Audio, video, and print information are then made available from the desired content experts who establish a classroom setting. Instead of focusing on specific instructional strategies that the teacher uses, the environment focuses on important aspects of the whole classroom. For example, the arrangement of the room, student and teacher interactions, classroom management/discipline, and use of technology are all presented as a context for the instructional strategies. This enables the user of the system to gain a deeper understanding of how all of these classroom aspects are integrated into an effective teaching/learning situation.

Once the user enters the hypermedia learning environment, the system immediately provides opportunities to view video examples of expert teachers who are teaching an entire lesson. Commentary in audio and video format made by the teacher in the video, other expert teachers, and researchers are provided at appropriate times during the video. These commentaries focus on the key components and contextual factors that comprise the classroom context. Examples of these commentaries might be from an expert teacher explaining, providing research support, and suggesting alternatives as to how the teacher in the video monitors homework, uses ill-structured problems, and employs collaborative learning techniques. The "think-aloud" format is often taped, so that the user can gain greater understanding of the processes used by the teacher in planning, monitoring and evaluating of his or her own instruction.

Consider a more specific example of how a second grade teacher might use the system in implementing some new teaching strategies in math. That teacher would likely choose to examine math classrooms for early-elementary grade levels. The teacher might then preview several of the 30 second summaries which briefly describe and show short segments of classes. Once a video is selected, the teacher could view it in one of several ways. First, the teacher might choose to watch it from start to finish (about 40 minutes).

Another choice would be to select a "tour" which would highlight certain classroom dimension such as management, problem-solving or teaching strategies. If the teacher chose the management tour, the video would play those events within the class that had attached expert commentaries about specific management issues of that class.

A third option would be for the teacher to view the video either straight through or as a tour, and then choose to view video elaborations. Periodically as the video plays, special symbol appears on the screen that the teacher can click to get an elaboration on the current event. For example, an elaboration might show a teacher utilizing an instructional strategy in a different classroom. Or an elaboration might show the classroom from another viewpoint, for instance, a group that is working together while the teacher is helping other groups.

Once the teacher views the elaboration, the system returns to the original point of departure and the video continues. A teacher can also access recorded voices of various people who present alternative perspectives on the classroom such as the strengths, weaknesses, alternatives and research for using manipulatives in teaching a math class.

Other features of the STF Hypermedia Library which are specifically designed to enhance learning are an electronic notetaking system which allows teachers to reflect on the important aspects of the video. The teacher can take "electronic notes" on the system and paste them to specific segments within each video. At a later date the user can come back to the system and receive a tour of those personal notes and events to which they are attached. Notes can be shared among all users, creating the potential to establish a network of peer commentaries. In addition, the user can access any of the text and graphics materials in the database. These materials are linked together in such a way that a teacher can simply follow an "associative link" from one document to another. For example, a teacher might notice a link marker within a lesson plan, click on it, so that they can view another document which relates to this lesson plan.

STF Dimensions Within the Hypermedia Library

The design of the STF Hypermedia Library is based on a constructivist perspective. The following provide some of the underlying concepts upon which the system has been designed.

1. Goals and metaphors that drive learning and instruction

Context: The meaning of any concept is determined by its use in a specific context (Wittgenstein, 1958). For example, developing an understanding of how and why a teacher uses a particular instructional strategy requires that the learner see the strategy within the context of the whole classroom. Consequently, the STF Hypermedia Library includes 1) full class periods which are approximately 40 minutes; 2) a rich array of teacher-student and student-student interactions; 3) the physical characteristics of the classroom; and 4) classroom examples from a wide range of contexts (i.e., well-equipped, large).

Our work is based partially on the notions of Cognitive Flexibility Theory (Spiro, this volume) which suggests that multiple cases and multiple goals within a case will promote successful learning. The STF Hypermedia Library provides the opportunity to engage in sustained analysis of various cases of excellent teaching.

The goals and metaphors of traditional staff development are usually based on the notion that the learner is a vessel into which information can be poured. The STF Hypermedia Library uses a diametrically opposed metaphor which attempts to situate all learning within authentic contexts.

2. Learner characteristics, responsibilities and values

The most fundamental learner characteristic that this project addresses is the beliefs about how people "know what they know." The vessel metaphor presented above suggests that learning is a matter of accumulating information from the environment. Our perspective is based on an alternate view of knowing.

Mental Models: Learners understand complex experience through the mental models that they have constructed of it. For example, it is often shown that teachers teach as they were taught. That is, over the course of their instructional experience, learners have experienced many different teachers. Taken together, they become abstracted into the learner's mental model of how teaching proceeds. Certainly, one of the goals of STF is to provide experience with alternate, strategic teaching approaches so that the mental model one holds of teaching is changed. Although principles and guidelines are important, professional action is strongly influenced by the mental model in which those principles and guidelines are embedded. Thus, the STF Hypermedia Library helps educators develop rich mental models of classrooms by presenting examples of exemplary classes for a full class.

Multiple Representations: The second aspect is related to the first and suggests that there are more ways to learn and understand than verbal and mathematical. Gardner's work on multiple intelligences (Gardner, 1983) suggests that intelligence is multidimensional. It not only includes the familiar mathematical and verbal intelligences but also visual/spatial, kinesthetic, interpersonal, intrapersonal, and musical. The STF Hypermedia Library presents content in many forms including motion video, still video, audio, prose, text and graphics. These are designed to aid participants in developing mental models that are comprised of knowledge in the most meaningful modes for each learner.

3. Teacher characteristics, responsibilities and values

Multiple Perspectives: Developing a thorough understanding of an event or concept is enhanced by having available multiple perspectives on the meaning of the event or concept. This alternative provides a basis for the learner to test his or her own understanding. The STF Hypermedia Library provides perspectives on activities in the classroom from various experts such as the teacher, teacher educators, researchers and administrators. Additionally, a user of the environment could add their own comments via an electronic notebook which could be shared with other users. Also it might be possible through various networks to interact with other teachers and experts throughout the United States.

4. Tasks that define the nature and level of achievement

Anchored Instruction: The STF Hypermedia Library is consistent with Bransford's concept of anchored instruction (See Cognition and Technology Group at Vanderbilt, this volume). The instructional tasks which the learner is given are defined. The environment also realistically situates the learner in the classroom and promotes flexible response (problem solving skills) in actual classroom interactions.

5. School characteristics (context) that support teaching and learning

Time: The issue of providing quality time for staff development work continues to be a barrier in improving education. The STF Hypermedia Library provides a great deal of flexibility in terms of where and how it can be used. This can be an asset in dealing with the common problem of inadequate time to learn about and practice new techniques.

Financial resources: For many schools, resources are not available to provide educators with the different perspectives from experts in the field. The STF Hypermedia Library can fill this need by providing different perspectives in a cost efficient manner. The STF Hypermedia Library can be housed in a school library or resource center and accessed by individual and small groups at any time. The system can also be used in large group staff development settings with follow-up time on the system and/or with videotaped segments of the classrooms and accompanying print materials.

6. Principles of sequencing

Sequences: The STF Hypermedia Library provides a rich array of resources to aid the learner in adapting the particular expert's approach to teaching. Instructional guidance for using these resources is designed to provide a skeletal framework for the teacher. The intent is that the learners will work to identify their own needs and will sequence their experience in a way which will maximize their own learning. For example, rather than participating in a sequential view of the classroom, educators can follow a tour of a particular topic or participate in concurrent and extended elaborations. Moreover, the user can use the system at any time and as often as necessary. The video classrooms are so rich that they can be used and studied for months.

7. Principles of assessment

Reflection Opportunities: The development of new skills is enhanced by the act of reflection on the learners' own experience and cognitive development. This act of "self-assessment" provides opportunities for the learner to make connections and relate learning tasks to their own situation. Through the use of a personal and shared electronic notebook, the STF Hypermedia Library provides the learner the opportunity to add personal commentary on each classroom and to go back to it at any time desired. The act of self-assessment serves to facilitate learning.

This notion of practice, analysis, and self-assessment is based on Schön's (1987) idea of the "reflective practitioner." In this process, the educator is continually engaged in a cycle of action, reflection, and action, which leads to the development of expertise in a domain.

Restructuring to Promote Learning In America's Schools

The nine part video conference series "Restructuring to Promote Learning in America's Schools" provides a comprehensive professional development activity for educators. It presents a systematic examination of the "what" and "who" of restructuring schools around a new vision of learning, and of schools as learning centered institutions.

The topics for the series were selected in part because they represent major areas of education research and in part because they are all relevant to the national education goals. Although each topic area in the series involves different departments and school staff, the schools are a part of a system and what happens in one area influences another area. Specifically the goals of the series are to:

- Examine the direct implications of current and projected societal changes for developing new models and strategies for schooling based on learning;
- Review the most recent evidence from research and practice that supports the need for and implementation of, new approaches to schooling;
- Review strategies for changing schools and instruction;
- Redefine current assumptions about effective strategies for addressing the needs of "at risk" students;
- Provide a wide variety of examples of innovations from schools throughout the United States.

The video conference series was developed for use by teachers, administrators, and curriculum specialists, as well as staff from state education and intermediate service agencies.

However, the series is also designed to appeal to school board members, parents, teacher educators and their students, policy makers, staff developers, and researchers interested in school improvement. These potential audiences include those individuals who are most instrumental to school restructuring efforts.

The nine video conferences contain three different elements: a video program, a guidebook and selected readings. Each of these represents a different learning approach to the topic of restructuring.

Each video program is a two and one half hour interactive video videoconference. An "uplink" satellite transmits a live conference program to a communications satellite which then transmits it to a downlink site. When combined with a telephone hookup, videoconferencing becomes interactive with one way video (viewers see the presenters on monitors although presenters cannot see the viewers) and two-way audio (viewers can call in and speak to the presenters).

The second component of the series, a guidebook provides a synthesis of key ideas, concepts, and examples presented, as well as a variety of exercises and assignments that can help viewers better understand and reflect on the program's content. The exercises are designed to be completed by either individuals or groups of participants working cooperatively and can be used both pre- and post-viewing the conference.

In addition to the guidebook, a two-volume set of selected readings is also available. Each volume contains readings that provide more in-depth discussion of the topics presented in each program, as well as a critical review that can assist participants in improving their reflective and critical analysis skills. The selected readings also contain additional assignments related to the topics of each video program.

The materials which comprise this program can be used in several different ways. It might be used as a self-contained, individual professional development activity or as a training activity for curriculum or other administrative or support staff. It might also be used as a part of an overall school improvement planning process for schools or districts. Additionally, intermediate agencies might use the series in professional development workshops or they might be used as a part of an induction or intern program for new teachers or administrators. The particular dimensions which have been utilized in the design process are as follows:

1. Goals and metaphors that drive learning and instruction

The entire series is based on the new directions and priorities for schools and schooling. The framework for the series is based on a new vision of learning that integrates the needs of a changing society with research about learning and instruction. Further, it is based on idea that models for educational change or school improvement must first focus on new expectations for the goals and outcomes of schooling, and only then, on the strategies for restructuring schools.

With a goal to promote learning in such a varied and complex environment as the schooling system in the United States, the approach suggested by a constructivist perspective is that it should provide a systematic examination of the critical dimensions of schooling through the perspective of learning and should provide a coherent, conceptual framework for thinking about the manner in which schools of the future should be organized. The videotape series attempts to do that by providing examples of professional practice through presentations by national experts and practitioners, discussions of key issues and concepts, and videotaped highlights from schools and classrooms around the country

This combined research and practice approach provides the diversity of perspectives that is critical to an informed understanding of educational problems and their solutions.

2. Learner characteristics, responsibilities and values

The audience and their characteristics will differ greatly due to the nature of the "Restructuring Video Conference". This requires that a variety of different instructional approaches as well as contexts must be provided to enable the learner to create a mental model of school in the future. A hallmark of this series was the number of pre-taped video interviews and classroom demonstrations across the United States. Learners would view the video, use the additional materials for reference, awareness and exploration, or in depth, sustained learning. Tasks were designed to use the array of "higher order" skills in the dimensions of thinking framework; accordingly they involved such skills as elaborating, representing, comparing, and problem solving individually and in small groups.

Additionally, each videotape contains an "urban" and "rural" epilogue which highlights learners in these particular settings. These provide specific examples which relate to this large population of learners.

3. Teacher characteristics, responsibilities and values

The videotape, guidebook and supplementary materials provide the primary teaching methodology for the restructuring series. The guidebook contains a variety of pre-video and follow-up activities for teachers, schools, parents, and community members. The activities vary greatly, depending on the content of the program. Some activities ask participants to create a product, others ask participants to participate in discussions around key program issues.

Another component of the videoconference programs is an opportunity to ask questions to the presenters. During the live satellite transmission, the live studio audience has an opportunity to ask their questions directly. Remote viewers can call in at any time during the program and give their questions to the telephone operator. In turn the moderator will ask selected questions to the presenters throughout the program. Questions not answered on the air may be answered by phone or print. For thirty minutes immediately following the satellite transmission of each videoconference, participants can call with their questions/comments and speak directly to the presenters. Because this segment provides one-to-one contact between presenters and participants, it is the key to the interactive "teacher role" within the series.

4. Tasks that define the nature and level of achievement

A variety of tasks which are provided within the series. The tasks center around a variety of knowledge, skills and values which participants will need to restructure a school.

5. School characteristics (context) that support teaching and learning

The availability of videoconferencing sites around the United States which can be used by schools is continually increasing. Videoconferencing, as a means of sharing information and ideas with those in a variety of locations is cost and time efficient for educators. The series also provides for direct interaction with experts and researchers which would generally be difficult for educators who come from many areas throughout the country. The additional materials, including the guidebooks and additional resources provides for additional learning separate from the videoconferencing program.

6. Principles of sequencing

The program was carefully sequenced in order to provide a systematic examination of critical dimensions of schooling through the perspective of learning, and to provide a coherent, conceptual framework for thinking about the manner in which schools of the future should be organized. Based on the belief that positive change in schools must be based on the end results to be achieved, the first five program units describe the "what" and "why" of school restructuring.

Program one explores the needs of an information-based, technological and socially diverse society, as well as the implications for the types of knowledge and skills tomorrow's adults will need. The presenters posit that the current focus on accumulating isolated facts and skills, finding right answers on multiple-choice tests and demonstrating only awareness of curricular content is no longer an adequate standard for defining student success. Based on discussions of critical distinctions between these "old" and "new" perspectives on what students will need to know and be able to do, a "new definition of learning" is proposed as the foundation for redefining the goals, purposes and process of schools and restructuring the organizational context within which they will be achieved.

The next four programs focus on the implication of these new perspectives in the areas of curriculum, instruction, assessment, and the relationship between schools and the larger community. Having defined new directions and goals for the restructured school, programs 6 through 8 focus on the "how" of the restructuring process by describing and providing examples of a variety of strategies for changing the structure, social organization, and cultural norms of schools to support the model of learning and instruction.

Program 9 addresses the special challenge of the growing number of "at-risk" students, those who have not only failed to achieve at minimally acceptable levels, but who have become, in many cases fully disconnected from the entire educational process.

Within each of the nine programs, the sequencing of the ideas presented is also important. Each program contains a sequence of perspectives from such researchers, administrators and teachers. The program ends with application epilogues which feature researcher and practitioners applying the ideas and concepts of each videoconference in small/isolated/rural communities and large/complex/urban school contexts. The sequencing of the entire program and each segment provides an important aspect of creating a productive learning environment for program participants.

7. Principles of assessment

The guidebooks contain a variety of ways for participants to assess their own knowledge, skills and values. Often, a series of "pre-conference" activities are provided which allows participants to begin accessing prior knowledge and create frameworks which are aligned with the concepts expressed in the video program.

Additionally each guidebook provides a series of follow-up activities for teacher, school, parent and community audiences. These activities aid participants in integrating the ideas presented in the video program and guidebook, as well as applying the ideas to their own particular setting. Such activities as using a checklist to evaluate their own setting, providing discussion questions, and suggesting survey efforts, are examples of the kind of assessment activities proposed. These activities provide an opportunity for participants to more actively approach this learning experience.

Conclusion

The examples above are just two of the many ways that the Strategic Teaching Framework can be implemented for staff development. As we continue to refine our conceptual framework and apply them in new components for constructivist learning environments, an overarching theme will persist: Helping educators to improve their practice amounts to helping them *learn* to become strategic teachers. This means that educators deserve staff development experiences that are commensurate with principles of *constructivist learning*.

References

AAAS (1989). *Science for all Americans: A Project 2061 report on literacy goals in science, mathematics, and technology*. Washington, DC: American Association for the Advancement of Science.

Bransford, J.D., Sherwood, o R., Hasselbring, T.S., Kinzer, C.K., & Williams, S.M. (in press). Anchored instruction: Why we need it and how technology can help. In D. Nix & R. Spiro (Eds.), *Advances in computer-video technology*. Hillsdale, NJ: Lawrence Erlbaum Associates.

Brown, J.S., Collins, A., & Duguid, P. (1989). Situated cognition and the culture of learning. *Educational Researcher, 18*(1), 32-42.

Carnegie Forum on Education and the Economy. (1986). *A nation prepared: Teachers for the 21st century.* New York: Author.

Cohen, E.G. (1986). *Designing group work: Strategies for the heterogeneous classroom.* New York: Teachers College Press.

Duffy, T.M. & Jonassen, D.H. (Eds.). (in press). *Constructivism and the technology of instruction: A conversation.* Hillsdale, NJ: Lawrence Erlbaum Associates.

Fishman, B. & Duffy, T. (in press). Strategic teaching frameworks: Hypermedia for strategic classroom change. *Educational Technology Research and Development.*

Gardner, H. (1983). *Frames of mind: The theory of multiple intelligences.* New York: Basic Books.

McCombs, B. (1989).Self-regulated learning and academic achievement: A phenomonological view. In B.J. Zimmerman & D.H. Schunk (Eds.), *Self-regulated learning and academic achievement: Theory, research and practice.* New York: Academic.

NCTM (1989). *Curriculum and evaluation standards for school mathematics.* Reston, VA: National Council of Teachers of Mathematics.

Pearson, P.D., & Raphael, T.E. (1990). Reading comprehension as a dimension of thinking. In B.F. Jones & L. Idol (Eds.), *Dimensions of thinking and cognitive instruction.* Hillsdale, NJ: Lawrence Erlbaum Associates.

Schön, D.A. (1987). *Educating the reflective practitioner.* San Francisco: Jossey-Bass.

Spiro, R. (1988). Cognitive flexibility theory: Advanced knowledge acquisition in structured domains. *Technical Report No.441.* Champaign, IL: Center for the Study of Reading.

Schlechty, P.C., Ingwerson, D.W., & Brooks, T.I. (1988). Inventing professional development schools. *Educational Leadership, 46*(3), 28-31.

Stiggins, R.J. (1991). Assessment literacy. *Phi Delta Kappan, 72*(7).

Wiggins, G. (1989). A true test: Toward more authentic and equitable assessment. *Phi Delta Kappan, May*, 703-713.

Wittgenstein, L. (1958). *Philosophical investigations, third edition.* New York: MacMillan Publishing Company.

7 Developing Literacy Skills Through Cooperative Computer Use: Issues for Learning and Instruction

Clotilde Pontecorvo

Università di Roma "La Sapienza", Rome, Italy

The research presented in this chapter discusses the use of technology as a medium within the ecology and organization of a second to sixth grade literacy curriculum in Rome and in Florence. This is an example of an epistemological approach to schooling which "argues that knowledge is not acquired as a collection of abstract entities but rather is constructed in the context of the environment in which it is encountered. Context is integral to understanding; meaning varies from context, and understanding is constructed through this experience. Essential to this view is the social nature of learning: people construct knowledge socially through collaboration (Duffy et al., 1993)." This new epistemology particularly underlines the role of social dimensions in cognition and the centrality of tool mediated actions (Zinchenko, 1985; Wertsch, 1990), i.e., of actions, even verbal ones, carried out by the participants, which are always mediated by tools, media and technology. In teaching, actions are more strictly dependent on the systems of signs (Vygotskij, 1934/1990) and methodologies which characterize different subject matters.

A change in the epistemological approach to knowledge in school also implies a change in the scientific approach to the study of school knowledge. Schooling can no longer be regarded as an applied field of a psychology developed elsewhere. It is a natural social context - as are families, work places, political groups, enterprises - where people learn, i.e. where they share meaning and construct knowledge by interacting with others, with objects of knowledge and with communication media. Thus, basic research into schooling must take into account all its contextual and social features.

However, since education is also a practical activity, a particular warning must be given regarding the distinction between "description" and "prescription". In the study of schooling, we want to gather as much full, objective information about the products and processes of a particular teaching-learning activity as possible. In addition, our subject of inquiry should be studied "juuxta propria principia" (according to its own principles), as a XVII century Italian philosopher said of nature.

This new conception of learning directly affects instruction and teaching. We look to *instruction* as systematic and planned activity which is aimed at learning and includes teaching. There is no opposition between the view of a constructivist learner and the view of a planning teacher. In order to have children free to find their own ways in a specific domain by interacting with each other and by directly engaging themselves in the activities that characterize it, the teacher has to carry out a great deal of analysis and planning. This means that subject matter needs to be analyzed not only in terms of methods and concepts but also in terms of *activities and operations* (Leont'ev, 1959/1963) which are usually carried out by experts and must be learned and practiced by novices (Greenfield, 1984). This analysis is needed in every domain (language, science, history, arts, etc.).

Theoretical Background

We will now describe, in general terms, how the three essential elements of schooling - interaction with an object of knowledge, with others, and with media - are addressed in our research.*

Firstly, written language was analyzed in order to determine what has to be learned in the primary school. Two main features that can both be developed through computer use were identified: a) The communicative functions of written language that are involved in a large range of activities in planning, generating, and revising different types of text, and; b) The skills of "reflecting about language", such as text planning and revising, text comprehension and summarizing, which are developed through literacy and at the same time foster its further acquisition.

Secondly, all studies carried out within this research framework were framed within Vygotskian theory. They were characterized by an extensive and dominant use of child interaction as a facilitator for learning. Children worked in pairs or in triplets when using the computer, and in teacher-led larger groups when discussing results and problems. A particular feature of all instructional interventions was to include the computer in usual school activities. This affected both the curriculum and classroom organization, thus confirming the observations advanced by many researchers (such as Newman, 1990) who emphasize the organizational impact of new technologies on the social and instructional activities carried out in schools. Although this aspect will not be overtly discussed here, we observed an enormous increase in autonomy and direct management of the learning situation on the part of the children who also acquired a high level of competence and motivation regarding the use of the computer.

Thirdly, the computer was used as a flexible tool for manipulating written materials, when both all-purpose (such as a word-processor) and didactic software were used. As a medium of communication that is typical of our culture, the computer produces an effect on cognitive development if individuals are allowed to use it as a "performative domain" and as a "means of

* This research project was supported by a 1988-1991 grant from the National Council of Research (CNR) given to Clotilde Pontecorvo on "Writing and Knowledge representation through Computer" (n. 88.00.3311.11).

expression and communication"(Olson, 1974) that (by conveying a specific information) transforms knowledge structures and develops particular skills. As regards the interplay between media and transmitted contents, it was assumed that each medium would be able to "make its own special contribution to child's learning and development" (Greenfield, 1987, p.17), if it were utilized appropriately in the educational process. In adding a new medium to an educational context, it is essential to consider how it can foster learning activities that are traditionally performed in school and how the introduction of the new medium can produce both an expansion of objectives and a strengthening of methodologies (Tornatore, 1987).

Collaborative Writing in a Computer Supported Interaction

The aim of the first study was to describe what kinds of procedures children follow during story completion in a collaborative computer task and what contribution social exchange makes to understanding and solving the task. This study was devoted to the analysis of planning and ideational processes (for more details on this research, see Pontecorvo & Paoletti, 1991a). Since the task had to be carried out in pairs using computer software, children had to express their proposals or evaluations verbally and support them with justifications if the other child did not comply.

It is frequently said that young children do not practice global planning when they write. Their texts are often lists of isolated sentences, which are not planned and not linked, except for the fact that all of them refer to the same general topic (Scardamalia and Bereiter, 1987). However, even though children do not explicitly use high level knowledge of text structure to plan their writing, it is likely that they practice some planning when they are constrained and guided by an existing framework which acts as a kind of plan outline.

The subjects were 18 second grade children in the same class in a school in Florence. They were from a middle class social background. Children were paired following the teacher's advice regarding their preferences in working together. They worked with a C64 computer with a standard keyboard and "Storiaperta" software. The children from whom we collected data were using "Storiaperta" for the first time. However, they were already familiar with the computer and with similar tasks.

"Storiaperta" requires children to select a story by its title from a list of stories. After the story has been selected, it appears on the screen without the title and with the gaps marked by empty blocks. Gaps are to be filled in with words or sentences that have to be produced by the children. Children have to review continuously both the single proposals and the completion plan by looking carefully at what comes before and what comes afterward in the story framework. In "Storiaperta" it is possible for the teacher to create a relationship between coherence and cohesion requests, in such a way as to affect planning strategies and textual completion.

In this study we collected interactional data on the story framework called "The golden castle". Figure 1 shows the story framework, followed by the categorization of the gaps according to the narrative and the syntactical aspects they involve.

Figure 1: The Golden Castle

1. ....had a magic crystal ball.
2. One day (he/she) decides to make...............(he/she) said
3. "........... a golden castle".
4. But the golden castle .... (.)
5. Repeated...... the castle appeared.
6. .... entered the castle
7. and............. (.)
8. At a certain point ..... a golden ghost!
9. .... ran away with legs flying, terrified.
10. .... and broke the magic crystal ball.

1. Narrative category: Minor setting; the main character should be introduced.
   Syntactical category : a subject is missing.
2. Narrative category: Initiating episode. The semantic referent is either provided in the preceding sentence (the magic crystal ball) or in the following one (you have to do or say something in order to get a golden castle).
   Syntactical cue : an object is needed.
3. Narrative category: Attempt.
   Syntactical cue: The direct form requires a verbal formula, not necessarily in the form of a verbal predicate.
4. Narrative category : Failed attempt suggested by the adversative.
   Syntactical cue: lack of verbal predicate.
5. Narrative category: New attempt.
   Syntactical cue: lack of an object of the verb.
6. Narrative category : Consequence of the new attempt.
   Syntactical cue: the subject is missing and there is a possible referential coherence with gap (1).
7. Syntactical cue: a verbal predicate is required.

8. Narrative category : New episode, with a problem.
   Syntactical cue: a verbal predicate is required. (in Italian the position of "a golden ghost" leave the possibility of its being either subject or object).
9. Narrative category : Consequence.
   Syntactical cue: The reference must come from the preceding sentence; the morphological agreement of the predicate requires a male gender for the referent.
10. Narrative category : Consequence.
   Syntactical cue: A verb in the past tense is required as well as a subject, which is not given.

Structural cues, semantic elements, and morpho-syntactical constraints direct the completion activities. For instance, as regards structural cues, the adversative which precedes gap 4 suggest a failed attempt, while the temporal indicator preceding gap 8 indicates the beginning of a new episode. On the other hand, the semantic content, which follows the first gap, suggests the choice of the character of the story and also guides the choice of the completion of the second gap. A syntactical constraint is offered by the gaps 5 and 7, because both require a verbal predicate.

As regards the ideational process, we wanted to see if and how there is a relationship between child interaction typology and metalinguistic level. Since we had found in previous research that overtness and justification are linked to different types of social interaction, we sought to investigate in this study whether this relationship could be hypothesized for the linguistic context as well.

Analyzing Planning Processes in Dyadic Work

Child interaction was observed, taped and fully transcribed in order to examine the textual analysis strategies which guided the planning and ideational components of the completion process. We evaluated each turn according to whether it made a new proposal of any type which was linked to the task. Repetitions, conversational moves, comments or suggestions on software functioning, and experimenter turns were excluded from this analysis.

The unit of analysis was the gap. It was the base line of the processing task and the point of departure for the computation of levels of planning. As there were 10 gaps to be filled, children's interaction protocols were divided into 10 parts, with each part containing all the interactions involving a particular gap. Within these parts we looked at the portion of the text which children process before writing (filling the gap-base line). The extension of the text which children analyzed before adopting a particular solution helped us to discriminate as to whether the children were using a local or global planning strategy. There was a minimum linguistic environment which the children had to consider in order to link the new elements with those already given, as in the following example:

Ex. 1 (gap 1):

.....HAD A MAGIC CRYSTAL BALL.

23 Ir: The, The king, I've got a lot of words in my head, but not those.

This example shows level 0 planning because the children are making a new proposal without mentioning any part of the framework, not even what follows immediately afterward. Level 1 planning is when planning is limited to the gap and to the linguistic context which immediately surrounds the gap. In both cases children are using a *local planning* strategy.

A *global* strategy occurs whenever children, while working on a particular gap and its surrounding elements, analyze (at the very least) how the proposed solution is coherent with what comes before and/or what comes next. As a function of the number of preceding and subsequent gaps under examination there can be a level 2,3... n of planning. A Level 2 analysis is regarded as an attempt to produce global planning because the text is being treated as a set of elements which presents cohesion and coherence requests and not as a list of isolated items.

Ex.2 (gap 8 and 9)

(AT A CERTAIN POINT ...... A GOLDEN GHOST!)

.... RAN AWAY WITH LEGS FLYING, TERRIFIED.

130 Eu: He saw a golden ghost and then ran away with legs flying, terrified. Here we are! We can say, the ghost ran away with legs flying, terrified! R2

This example shows level 2 planning because the children review (R2) what had been inserted in the previous gap. Data analysis shows that there is a very high degree of use of information presented in the immediate textual context. However this does not exclude other levels of analysis being used. Previous and subsequent units introduced are also brought into play by children.

It is interesting to note that there were more anticipations (A) than reviews (R). In general the number of anticipations was greater than the number of reviews, both in the total amount of turns and for five particular dyads out of nine. This means that a certain control over the text as it is being presented on the computer screen and the habit of going forward to find subsequent textual elements which might affect previous ones is widespread even at this age. There is also an alternate use of Anticipations and Reviews in the same turn or in subsequent and connected turns. This is especially true in attempts to fill particular gaps, for example gaps five and ten. Only two groups (dyads six and seven) processed the units according to the gaps of the framework in the foreseen order, i.e. following the given constraints in a linear way and trying to solve each of them one at a time. In other cases, children went for larger blocks and planned more gaps at the same time, modulating their planning with elements which they had already used.

One of our aims was to check how much the use of a more or less global strategy was dependent on the composition style of the dyads or on the linguistic requirement of the gap. Some gaps were more stimulating for reflection, as is the case for gap nine, where the morphological constraints make the children think back to previous parts of the story. But the results also depend on dyad style. Some dyads wait for the critical gap to arrive; others plan the text in advance, before the arrival of a critical gap, and do not proceed from gap to gap, but distribute their work over two or three planning blocks. This is shown by the proportion of global planning over the total number of new proposals (between 35% and 50%). But there was one dyad (dyad five) which performed 73.5% global planning.

Effects of the Interactive Setting on the Ideational Process

The collaborative setting makes the ideational process an interactive one. Children are required to construct solutions together and share their effort. Each child can benefit from his/her partner's competence. The ideational flow found in verbal interaction was analyzed according to two dimensions, metalinguistic and social.

The metalinguistic dimension is how much children propose, evaluate, defend or justify their choices in a more or less overt way. We distinguished three main metalinguistic levels in the attempts children make to solve the story completion. The first (M1) is when the new proposal is expressed without giving any reason, nor any explicit reflection or evaluation or justification. The second (M2) is when the new proposal is made by referring to framework constraints which help or hinder certain choices and/or by evaluating a previous proposal negatively:

Ex. 3 (dyad 1)

> 42 Ir: no, it doesn't fit, look. A witch had a magic crystal ball, one day she decided to do, to do, and she said, a magic castle, how.

The third (M3) might be regarded as properly metalinguistic: children give overt semantic or syntactical reasons for their proposals by referring to what is written, to the internal coherence of character or of the story itself, or to linguistic rules:

Ex.4 (dyad 1)

184 Ir: it's the ghost, terrified, not the witch can you see what's written, "terrified"?

185 Da: No. The ghost, went into the castle and said, nice. Then he saw the ghost, didn't he, otherwise it would have been written the ghost saw the witch.

Thus the ideational process is more or less overt. It is possible to distinguish between levels of explicitness ranging from a totally covert level, in which proposals are made without giving any reason, to justified proposals in which even metalinguistic statements are present.

The social dimension is made up of the continuum between agreement and opposition within the dyads. Previous research on social interaction (see Orsolini & Pontecorvo, 1989) has shown that opposition between children in teacher-led discussions is related to higher levels of cognitive activity and particularly to the production of explanations. We hypothesized that the distinction between "agreement" and "opposition" might be related to the metalinguistic dimension, because the disagreeing situation requires judgements in favor of a particular choice to be made more explicit. Operationally the sequence is identified by at least three turns which share the same topic and/or are pragmatically linked. The first proponent takes up or opposes the proposal of the other member of the dyad in his/her second turn.

Two main typologies were identified. In the first, children co-construct the filler by adding their pieces to the common verbal construction or by producing variants. In the second, children oppose each other and propose different alternative ways of solving the problem. They do this by strongly opposing each other and arguing through evaluations, literate judgements and metalinguistic observations regarding the appropriateness of the proposed text.

In the *co-constructing situation*, proposals are juxtaposed in a rich and flexible spurt of linguistic invention, although children hardly ever give reasons for their temporary and final choices, direct verbal proposals are generally introduced without external cues of evaluation or justification.

In the *opposing situation*, proposals are overtly justified and often strongly argued, sometimes with clear metalinguistic reasons. In the following examples of the two typologies the metalinguistic code for each turn containing a new proposal is marked M1,M2,M3.

Ex.5: Co-constructing sequence

Dyad 4

356 Em: The ghost saw his shadow, and ran away with legs flying. And he was so scared M1

357 Ca: and, and

358 Em: and

359 Ca: and he was so scared

360 Em: he was so scared

361 Ca: he was so scared and broke the magic crystal. It doesn't fit M2

362 Em: wait, I might have an idea. The ghost M1

363 Ca: the ghost

364 Em: wait I'll read it all again

365 Ca: come on, the ghost ran M1

366 Em: it's one and a half lines M2

367 Cat: no the ghost ran away, no, he bumped into the crystal ball by mistake, no M2

368 Em: wait an idea, an idea

369 Ca: and broke

370 Em: wait,the ghost was frightened in a way so in the end he broke it by mistake M1

378 Em: he was very frightened and broke the crystal ball M1

379 Ca: the ghost was very frightened and broke the magic crystal ball, dictate it to me .

Ca. (361) looks for a solution to the constraint represented by the conjunction (e=and) and in (367) discovers both the semantic and syntactic filler (another verb and a coherent action). Em. (370) produces a causal clause which is coherent as regards the gap but forgets the constraint "and". Subsequently in (378) Em. can only work on the last proposal by changing the subordinate clause into a coordinated one. In the whole sequence only once, in (361), is Ca. evaluating their shared proposal. What prevails is the working together on the same linguistic material.

The following is an example of the opposing typology in the same dyad.

Ex.6. Opposing sequence

Dyad 4

158 Ca: Then?, Then?, Then here he meets a man because otherwise the fairy, the castle, the fairy castle, the castle, then they saw a golden ghost. The king run away with legs flying, terrified and broke the crystal ball. M3

159 Em: Now I'll tell you why I'd like to write the king, because if she had made the castle appear, when she made it appear, in the castle there's always a king, anyway M3

160 Ca: But

161 Em: Then the son of the king M1

162 CA: But, in those times there weren't any kings in the castle anymore were there? M3

In this short opposing sequence Ca. in (158) is planning the final part of the story far ahead and is at the same time giving a clear metalinguistic reason for the fact that a male gender is needed for gap 9, while Em. (159) supports the choice of a king as a good character for the castle (in a castle there is always a king), Ca. (162) opposes an "historical" reason: ("in those times, in the castle there are no more kings").

Learning About Language Through Computer Use

The second study aimed at studying ways and effects of introducing computer use within a context of metalinguistic education. Research on metalinguistic abilities (Bialystock, 1986; Zucchermaglio, Pontecorvo, Tonucci, Blachowitz, 1986; Tunmer, Pratt & Herriman, 1984) has shown that it is educationally relevant for school to develop metalinguistic skills in children as dimensions that can foster more general linguistic development, particularly since all the complex cognitive components of reading and writing are required for literacy development. Indeed, metalinguistic skills are required both by reading comprehension of complex material as well as in summary production and text revision.

Computer informational features are particularly suitable for developing a kind of artificial context for metalinguistic work in school. Notwithstanding the importance of focusing on the different functional and communicative uses of written language which can also be developed through computer use, it also seems important to use the computer as a flexible tool for manipulating written materials and for "playing with language" more or less independently from the meaning dimension so as to enable users to reflect on language form and learn to separate form from meaning (Pontecorvo, Orsolini, Zucchermaglio, 1989).

Following our general principle of introducing computer use to the traditional classroom activity, teachers were stimulated to *integrate* the software within a curriculum activity about "reflection on language". This was also carried out, without the computer, in a control class. In our experimental group there were two types of "activities without computer":

a) preliminary activities that were preparatory to those done with the computer, (e.g. "cutting" sentences and recomposing them in all possible ways, classifying the different "parts" and discussing acceptability) and;
b) activities in which the whole group of children "come back" to the linguistic products at their work with the computer (eg. they engage themselves both in the production of new "vocabularies" that have to be inserted into the software and in the analysis of sentences produced by other children with a given vocabulary).

The study also aimed to develop an *ecological account* of what happens in a classroom when a computer is introduced as a part of the normal teaching activity and within a curriculum aimed at developing reflection on language through a range of curriculum activities. In particular we were interested in obtaining data from observational and experimental types of assessment. The observational type is aimed at discovering the cognitive and linguistic strategies developed by children through their interaction with the computer and with each other. It requires the development and use of an instrument for observing children's interactions appropriate to the cognitive/linguistic characteristics of the computer courseware. The experimental type is aimed at testing the effectiveness of computer use within a linguistic curriculum unit, using an individual measure of metalinguistic ability that had been administered to the experimental and to the control group as pre- and post-test.

The subjects of the experimental treatment were 19 third grade children enrolled in a school located in Rome. All children were from a middle-class background. The same number of children, the control group, were taken from another third grade class in the same Montessori school. A general linguistic curriculum, planned at the school level between teachers, was shared by both groups (for more details on this research, see Pontecorvo & Zucchermaglio, 1991).

The experimental treatment involved the use of specific computer software, introduced as an additional aspect of a general linguistic curriculum, fostering social interaction among children. The computer software was not used as a means for auto-instruction nor as an exclusive tool versus more traditional media. Rather, it provided an "artificial" context for children's linguistic activity for which the computer is particularly suited, owing to its ease in making fast revisions of words and texts and its ability to process and manipulate linguistic material. This enables children to carry out a series of *activities* on language, that involved play and metalinguistic analysis. It also fosters language production through the breaking of some linguistic constraints. It could be said that *all* the software "affords" the production of texts of different types, using what is already given - in a more or less constraining way - and linking it to the new elements. The presence of different constraints encourages metalinguistic reflection because one has to compare the proposed choice with a frame of reference made up of an already existing vocabulary, the structure of a story, a given number of lines, and so on.
The software used was of two kinds:

A) "*Stories*" . This group required the following: a) planning in a given context; b) maintaining semantical and syntactical coherence; c) using verbal fluidity in constructing and re-constructing texts.

B) "*Composition*". This group required: a) planning; b) using verbal flexibility; c) restructuring. The activity of composing sentences and texts is required within a context in which *ad hoc* constraints are set up. These include lack of punctuation and connectives, the need to use a given "vocabulary", the presence of verbs that cannot be modified, the need to follow a compulsory order of choice, etc. In order to reach the goals given by the software, it might be necessary to produce sentences and stories that are semantically unacceptable. Software of this group (COMPFRASI) was used for pre-test and post-test observations.

The second component of the treatment was provided by social interaction. Children worked with the computer software in small groups of three. Groups were heterogeneous with regard to sex, general linguistic skill and initial metalinguistic levels. Children freely used the software they enjoyed the most during the school year (six months). The first presentation of each piece of the courseware was observed and recorded Group observations were carried out within the normal school time.

Ecological Observation Systems

Observation was used as an internal measure of processes elicited by the software in order to describe the type of linguistic and interactional processes activated during work with the software.

All child interactions were observed as children worked with the same software (COMPFRASI) at the beginning and at the end of the experimental treatment. This software, which is graded in four levels, asks the child to construct sentences with words representing nouns, verbs, adjectives, articles and prepositions which are organized under a common heading. The challenge is to build as long a sentence as possible and the task is constrained by the fact that the software does not offer conjunctions, relative pronouns and punctuation. Thus, the software requires sentence planning and restructuring and develops syntactical coherence, semantic fluidity, and the ability to distinguish between classes of words. At the fourth level children are required to invent their own vocabulary, with which they are then required to construct the sentences. This activity demonstrates how much children try to overcome previous constraints, and develop awareness of the criteria to be followed in order to construct "good" vocabulary.

The groups were analytically observed for 30 minutes at the beginning and at the end of the school year. Observations were audiotaped, fully transcribed and categorized independently by two judges who discussed their disagreements. Observations were categorized according to two different systems of analysis: one for the cognitive linguistic dimension and another for the social dimension.

The first system of categories was developed through both a "top-down" and a "bottom-up" process: the categories in most cases are common to the entire courseware while few are specific to each software and are not described here (see Pontecorvo & Zucchermaglio, 1987). The common categories are:

A: identifying/reading words

B: choosing words or sentences without planning or giving reasons

C: choosing words or sentences with planning

E: restructuring/revising what has been produced or planned previously

F: giving metalinguistic explanations (both morphosyntactical and semantical)

S: questions, remarks or commands about the software

We categorized any observer intervention and children's turns regarding the hardware or conversational aspects as OFF/TASK. To illustrate how this system is applied, a categorized interactional sequence taken from an initial observation with COMPFRASI is presented below:

Group 1 - Daniela (at the keyboard), Simona e Michele

10 Daniela (at the keyboard): Yes, but let's read them! (she reads the word list) S

11 Simona : So / Franco cleans the cat belonging to.../ C

12 Daniela: /to...monkey/..../ Franco talks to the monkey.../ E

13 Simona : Oh! /Antonio's!/ (cat) E

14 Michele: Where do you see that /Antonio/? A

15 Daniela: /Franco cleans Antonio's cat with the monkey.../ E

16 Simona: But how can he clean the cat with the monkey? Daniela!!! F

17 Daniela: It's all right, it can be imaginative or impossible!!! F

18 Michele: No, wait / Franco waits the monkey for a snack/... "for" it' there! E

19 Daniela: Yes , "for" "the" there are! C

20 Michele: So, /Franco waits the monkey for a snack/...No, there is/ milk/ So let's do /Franco waits the monkey for..../ C

21 Daniela: / for the snack with the milk/ C

22 Michele: Let's just write this for now B

23 Simona: Yes, how was it / Franco ....waits the monkey for a snack... C

24 Michele: Perhaps/for Antonio's snack/ E

This system was used to carry out both qualitative (based on sequences of utterances) and quantitative analysis. With regard to quantitative analysis, the categories were ordered according to the level of cognitive complexity of the corresponding linguistic activities or levels of explication of the speech activity. The categories were then transformed into ordered scores and a group score was computed (see Pontecorvo and Zucchermaglio, 1991 for a full presentation of this study).

The second system of categories involved the social aspect of the interaction and aimed to describe the type of social interaction produced by the children when working with computer software. The unit of analysis is a turn linked to a previous one, in an exchange defined as "the pragmatic link between two not necessarily contiguous conversational contributions" (Orsolini, & Pontecorvo 1989). It distinguishes between :

1) converging exchanges (CONV): expressions of agreement, repetitions and reformulations, elaborations of the information introduced by a previous speaker, requests for information;
2) questioning exchanges (QUEST): introduction of new information and delimitations, requests for explanation or justification;
3) opposing exchanges (OPPOS): opposition with a previous utterance, counter-oppositions (that reject a previous opposition), defense of a point of view which had received an opposition.

It was expected that the opposing exchanges would correspond to a higher cognitive level and more productivity in the learning process. Thus, the two systems of analysis were related by computing the frequencies of each linguistic-cognitive category in each exchange type.

Linguistic and Social Interaction

As regards the general experimental context, it is not possible to separate effects due to the insertion of the computer software alone from those due to the socio-interactional context of learning. By hypothesizing that the experimental group would obtain higher results at the end of the school year, we expected this increase to be due to the cumulative effect of computer use in an interactional context. Working in groups on linguistic software requires the negotiation of single linguistic and non-linguistic proposals for the construction of the text. The group situation produces the need "for granting" as in previous research (Orsolini, Pontecorvo & Amoni,1989; Pontecorvo & Orsolini, 1992). Opposing and alternative proposals require justification and explanation in order to be taken into account by the other members of the group.

Linguistic interaction levels increased for all groups of children after the educational activity with the courseware. ANOVA analysis carried out on the mean scores of children's interaction with the same software (COMPFRASI) at the beginning and at the end of the school year showed a statistically significant effect while no significant differences were observed between the groups.

In analyzing the frequency distribution of these data in the linguistic categories an evident decrease in low cognitive-linguistic level categories and software categories was noted. Conversely, the frequencies of high cognitive-linguistic level categories and metalinguistic category more than doubled from pre- to post-test.

Children produced a greater number of planning and restructuring processes as well as increased explanations at a metalinguistic level when observed at the end of the year. The fact that this strong effect was found when comparing frequencies of interactions with the same software used at the beginning of the year needs to be interpreted. As the children became more familiar with it, it was to be expected that cognitive demand would be lower and that children would operate at a lower cognitive level. In fact, the familiarity effect with the software allowed the children to work *only* on the linguistic content proposed by it, without being particularly involved in the procedural requests. This is shown by the decrease in the frequencies of the "software" category. The focusing on the linguistic content of the software, the mastery of the "play" and the more productive use of the social interaction could explain the strong increase in the frequencies for the high level and metalinguistic categories.

Changes were observed in the distribution of the cognitive and linguistic categories across the social dimension. Whereas the low cognitive level categories were mainly concentrated in the converging exchanges, the high cognitive level ones were almost equally distributed across the different exchange types, with a preference for the questioning exchange. On the other hand we only found metalinguistic categories in the questioning and in the opposing exchanges. To summarize, based on the high cognitive level and the metalinguistic categories, we can support the hypothesis that opposing exchanges between children are linked to a higher cognitive level. In this context of reflection on language, as in others, opposing interactions were more productive for the reasoning and learning processes carried out by the children; this is shown in the following excerpt taken from a COMPFRASI observation, in which children were requested to invent their own vocabularies.

Group 5 - Marta (at the keyboard),Vittoria and Giovanni
94 Marta: A name now F CONV
95 Giovanni: We put so many! F OPP
96 Marta: No, a girl's name E OPP
97 Giovanni: /Giacomo/ C OPP
98 Vittoria: Wait then/Barbara/all right? let's put some actions now, we didn't put many!! F QUEST
99 Giovanni: / violet/ B QUEST
100 Marta: But we only put two names! F OPP
101 Vittoria: Yes, but we also put /children, birds, trees .../ E OPP
102 Giovanni: We can put /violet/... /violet flowers smell good/ C QUEST
103 Vittoria: That is /violet/ to say how they are? Or it could also be the flower F QUEST
104 Giovanni: Yes, we could also do /the violet smells good/ isn't it? E QUEST
105 Vittoria: Then, let's put /spring/ C CONV
106 Giovanni: /beautiful /.../ flowers are beautiful/ C CONV
107 Marta: No, wait /they pick up/ .../they pick up flowers/ E OPP

108 Vittoria: Sure and what else! C OPP
109 Giovanni: Well, they could pick up dirt too! F OPP
110 Vittoria: Yes, but... B QUEST
111 Giovanni: /meadows/ C CONV
112 Vittoria: Oh, yes /meadows/ we can put that or /meadows C CONV
113 Giovanni: No, Let's put /meadow/ C QUEST
114 Vittoria: Yes, but we must be careful because we put too many... E QUEST
115 Giovanni : too many names F CONV
116 Marta: Yes, but also children's names F QUEST
117 Giovanni: We didn't put many plural nouns F QUEST

The opposing interactions, which require children to create and provide sound arguments to support their proposals, elicits the metalinguistic competence to become a social, overt, and explicit activity.

Metalinguistic Level

An external measure of metalinguistic level was taken as a pre-post treatment test of the effectiveness of the computer based curriculum. A metalinguistic task was also administered to the control group through individual interviews at the beginning and at the end of the school year. It had been tried out in previous research (Pontecorvo, Orsolini, Zucchermaglio, 1989) and was based on explanations given by children on the acceptability judgments of four different types of sentences. The sentences were created for each of the four items by the child through the substitution of a given word in a sentence proposed by the experimenter. In the sentences there could be more or less of a conflict between the form and the meaning. For each new sentence the children were required to give acceptability judgments and to provide reasons for their judgments, which received a score from 0 (No explanation) to 4 (use of morpho-syntactical rules) with a maximum score of 64 (16 for each of the four items) for each subject.

Analysis of the metalinguistic interviews showed a statistically significant effect of interaction between group and time. Moreover, the experimental group did significantly better than the control group by the end of the school year. The level of explanations given on acceptability judgments by the experimental children was higher than those obtained at the beginning of the school year. This is based on the consideration of the morphological aspects of the sentences. Conversely, the level of explanations offered by the control group showed a decrease by the end the school year. These children experienced more difficulties in handling the grammatical aspects of the sentences and never "forgot" the semantical aspects of them. It might be claimed that the increase shown by the experimental group was not dependent upon age or development, but rather on the work with the software supported curriculum that focused on handling the formal aspects of language. This result is due to the whole integrated linguistic curriculum and cannot be attributed solely to the effects of interaction with the computer software, but it supports the strong differences found in the cognitive-linguistic interaction between pre- and post-tests within the experimental group presented above.

Cooperative Computer Use in Text Revising

The third study was carried out with the double aim of: a) controlling whether use of the computer could modify children's text revision in starting from 4th grade, and; b) checking whether there were differences in text revision, within the experimental groups between children who used the computer during the test administration and those who did not.

We wanted to verify, in a different context, the thesis advanced by Salomon (1990) that, beyond possible *effects of* the computer on cognitive development, there are much stronger *effects with* the computer; i.e. effects that can be only detected if the subject is working with the proper support of the technology.

As in previous studies, the computer was ecologically inserted into the normal activity of the classrooms. In this case, computer use mainly involved a collective text producing activity. Children worked at the computer at different writing tasks (stories, recounts, notes, summaries) using a word processing program and a program for producing a school newspaper. They worked mainly in dyads or triads. The computer writing activity included composing, reading, discussing and revising texts and organizing the layout of text and graphics for the newspaper.

While the computer was usually used by children in interaction with others, we also wanted to control whether the revising was better done in pairs or individually. Moreover, the use of the computer in cooperation requires verbal expression of reasons for revising proposals, basing them on convincing reasons and sometimes giving up one's own personal point of view. At the same time it is possible to observe the communication and reasoning developed by the children in their interactions. Such an observation requires the development of a system for analyzing the revision process as a collaborative activity in order to understand how revising is carried out by children at different levels of competence (as was done in Paoletti & Pontecorvo, 1991).

In order to control knowledge content, children were asked to watch the same structured video-taped documentary. All children thus received the same information. They then had to revise a standard expository text which summarized the documentary and contained different kinds of errors. While the control groups corrected it with paper and pencil, the experimental groups were put under different conditions (with or without a computer, in pairs or individually).

We collected revision products from 266 children which had been produced individually, in pairs, and with and without the computer. Revision products were studied using a coding system already applied in Paoletti & Pontecorvo (1989). As described earlier, we developed a system for analyzing revision products based on four levels of error detection:

1. Macrostructural (Macro) detection required the analysis of an extended part of the text and consequent changes affect the structure of the text itself.
2. Comprehension (COMP) detection also requires the analysis of an extended part of the text, but changes do not affect text structure.
3. In-phrase (INF) detection concerns a syntactical or a morphological error, and its solution requires analysis of one sentence only.
4. Convention (CONV) detection concerns written language conventions e.g. word segmentation, spelling, some conventional uses of the comma.

Children who revised the standard text had to face 20 errors of different detection difficulty: six at the Macro level; four at the Comp level; eight at the Inf level; and two at the Conv level. On the basis of an item analysis carried out on the pre-test scores, we attributed a score to each error based on its difficulty index produced from this analysis. A total score was then computed for each subject.

Effectiveness of Collaborative Revision Done with Computer

Children's revising ability was expected to increase with:

1) age: older children would have better results in revision than younger children;
2) use of the computer as treatment and tool for the test:
   a) children who learned to use a word processor and use it in their daily experience would have better results than control children;
   b) as a sub-hypothesis, experimental children who carried out the test with the computer would have better results than those who did it without the computer.
3) cooperation: children who worked in pairs would have better results than those who worked alone because the need to explain and negotiate the decisions would foster text revision.

Statistically significant results were obtained for all the hypotheses mentioned above (for a full presentation of data see Pontecorvo & Paoletti,1991b).

Age-and-grade. The analysis we carried out had grade (4 levels) as a between-subject variable and time (pre-post test) as within-subjects variables. There was a statistically significant difference ($p>.001$) due to grade level. In 4th and 5th grade there was a strong increase between pre- and post-tests.

Computer as treatment. The analysis had treatment (2 levels) as a between-subjects variable and time (pre-post test) as a within-subjects variables. There were statistically significant differences in revision (p>.05) due to the treatment and due to the interaction between treatment and time as regards the total scores.

Computer as tool. Children who used the computer *during the tests* had a higher score both in the pre-test and in the post-test, and showed a greater improvement. The analysis used the test conditions (computer/non computer) (2 levels) as between-subjects variables and time (pre-post-test) as within-subjects variables. There was a statistically significant difference (p>.001) due to the use of the computer during the test, and a difference at p>.05 due to the interaction between treatment and time.

Collaborative versus individual revision. Total scores were compared for individual and collaborative revision for 4th and 5th grades. Pairs had a higher score both in the pre-test and in the post-test, and showed a greater improvement. The analysis we carried out had individual or collaborative work (2 levels) as between-subject variables and time (pre-post test) as within-subjects variables. There was a statistically significant difference (p>.001) for the unexpected changes due to the pair condition.

There was also a strong effect for age-and-grade, which is particularly relevant in the passage from the 4th to the 5th grade. A real quality jump occurs in the revision competence in children at this time. It would be interesting to compare this result with what happens in other languages and in other school systems.

As regards the effect attributed to the *computer as an experimental treatment*, experimental groups scored lower than control groups in the pre-test revision task. It is interesting to note that the use of computer for text revising had a very positive effect in increasing the awareness of error detection in children. Computer use had both a motivational and a facilitating effect for less competent children.

The positive effect of the *computer as a tool* for accomplishing the revision task is clear from our results. Experimental groups who used the computer in order to carry out the revising activity always had better results in the pre-test task. Moreover their results increased significantly in the post-test task.

Last but not least, there are strong positive effects of working in pairs as compared to individual revision work. As in the effect of working *with* the computer, the positive effects significantly increased in the post-test task.

Collaborative Language Learning in Constructivist Environments

The main aim of our research was to show how a new epistemology of schooling can be implemented, and how it is possible to make an ecological study of what occurs in such a situation, which is coherent with that epistemology. For this reason we always used different types of "measures" in order to understand better what really happens when children use different types of hardware and software in the "natural" context of school life and learning.

As regards the first study, the collaborative situation, which is facilitated by the sharing of the computer screen, opens a new perspective on the study of some unexplored dimensions of the writing tasks of young children for two main reasons: the effect that it can have on learning, and; the view that it provides of internal processes becoming overt.

Children are often said to plan their writing tasks by following an ideational flow which does not connect subsequent portions of the text. Thus they do not produce an overall plan, and very rarely refer to an overt analysis of linguistic choices suited to the communicative aims of their writing tasks. Collaboratively working on completion tasks becomes collaborative learning since it forces the child to explain to his/her partner the reasons for his/her alternative proposal. This produces a better understanding of the logical and linguistic implications of the proposed solution. It also plays a role in reciprocally exchanging the linguistic knowledge which the individual child already possesses (though without being aware of it).

The situation in which the child understands better what he/she already knows in an unconscious way, and the situation in which there is mutual enrichment, were clearly revealed in the co-constructing and opposing sequences we found in child interaction. They also showed how the presence of one partner helps the other even when it apparently limits the freedom of invention by simultaneously reducing the burden of the problem solving task of story completion. Moreover, the presentation of the task through the medium of the computer is a facilitator of child interaction and discussion during the writing task, because of both the sharing of the screen and the easy editing of the text. Thus, children are constructing their linguistic knowledge in an instructional context that, although designed by their teachers, is autonomously managed by themselves in a socially supported situation.

The results of the second study confirm the educational relevance of introducing computer use within a curriculum perspective as a medium for literacy learning aimed at both linguistic and metalinguistic development. Both interview and observational results have confirmed the effectiveness of the experimental intervention. However, given our research "philosophy", we cannot distinguish which effects are due to the work on the computer courseware and which are due to the whole curriculum.

This study was also aimed at developing and trying out a system of analysis of children's linguistic interactions with software for composing texts and stories which could measure differences in children's linguistic activities. Thus, we were interested in describing the processes fostered by the software in children's work with it. We found that the systems were sensitive to the increases in the cognitive and linguistic level of children's interaction. This result is consistent with the aims of the curriculum. On this basis, giving an ecological account of the children's interaction with the computer software might be one of the main methodological instruments for testing whether the software is educationally effective and appropriate. Moreover, research aimed at gathering this type of information is essential in order to design more constructivist computer environments.

Overall results of the third study are in agreement with the hypothesis drawn from Salomon (1990) that more than looking for effects of the computer on individual's performance, we have to look for effects with the computer as a supporting tool for performing different types of literacy activities. There are also, most likely, long term effects of the computer on our "normal" way of writing (which we have not measured in this research). But these effects are much more present when the subject is working with the computer and in particular if this work is done in collaboration with a partner.

The use of the computer for literacy acquisition which we are proposing is very flexible and has a large range of different applications, according to the competence of children and to the curriculum choices of teachers. In any case, it brings about a deep change in classroom organization. Indeed we regarded the full participation of teachers in activity planning and in the choice of a constant and differentiated use of social interaction as an integral part of the educational proposal.

In addition, both qualitative and quantitative results show that working in dyads or in groups with computer software produces relevant cognitive and linguistic interactions which foster the supporting and scaffolding possibilities that are already embedded in the computer software. Our research is a modest contribution to the theory of situated and distributed cognition, in which "distribution" is offered both by the computer and the active presence of the others.

These results also show how a complex activity can be developed by children with very simple software, such as that used in these studies or with all-purpose software such as a word-processor. Once again, it is not so important to have "intelligent" programs: what is more important with educational technologies is that they can solicit intelligent, conscious, and intrinsically motivated activity from the learner.

References

Bialystock, E. (1986). Factors in growth of linguistic awareness. *Child Development, 57* (2), 498-510.

Duffy, T.M., Lowyck, J. & Jonassen, D.H. (Eds.) (1993). *Designing environments for constructivist learning.* (NATO/ASI Series F, Vol. 105.) Berlin: Springer-Verlag

Greenfield, P. (1984). A theory of the teacher in the learning activities of everyday life. In B. Rogoff & J. Lave (Ed.), *Everyday cognition.* Cambridge, MA: Harvard Univ. Press.

Greenfield, P.M. (1987). Electronic technologies, education, and cognitive development. In D.E. Berger, K.Pezdek & W.P. Banks (Eds.), *Applications of cognitive psychology.* Hillsdale, NJ: Erlbaum.

Leont'ev A.N. (1959/1963). *Problemi dello sviluppo psichico.* Roma: Editori Riuniti.

Newman, D. (1990). The impact of technologies in the classroom. *Educational Researcher, 19* (6), 19-26.

Olson, D. R. (Ed.). (1974). *Media and forms of information, communication and expression.* Chicago: NSSE.

Orsolini, M. & Pontecorvo, C. (1989). Arguing versus co-constructing in children's verbal interaction. *Dossiers de Psychologie, 37,* 53-60.

Orsolini, M., Pontecorvo, C. & Amoni, M. (1989). Discutere a scuola; interazione sociale e attivita' cognitiva. *Giornale Italiano di Psicologia, XVII* (3), 479-511.

Paoletti, G. & Pontecorvo, C. (1991). *Children revising text with and without computer: A system for analyzing revision.* Proceedings of IIIrd EARLI çonference(Madrid, 1989), Oxford: Pergamon Press.

Pontecorvo, C. & Orsolini, M. (1991). Discussing and explaining a story in preschool. In F. Danesi & M.A. Pinto, *Festschrift for R.Titone,* Roma: Bulzoni.

Pontecorvo, C. & Orsolini, M. (in press). Children's talk in classroom discussion. *Cognition and Instruction.*

Pontecorvo, C. & Paoletti, G. (1991a). Planning story completation in a collaborative computer task. *European Journal of Psychology of Education, VI,* 2, 199-212.

Pontecorvo, C. & Paoletti, G. (1991b). *Studying the revision process: effects of computer in cooperation,* Paper presented to the 4th EARLI conference, Turku, Finland (24-25 August, 1991).

Pontecorvo, C. & Zucchermaglio, C. (1987). The computer in a metalinguistic education context (Il computer inserito in un contesto di educazione metalinguistica). *Rassegna di Psicologia, 2/3,* 151-172.

Pontecorvo, C. & Zucchermaglio, C. (1991). Computer's use in learning about language. In *European Journal of psychology of education, VII* (1), 15-27.

Pontecorvo, C., Orsolini, M. & Zucchermaglio, C. (1989). Metalinguistic skills in children: what develops? *Infancia y Aprendizaje 47,* 55-65.

Salomon, G. (1990). Studying the flute and the orchestra: Effects of and with the computer. *International Review of Educational Research 13.*

Scardamalia, M. & Bereiter, C. (1987). Knowledge telling and knowledge transforming in written composition. In S. Rosemberg (Ed.). *Advances in applied psycholinguistics.* Cambridge, U.K.: Cambridge Univ. Press.

Tornatore, L. (1987). Il fare e il parlare. *Rassegna di Psicologia, IV* (2/3), 135-150.

Tunmer, W.E., Pratt, C., Herriman M.L. (Eds.). (1984). *Metalinguistic awareness in children.* Berlin: Springer-Verlag.

Vygotskij, L.S. (1934/1990). *Pensiero e linguaggio.* Nuova traduzione a cura di L Mecacci. Bari: Laterza.

Wertsch, J. (1990), *Voices of the mind.* Cambridge, MA: Harvard University Press.

Zinchenko, V. P. (1984). Vygotsky's ideas about units for the analysis of mind. In J.V. Wertsch (Ed.), *Culture, comunication and cognition: Vygotskian perspectives.* Cambridge, U.K.: Cambridge University Press

Zucchermaglio, C., Pontecorvo, C., Tonucci, F., Blachowicz, C. (1986). Linguistic awareness and literacy. *Reading Psychology, 1* (7), 11-25.

Part II

Design Issues

8 Tools for Constructivism[1]

Randy A. Knuth* and Donald J. Cunningham** [2]

* North Central Regional Education Laboratory, Oak Brook, Illinois, USA
** School of Education, Indiana University, Bloomington, Indiana, USA

Over the years, those laboring in the field of instructional design and development have drawn upon insights offered from a variety of theories of learning and cognition. Behavioral theories held sway for many years (as embodied, for example, in programmed instruction and computer managed drill and practice) and are only now being supplanted by cognitive information processing theories (e.g., levels of processing, schema theory, production systems, metacognition). More recently, a variation of cognitive information processing theory has begun to attract attention -- connectionism (see Bereiter, 1991).

We have argued elsewhere (Bednar, Cunningham, Duffy & Perry, 1991; Cunningham, Duffy & Knuth, in press) that all of these models treat instruction as a process of systematic communication where some content and/or set of skills is communicated to or instilled within the student. Knowledge, that which we wish the learner to know, is contained in the teacher's lessons or in the text book, film, computer data base, and so forth. Instruction is essentially a process of engineering learning environments so that transmission of this knowledge from these sources to the student is efficient and effective. Much of our theory and research on the learning process is embedded within this view: what is the best way to present material to students, whether by live teacher, in a text, in some CAI software, etc., to maximize the amount learned? Theoretical concepts derived from these theories have even crept into our everyday language about schooling: "Mary, you aren't getting the message!"; "I knew the answer, but I couldn't get it out of long term memory"; "Billy just doesn't have a schema for learning geography"; etc.

Within the last few years, a distinctly different body of theory has begun to attract the attention of the field of instructional design and development -- constructivism. A recent publication (Duffy and Jonassen, in press), as well as this volume, attests to the willingness of the field to explore the implications of these theories for instructional design. As with most labels, the term constructivism (as well as other labels often regarded as synonymous with it like experientialism, semiotics, relativism, etc.) hides the diversity of viewpoints that one will find, from moderate to extreme, to use Merrill's (1991) characterization. In this paper, we

---

[1]This paper is a collaborative effort of the authors. The order of authorship is arbitrary and was decided by an arm wrestling match.

[2]This paper was written during the period when the second author was a visiting professor at the University of Ulster, Coleraine, Northern Ireland.

would like to explore the implications of an undoubtedly extreme version of constructivism, in part because we believe it is a very powerful model, but also because it questions the very foundations underlying such diverse disciplines as biology, psychology, cognitive science and education. In other words, we relish the debate that this model usually provokes and feel strongly that such debate will cause others, even those not persuaded to our view, to rethink their own theoretical preferences.

Learners and Learning

A hallmark of traditional models of learning and cognition is that they assume that knowledge is external to the learner and can be objectively specified (e.g., by task analyses, schema, semantic networks, production systems, etc.). That is, they rely on the existence of information "objects" that can be passed through mental structures by cognitive mechanisms in an analogous way that a message flows through a telephone wire. The process of learning becomes one of mapping this external knowledge into some form of internal representation that more or less approximates the external "objects." To see if the transmission process has been successful we check the match between the student's cognitive representation and the knowledge as previously defined.

Constructivism, on the other hand, argues that instruction is more a matter of nurturing the ongoing processes whereby learners ordinarily and naturally come to understand the world in which they live. In this view, knowledge is an active process of construction, not the receipt of information from external sources. The role of teaching and other instructional media shifts from one that seeks to maximize the communication of fixed content and/or skills to one in which students are led to experience the knowledge construction process: to construct interpretations, appreciate multiple perspectives, develop and defend their own positions while recognizing other views, and become aware of and able to manipulate the knowledge construction process itself. An important aspect of this approach is the insistence that learning take place embedded in the contexts to which it is most relevant in everyday life and with which the students are personally involved.

As promised, in this paper we will take a rather extreme view of constructivism, one that questions the very notion that the environment can be "instructive" in any real sense of that word. For our view, we will draw upon the writing of the Chilean biologist, Humberto Maturana. Our purpose is not to reject other versions of constructivism (or behaviorism, cognitive information processing, etc., for that matter) but to assess the implications of this view for existing and possible new instructional systems. In other words, would instructional design and the use of technology look different based upon Maturana's notion of autopoiesis?

In what way can we design instruction that is synomorphic[3] with this process? But first, a few words about Maturana.

Maturana (e.g., Maturana & Varela, 1987) begins with the seemingly simple question "What is the organization of living systems?"; that is, what characterizes systems as living as opposed to non-living? After years of research and thought, Maturana has concluded that the single most important characteristic that distinguishes the living from the non-living, in regard to their unitary character, is autopoiesis (a term he coined). In brief, an autopoietic unity is self organized and structurally closed. Their behavior and internal processes are governed by their internal organization (embodied in a particular structure) that must be maintained (conserved). That is, their structure can and will change as a function of internal processes and environmental influences, but the basic unity of the organism and its adaptation must be conserved. With respect to humans, the following, highly integrated points may be noted:

1. Humans are structurally determined systems; that is, they are autonomous and recursively organized living systems that behave as a function of their organization and particular structure (Goolishian & Winderman, 1988). Instead of responding in a cause-effect manner to objective environmental stimuli, living systems, when perturbed by structured patterns of energy, respond in their own idiosyncratic way -- they determine their own response. Thus, there are no cause-effect relationships between the world and the learner, and the patterns exhibited by the perturbed living system do not reflect the structure of the perturbing stimuli. Behavior, whether internal or external, emerges within a context in which the human organism conserves its adaptation and organization.

2. Living systems are informationally closed. Humans cannot take in information from the outside world and map it onto mental symbols that are then manipulated and processed (e.g., see Newell & Simon, 1976). Rather, people are always immersed in a sea of structured energy that is interpreted and made sense of by an active observer. For example, light, that enters our eyes and perturbs the structure of our nervous system by triggering chemical changes, is organized by our nervous system into edges, light-dark gradients, bars, intense spots, etc. (Marr, 1982) that our cognitive system actively interprets. In other words, we "objectify" our "subjective reality"; "objects [that] we think we see and study are [actually] products of the activities of our own nervous system" (Efran & Lukens, 1985, p. 24). Light energy from the environment can "trigger" but not determine the visual experience.

Notions such as these have led Maturana to argue that if we want to understand human learning we need to focus on the interactions within the learning system, not on the structure of

---

[3]Synomorphy is a term coined by Roger Barker, an eco-environmental psychologist which stresses the closeness of fit between entities. For example, a glove is highly synomorphic with a hand but not with a foot.

the environment. Winograd & Flores (1986, p. 44) make the same point: "...it is the structure of the perturbed system that determines, or better, specifies what structural configurations of the medium can perturb it."

3. Organisms are structurally coupled to the medium in which they are embedded. That is, living systems survive by fitting with one another and with other aspects of the surrounding medium in a manner that conserves their organization and adaptation. Life is a succession of dynamic interactions or activities in which people are structurally coupled to each other and/or the world (Leont'ev, 1981) and in which there are no stops and starts but rather continuous activity. "People do what they do because of how they are put together, and they do it in connection with (but not on direct instruction from) the medium in which they exist, which includes other people." (Efran & Lukens, 1985, p. 25).

4. Humans are observing systems who describe, distinguish, and delineate in words and symbols. Without the observer, for example, the very notion of behavior in response to external "instructions" from the environment ceases to exist. It is the human observer who imposes some sort of conceptual system upon the phenomena he/she observes and thereby brings forth a world that includes those phenomena. We do not perceive an objective universe but rather it is through observing that humans are capable of generating meaning. Further, all kinds of cause- effect thinking are just verbal formula we use to make sense of our experience.

What do Maturana's notions of the learner imply for instructional designers? Efran & Lukens (1985, p.23) highlight Maturana's belief that instruction in the traditional sense is simply not possible. They suggest that "you do not change organisms -- you design an environment in which organisms thrive, respond, and change themselves." The idea that we can prescriptively design instruction is based on the belief that it is possible to predict a learner's behavior, a concept that has been convincingly argued against by Maturana. He believes that we cannot determine a student's learning, that is directly produce the behaviors we want, when we want them. When we believe we are doing a pretty good job of instructing, students may simply be accommodating to the situation in which they find themselves, acting in the way they think we want them to act (i.e., in terms of the world that we have brought forth with them) so as to conserve structural coupling and adaptation. Whether this is "instruction" in the sense that most of us feel is important, is open to question.

Some Principles of Constructivism

Winn (1989, p.40) expresses a sentiment that a number of you may be feeling at this time. If Maturana is correct, the very existence of traditional instructional design is threatened: "Indeed, the very idea that instruction can be designed in the first place must be abandoned unless one subscribes to the belief that how students will react to instruction can be predicted with reasonable accuracy." But the idea that humans are structurally closed need not inevitably lead to the notion that they can not be "influenced," and influenced in predictable ways. The ideas underlying constructivism suggest that we shift from designing environments that instruct to designing environments that influence the structure of autopoietic unities in ways that conserve organization and adaptation. Thus, while the organization of, say, the human nervous system is fixed, its interconnectivity allows for nearly infinite structural flexibility. Through structural coupling with its environment (that includes other beings), the organism literally brings forth the world in which it finds itself, a world constrained by the organization of the environment and by its own organization. But within those limits, an incredible variety of "worlds" are possible[4].

The key to understanding the relevance of this view for human instructional design is to recognize the importance of a uniquely human form of structural coupling with the environment: social coupling through language. In a very real sense, the environment is entirely independent of us. Living systems are organized to generate internal regularities like neuronal activities and their interconnections that conserve adaptation. The environment is a source of perturbations that the organism may "select" in order to preserve autopoiesis. In other words, throughout its phylogeny and ontogeny, organisms have come to select those aspects of the environment that are or can become structurally coupled to its internal organization, and by doing so have brought forth a world in which autopoiesis is conserved.

In humans, these structural couplings include social couplings brought forth in a network of conversation and dialogue, a unique dimension of operational closure that permits us to experience what we have come to call consciousness: the experience of "mind" and "self" and its reciprocal, "other". The mind is not located in the brain -- it along with consciousness and notions of self and other exist in the domain of social coupling that we continuously weave, through the linguistic interactions that we generate with others. And it is through this means that we generate ourselves as describers and observers of the world in which we find ourselves. It is perhaps natural to assume that this world is the same for everyone, an objective world that exists as a point of reference independent of each of us. But the same linguistic couplings also allow us to see not *the* world, but *a* world that we bring forth with others. And we can see that many worlds are possible, that the world can change if we live differently. In Maturana's words, "the knowledge of knowledge compels". (Maturana & Varela, 1987, p. 245).

[4]It should be noted that humans cannot simply decide which aspects of the environment to perceive and which to ignore. Humans by nature live in a relatively narrow band of perceivable energy; without special tools, we can't "see" infrared or ultraviolet light nor hear ultrasonic vibrations. Further, we can't interact at the level of bacteria nor at the level of solar systems. It quickly becomes obvious that there are infinite worlds possible, each depending on an enormous array of observer properties -- the worlds that humans can bring forth because of their particular properties are but one relatively narrow subset among the possibilities.

This is the essential insight of constructivism: to know not only *that* we know but *how* we know. To emphasize this point, we would like to state and briefly discuss seven constructivist principles that are consistent with Maturana's views. In the section to follow, we will review some "tools" that purport to be in the constructivist mold and evaluate the extent to which they embody these principles.

1. All Knowledge is Constructed

Among the most quotable phrases from Maturana is the following: "Everything said is said by someone". (Maturana & Varela, 1987, p. 26) This sounds obvious, but consider its implications. Every distinction, every observation that we make brings forth a world. Every reflection is a human action by some particular person in some particular context. And this bringing forth of a world (knowledge) is essential if we are to understand it. But often we take this world as objective, independent of us -- its constructedness is hidden. Scientists, for example, are often perceived as investigating phenomena in the physical world. They aren't. They are investigating the distinctions and observations of themselves or other scientists, based upon a social and linguistic domain that specifies what they say and do. Scientists bring forth a world through their structural coupling in the same manner as we all do, and the constructedness of this world is no less than that brought forth by humanities scholars, for example.

One goal of instructional design derived from this principle might be to allow or encourage the experience of the "constructedness" of our knowledge of the world, a feature that is usually invisible to us in our ordinary daily interactions. By inviting students to adopt the perspectives and roles of a variety of individuals, we attempt to show them that different people can have different views of a situation and that these views can have a sense or logic independent of their own views. Truths that the students hold are shown to be only one of many possible truths.

A rather interesting way to provide such experience is to introduce the concept of metaphor. Lakoff and Johnson (1980) have argued convincingly that much, perhaps all of our thinking is metaphorical in nature. The strategy is to probe a student's existing metaphor for a particular situation, then show how changing the metaphor can change one's view of that situation. For instance, many teachers and students tend to view the classroom as a workplace, where tasks have to be completed in exchange for some sort of reward (e.g., a good grade in the course). Even the language we use to talk about classrooms is embued with this metaphor: homework, classroom management, reading gains, teacher accountability, and so forth. In consequence, learning tends to be regarded as a phenomena that takes place in classrooms, not elsewhere, much as work takes place in the workplace.

But suppose we adopt a different metaphor, say, the classroom as providing a consulting service. Now the agenda of tasks to be completed shifts from ones imposed by the teacher to ones generated by the students themselves. The classroom becomes one of only many places where work on this task takes place. The role of the teacher and other students shifts; they are now sources of insight and assistance, not authoritarian wisdom or competition. No doubt you can think of other differences that would emerge from such a shift in metaphor[5].

Another useful strategy is to expose students to cultures different than their own. Exposure to different cultural practices varying from the mildly odd (in most of Europe, for example, one shakes the hand of a friend upon meeting, but not a stranger, while the opposite is true in the U. S.) to the extreme (some Africans are circumcised at puberty, while in the U. S. this is done soon after birth) invites students to reconsider the inevitability of their own cultural practices.

2. Many Worlds Are Possible, Hence There Will be Multiple Perspectives

The notion that we bring forth worlds through our structural coupling leads directly to the issue that no one else sees the world exactly as we do. Of course, because the organization of human autopoiesis and the environment in which it exists are determined, it would be unlikely to find extreme differences where, for example, we would see the trees as made of green cheese. But these commonalities should not obscure the differences. There is great comfort in the certainty that one's view of the world is correct, but this certainty is obtained at the expense of failing to consider the perspective of others. Instead of assuming there is a fixed reference point (i.e., an external world) to which we can anchor our knowledge in order to affirm its validity, we have to accept the fact that our experience will be a mixture of stability and change, of regularity and conflict.

In constructivist instructional design, our aim is to find a way to bring forth worlds with others that accommodate or at least reflect the views of others. Few issues in the world have a single "correct" resolution. But young children (and many adults as well) tend to think that knowledge is either right or wrong, that all valid questions have answers, that authority figures (e.g., teachers, textbooks, etc.) have the answers to these questions and that experts know the truth or have ways to figure it out (Perry, 1970). Instruction designed under constructivist influences should again reveal the constructedness of knowledge, that any "truth" begins with a set of untested assumptions that can be examined to evaluate the adequacy of the position taken. What we take as "true" in a situation is very much a product of a process of negotiation, often taking the form of some sort of dialogue. Positions are something we commit ourselves to, not

[5] Our purpose here is not to argue for one metaphor or the other (although we certainly favor the second over the first). Our point simply is that under constructivism, a primary aim is to provide the students the opportunity to experience the constructedness of their world view.

something we adopt because (or certainly not only because) an authority figure decrees that we must.

Multiple perspectives are most commonly encountered in dialogue with other individuals. Certainly not all forms of dialogue will accomplish this goal. If one member of the group is "certain" about her position (i.e., is an expert, or simply dogmatic) and the others not, that member will usually dominate. If the group contains more than one "certain" individual, none of whom are willing to compromise their beliefs, then once again the dialogue will be unproductive in terms of this goal (although others in the group who are less certain may benefit). What we are interested in here is the situation where a group member is willing to reconsider his beliefs in terms of another's position and try to find a new view that accommodates them both. Surely not all views are equally accommodatable (we can not imagine finding common ground between our views and those of the KKK, for example). But the development of the realization that our view is only one of many and that an attitude of acceptance toward other views allows for the growth of our views, is fundamental under constructivism.

3. Knowledge is Effective Action

According to Maturana, "every act of knowing brings forth a world ... [so] all doing is knowing and all knowing is doing". (Maturana & Varela, 1987, p. 26). This is a key point. Knowledge is effective action. We observers regard an action as effective in a particular context. There is no real distinction between knowing and doing. Behavior is a result of the organism's attempt to conserve its autopoietic organization. The environment does not cause behavior, it only triggers it based upon the structural coupling between the unity and the environment.

This idea resonates nicely with the notion of situated cognition that is so passionately endorsed in the educational literature today (e.g., Brown, Collins, & Duguid,1989). So much of what passes for education these days is relevant only to a single context -- the school. Study after study shows a lack of transfer of knowledge acquired in the classroom to the real world (e.g., Bransford et al., 1990). Thus, while students are able to complete the word problems at the end of the chapter in their science textbook, they are unable to use that knowledge to calculate the time it will take them to travel to Grandmother's house at a certain speed and distance. Instruction derived from a constructivist framework must be designed to address issues and be embedded in contexts with which the students are familiar and about which they care. For knowledge to be "effective action", the context of its embodiment must be veridical to the world in which the child finds him/herself.

To be sure, we can manipulate the process of negotiation through which worlds emerge to insure that the school context is a source of "perturbations" to which the child must adapt (to the extent that autopoiesis is conserved). So much of what we ask students to learn is of *our* choosing. They experience little ownership of the ideas, little sense that they are an active participant in their own learning processes. We feel that the students must come to feel some personal sense of responsibility for the products of their thinking, where their views are heard and respected by others in the situation. In other words, students must come to see that the tasks they are performing will help them accomplish the things they want, will empower them to take more complete control over their lives, to know how they know. In essence, we are suggesting that the children become the observers of their own behavior, the judge of the extent to which their knowledge is effective action.

4. Human Learning is Embedded Within Social Coupling

Humans learning is a distinction made by observers of effective action in a particular context. Our commonsense notion that to learn means to internalize some object from the environment is simply wrong. Actions emerge based upon the structural changes brought about by interactions between the autopoietic unity and its environment. The most interesting of these, from the perspective of humans, are social couplings based in language. In a very real sense, human learning is human languaging, the exchange of conversation and dialogue. Even where language is not present in an interaction, its influence is still present in the distinctions and differentiations that are used in the interactions (i.e., in the world brought forth).

The importance of discussion and dialogue for instructional design has been recognized recently with the rediscovery of Vygotsky's (Vygotsky, 1978) views of cognitive development and Freire's (Freire, 1970) pedagogical writings (see Cunningham, in press, for an elaboration of this point). Many of the examples given so far have focused on dialogue as an important pedagogical strategy for constructivist instructional design. This is no accident because dialogue is a major medium for providing experience in the knowledge construction process. While the individual learner is the only one who can construct his or her unique understanding of the world, this understanding emerges in a social context. Concepts take on meaning through a process of social negotiation. The differentiations that a person makes in the world -- mother versus father, democracy versus dictatorship, computer versus teacher, etc. -- arise from the contrast of one thing with another in some sort of social experience. Language is the key to understanding the development of these processes in humans.

While it is possible to "have a conversation" with oneself (and even desirable in some circumstances), dialogue between individuals is the primary mechanism that allows the social construction of meaning. According to Vygotsky, it is the internalization of social speech into inner speech, that is, the ability to engage in a socially appropriate dialogue with oneself, that allows one to plan and monitor cognitive progress. Inner speech, Vygotsky maintains, is developed by participating in social dialogue.

5. Knowing is not Sign Dependent

This particular principle is not explicit in Maturana's writing but we think it is consistent with it, and essential. His emphasis on social coupling through language could lead some to characterize his views as logocentric; that *all* knowing is languaging. Certainly, learning and cognition, and ultimately living, is always embedded within a social context mediated, in part, through language. Language is one of the most powerful means through which humans become structurally coupled to each other, each acting as perturbations for the other. In addition to language, however, human interaction also involves the formation and interpretation of other complex sign systems (e.g., speech, gestures, writing, music, etc.). We use *many* sign systems to socially construct our world (Goolishian & Winderman, 1988), a world in which we come to believe in the objectivity of our observations.

Multiple sign systems should be exploited in terms of what they can contribute to the knowledge construction process (e.g., see Howard Gardner's (1983) discussion of multiple intelligences). Within the computer context, for example, many modes of representation can be captured (e.g., graphics, photographs, animation, video, sound, etc.) and each of these can be assessed in terms of what they can reveal and what they might obscure. In another example, Michael Roth (1990) makes sure that his science students experience multiple ways of representing their experiences while conducting laboratory experiments (e.g., verbal description, equations, pictures and diagrams, demonstrations, tables of numbers, graphs, etc.), all the while encouraging them to point out the strengths and weaknesses of each mode, what is foregrounded in one representation, obscured in another.

The important point to stress here, and the aspect that we think is most compatible with Maturana's views, is that the use of varieties of sign systems can enhance still further our understanding of the constructedness of knowledge, the value of considering multiple perspectives, and so on for each of the other principles listed here. No doubt we become aware of and reflect upon these factors in large part through language. But we must avoid the conclusion that only language can provide the structural social coupling through which we bring forth our world.

6. World Views Can Be Explored and Changed With Tools

This is another principle not explicitly discussed by Maturana but with which we believe he would find sympathy. Writing long before the advent of computers, Vygotsky (1978) defined tools as "mediating" devices that allow humans to manipulate their physical world for the purposes of labor. (It was labor that necessitated the development of tools in the first place.) Thus, "man uses the mechanical, physical, and chemical properties of objects so as to make them act as forces that affect other objects in order to fulfill his personal goals" (Marx, 1936, cited in Vygotsky, 1978, p. 54). Thus, for example, a hammer mediates the achievement of the physical goal of driving a nail into wood.

According to this definition, the object of tool use is always external to the user. Although using a tool certainly affects the user psychologically (for instance, with experience a hammer becomes a transparent extension of the arm), the purpose of tool use is to affect the physical world. On the other hand, that which is used by humans to purposefully affect one psychologically is designated by Vygotsky (1978) as a "sign." For example, when one ties a knot in a handkerchief as reminder to do something, the person has created a sign that is intended to affect the person psychologically, i.e., to remember something.

Sign usage by humans is so ubiquitous that it, like tool usage, quickly becomes transparent. The two year old son of one of the authors (RK) is still aware of the signification of traffic lights: "Green says go, daddy?" In contrast, his four year old son, who has internalized traffic light sign systems simply says, "Go, daddy, the light is green!" The function of the traffic light is to psychologically affect the driver by acting as a perturbation. The driver then, due to structural coupling, is "reminded" of and takes appropriate action -- to go (or to honk if the driver ahead misses the sign!)

According to Vygotsky, the characteristic common to both tool and sign use is their mediating nature. In order to achieve a physical goal, humans use tools to mediate its achievement. (Except for the most rudimentary tasks such as digging in the sand with one's hands[6], all physical goals require the mediating use of tools.) Similarly, signs act as mediators for mental activity, that is, activity that would be nearly impossible (or at least significantly more difficult) without employing signs. Further, the creation and use of sign systems (such as certain computer applications) allow humans to engage in mental activity not otherwise possible (Pea, 1985).

One distinct difference between tools and signs should be highlighted. That is the cause-effect relationship of the mediating device to the intended object. As observers, it is easy to point to the effect that the hammer will have on the nail -- the result is predictable and only depends on the use and observation of the tool, not on the the nail's "knowledge" of the hammer. On the other hand, signs work only if the observer has prior experience and knowledge of the sign system. An Eskimo who has never been to a village would be able to be

[6]It can be argued that even hands can be classified as tools, but that is another story.

perturbed by a traffic light changing color but would have absolutely no idea of what it signifies. In other words, the Eskimo, due to history, is not structurally coupled with that particular sign system. Thus, as Maturana points out, the sign does not instruct the observer; any response is determined entirely by the structure and history of the observer. Whether or not the sign has its intended effect is solely determined by the Eskimo's ability to perceive the sign in conjunction with his prior knowledge of and experience with traffic light sign systems.

Perhaps it was because that, during his time, tools were used almost exclusively for physical labor and signs for mental activity, that Vygotsky was adamant about their distinction. Since the mid-fifties, however, the nature of work (at least in western nations) has shifted from industrial to informational. Even before the launch of Sputnik, the number of white collar jobs outnumbered blue collar jobs in the United States for the first time in history (Naisbitt, 1984). And, since 1984 over half of the US GNP was generated through information/service related jobs. This means that the object of labor is no longer predominantly physical, but rather has shifted toward the various means and purposes of knowledge development.

Because of this qualitative change in labor, its requisite change in the nature of tools, and the ubiquitous use of sign systems, we have broadened Vygotsky's definition of tool to include all mediating devices that can potentially affect both physical and mental activity[7]. The tools we will describe below are of this character.

7. Knowing How We Know is the Ultimate Human Accomplishment

This is perhaps the most important principle of all and has naturally arisen in discussion of previous goals. Providing experience in the knowledge construction process is an important goal, but the outcome we hope will eventually occur is awareness of the constructedness of much of our knowledge and active control over that construction process: To know how we know. In other places (e.g., Cunningham, in press) this has been referred to as the development of reflexivity. There is no higher educational goal.

---

[7] An illustrative example of an existing tool that clearly serves both mental and physical activity is the use of computer-assisted design/computer-assisted manufacturing (CAD/CAM) systems. A designer uses a CAD/CAM system to design, that is, to manipulate three dimensional graphical representations of an object which is to be manufactured. The image is not the object but rather stands for it; thus it is a sign (either an icon or a symbol) of the object. The designer works with this sign system by manipulating it along many dimensions, by making decisions, by considering ramifications, by checking it with specifications, by imagining it in relationship to other components, and so on. In other words the CAD/CAM system allows the designer to engage in creative, complex mental activity which would arguably be impossible without it. At this point no physical object has been created with the tool. The image is simply a particular arrangement of symbols that helps the designer think about the real object. Once the design is complete, however, the designer can use the CAD/CAM system to transform the design into a physical object. The designer "tells" the CAD/CAM system to "read" the image and to create the specified object. The tool has clearly served two purposes: (1) it has allowed the designer to think in new ways about designing; and (2) it has allowed the designer to actually affect the physical world by creating the object.

If reflexivity were to come to serve as a primary goal in our school curricula, the subject matter of each of our courses would be the mind itself. A course in history would emphasize not simply history, but how historians know, the sign structures or systems of belief that historians use in their discipline, and skills and tools used to construct knowledge. What are the potential effects of those beliefs on the historical analyses that are regarded as acceptable? Or take physics. How do our assumptions about the nature of matter influence our experimental methodologies, and vice versa? How do the various forms of representing our knowledge of the universe influence our theories?

One consequence of an emphasis on reflexivity in our courses would be to coalesce the various subject matters, revealing the unity underlying them and rendering their separate treatment ill advised. More classes would be taught by teams of teachers, say a mathematician, a geographer, and a historian. The systems of belief of each of these disciplines could be juxtaposed so that, for example, the logic used to fashion some particular analysis could be examined against the tools provided by another discipline. We could ask questions like the following: Is adding amendments to the U.S. Constitution like adding 3 apples and 2 apples, or can we think about a mathematics problem in which not only the number of elements but their character is represented? What does it mean to count people, as the U.S. Census Bureau currently does? Is our use of mathematics value neutral? Does it have a historical dimension?

One hears quite a lot these days about the development of critical thinking and reflection in students, and we would agree with this emphasis. But we want to stress that reflexivity is not a skill existing independent of the learner that must somehow be transferred inside (e.g., the SQR3 method of reading, the method of loci, etc.). Rather we argue that reflexivity must emerge naturally as a function of all the other principles we have mentioned (experience of constructedness, multiple perspectives, tool use, etc.).

Education and Scientific Knowledge

Before we take account of the above principles with respect to "constructivist tools," we want to pause, for a moment, and consider the function of education. We want to be clear that we regard schools and other educational contexts as an appropriate milieu for learning in our version of constructivism. We agree with Vygotsky (1978), who regarded schooling as the means of helping children develop "scientific" processes and knowledge. Science here refers not only to the narrow, stereotypical view of science as disciplines such as physics, biology, and chemistry, but more generally to the notion of science as conventionally defined systems and processes of knowledge. Scientific knowledge may be contrasted with practical knowledge that a child develops through informal, everyday experience. For example, even without schooling children develop remarkable (practical) proficiency in oral language through their informal interactions with adults and peers. On the other hand, to practice law requires that the lawyer develop understandings and skills in a specifically defined system of oral discourse.

While it can be argued that a lawyer, or anyone else for that matter, can develop proficiency in scientific understanding outside of formal schooling, we believe that this is by far the exception and not the rule for two main reasons. First, we are committed to the notion that learning is inextricably embedded in social settings. Thus, in the case of our budding laywer, in the absence of simulated courtroom practice where the student not only participates in the conventionally defined systems of courtroom debate but also receives analysis from experts and peers, a knowledge of law developed through the study of textbooks alone will most likely be deficient. Second, schooling provides an ideal opportunity for integrating all kinds of learning experiences, both formal and informal, that is simply not possible for the vast majority of learners outside of formal schooling. It is indeed true that many schools do not provide such an idealized integration of learning experiences. However, it is our goal to help redefine currently held metaphors of schooling by suggesting various tools and situations that we believe support the constructivistic nature of learning.

A key point about scientific knowledge must be reiterated: Scientific knowledge is created and defined by observing humans and does not exist independently of people who engage in the scientific process. Maturana (1978, p. 28) states that "... scientists make scientific statements. These statements are validated by the procedure we use to generalize them: the scientific method." At the very outset of this method the "observer specifies a procedure of observation that, in turn, specifies the phenomenon that he or she will attempt to explain" (p. 28). In other words, how an observer "observes" (that is always mediated and never direct) dictates that which is to be explained. Maturana (1978, p. 28) continues:

> ... we are seldom aware that an observation is the realization of a series of operations [i.e., the scientific method] that entail an observer as a system with properties that allow him or her to perform these operations, and, hence, that the properties of the observer, by specifying the operations that he or she can perform, determine the observer's domain of possible observations.

The point is that scientific knowledge is socially defined and determined entirely by the properties of human observers. If we had eyes that were sensitive to infrared electromagnetic radiation or ears that could detect ultrasonic waves, the world we would observe and the scientific knowledge we would use to explain it would be extremely different than our present real world conceptions. "Instructing" students in the processes and knowledge of science, then, amounts to enculturating them into the conventionally held methods of observing the world. It is equally important, however, to help students become aware of their *ways* of observing and how they may create new ones such that they become empowered to re-define scientific knowledge.

Tools to Think With

The extent to which the tools we design actually support the constructivist nature of learning is a function of (1) the affordances for knowledge construction that they provide in terms of the principles described above, and (2) how they are employed by both teachers and learners in the learning environment. For example, hypermedia environments can provide incredible opportunities for learners to engage with complex problems for extended periods of time, a requirement for students to develop rich understandings and to transfer their learning to other domains. On the other hand, hypermedia can also be structured in such a way that it becomes little more than a traditional CAI tutorial, or worse, an electronic page turner. The purpose of this last section is to describe a limited number of tools that we believe afford powerful opportunities for learning when employed thoughtfully.

Of the numerous dimensions of learning environments, we have identified three that can be particularly well supported by tools: (1) information[8]; (2) process; and (3) reflexivity. The first dimension deals with the information that is required to accomplish learning tasks. What we are concerned with here is how the information is structured, that is, what particular sign systems are used to represent the information. In addition to the various media that can be used (audio, video, text, graphics, etc.), alternate forms and organizations of knowledge can be represented. For example, video can present case studies, documentaries, movies, demonstrations, interviews, etc., all of which have their own unique ways of being interpreted by learners. Another aspect of this dimension has to do with access; that is, how rapidly can the particular instances be retrieved and how easy are they to find it? A final aspect deals with how "plastic" these various sign systems are. In other words, can the learner modify the existing structures? Can new structures be created? Can the learner work with the information in any setting (or only in a special laboratory)?

The second dimension, process, concerns the cognitive processes required to engage in the task. That is, in accomplishing a learning task such as reading, are there cognitive actions that the learner can take to make the experience meaningful? Can we help learners develop more effective ways of thinking about and engaging with their worlds? Can we support the development of these processes and increase the probability that they will transfer to new

---

[8]We do not consider information to be synonymous with knowledge; information , in the form of structure energy, resides in the organized environment but does not embody meaning. Knowledge, on the other is constructed via the dynamic structural coupling with information as humans act as autopoietic beings.

domains? Can we explicitly model them in a social setting and then encourage their internalization into individual use?

The third dimension, reflexivity, concerns the ability to consciously be aware of one's own learning, belief systems, actions, and knowledge. We want our learners to be able to step back and take notice of how they are learning and to think critically about their thinking in order to become empowered members of society.

These three dimensions form a framework by which we can classify tools at a gross level. We believe that successful learning environments provide support for the learners along each of these dimensions. Any particular tool used in the learning environment, however, may support only one of these dimensions, support for the other dimensions residing in some other, perhaps more traditional form.

Intermedia

The first tool we will describe is Intermedia, developed at Brown University (e.g., see Yankelovich, Landow,& Heywood, 1987). Intermedia is a hypermedia system that primarily falls within the information dimension described above. It is a tool designed to allow access to large databases containing information represented in three kinds of sign systems: text, graphic, and timeline. What makes Intermedia powerful is the way in which information is accessed: documents are accessed from documents rather than indices or boolean search routines. That is, by clicking on a link marker, a learner can simply follow links from one document to another. The links are established between documents according to the teacher's or student's beliefs about their relationship.

Usually, some kind of a graphic organizer is used as a table of contents to aid in document selection. The learner can use the organizer as a jumping off point to access a particular document, and follow an unspecified path from document to document, or she may return back to the overview to choose new documents. In a hypermedia system such as Intermedia, the learner has complete control over what is seen and how much time is spent on any particular document.

How does Intermedia support the construction of knowledge? The first issue that should be pointed out is that given the amount of control they have over their learning, learners must know how to employ effective cognitive processes. Our study (Knuth, in preparation) of Intermedia users (students in George Landow's course at Brown) is revealing that one particular and widespread cognitive process employed can be characterized as "internalized social speech." That is, think aloud protocols indicate that users engage in arguments with themselves in order to make the learning decisions listed above. They state their beliefs, provide evidence, debate the merit of evidence and how it affects their beliefs, posit conclusions, evaluate conclusions, and finally make the decision.

Although not explicitly supporting this form of cognitive activity, Intermedia requires its use for a successful learning experience. In this particular study it appears that argumentation is modelled socially within the more traditional structure of the classroom. Within his classroom, Landow moderates a dialogue in which argumentation is the social mechanism that allows students to negotiate meaning with each other. It also provides a model for choosing directions in the collaborative learning process. Thus, the structural coupling between students and professor that is supported within the classroom through social engagement is internalized in the Vygotskian sense and allows individuals to engage critically in their own learning process both within the classroom and while using Intermedia.

One of the most obvious affordances of Intermedia is its ability to represent many perspectives on a single issue (i.e., multicausal thinking). For example, when developing an understanding of educational psychology, it would be a disservice to only allow access to or advocate the exclusive use of a single theory or paradigm (see Cunningham, in press, for an elaboration of this example). Intermedia can house a huge store of perspectives not only representing the different theories but also perspectives from many different people. For any given theory, commentary and analyses from theoreticians, researchers, and teachers can be augmented by collections of perspectives from students. The utility of particular theories to provide insights into the solution of realistic or actual problems can then be evaluated

Ultimately, Intermedia affords the opportunity to contribute to the database -- the student can participate in the social construction of knowledge. He has the opportunity to create sign systems within Intermedia to represent and work out his own perspectives on the issues he is toiling with. He has the opportunity to share these reflections and consider those of others by simply linking them together. One of the recurring comments we receive by students who use Intermedia is that they like the idea of the database containing their works in addition to the "experts". What they see is that their writings, although not often as eloquent or deep, have worth for others just as the papers the professors and other established authors do. Credibility and confidence in one's work is an extremely valuable quality to nurture in our students.

Students using Intermedia may also be encouraged to find new relationships between documents in the corpus. The class, then, can debate the merit and usefulness of these relationships and, if they are determined to be appropriate, they are entered into the database. In this way the students have voice not only in contributing their works to the database but also in re-shaping its existing form.

Intermedia comes out of the box as an empty "shell" that is then filled with a database of information and integrated into the teaching/learning situation. Not all of the Intermedia applications that we have seen support the constructivist nature of learning. For example, some databases consist mainly of the professor's lecture notes, acting much like the reserve desk at the library. This is certainly a convenience for the student (and professor), but doesn't take advantage of Intermedia's ability to house many alternate perspectives on the issues at hand. It completely ignores the organizing capability of the timeline and promotes the predominant metaphor of the teacher as the information broker.

In another application, primary works (large research documents) make up the database. Students are required to search the database to find an area to research, and then to pursue it on their own. Students are evaluated on the "publishability" of their research papers. This is certainly a creative use of Intermedia but not terribly constructivist -- students use the database as a source of information but do not use it to actively construct knowledge in the same manner as Landow's students.

RoundTable

If Intermedia supports the access and representation of information in alternate sign systems, RoundTable supports the explicit development of cognitive processes. RoundTable is a "tool set" that we have developed at Indiana University (e.g., see Knuth & Goodrum, 1991) to support the following processes in a social environment: comprehension, idea generation, analysis, composition, reflection, and communication. When engaged in a RoundTable session, all students are networked together allowing each person to see the contributions of all the others. We have designed three social-cognitive tools within RoundTable: Brainstormer, Argument Analyzer, and Papers.

Before describing how RoundTable works and how it supports the constructivist nature of learning, it is important to understand the rationale behind its development. The first issue is that in typical group settings not everyone gets an equal chance to contribute, and hence to construct rich understandings. This is a result of the social dynamics of most ordinary group work. One RoundTable user eloquently described the problems associated with group discussion and how a technology that mediates collaboration can help:

> [...] It [RoundTable] has definitely made me think more critically because sometimes when talking in small groups, it is hard to get your opinion stated either because someone else may say what you wanted to say or your thoughts just get stirred up in your head and you cannot verbally say what you are thinking. It is much easier to write down my thoughts because I can type as I think. I don't have to wait my turn to talk. It is so beneficial to see everyone else's opinions on the subject. It helps to have it right their in front of you because I can always go back and refer to someone else's statement as well as my own [...]

We are certainly not advocating the exclusive use of mediating technology. In fact one goal is to enable all students to collaborate successfully on social tasks *without technology*. In support of this RoundTable is designed to minimize the stifling effects of group interaction at a time when students are learning new ways to think about their worlds.

The second goal for this design was to make cognitive processes explicit in a social setting such that students would be able to internalize and use them individually. Cognitive processes that we want students to develop must necessarily be modelled for students; that is, students must practice them socially, and then individually. Equally important, these cognitive processes must always be embedded within authentic tasks so that the students are using them to construct meaningful knowledge. The goal here is similar to that of cognitive apprenticeship in which experts model a cognitive task and then gradually increase each students' responsibility for doing the task on their own. Our aim is to help each student work within her "zone of proximal development" (Vygotsky, 1978), allowing the student to complete tasks with a group that she could not presently accomplish on her own.

An example of how RoundTable is used is perhaps the best way to illustrate what it is. One of the tasks that RoundTable supports is argument analysis in which students read, for example, a case study in which varying views on testing are played out in a narrative fashion. Each character in the story, (e.g., teacher, principal, parent, etc.) converses and acts with the other character. The task for the students is to identify the conclusions that each character makes and then find the evidence and premises on which they are based. In this way each student can judge the relative merits of each position presented. Ultimately each student will then turn the analysis on himself, uncovering the premises and evidence behind his own conclusions thus making possible the critical taking of positions on important issues.

While at the computer each student enters a statement about the evidence, premise, or conclusion that they have identified for one of the people in the case study. Once entered, the student "publishes" the statement that is immediately displayed on every other computer on the network. It appears in one of three windows (premise, evidence, or conclusion) depending on how it was classified by the writer. At this point, everyone can see what everyone else is writing. This is intended to stimulate new ways of thinking about the issues in the case. Students can comment on any statement that has been made by any person and publish it for all to see. In this way, RoundTable is making one form of social-cognitive process -- argument analysis -- explicit and allowing each person to have an equal opportunity to contribute. More importantly it is promoting the social negotiation of meaning by providing a dialectical forum.

RoundTable also possesses the capability to contain a hypermedia database similar to Intermedia although on a much reduced scale. We have scanned the case studies into this database. Thus, students can publish their statements and then link them to the specific sections within the case study document that supports their statement. While reading a published statement, any reader may simply follow the link to the case study, read the highlighted passage, and then return to the Analyzer, providing an immediate contextual reference for the statement.

Many other features and tools of RoundTable, such as individual and group mail, the BrainStormer, Group Papers, and Individual Papers, merit discussion but are beyond the scope of this paper. However, the point to be made is that RoundTable is designed to explicitly support the social construction of knowledge. It is not a tool for information presentation -- without the active, social use by students, nothing is accomplished.

RoundTable by design engages learners in social action, bringing to the forefront the varying perspectives held by peers and teachers. Thus, it helps learners realize that the truth of an issue is a negotiated matter, that what they know is constructed in relation to other constructed positions held within the group. We are aiming at helping learners explore and change their views of the world; that is, to make visible their tacit beliefs about reality, and ultimately to help each learner form an awareness of their methods of knowing.

Bubble Dialogue

Whereas Intermedia supports the information needs and RoundTable the cognitive processes of a task, Bubble Dialogue (e.g., McMahon, O'Neill & Cunningham 1991) is designed to foster reflexive thinking in our students. Bubble Dialogue, described in detail elsewhere in this volume, is a HyperCard-based technique that combines elements of role play, comic strip creation and reflexive dialogue analysis. Users play out the parts of characters on the screen, creating dialogue in the characters' private domain (their thoughts or 'inner speech') as well as in the public domain (their public speech). A graphic showing two or more characters is presented on the screen along with a prologue that sets the scene. For instance, portraits of Skinner and Piaget could be presented along with a prologue like: "Two of the great figures of psychology meet to discuss their differences." Students then are invited to construct a dialogue between the characters. Clicking on an icon brings up an empty speech or thought bubble for the chosen character, just as in a comic. To accomplish the task, the students must be able to adopt the perspective of the characters, realize the difference between public speech and private thought, and sequence the dialogue in terms of the public speech (since we can't read each other's thoughts), etc. Notes can also be added to the sequence where the students can annotate or provide a running commentary of the dialogue, much as the banner in a comic does. Researchers and teachers can use the notes in a variety of ways: as field notes, commentary, reminders, questions for the students to consider, etc.

Bubble Dialogue is not designed to communicate any particular learning objectives. It is more a tool to think about issues and one's thinking rather than communicate any information directly about them. By inviting students to adopt the perspectives and roles of characters on a computer screen, we are attempting to show them that different people can have different views of a situation and that these views can have a sense or logic independent of their own views. In one of our projects, for example, we have probed children's understanding of computers. Playing the role of one of the characters, we ask questions like "Is the computer like a teacher?" Through their answers, the children reveal the underlying metaphors that guide their thinking about computers. To some children, the computer *is* a teacher, for others, there are important differences between a computer and a teacher. The way we view a situation, therefore, depends heavily upon the metaphors we bring to bear. Bubble Dialogue and other software of this type allows the students to experience this characteristic of their thinking.

Another aspect of our work is revealed most clearly in the project Education for Mutual Understanding (EMU) being carried out within the Northern Ireland context. The pub and soap-box rhetoric about the "Troubles" between Catholics and Protestants in Northern Ireland may come down to a simple lack of appreciation of the different perspectives that each side has. Through the use of Bubble Dialogue, we have been able to foster some cross cultural thinking by having groups within and across each of the communities adopt the perspectives of Catholics and Protestants depicted on a computer screen. Dialogue and negotiation of differences are stressed, rather than an absolute resolution in favor of one group or the other.

In another example, during a group session using the Bubble Dialogue tool, one of the boys in the group became angry when the rest of the group, two girls and a boy, disciplined him for inappropriate behavior. A fight broke out afterwards between the two boys, and although the teacher talked with them afterwards, she asked us to use the Bubble Dialogue tool to find out what had happened. We produced an appropriate graphic, prologue and opener and each of the boys were individually asked to construct a dialogue between the two boys on the screen, who had been given the same names as the two protagonists. The boys were given the choice of playing themselves or the other, with one of us playing the opposing role. Interestingly, the boy who started the fight, chose not to play himself. Yet he showed considerable insight into the feelings of the aggrieved party. The victim likewise showed considerable compassion for his attacker and in the end a new understanding was reached about how to handle such occurrences in the future. All parties seemed pleased with the outcome.

One of the reasons that users find Bubble Dialogue so appealing, we believe, is the experience of seeing their words put into the characters' thoughts and speech. The character is made to say/think what the user believes is important, or the user is asked to describe via the notes procedure what the character is feeling or doing. This kind of active involvement in the

not complicate it and we have a lot of work to do in this regard. It is important to stress once again that these tools are simply devices to assist the structural coupling of autopoietic unities as they bring forth their worlds. Technology can assist this process, but not replace it. Our overall goal is to promote reflexivity throughout the student's autopoiesis, whether technology is available or not.

Finally, we would like to suggest, as Maturana has done, that knowledge of the knowledge construction process entails a strong sense of responsibility for the state of the world in which we find ourselves. If many worlds are possible, then worlds can change. We have within our capability the constant renewal of our world view. Human reflection is the key to understanding and creating anew a world in which we co-exist with others. Assuming we wish to co-exist with these others (Catholics and Protestants in Northern Ireland, African Americans and whites in the U. S., Jews and Arabs in Israel, etc.), then we must come to realize that someone's else's world view, her certainty, is as legitimate as our own. To co-exist, a broader perspective is necessary, one in which both parties cooperate to bring forth a common world where many perspectives are valid. Tools for constructivism can assist this process.

References

Bednar, A. K., Cunningham, D. J., Duffy T. M., & Perry, J. D., (1991). Theory into practice: How do we link? In G. J. Anglin (Ed.), *Instructional technology: Past, present, and future*. Englewood, CO: Libraries Unlimited.

Bereiter, C. (1991). Implications of connectionism for thinking about rules. *Educational Researcher, 20,* 10-16.

Bransford, J., Sherwood, R., Hasselbring, T., Kinzer, C., & Williams, S. (1990). Anchored instruction: Why we need it and how technology can help. In D. Nix & R. Spiro (Eds.), *Cognition, education and multi-media: Explorations in high technology*. Hillsdale, NJ: Lawrence Erlbaum Associates.

Brown, J. S., Collins, A. & Duguid, P. (1989). Situated cognition and the culture of learning. *Educational Researcher, 18,* 32-42.

Cunningham, D. J., Duffy, T. M., & Knuth, R. K., (in press). The textbook of the future. In McKnight, C. (Ed.), *Hypertext: A psychological perspective*. London: Ellis Horwood.

Cunningham, D. J. (in press). Beyond educational psychology: Steps toward an educational semiotic. *Educational Psychology Review*.

Duffy, T. & Jonassen, D. (in press). *Constructivism and the technology of instruction: A conversation.* Hillsdale, N.J.: Lawrence Erlbaum Associates.

Efran, J. & Lukens, M. D. (1985). The world according to Humberto Maturana. *Family Therapy Networker; 9,* 22-25, 27-28, 72-75.

Freire, P. (1970). *The pedagogy of the oppressed.* NY: Herder and Herder.

Goolishian, H. A., & Winderman, L. (1988). Constructivism, autopoiesis and problem determined systems. *Irish Journal of Psychology, 9*, 130-143.

Gardner, H. (1983). *Frames of mind: The theory of multiple intelligences.* NY: Basic Books.

Knuth, R. A. *Embodying the new epistemology: An investigation of Intermedia.* Bloomington, IN: Indiana University (Doctoral dissertation in progress)

Knuth, R. A., & Goodrum, D. A. (1991). *Collaborative process tools: The case of roundtable.* Paper presented at the annual meeting of the American Educational Research Association, Chicago, IL, April, 1991.

Lakoff, G. (1987). *Women, fire, and dangerous things; What categories reveal about the mind.* Chicago: The University of Chicago Press.

Lakoff, G. & Johnson, M. (1980). *Metaphors we live by.* Chicago: The University of Chicago Press.

Leont'ev, A. N. (1981). The problem of activity in psychology. In J. V. Wertsch, (Ed.), *The concept of activity in Soviet psychology.* Armonk, NY: M. E. Sharpe.

Marr, D. (1982). Vision. In N. A., Stillings, M. H. Feinstein, J. L. Garfield, E. L. Rissland, D. A. Rosenbaum, S. E. Weisler, & L. Baker-Ward (Eds.), *Cognitive science: An introduction.* Cambridge, MA: MIT Press.

Maturana, H. R. (1978). Biology of language: The epistemology of reality. In G. A. Miller & E. Lenneberg (Eds.), *Psychology and biology of language and thought: Essays in honor of Eric Lenneberg.* NY: Academic Press.

Maturana, H. R. & Varela, (1987). *The tree of knowledge: The biological roots of human understanding.* Boston: New Science Library.

McMahon, H., O'Neill, B., & Cunningham, D. (1991). Bubble dialogue. *Paper presented at the annual meeting of the American Educational Research Association*, Chicago, April, 1991.

Merrill, M. D. (1991). Constructivism and instructional design. *Educational Technology, 29*, 45-53.

Naisbitt, J. (1984). *Megatrends: Ten new directions transforming our lives.* New York: Warner Books, Inc.

Newell, A. & Simon, H. (1976). Computer science as empirical inquiry: Symbols and search. In J. Haugeland (Ed.), *Mind design.* Cambridge, MA: MIT Press.

O'Neill,B., McMahon, H., & Cunningham, D. J. (1991) *Bubble dialogue as a tool for literacy.* Paper presented at the annual meeting of the American Educational Research Association, Chicago, April, 1991.

Pea, R. (1985). Beyond amplification: Using the computer to reorganize mental functioning. *Educational Psychologist, 20*, 167-182.

Perry, W. (1970). *Forms of intellectual and ethical development in the college years: A scheme.* New York: Holt, Rinehart and Winston.

Roth, W. M. (1990). *Collaboration and constructivism in the science classroom.* Paper presented at the annual meeting of the American Educational Research Association, Boston, April, 1990.

Vygotsky, L. S. (1978). *Mind in society: The development of higher psychological processes.* Cambridge, MA: Harvard University Press

Winn, W. (1989). Towards a rationale and theoretical basis for educational technology. *Educational Technology: Research and Development, 37,* 35-46.

Winograd, T. & Flores, F. (1986). *Understanding computers and cognition.* Norwood, NJ: Ablex Publishing Corporation.

Yankelovich, N., Landow, G., & Heywood, P. (1987). *Designing hypermedia ideabases -- The Intermedia experience.* (IRIS Technical Report 87-4). Providence, RI: Brown University, IRIS.

9 A Constructivist Critique of the Assumptions of Instructional Design

William Winn

University of Washington, Seattle, Washington, USA

Any analysis of constructivism is difficult because there is a great range of ideas and a great variety of theoretical positions whose proponents call "constructivist". The idea that is common to all these flavors of constructivism is that students construct knowledge for themselves. The divergence of opinion among constructivists arises from differences in perception of the instructional implications of this basic tenet. For some, knowledge construction requires little more than the addition of coaching or help systems to traditional instructional strategies. For others who take a more radical position, knowledge construction implies that each of us knows the world in a different way, that there is therefore no shared objective world to teach about, and that consequently instructional analysis and prescription make no difference to what and how students learn. I must also point out that there is great diversity in the opinions and theoretical stances of instructional designers. These range from hard-core behaviorism to a cognitive orientation which, adopting the same tenet of knowledge construction, coincides with the position of "moderate" constructivists, as Merrill (1991) has pointed out. Only at their extremes are the positions of constructivists and instructional designers truly adversarial.

Yet extremism has its uses. It helps clarify fuzzy issues by throwing differences of opinion into sharper relief, and it occasions useful debate (Cunningham, 1991b). This chapter therefore characterizes both constructivism and instructional design in terms that some might find extreme. In much of what follows, constructivism is portrayed as mistrusting claims for the existence of an objective world, and discounting the predictability of human behavior. On the other hand, instructional design is assumed to espouse both objectivism and predictability, and to use theory and tools that embody these very assumptions to analyze, prescribe and assess instruction. Only in the last section of this chapter will a more moderate stance appear, allowing us to identify ways in which instructional design can contribute to the efforts of constructivists.

The Problem

The claims of the more extreme constructivists are disturbing for anyone who believes that it is possible to design instruction that has predictable outcomes. If knowledge is constructed entirely by students, there being no objective reality to teach them, there is nothing that instructional designers (or teachers for that matter) can do to affect student understanding and behavior. Instructional design is based on the assumptions that students react in predictable ways to instruction and that what is taught has some factual, conceptual, rule-based or procedural foundation in the real world. If constructivists are right and these assumptions do not hold, then it is pointless to try to design instruction.

Yet there is evidence that students can learn from "designed" instruction. Students learn from computer-assisted instruction, for example (Kulik, Kulik & Cohen, 1980; Kulik, Kulik & Bangert-Drowns, 1984; Kulik, Bangert & Williams, 1983). And students certainly learn from a variety of other media (Kozma, 1991). The purpose of this chapter is to examine the contradiction that arises when relatively extreme constructivist ideas are compared to the tenets of traditional instructional design. I begin by identifying the assumptions that underlie instructional design (ID). Then I critique these assumptions from a constructivist point of view. As a conclusion, I look at roles for design both within and outside a constructivist framework.

Assumptions of ID

Instructional Principles

Instructional design proceeds from what Reigeluth (1983) has called "instructional principles". A principle makes a statement about the outcomes instruction is intended to attain, the conditions under which it is to occur, and the methods that are to be used to attain the instructional outcomes. Because the purpose of ID is to produce plans for teaching, design principles prescribe which instructional methods to use given information about outcomes and conditions. The designer's job is to find out as much as possible about the outcomes and conditions of instruction and then to select or develop instructional methods that will help students reach the intended outcomes. Collectively, the principles the designer uses form a prescriptive theory of instruction.

Instructional designers use a number of techniques to determine which instructional methods are most likely to be effective. Since a designer's chances of selecting the best methods increase as more is known about the conditions and intended outcomes of instruction, one group of techniques is concerned with the analysis of outcomes and conditions. A second group of techniques matches the results of this analysis to methods in ways set down in prescriptive instructional theory. Finally, ID makes provisions for the empirical evaluation of decisions about methods and the revision of those decisions if selected methods do not work. Instructional design procedures therefore consist of analysis, method selection, and evaluation (see Andrews & Goodson, 1981; Nord, 1971).

The assumptions that underlie instructional analysis, method selection, and evaluation are different though related. I shall examine each in turn.

ID Procedures: Analysis

The instructional designer needs information about the outcomes instruction is intended to attain and the conditions under which it is to occur. Information about outcomes is obtained by means of task or content analysis. These analyses are intended to identify every subtask and every piece of knowledge the student must learn in order to reach the outcome. Information about instructional conditions is obtained mainly from analysis of the students. At the very least, instructional designers need to find out what students already know about a topic (Gagne, Briggs & Wager, 1988). Often, too, they like to know something about students' learning styles, aptitudes, motivation, self-confidence and other relevant factors. Sometimes, other types of instructional conditions need to be analyzed, such as available resources, whether students are present during instruction or learning at a distance, or whether they are learning with a teacher or on their own. Because these conditions have to do primarily with instructional management, they will not be discussed further.

The assumption that underlies task analysis is that a student must master the parts of a task or of a body of knowledge in order to master the whole. Task analysis is therefore largely *reductionistic*. However, constructivists claim that understanding can only come about when each piece of a knowledge domain is considered in its relations to other pieces of knowledge. Knowledge has "emergent properties" that defy analysis.

The assumption that underlies the analysis of students' existing knowledge of a domain is that there is a verifiable correspondence between the way a student understands or does something and the way the designer or teacher understands it or does it. This assumption implies that designers, teachers and students know and do the same things in the same way, requiring a common standard against which to assess the extent of student compliance with what they have been taught. Instructional designers therefore assume there is an *objective reality* that can be described and taught. A major argument made by some constructivists (e.g. Duffy & Jonassen, 1991), however, is that there is no trustworthy objective reality to learn about.

ID Procedures: Method Selection

Instructional research, experience and conventional wisdom provide designers with a great deal of information about which instructional methods to select given various outcomes and conditions. This information is embodied in prescriptive theories, as we have seen. If the designer has obtained reliable information about instructional outcomes and conditions, a good instructional theory will make it easy to determine which method (Gagne, Briggs & Wager, 1988) or model (Merrill, 1983; Reigeluth, 1983; Reigeluth & Curtis, 1987) to use.

Because the prescriptions of an instructional theory have worked in the past, in the classroom or in the laboratory, designers assume that there is a good chance they will work again. Instructional theories that guide the selection of methods are therefore to some extent *deterministic*. Of course, no instructional designer expects that the principles of an instructional theory will work perfectly all the time. Yet designers maintain that there is a good *probability* that they will work (Gagne & Dick, 1983; Reigeluth, 1983). To believe otherwise would be to deny the validity and value of prescriptive instructional theory.

The deterministic flavor of instructional theory implies that human behavior and cognition are to some extent predictable. If a given instructional method reliably produces the same gain in performance or knowledge when it is used under similar conditions, then it is tempting to assume that the change in behavior or knowledge can be predicted with reasonable probability from the method. However, there are arguments and evidence that human behavior is not predictable in this way. If knowledge is constructed by students, and particularly if humans are "structurally closed" (Cunningham, this volume; Maturana & Varela, 1987), then it is not possible to predict how students will behave. Instructional theory then has no predictive power.

ID Procedures: Evaluation

The fact that students' behavior is probabilistic rather than fully determined makes it necessary to verify whether the methods instructional theories prescribe work as predicted in each particular application. Instructional designers have always recommended the iterative testing and revision of instructional prototypes until a pre-determined criterion for student performance has been achieved.

The assumption that underlies the evaluation and revision of instructional prototypes is that the effects of instructional methods are *replicable*, in two senses. First, it is assumed that methods will have similar effects on the same students at different times. When prototypes are re-tested after revision, it is expected that what worked well the first time will still work well. Because "bugs" have been fixed, some of the things that did not work well before will now work and overall performance will improve. Second, it is assumed that once an instructional prototype has been revised until it brings students' knowledge and skill to the intended criterion, the instruction can be "packaged" and used with other students with similar results. The argument that carefully designed instruction is replicable has often been given in support of the use of technology in education (Heinich, 1970, 1984).

The arguments that constructivists make against the replicability of instruction are similar to those made against instructional determinism. (The assumption that well-designed instruction is replicable is little more than a variant of the assumption that human behavior is predictable.) If students construct their own knowledge, it is likely that instruction will have different impacts on the same students at different times and different impacts on different students.

A Constructivist View of the Assumptions of ID

I have said that the more radical constructivists would disagree with the three assumptions underlying ID which I called reductionism, determinism and replicability. I now turn to a more thorough critique of these assumptions.

Reductionism

The reductionism inherent in task and learner analysis is challenged by any evidence or argument that knowing something or knowing how to do something depends on knowing how pieces of knowledge are related or skills articulated. Arguments to this effect can be found in many places. I shall look at three: Arguments from system theory, arguments for "downward causation", and arguments from constructivists themselves.

System theory has been part of instructional technology since the 'sixties (Heinich, 1970; Finn, 1960; Hoban, 1965). The "systems approach" was adopted by instructional developers for large-scale projects whose complexity defied management by conventional means. But because the emphasis was on instructional management rather than on learning, the most important features of system theory were largely neglected with the result that system theory has been misunderstood and misused in instructional design.

System theory was developed by von Bertalanffy (1968) as a series of mathematical models that explain the dynamic interactions among all of the parts of living organisms. It was therefore intended as a way to explain complexity. Its capability for explaining complexity made it attractive to instructional developers, who needed a tool for managing complex educational systems. However, ID is a prescriptive activity. Von Bertalanffy's theory is descriptive. System theory therefore came into education in a role it was not designed to play, namely to prescribe how to develop and manage complex instructional systems. As a result, the systems approach to ID has become little more than a set of procedures for instructional analysis, method selection and evaluation. The essential idea of the description of complexity has been lost. As Davies (1981) would say, ID has become a "systematic" way of making instructional decisions, not a "systemic" way of looking at learning.

Attempts to apply system theory to learning in its original "systemic" sense (Beckwith, 1983; Fosnot, 1984; Winn, 1975) have returned to von Bertalanffy's original ideas, (as well as to similar ideas developed by Piaget [1968]). These authors stress the importance of the dynamic interactions of whole systems of factors focussing, like von Bertalanffy and Piaget, on learning processes that change a student's entire cognitive makeup. There are therefore two implications of this conception of system theory for learning. The first is that it is the *interactions among* the pieces of knowledge and the subskills, not merely their acquisition, that determine what is learned. Task analysis does not identify these relations, except insofar as it indicates the sequence in which knowledge and skills may be taught. The intention of task analysis is to produce sequences or hierarchies of tasks (Dick & Carey, 1985; Gagne, Briggs & Wager, 1988). However, knowledge is not built in neat hierarchies and sequences. The reduction of knowledge and skills to sequences and hierarchies is a gross oversimplification of the knowledge students will construct.

The second implication of system theory for learning is that the interactions among knowledge and skills are *dynamic*. This means that the knowledge and subskills that task analysis describes are not stable. As soon as a student starts to learn a hierarchy or sequence, how the student understands the information changes and the results of the analysis are no longer valid. What a student learns changes what the student knows and what the student still needs to learn. Reductionism ignores the dynamic nature of knowledge while it is being learned.

Downward causation is explained by Popper (1977, pp.14-31) as the opposite of reductionism. As we have seen, reductionism explains events in terms of their separate parts and causes. A reductionist might explain reading comprehension in terms of the comprehension of text structure, the comprehension of text structure in terms of syntax and semantics, semantic and syntactic interpretation in terms of the construction and retrieval of schemata from memory, memory in terms of neural networks, neural networks in terms of cerebral functions, and cerebral functions in terms of the physics and chemistry of brain cells. For the reductionist, events are caused by what happens at a "lower level" in the system. Causation is "upward".

Popper makes the case that many phenomena exhibit the reverse of the upward causation. For example, an animal may well survive the loss of a limb. However, when the animal dies, all of that animal's parts will also die. The death of individual organs and cells is therefore "caused" by the death of the animal. Causation is now "downward".

A second way of looking at this is that many events are "emergent" and defy explanation in terms of their parts. Popper claims that the products of human creativity, such as works of art, cannot be accounted for just by activity at the level of cells and atoms. Koestler (1967) makes a similar argument for the emergent nature of human creativity and of cognition generally.

More recently, empirical evidence has been found for the emergent nature of cognitive events. Pomerantz (1981, 1986) has demonstrated that early perceptual organization relies on the emergent properties of configurations in the visual field. We see triangles, not their separate lines and angles. "Triangleness" is an emergent property of the percept. Research on higher-level cognitive processes has shown that experts solve problems as efficiently and effectively as they do because they have compiled a great deal of information into well-formed schemata, the application of which as wholes is necessary to solve the problem. Expert chess players look at patterns on the chessboard, not at individual pieces (Chase & Simon, 1973). Expert bridge players likewise recognize groups of cards as "chunks" and attend to the distribution of cards among suits (Charness, 1989). Expert magistrates make legal decisions by using patterns of information (Lawrence, 1988).

Whether emergent properties are the result of the complexity of interacting processes in human cognition, as Chaos Theory (Gleick, 1987) might lead us to conclude, or the result of random interactions (Bateson, 1979) is beside the point. What is important is that a lot of what students learn may not be understood in terms of their parts, such as subcomponents in a learning hierarchy.

Constructivists themselves, or course, make similar arguments against reductionism. For example, Spiro (Spiro, Feltovich, Jacobson & Coulson, 1991; Spiro & Jehng, 1990) claims that the construction of advanced knowledge in complex domains cannot be accomplished in a single pass through the material. Knowledge of complex domains requires an understanding of many possible relations among ideas. This requires that any idea must be revisited many times so that a student may understand it in the context of other ideas that have been encountered in the meantime. The material cannot be studied in a linear manner because understanding each piece of knowledge changes the meaning of all other knowledge in the domain. Knowledge acquisition is therefore dynamic rather than static, multidimensional rather than linear, "systemic" rather than "systematic".

Spiro's approach has students construct knowledge by "crisscrossing a landscape" many times and in many ways. (The metaphor is borrowed from Wittgenstein [1953]). The knowledge that each student constructs is not predictable from the individual pieces of information in the landscape. Rather, it emerges from the sum of the encounters and from the relations established by the student within the knowledge domain.

The link among these three arguments against reductionism is that "the whole is greater than the sum of the parts". The thinking, learning, imagining, creating student is a complex system of interacting factors whose behavior cannot be predicted. How the student understands what is learned depends on the entire structure of a knowledge domain not on the isolated pieces within it. The learning process itself is dynamic and complex, requiring non-linear approaches knowledge acquisition.

Determinism

The assumption that human behavior is predictable and that the prescriptions of instructional theory can, to a degree, determine student performance is challenged by any argument or evidence that students do not learn what it was intended that they should learn nor in the manner in which they were intended to learn it. I shall look at a number of examples from research in individual differences, metacognition, plausible reasoning and, again, from constructivism itself. I begin, though, with a relatively trivial point.

Instructional theory is incomplete. There is a lot of human behavior and many areas of knowledge for which instructional principles have not yet been formulated. The effect of instructional methods used to teach this behavior and knowledge is therefore unpredictable.

People learn in idiosyncratic ways. A major difference between determined, physical systems, and social or cognitive "systems" is that the latter are highly heterogeneous. All hydrogen atoms are more or less the same. But common experience tells us that there are a great number of important differences among the ways in which different people think and act. Individual differences that have been considered relevant to instructional design include: Prior achievement (Tobias, 1976), aptitude (Cronbach & Snow, 1977), learning and cognitive style (Dunn & Dunn, 1979), motivation (Keller, 1983), anxiety (Tobias, 1989) and self-efficacy (Schunk, 1984). Variation on these factors creates a great deal of heterogeneity among students that makes it extremely hard to select instructional methods and to predict how each student will behave.

Instructional designers have taken three approaches to individual differences: They have ignored them; they have attempted to develop prescriptive principles to take account of individual differences; they have acknowledged the difficulties individual differences create for the designer and have turned over to students the decision about how they should be taught.

Early, behaviorally-based, instructional theories did not often make prescriptions for instructional methods based on individual differences. At the very best, they required that student's prior knowledge and skill in an area be assessed and form the basis for instructional activities aimed at teaching new knowledge and skills (Gagne, 1985). Different students would receive different types of instruction based on how much they already knew.

The reason for ignoring most individual differences was that not enough was known about how individual differences mediate methods to affect instructional outcomes. Also, there was evidence from experimental research that a greater amount of variance in performance could be accounted for by differences in task and method than by individual differences (Rhetts, 1974). This gave priority to task analysis over learner analysis, and to prescriptions to do with methods rather than with types of student. The "conditions" component of prescriptive principles received little, if any, attention.

The problem with this approach is that individual differences do affect how students learn and how well. And even if students can be made to attain instructional outcomes without attention to individual differences, it is likely that there will be undesirable side-effects. For example, if learning style is neglected, students might still be taught to perform a task. But they may dislike performing it so intensely that it will be difficult to motivate them to learn another task.

The realization that individual differences do affect student performance encouraged instructional designers to take a second approach and develop instructional prescriptions that accounted for relevant individual differences. The problems with this approach were the inordinate number and conditional nature of the prescriptions that would be necessary in a practical theory of individual differences, and the exponential increase in uncertainty of performance for even slight deviations from assessed individual characteristics.

The unmanageable complexity of a prescriptive theory of individual differences is acknowledged by Cronbach & Snow (1977). Ideally, everything about the student that is relevant to the attainment of an instructional outcome should be accounted for in the instructional model. Clearly, this is impossible to achieve. What is more, most studies of the interactions of individual differences and instructional methods, and most prescriptions for methods that ensue from this research, involve just one factor. Few prescriptions distinguish among methods recommended for combinations of even two factors, such as low-verbal motivated, high-verbal motivated, low-verbal unmotivated, and high-verbal unmotivated students. While the number of prescriptions for methods might be manageable with such an approach, so many factors are ignored that the approach is little better than not considering individual differences at all.

Perhaps the impossibility of a useful prescriptive theory of individual differences is best illustrated by an idea from Chaos Theory (Gleick, 1987). The behavior of complex non-linear systems (such as students) is impossible to predict because of "sensitive dependence on initial conditions" (Lorenz, 1979). The idea is that miniscule, even undetected, inaccuracies in the assessment of the state of a system at a particular time are rapidly magnified to such an extent that the system soon begins to behave unpredictably. Given the psychological complexity of students and the relative crudeness of the instruments we use to assess them, any instructional models we develop from our knowledge of individual differences are also sensitively dependent on initial conditions. They cannot therefore predict what students will learn.

The difficulty of the prescription of instructional methods on the basis of individual differences has led some instructional designers to place the selection of methods, to some extent at least, in the hands of students themselves (Merrill, 1975). Learner control over instruction has become a prominent feature of much computer-assisted learning (Merrill, 1988; Tennyson & Park, 1987).

For learner control to work, two conditions must be met. Students must know the extent of their own capabilities. And they must be capable of acting wisely on that knowledge. If students do not know what strategies are available to them, which work best for them, and when it is appropriate to use them, learner control will be exercised arbitrarily with unpredictable results.

One way around this problem has been to use what Tennyson (1981) has called "advisement". If students make inappropriate pedagogical decisions, the system advises them, but does not compel them, to reconsider the decision. Most of the time, students follow the advice. However, the judgement by the system of what is appropriate for the student, and the decision about what advice to give, are open to the problems concerning prediction and prescription that surround any instructional model.

Finally, there is evidence that, given a choice, students will opt for the least effective instructional method. Clark (1982) has suggested that students learn least from the methods they like the most, methods that require them to expend the least amount of effort. However, students learn most when they engage in "effortful elaboration" (Salomon, 1983) of the material they are to learn. It is safe to assume that students will often exercise learner control by selecting the methods they like the most. They will therefore expend the least amount of effort elaborating the material, with the result that they will not learn it well.

In sum, none of the approaches instructional designers have taken to dealing with individual differences has really worked. Ignoring them makes it difficult to prescribe effective methods because a lot of factors that might improve the methods' success are not considered. On the other hand, trying to construct a useable prescriptive theory of individual differences is virtually impossible. Such a theory would also be susceptible to sensitive dependence on initial conditions. Lastly, for students themselves to make decisions about methods requires abilities that they may not have, and may lead to shallow processing. It can therefore be argued that the existence of individual differences makes it virtually impossible to predict student behavior in any way that is useful to the instructional designer.

Metacognition. Metacognitive skills are skills that allow students to monitor how successful they are as they learn something and to change learning strategies if they find they are not succeeding (Brown, Campione & Day, 1981). We saw above that such skills are necessary for the exercise of learner control and that their absence may sometimes be compensated for by advisement. We also saw that learner control is not without its problems. Nonetheless, it is generally acknowledged that it is good for students to have metacognitive skills, and effort is often expended to help students acquire them (Sternberg, 1983).

On the other hand, we need to consider the problems that can arise for the instructional designer as a result of the *presence* of metacognitive skills. Instructional designers assume that if they select a particular instructional method because it is appropriate for the instructional outcomes and conditions, it will be used as prescribed. For example, if a unit of instruction uses mental imagery as an instructional method to teach about maps (see Thorndyke & Stasz,

1980), and if the material includes instructions to students to create a mental image of the map, mentally divide it into quadrants, learn the contents of each quadrant, then put the quadrants together again, it is assumed that superior performance will ensue because students use the imagery strategy. However, this strategy may not work for some students. If these students have metacognitive skill, they will be able to determine that they are not learning the map well. In such cases, it is likely that the students will switch to another method. Once this occurs, the student is not using the method the designer prescribed, nor, more broadly speaking, the instruction the designer designed. No-one can therefore predict what the outcome will be.

In one sense it is paradoxical that developing metacognitive skills should be problematic. However, the paradox ceases when we realize that the intentions of instructional designers and advocates of metacognitive skill are quite different. Instructional designers are by and large attempting to get all students to achieve the same objectives. For that reason, any deviation from prescribed instruction becomes an impediment to learning. The encouragement of metacognitive skill, on the other hand, can lead to diverse approaches to learning. Different approaches can lead to the same outcome. But they can also lead to different outcomes determined in part by student choice. This, of course, is one characteristic of constructivist approaches to learning. Metacognitive ability can help students construct their own understanding of a knowledge domain.

Plausible Reasoning. People do not think logically. They make decisions on the basis of incomplete information, intuition, experience, hunches and guesses. Collins (1978) has called this kind of thinking "plausible reasoning". If we waited for complete information before making a decision, we would never make one because no information is ever complete (Hunt, 1982).

This picture of decision making has been reinforced by more recent research in situated cognition (Brown, Collins & Duguid, 1989; Lave, 1988; Suchman, 1987). This work has shown that people do not solve problems by using the kinds of problem-solving skills they have been formally taught, but by using, sometimes quite arbitrarily, the materials and information that they find in the context in which the problem presents itself. Thus, people try to make a copy machine work by randomly pushing buttons, or calculate the best buy in packaged cheese by hefting it in their hands rather than by calculating the price in cents per pound.

Instructional theories proceed from the assumption that students will solve problems with the same logic that task analysis uses to break them apart. It is assumed that the student will see and learn the same logical structure in a procedure or task hierarchy that the designer does. From the evidence of plausible reasoning and situated cognition, however, this will probably not occur. On the one hand, people do not typically use formal academic logic for solving real-world problems (Streibel, 1989). On the other hand, instructional designers cannot possibly foresee all of the situations in which the knowledge and skills they teach can be applied. Again, the predictability of human behavior comes into question.

Constructivism. As might be expected, the ideas of some constructivists themselves run counter to the determinism assumed to underlie instructional theory. We have already seen, in the work of Spiro and his colleagues, that students can follow unique paths as they crisscross a knowledge domain. Indeed, any instructional system that has hypermedia characteristics permits students to follow a limitless number of different paths through material. Since students have a great deal of choice in such systems, it is impossible (and unnecessary, constructivists would argue) to predict which paths they will take.

If learning does not depend in any predictable way on instructional methods, is there an alternative explanation for how learning occurs? The following account is reasonably consistent with the more extreme constructivist position (see, for example, Cunningham, 1991a, this volume; Bednar, Cunningham, Duffy & Jonassen, 1991). Learning occurs as people build interpretations to account for their experiences. This construction is based on each person's prior experiences. It is not achieved by transferring information into that person's cognitive apparatus from the outside. Learning therefore does not consist of a person constructing and assimilating representations of "real-world" experiences. Indeed, the world is not knowable in any objective sense at all. For this reason, each person constructs a different interpretation of the world which only that person can know. Other chapters in this volume go into constructivists' views of learning in great detail and provide numerous examples.

Cunningham (1991b) acknowledges the influence of Maturana on some constructivists' accounts of learning. A biologist, Maturana (Maturana & Varela, 1987) has provided an account of the actions and development of living organisms and of their cognitive activity. The key to Maturana's position is that the behavior, knowledge and development of an organism are determined by its own individual structure and not by anything in the environment in which it exists -- they are determined phylogenetically. However, an organism is capable of detecting "perturbations" in its environment. The organism reacts to these perturbations, not by taking them into itself, but by adapting to them in terms of what its structure allows it to do. The ontogeny of the organism therefore consists of the history of its adaptation to perturbations, constrained only by the limitations of its structure..

When constructivists apply Maturana's ideas to learning, two reasons emerge for why human behavior and understanding cannot be predicted. First, people's biology simply does not permit them to take in experiences from outside and create representations of them that can be shared by others. People are informationally closed systems, (the argument from phylogeny). Second, the way people construct interpretations depends entirely on their unique, personal adaptations to perturbations, made entirely within the limits of their internal structure (the argument from ontogeny).

We have given a number of arguments against determinism and the predictability of human behavior which undergird prescriptive instructional theory. If these arguments prove to be true, then the reliable selection of instructional methods will turn out to be impossible.

Replicability

Finally, we turn to the instructional designer's assumption that carefully designed instructional systems are replicable. This analysis will be brief, because the arguments have already been made.

First, instructional designers assume that, when they iteratively pilot-test instructional prototypes, bug-free instruction remains bug-free. Re-analysis and selection of different methods to deal with troublesome instructional episodes will lead to an improvement in learner performance. However, if task analysis produces an oversimplified and fragmented description of what the student is to learn, and if the predictions of instructional theory are unreliable, it is very likely that new bugs will occur in what was thought to be bug free, and that the corrections made to earlier instructional models will not necessarily lead to improvements.

Second, instructional designers assume that instruction continues to perform to criteria once it has been developed and tested to meet those criteria. Yet if students work with the instruction who have different abilities, aptitudes and styles from those with whom the instruction was tested, or if they exercise metacognitive ability and opt for strategies other than those prescribed by the designer, if they reason differently about the content from the designer, if, in short, they act as constructivists say they must, then there is no reason why an instructional system should behave effectively in each situation where it is used. The claim that instruction is replicable is therefore open to serious question.

If Students Construct Their Own Knowledge, What is There to Design?

So far, I have identified three assumptions that underlie instructional design as traditionally practiced, and have critiqued them as a more extreme constructivist might. In this concluding section, I suggest some implications for design if the constructivist views I have described are correct. I therefore assume that students construct knowledge for themselves and that attempts to instruct them using prescribed methods have little predictable impact on the knowledge they construct nor on how they construct it. I also assume that there is no reliable reference point external to students and teachers against which to assess objectively what the student has learned.

The Objective World as a Teaching Device

I begin with an argument for doing ID the way it is done now. Although there may be no objectively knowable world, it is sometimes useful for instructors and students to act as if there were. This occurs when students simply want, or simply need, to be taught *how* to do something without having to understand *why* they are doing it. The assumption is that some instructional goals simply require students to perform a task consistently without transferring what they have learned to new tasks or contexts. Salomon and Perkins (1989) have characterized this kind of learning as leading to "low-road" transfer. It is acquired through practice leading to automaticity. It can therefore be readily achieved from instruction built from the kind of behavioral theory (Clark and Voogel, 1985) to which instructional designers traditionally subscribe.

Salomon and Perkins (1989) contrast learning leading to automatic performance with "high-road transfer", which is acquired through mindful (Langer, 1989), effortful (Salomon, 1983) processing leading to abstraction. Salomon and Perkins state that abstraction is necessary so that what students learn can be applied in different contexts. Mindfulness is required so that the relations between the abstract representation and its applications in specific contexts can be "genuinely comprehended, not just learned as a formula" (Salomon and Perkins, 1989, p. 126). My argument is that traditional instructional design is best suited to improving automatic performance. Genuine comprehension requires that students construct their own knowledge in ways that I have argued often lead to unpredictable outcomes that can undermine instructional prescriptions.

Performance without genuine comprehension, thus defined, requires an agreement between student and instructor that defines a standard for the student to attain. The student agrees that the instructor shall determine what is in the student's interest. The instructor agrees to design instruction that will enable the student to attain the agreed-upon standard. Established ID procedures are used to create a set of learning experiences.

This appears to be no different from what happens when instructional designers create training materials. From a constructivist's point of view, however, there are some important differences. First, the student concedes that learning will not lead to genuine comprehension. (It might. But that is an added bonus rather than a guaranteed outcome.) Second, the student agrees to accept the instructional designer's version of reality even if it may not make sense. This means that the student will often behave *as if* comprehension has occurred even if it has not. Third, the instructor concedes the impossibility of ever knowing whether the student has really understood what has been learned. An example will illustrate these points.

Recreational scuba divers learn a number of safety procedures to prevent nitrogen bubbles from forming in their blood. They learn how long they can safely stay in various depths of water and how fast they should ascend to the surface. These safety standards have been developed from years of study of human biology and of the physics and chemistry of gases. They are enshrined in tables relating time to depth of water. The world that the tables describe is assumed to be real and objective. Insofar as the effects of nitrogen are basically the same for all humans and that the effects of individual differences, such as divers' age, weight and fitness, can be factored into calculations based on the tables, the world described by the tables appears to be standard.

Scuba instruction places a great deal of emphasis on learning how to use the tables. Students accept that they will learn to use the tables without necessarily understanding physiology or the theory of gases. They accept that the information in the tables will apply to their own bodies as to everyone else's and that adhering to the tables' prescriptions will save their lives. Instructors accept that students will probably not understand why the tables work, but that they will not suffer as a consequence. Low-road transfer is perfectly acceptable. The relatively low number of injuries and deaths from diving accidents attests to the success of this curriculum and the harmlessness of what students and instructors concede.

Two important points arise from this example. The first concerns the role of the diving tables. If they do not describe an objective world about which students need to construct an abstract representation, they still serve as a useful learning device. Now, however, the outcome of instruction (saving lives) is really little more than a by-product of an essentially automatic performance with that device (using the tables in a "mindless" manner) rather than of genuine comprehension (understanding the amount of residual nitrogen in the blood and its physiological effects). If we generalize from this, we conclude that students and instructors can agree, when it suits them, to pretend that there is a standard objective world. However, the artifacts that this world contains can only lead only to incidental learning. In the case of learning to dive, this is perfectly acceptable.

Second is the problem of assessment. There is no way of knowing whether a student genuinely comprehends something or not. By accepting that comprehension is not the intended outcome of learning, and by agreeing to follow instructional prescriptions even if they do not make sense, the student is playing along with the idea that the diving tables describe an objective, standard world. When the student is asked to demonstrate comprehension, one of three things can therefore happen. The student can pretend to understand by performing in the expected way and make a rote calculation from the tables. The student can perform in the expected way even though the student has constructed an understanding of the tables which dictates a different performance. The student can understand the abstractions behind tables and perform according to that understanding. (This case of genuine comprehension might lead, for example, to students arguing about the accuracy of the tables, or would permit students who have forgotten how to use the tables to recover the procedures from basic principles.) Since the agreed-upon standard of performance is the same in each case, and is external to the student, it is impossible to determine whether the student really understands the tables or just seems to.

I have implied that by agreeing to act as if there were an objective world, students and instructional designers sacrifice the ability to make a distinction between genuine comprehension and seeming to comprehend. In learning to dive, this does not matter. In school it does. Students can seem to understand something for a variety of reasons. They can cheat on tests and assignments. They can tell the teacher what they think the teacher wants to hear, not what they really know. They can memorize material and give it back verbatim. Or they can perform on the basis of the understanding they have constructed. The inability to distinguish among these apparent demonstrations of comprehension often means that students are advanced through the grades, enter college and even graduate school without really understanding what they appear to have learned. The reasons for this are complex, involving weaknesses in our testing technologies, the reluctance to fail students, and the lack of clarity about what students really need to understand in the first place. It remains clear, however, that accepting the semblance of comprehension when genuine comprehension is called for, and imposing a fictive objective standard that conflicts with the world constructed by students, pose enormous ethical problems.

The Negotiation of Meaning

The case of students and instructors expediently agreeing to accept objective standards reminds us of a more fundamental principle: If people did not agree about what concepts mean, no communication would be possible. Obviously, this is not the way the world is. People communicate with each other all the time. Meaning must therefore be shared among people. Deciding what concepts mean becomes a social activity.

The scope of the negotiation of meaning among people, and the permanence of what is agreed upon, varies considerably. Pask (1975) describes learning as a conversation between two participants, the purpose of which is to arrive at "an agreement over an understanding". McMahon & O'Neill (this volume) describe the construction of conversations between pairs, or at most small groups of people. On the other hand, some constructivists (Cunningham, 1991a; Duffy and Bednar, 1991) subscribe to a point of view that common meanings emerge from negotiations in entire societies. (The acknowledged source of this notion is the work of Vygotsky [1978]). In this case, meanings are culturally determined and relatively permanent.

Acceptance of the social nature of understanding opens the way for instructional design. If socially-accepted meanings exist for concepts, then these can be taught explicitly, and instruction to teach them can be developed. The way this is done, and what it implies, are no different from what I described in the previous section. Also, genuine comprehension of such socially-defined concepts can be achieved through Socratic dialogs and apprenticeships. Learning is conceived here to be synonymous with acculturation, and is encouraged through practices no different from those found in societies having no formal system of schooling.

In cases where meaning is negotiated locally, as between a student and a computer program for instance, it is less important that understanding should be shared with the society at large. In such cases, the educational goal may stress the process of making meaning rather than the end of arriving at a particular understanding. Here the designer needs to put effort into facilitating the negotiating process itself and not in guiding the student towards any particular understanding. The next section describes one way in which this might be achieved.

Designing Shells

I turn now to design within a constructivist framework. I begin with the design of systems that contain the environments within which students construct understanding. I confine this discussion to the design of systems that are in some way or other supported by technology. This constraint is consistent with the majority of projects described in this volume.

Zucchermaglia (this volume) makes a distinction between full and empty technologies. Full technologies are those, like intelligent tutoring systems, that contain specific content to be taught to students in ways that have been designed on the basis of instructional principles. They are clearly fraught with all the problems surrounding traditional ID that I discussed above. Empty technologies are those that are not designed with any particular content or instructional method in mind. For example, hypermedia systems of the type described elsewhere in this volume can be used with any information presented in any way. These may be thought of as shells that can contain anything a teacher or student wishes to place in them.

There are several guidelines for the design of shells that will make it easier for students to construct understanding for themselves. These include:

1. Make the shell as flexible as possible so that the student can easily move around inside a knowledge domain. The necessity of constructing relationships and revisiting ideas many times requires complete freedom of movement. The shell should not constrain any action the student wishes to take.
2. Allow students to record where they have been and to retrace their steps. The disadvantage of complete freedom of movement is that it is easy to lose your way (Kerr, 1986). Rather than having the shell itself provide wayfinding aids or impose constraints on where the

student can move to, the shell should allow the student to create them. These might be as simple as "signposts" students can erect as reminders of paths previously traversed, or barriers that prevent the student taking some access routes to particular areas in the domain. Put another way, there must be a means for students to preserve what they construct. Perkins' (1991) "symbol pads" and "construction kits" serve this purpose well.

3. Allow networking. It should be simple for students to share what they have constructed with others. A number of projects described in this volume emphasize the social nature of constructed meaning.

Designing Interfaces

Students interact with shells in a number of ways. These include keyboards, pointing devices, touch screens and, increasingly, speech. The extent to which these devices facilitate or interfere with the construction of knowledge varies with a number of factors, ranging from the reliability of the software to students' familiarity with the devices. To avoid creating interfaces that impede knowledge construction, the designer should:

1. Use the interface device with which the student is most comfortable. It is likely that younger students will be better off with pointing devices than with a keyboard, for example. This guideline also requires the designer to provide a choice of interface devices when the audience is unknown or heterogeneous with respect to its skill and familiarity with devices.
2. Follow the precepts of good screen design. For example, what students see on a computer screen must be legible. The interface must also be consistent so that the same actions always produce the same kinds of result.
3. Make the interface as transparent to the student as possible. The interface is simply a device that allows the student to explore a knowledge domain and to come to understand it. If the student's attention is focussed on the interface itself, then it gets in the way of exploration and knowledge construction. The first two guidelines will go a long way to reducing this problem. However, the ultimate goal should be to get rid of the interface altogether so that the student can interact directly and naturally with the knowledge domain. The technology of Virtual Reality achieves this (Bricken, in press). Students inhabit the world that the computer creates and can interact with it just as they interact with the real world, by moving around, picking things up, pointing. There is in effect no interface at all.

Designing Learning Environments

The design of the learning environments that are put into the shells is not a simple business. Other chapters in this volume give specific guidelines. Here, I offer some more general considerations.

The first thing that has to be established is whether the learning environment is intended to help students develop an understanding of what it contains or of something else. For example, Driver's simulations are intended to help students understand physics. They consist of objects whose behavior directly embodies the rules of physics, interaction with which leads to an understanding of physics. On the other hand, Bubble Dialogue (McMahon & O'Neill, this volume) is not intended to help students understand the nature of dialogue itself. Rather, it allows students to use their imaginations to achieve understanding of virtually any domain they care to dialogue about. In the first example, the learning environment is limited to the domain of physics. In the second, the environment is a highly flexible tool independent of any domain. Any guidelines for the design of learning environments must be sensitive to this distinction.

A second distinction to make is whether the domain is provided for or constructed by the student. The Jasper videodiscs (Cognition and Technology Group at Vanderbilt, this volume) are provided for the student. The contents of a bubble dialogue are created by the students. Design guidelines are easiest to provide for the former. All that can be required when students construct their own learning environments is to have them set a goal and to answer their requests for help.

Finally, the designer must decide to what extent the learning environment is to be governed by rules. Here, a delicate balance must be maintained between imposing structure and helping the student discover structure. In an environment that simulates physics, should a student's interaction with it be constrained by physical laws, or should it allow students to experiment with breaking physical laws? For example, should a violation of the laws of gravity cause a simulated object to crash into the ground? Or should the student be able to turn gravity off to see what it would be like to float in space? Decisions such as these have to be made on pedagogical grounds. Even in a constructivist framework, students still have goals to pursue, some of which may be set by the teacher.

The following guidelines serve to summarize these points. I begin with material produced for, rather than by, students.

1. If the intention is for students to learn about the learning environment itself, the main issue facing the designer is the degree to which the students' interaction with the environment should be governed by rules. If students are expected to understand the domain in particular ways, the rules should eventually be enforced.

2. If the intention is for students to use the learning environment as a means to exercise their imaginations or to solve problems, the rules should not be enforced. This means that the only "correct" outcomes of interaction with the environment are those that satisfy the student.
3. If students are to construct their own learning environments, then they need to decide for themselves how rule-governed those environments shall be. For example, a bubble dialogue might follow a path that is logical and predictable to the students who wrote it, in which case it is "lawful" on their terms. On the other hand, they might decide to write a dialogue replete with non sequiturs or in which they deliberately speak at cross purposes.
4. Requests for suggestions and help should not be refused. Unsolicited help should only be given when students are having difficulties that clearly prevent them from constructing their understanding of the learning environment.

These guidelines are not intended to impose unnecessary constraints on students. They are offered in the belief that learning does need some organization, even if only to give students more freedom. We cannot simply turn students loose and tell them to understand the world. They need guidance in their search for meaning. The remarks in this section are intended to suggest the form that this guidance might take.

References

Andrews, D.H., & Goodson, L.A. (1980). A comparative analysis of models of instructional design. *Journal of Instructional Development, 3* (4), 2-16.

Bateson, G. (1979). *Mind and nature.* New York: Dutton.

Beckwith, D. (1983, January). *The nature of learners as total systems with implications for research and instructional development.* Paper presented at the annual meeting of the Association for Educational Communication and Technology, New Orleans.

Bednar, A.K., Cunningham, D., Duffy, T.M., & Perry, J.D. (1991). Theory into practice: How do we link? In G. Anglin (Ed.), *Instructional Technology: Past, present and future.* Denver, CO: Libraries Unlimited.

Bertalanffy, L. von. (1968). *General system theory.* New York: George Braziller.

Bricken, M. (in press). Virtual worlds: No interface to design. *Cyberspace.*

Brown, A.L., Campione, J.C., & Day, J.D. (1981). Learning to learn: On training students to learn from texts. *Educational Researcher, 10* (2), 14-21.

Brown, J.S., Collins, A., & Duguid, P. (1989). Situated cognition and the culture of learning. *Educational Researcher, 18,* (1), 32-43.

Charness, N. (1989). Expertise in chess and bridge. In D. Klahr & K. Kotovsky (Eds.), *Complex information processing: The impact of Herbert A. Simon.* Hillsdale, NJ: Lawrence Erlbaum Associates.

Chase, W.G., & Simon, H.A. (1973). The mind's eye in chess. In W.G. Chase (Ed.), *Visual information processing*. New York: Academic Press.

Clark, R.E. (1982). Antagonism between achievement and enjoyment in ATI studies. *Educational Psychologist, 17*, 92-101.

Clark, R.E., & Voogel, A. (1985). Transfer of training principles for instructional design. *Educational Communication and Technology Journal, 33*, 113-125.

Collins, A. (1978). *Studies in plausible reasoning: Final report, October 1976 to February 1978. Vol. 1: Human plausible reasoning.* Cambridge MA: Bolt Beranek and Newman, BBN Report No. 3810.

Cronbach, L.J., & Snow, R.E. (1977). *Aptitudes and instructional methods.* New York: Irvington.

Cunningham, D.J. (1991a). Assessing constructions and constructing assessments: A dialogue. *Educational technology, 31* (5), 13-17.

Cunningham, D.J. (1991b). In defense of extremism. *Educational Technology, 21* (9), 26-27.

Davies, I.K. (1981). Instructional development as art: One of the three faces of ID. *Performance and Instruction, 20* (7), 4-7.

Dick, W., & Carey, L. (1985). *The systematic design of instruction* (second edition). Glenview, IL: Scott Foresman.

Duffy, T.M., & Bednar, A.K. (1991). Attempting to come to grips with alternative perspectives. *Educational Technology, 31* (9), 12-15.

Duffy, T.M., & Jonassen, D.H. (1991). Constructivism: New implications for instructional technology? *Educational Technology, 31* (5), 7-12.

Dunn, R.S., & Dunn, K.J. (1979). Learning styles/teaching styles: Should they, can they be matched? *Educational Leadership, 1*, 238-244.

Finn, J.D. (1960). Technology and the instructional process. *AV Communication Review, 8*, 5-26.

Fosnot, C.T. (1984). Media and technology in education: A constructivist view. *Educational Communication and Technology Journal, 32*, 195-205.

Gagne, R.M. (1985). *The conditions of learning*. (Fourth edition). New York: Holt, Rinehart and Winston.

Gagne, R.M., Briggs, L., & Wager, W. (1988). *Principles of instructional design* (third edition). New York: Holt, Rinehart & Winston.

Gagne, R.M., & Dick, W. (1983). Instructional psychology. *Annual Review of Psychology, 34*, 261-295.

Gleick, J. (1987). *Chaos: Making a new science.* New York: Viking.

Heinich, R. (1970). *Technology and the management of instruction.* Washington DC: Association for Educational Communication and Technology.

Heinich, R. (1984). The proper study of educational technology. *Educational Communication and Technology Journal, 32*, 67-87.

Hoban, C.F. (1965). From theory to policy decisions. *AV Communication Review, 13*, 121-139.

Hunt, M. (1982). *The universe within.* Brighton: Harvester Press.

Keller, J.M. (1983). Motivational design of instruction. In C.M. Reigeluth (Ed.), *Instructional design theories and models*. Hillsdale NJ: Lawrence Erlbaum Associates.

Kerr, S.T. (1986). Transition from page to screen. In S. Lambert & S. Ropiquet (Eds.), *CD ROM The new papyrus*. Redmond, WA: Microsoft Press.

Koestler, A. (1967). *The ghost in the machine*. New York: Macmillan.

Kozma, R.B. (1991). Learning with media. *Review of Educational Research, 61*, 179-211.

Kulik, J., Kulik, C., & Cohen, P. (1980). Instructional technology and college teaching. *Teaching of Psychology, 7*, 199-205.

Kulik, C., Kulik, J., & Bangert-Drowns, R. (1984). *Effects of computer-based education on elementary school pupils*. Paper presented at the annual meeting of the American Educational Research Association, New Orleans, LA.

Kulik, J., Bangert, R., & Williams, G. (1983). Effects of computer-based teaching on secondary school students. *Journal of Educational Psychology, 75*, 19-26.

Langer, E.J. (1989). *Mindfulness*. Reading, MA: Addision-Wesley.

Lave, J. (1988). *Cognition in practice*. New York: Cambridge University Press.

Lawrence, J.A. (1988). Experts on the bench: Modeling magistrates' judicial reasoning. In M.T. Chi, R. Glaser, & M.J. Farr (Eds.), *The nature of expertise*. Hillsdale, NJ: Lawrence Erlbaum Associates.

Lorenz, E.N. (1979, December). *Predictability: Does the flap of a butterfly's wing in Brazil set off a tornado in Texas?* Paper presented at the annual meeting of the American Association for the Advancement of Science, Washington DC.

Maturana, H., & Varela, F. (1987). *The tree of knowledge*. Boston: New Science Library.

Merrill, M.D. (1975). Comprehensive statement of a systematic analytical approach. *AV Communication Review, 23*, 446-449.

Merrill, M.D. (1983). Component display theory. In C.M. Reigeluth (Ed.), *Instructional design theories and models*. Hillsdale, NJ: Lawrence Erlbaum Associates.

Merrill, M.D. (1988). Applying component display theory to the design of courseware. In D. Jonassen (Ed.), *Instructional designs for microcomputer courseware*. Hillsdale, NJ: Lawrence Erlbaum Associates.

Merrill, M.D. (1991). Constructivism and instructional design. *Educational Technology, 21* (5), 45-53.

Nord, J.R. (1971). A search for meaning. *Audiovisual Instruction, 12*, 11-17.

Pask, G. (1975). *Coversation, cognition and learning*. Amsterdam: Elsevier.

Perkins, D. (1991). Technology meets constructivism: Do they make a marriage? *Educational Technology, 35* (5), 18-23.

Piaget, J. (1968). The role of the concept of equilibrium. In D. Elkind (Ed.), *Six psychological studies by Jean Piaget*, New York: Vintage Books.

Pomerantz, J.R. (1981). Perceptual organization in information processing. In M. Kubovy & J.R. Pomerantz (Eds.), *Perceptual organization*. Hillsdale NJ: Lawrence Erlbaum Associates.

Pomerantz, J.R. (1986). Visual form perception: An overview. In E.C. Schwab & H.C. Nusbaum (Eds.), *Pattern recognition by humans and machines. Volume 2, Visual perception.* New York: Academic Press.

Popper, K. (1977). Materialism transcends itself. In K. Popper & J. Eccles (Eds.), *The self and its brain.* New York: Springer.

Rhetts, J.E. (1974). Task, learner and treatment variables in instructional design. *Journal of Educational Psychology, 66,* 339-347.

Reigeluth, C.M. (1983). Instructional design: What is it and why is it? In C.M. Reigeluth (Ed.), *Instructional design theories and models.* Hillsdale, NJ: Lawrence Erlbaum Associates.

Reigeluth, C.M., & Curtis, R.V. (1987). Learning situations and instructional models. In R.M. Gagne (Ed.), *Instructional technology: Foundations.* Hillsdale NJ: Lawrence Erlbaum Associates.

Salomon, G. (1983). The differential investment of mental effort in different sources of learning material. *Educational Psychologist, 18,* 42-50.

Salomon, G., & Perkins, D.N. (1989). Rocky roads to transfer: Rethinking mechanisms of a neglected phenomenon. *Educational Psychologist, 24,* 113-142.

Schunk, D.H. (1984). Self-efficacy perspective on achievement behavior. *Educational Psychologist, 19,* 48-58.

Spiro, R.J., Feltovich, P.L., Jacobson, M.J., & Coulson, R.L. (1991). Cognitive flexibility, constructivism and hypertext: Random access instruction for advanced knowledge acquisition in ill-structured domains. *Educational Technology, 35* (5), 24-33.

Spiro, R.J., & Jehng, J.C. (1990). Cognitive flexibility and hypertext: Theory and technology for the multidimensional traversal of complex subject matter. In D. Nix & R.J. Spiro (Eds.), *Cognition, education and multimedia: Exploring ideas in high technology.* Hillsdale, NJ: Lawrence Erlbaum Associates.

Sternberg, R.J. (1983). Criteria for intellectual skills training. *Educational Researcher, 12* (2), 6-12.

Streibel, M.J. (1989, February). *Instructional plans and situated learning: The challenge of Suchman's theory of situated action for instructional designers and instructional systems.* Paper presented at the annual meeting of the Association for Educational Communication and Technology, Anaheim, CA.

Suchman, L. (1987). *Plans and situated actions: The problem of human/machine communication.* New York: Cambridge University Press.

Tennyson, R.D. (1981). Use of adaptive information for advisement in learning concepts and rules using computer-assisted instruction. *American Educational Research Journal, 4,* 425-438.

Tennyson, R.D., & Park, O.C. (1987). Artificial intelligence and computer-based learning. In R.M. Gagne (Ed.), *Instructional technology: Foundations.* Hillsdale, NJ: Lawrence Erlbaum Associates.

Thorndyke, P.W., & Stasz, C. (1980). Individual differences in procedures for knowledge acquisition from maps. *Cognitive Psychology, 12,* 137-175.

Tobias, S. (1976). Achievement treatment interactions. *Review of Educational Research, 46,* 61-74.

Tobias, S. (1989). Another look at research on the adaptation of instruction to student characteristics. *Educational Psychologist, 24,* 213-227.

Vygotsky, L. (1978). *Mind and society*. Cambridge, MA: Harvard University Press.

Winn, W.D. (1975). An Open System Model of Learning. *AV Communication Review, 23*, 5-33.

Wittgenstein, L. (1953). *Philosophical investigations*. New York: Macmillan.

10 Transitions in the Theoretical Foundation of Instructional Design

Joost Lowyck and Jan Elen
Catholic University Leuven, Leuven, Belgium

In the literature, it is generally agreed upon that the roots and theoretical base of Instructional Design (I.D.) can be found in behaviorism (see Andrews & Goodson, 1981; Case & Bereiter, 1984; Merrill, Kowallis & Wilson, 1981; Jonassen, 1990; Spencer, 1988). I.D. originates from the endeavors of behavioristic learning psychologists, like Skinner (1954) and Pressey (1960) to make instruction more controllable, efficient and effective by applying behavioristic learning principles. In addition, for the construction of particular I.D. models, derivates and aspects of General System Theory (Jonassen, 1984) were added to basic learning principles.

For more than twenty years now, learning psychology has shifted from a behavioristic view toward a cognitive perspective (Greer & Verschaffel, 1990). It took several years before I.D., as an applied discipline, recognized the need for seriously considering this shift both in theory and practice (Jonassen, 1990). Though cognitive oriented theories aroused the awareness that the content of I.D. models had to be changed, experienced deficiencies in the applicability and scope of traditional I.D. models have been equally important (Lowyck, 1988). Merrill, Li, and Jones (1990) for instance, identified some limitations of the 'first generation of instructional design'. These limitations pertain to all aspects of instructional design (theoretical background, scope, characteristics of prescriptions, and instructional developmental process), and can be briefly summarized as follows:

- Limited attention for integrated wholes in content analysis, course organization and teaching (see Gagne & Merrill, 1989).
- Limited prescriptions for knowledge acquisition.
- I.D. theories are closed and inflexible systems.
- Instructional development remains separated from instructional design (see Winn, 1987).
- Instruction prescribed is often passive rather than interactive, it primarily focuses on presentation variables (see Jonassen, 1990; Reigeluth, 1989).
- Instructional design is labor intensive.

In this contribution, an attempt is made to review endeavors to integrate cognitive research outcomes in I.D. by categorizing the different positions taken (Section one). It will further be shown that taking the cognitive shift in learning psychology seriously, implies the reconceptualization of I.D. How I.D. is affected by the cognitive shift is illustrated by pinpointing the transition points in I.D. models and investigating the importance of the cognitive skills of instructional designers (Section two).

A Cognitive Perspective Toward Instructional Design

In order to categorize the different positions taken toward the integration of cognitive research outcomes into instructional design, a distinction is made between three (not completely independent) dimensions (see Figure 1):

1. Instructional design is a prescriptive discipline (see Reigeluth, 1983; Landa, 1983; Bonner, 1988; Merrill, 1971; Lowyck & Elen, 1990). Both theoretical and empirical research outcomes are translated into if-then-rules, instruments and/or procedures enabling practitioners to make more deliberate and theoretically sound decisions. The transition from description to prescription, however, is conceived by various authors to be a problematic one. Bonner (1988), for instance, argued that learning psychology and instructional design aim at answering different questions. And even the answers provided by one discipline do not necessarily offer valuable insights to the other (see Merrill, 1971).

   The degree to which, implicitly or explicitly, the transition from description to prescription is recognized to be problematic, constitutes the first dimension.

2. Cognitive psychology, though unified by its acceptance of the importance of mental activities (e.g. Calfee, 1984), nevertheless encompasses a broad range of theoretical 'schools', which hold divergent views on concrete cognitive processes and structures involved in learning, as well as different assumptions about the relative importance of these processes and structures (for a discussion in mathematics, see Cobb, 1990).

   With respect to the integration of cognitive outcomes into instructional design, Bednar, et al. (in press) stress the importance of the epistemological nature of the specific cognitive theories upon which I.D. models are based. Roughly speaking, cognitive theories can be positioned on a continuum. Strong constructivist theories view learning as an essentially cognitive activity which is completely and deliberately initiated and monitored by the learner him/herself. It rests upon the epistemological assumption that knowledge is not tied to external reality, but based upon personal experiences of the individual (Jonassen, 1990).

   Mild constructivists argue that, though self-regulated learning might be an ideal, most learning involves the interaction between internal (cognitive) and external (e.g. instructional materials) monitoring and that learning processes can be initiated both internally and externally. Theories which are weakly constructivist, assume cognitive activities and processes to be essentially mediating variables. The learning process itself results from and is monitored by external stimuli. Weak constructivist theories rest upon an objectivist epistemology.

It is clear that the peculiar cognitive perspective toward learning determines the role and impact of instructional interventions as well as the scope and content of instructional design (see Winn, 1990).

3. As already mentioned, I.D. belongs to a strong behavioristic tradition. Most of the I.D. models aim at controlling specific learning outcomes by offering guidelines that enhance the probability that (particular kinds of) learning outcomes will appear. An essential feature of I.D. models, therefore, is their controlling, rather than enabling nature. In most cognitive theories, and especially in the more constructivist ones, the importance of self-regulation and learner activity is stressed (Shuell, 1986, 1988).

   A final dimension on which the various positions differ refers to the compatibility of cognitive theory with instructional design. The question is raised whether I.D. is not in itself an a cognitive discipline. A negative answer to this question enables the simple integration of cognitive findings in existing I.D. models, whereas a positive answer urges for the construction of cognitive instructional design models (C.I.D. models) outside the traditional I.D. framework.

Transition from Description to Prescription

problematic--not problematic

Constructivism

strong---------------------------------------mild---------------------------------------weak

Compatibility Cognitive Psychology - Instructional Design

problematic--not problematic

Figure 1: Three dimensions on which I.D. models might differ

Given these three dimensions, at least twelve different positions toward the relationship between cognitive psychology and instructional design could be distinguished. As previously mentioned, however, the three dimensions are not completely independent. In the remainder of this section an exhaustive discussion of all possible different positions will not be offered. Five positions will be discussed in order to exemplify the complexity of the problem and to clarify the distinctions made.

First Position: Translation

A first and perhaps mainstream position is taken by those researchers who directly translate descriptive research findings into prescriptions. Within this position, it is, either explicitly or implicitly, assumed that both descriptions can be easily transformed into prescriptions and cognitive research outcomes incorporated into instructional design. Some researchers acknowledge the importance of cognitive research for instructional design, and formulate 'cognitive instructional design' prescriptions within the traditional I.D. framework.

Researchers within this position who have a weak constructivist position toward learning, seem to assume that cognitive research offers more precise information and enhances understanding of cognitive processes or structures, as mediating variables. The outcomes of cognitive research, within this position, enable a precise control of the learning process. They are applied in order to make instruction more effective and/or efficient. The integration of new elements from the descriptive knowledge base into I.D. occurs by adding new parameters to existing I.D. models, replacing parameters, subsuming parameters, and adding or replacing design and analysis instruments.

Posner (1978), for instance, illustrates the necessity and applicability of the analysis of both cognitive and content structure for design purposes. Taking a similar position, Wildman (1981) elaborates upon the consequences of the information-processing approach to instructional design (see Wildman & Burton, 1981; Gallini & Fisk, 1986). Though cognitive research outcomes are applied in all these efforts, the basic I.D. framework, and especially the rigid steps in the developmental process, remain unquestioned.

Second Position: Adaptation

A second position is mostly taken by mild constructivists. They accept that learning processes require mental activity and active monitoring by the learner (e.g . Resnick, 1983). Cognitive processes and structures are not solely mediating variables but independent variables as well. Crucial, in this position, is the need for external control of learning processes. The outcomes of cognitive research are taken for granted and are directly translated into practical advice. Learning is viewed to be a problem-solving process that can be learned. In this position, it is implicitly accepted that the transition from description to prescription is not problematic. The prescriptions offered, however, are generally vague and encompassing. They are integrated in the traditional I.D.-framework. It is therefore accepted that learning goals are externally defined and that the usual I.D. developmental process is a suitable one. Within this position, Tennyson & Rasch (1988) propose:

> an instructional design model that integrates cognitive learning theories and instructional prescriptions to achieve an effective learning environment that improves both knowledge acquisition and employment (p. 369).

They argue that time allocation is the most crucial factor in instruction and propose that 70% of it would be devoted to the acquisition of higher-order thinking skills and processes instead of to the acquisition of declarative and procedural knowledge. A similar position is taken by Resnick (1983). She argues that a constructivist intervention theory should address all the traditional concerns of instructional design, like instructional representations and interventions that build upon previous knowledge and practice in learning. (see Schmitt & Newby,1986 for an example on the integration of metacognition in I.D.).

Third Position: Separation

From a mild constructivist perspective toward learning, the third position argues that there might occur strong transition problems due to the number of variables to be taken into account by fundamental and applied disciplines, or the divergence in the research questions within both categories of disciplines.

Descriptive sciences, like cognitive psychology, aim at solving problems different from prescriptive disciplines, like instructional design. A mere translation of descriptions into prescriptions is hardly possible (Clark, 1989; Landa, 1983). Cognitive psychology and instructional design each view learning from very distinct perspectives (e.g. Bonner, 1988). Whereas cognitive theory intends to describe how learning occurs and to identify the learning variables, instructional design examines conditions which influence effective and efficient learning (see Reigeluth, 1983).

Fourth Position: Reconceptualization

A fourth position holds an equally mild constructivist position towards learning. It is accepted that learning is an active process, but also that instruction influences learning by setting goals and monitoring the process. The position also recognizes that the transition from description to prescription is a problematic one. The observation that a phenomenon 'is', does not imply it's necessity. Cognitive research outcomes are seen as offering parameters to consider in facilitating, generating and monitoring learning processes. In contrast to the third position, however, the incompatibility between cognitive outcomes and the behavioristic background of the I.D. framework is focussed upon in this position.

The incorporation of cognitive research outcomes into instructional design is hardly possible due to both the description-prescription problem and the behavioristic nature of instructional design itself (Clark, 1989; Winn, 1989; Lowyck & Elen, 1990). The parameters, procedures and processes in traditional I.D. are so deeply influenced by its behavioristic background that an integration of cognitive outcomes seems impossible. A basic assumption of this position is that cognitive theory conceives the student to be an active member in the instructional process with idiosyncratic reactions toward stimuli (Shuell,1986;1988), while instructional design heavily depends upon the assumption that student's reactions can be anticipated and controlled. Cognitive psychology and instructional design differ in their research questions and, most importantly, in their perception of the learning process. Not an integration but a complete reconceptualization of I.D. is needed, which implies (1) selection of cognitive design parameters, (2) construction of a suitable developmental process and (3) adequate instrumentation of the selected parameters.

To our knowledge this position, until now, did not offer real I.D. models. Rather new kinds of instruction were constructed or empirically investigated in order to discover the fundamental characteristics or parameters of so-called 'powerful learning environments'. There are ample examples of this position in various fields, like process-oriented instruction (Vermunt, 1989), mathematics (Palincsar & Brown, 1984) and cognitive apprenticeship (Collins, Brown & Newman, 1989). The outcomes of these research endeavors suggest some general characteristics of how a cognitive oriented instruction should look:

- The activity of the learner is stressed (e.g. Di Vesta & Rieber, 1987; Shuell, 1986; 1988).
- Construction rather than instruction seems to be important (e.g. Reigeluth, 1989).
- The delivery of information should continuously be tuned to the audience, the learners, and consequently interactivity or dialogue seems to be of major importance (Winn, 1989; 1990).
- Cognitive, metacognitive, motivational, social and cultural processes should be addressed.

Fifth Position: Revolutionary

Recently a fifth position has been taken. This position holds a strong constructivist perspective towards learning. It is argued that learning in itself is indeterministic and, therefore, unpredictable (Cziko, 1989). This position stresses the epistemological and ethical problems in the traditional controlling nature of I.D. Closely related to this position, is the perception of learning as a situated process. Learning, in this view, implies continuous negotiation of meaning in social interaction within specific contexts. It is not, as traditionally perceived, pre-existing and exclusively subject to coding, transmission, and decoding processes.

Within this position, Streibel (1989) argues that cognitive research and I.D. are completely incompatible. Rather than teach, resources should be made available to aid learners in negotiating and constructing meaning. The epistemological shift in the perspective towards learning induces the view that:

> Learning is no longer a matter of indigesting externally-defined, decontextualized objects, but a matter of developing context-bound practices. (Streibel, 198 9, p. 22)

It is concluded that I.D. should limit its endeavors to the construction of instructional systems that help learners to develop their self-teaching skills and to offer learning environments to be used by learners as resources.

Summary

Table 1 summarizes the positions discussed. It should be noted, however, that the positions are not mutually exclusive. The relationship between cognitive psychology and instructional design is a fairly complex one.

Position	Transition description prescription problematic		Constructivism			Compatibility cognitive psychology I.D. problematic	
	Yes	No	Strong	Mild	Weak	Yes	No
1		x			x		x
2		x		x			x
3	x			x			x
4	x			x		x	
5	x		x			x	

Table 1: Five positions toward the relation between cognitive psychology and instructional design situated along three dimensions.

It seems that there is an historical evolution in these positions from not problematic to highly problematic due to the growing awareness of the epistemological issues involved. It is recognized now, even by authors who earlier took different positions, that learners are active beings and that rather than having to control the entire learning process, instructional design should foster their learning capabilities. The evolution towards a strong constructivist perspective on learning leads, based on epistemological grounds accepted in the fifth position, to the proclamation of the death of I.D. as its inherently controlling nature interferes with and deteriorates the learning process.

In our research, we start from the assumption that designing instruction does not necessarily imply a complete control of the learning process. From the moment that it is accepted that there should be something like 'instruction', instruction has to be designed. This might imply a certain amount of control. It is the task of I.D. to indicate how this can happen and how the outcomes of fundamental research can be applied to practice. Both context-boundedness and historical situatedness do indeed constrain the degrees of freedom in the personal construction of meaning. It seems to us, therefore, that the fourth position offers a promising approach to the issues involved in I.D. This position, conceiving learning as an active and constructive process, acknowledges; (1) the deficiencies of traditional I.D., (2) the difficulties of translating descriptive research outcomes into design prescriptions, and (3) the problematic nature of the relationship between cognitive psychology and instructional design. It urges, therefore, a reconceptualization and not only an adaptation of I.D. models.

Consequences of a Theoretical Shift in Instructional Design

Since the fourth position offers a challenging approach toward I.D., its reconceptualization of I.D. is elaborated upon in this section. First, a definition of I.D. is offered which sets the limits and enables a more precise specification of the characteristics of I.D. As the reconceptualization of I.D. models pertains to all aspects of such models, the structural components of instructional design models are identified. Finally, necessary transitions within and between the components are discussed.

Instructional Design Defined

In our view, instructional design is a discipline that links descriptive research outcomes with instructional practice by: (1) identifying design parameters, (2) instrumenting these parameters and (3) prescribing processes for instructional development in order to optimize learning and instruction.

This definition leads to the specification of the following characteristics of instructional design:

- It is a theory based discipline. The aim of I.D. is not only to offer 'procedures that work', but equally to understand why they work in given circumstances (see Briggs, 1982; Clark, 1990a; Bednar, et al., 1992).
- I.D. is prescription oriented, which implies that theory-based and empirically validated rules, procedures and/or instruments are built which enable more deliberate decision-making in concrete design situations (Shuell, 1982; Glaser, 1971; 1976).
- I.D. is an applied discipline. It does not focus on fundamental cognitive or instructional processes but on the applicability in concrete situations of outcomes from basic research.

Research within I.D. therefore encompasses two essential features. It is replicative and synthetical (Elen & Lowyck, 1989). It is replicative because the generalizibility of particular theories and outcomes over specific situations is investigated. It is synthetical because specific theories and disciplines offer detailed explanations of limited aspects of the learning and instructional process, while instructional design takes into consideration all aspects of the learning and instructional process.

Structural Components of I.D. Models

Clark (1990a) argued that there are too many I.D. models which only differ on minor features. There remains a difficulty, however, in identifying those features. There is a need for an overall framework by means of which I.D. models can be compared (Gropper, 1983). This is especially useful when reconceptualizing I.D. Such an overall framework does indeed offer the basic elements of I.D. models and facilitate the construction of new ones. An in-depth study of I.D. models would then enable us to identify those aspects that belong to C.I.D. models.

In our research we assume I.D. models differ from each other in their answers to the following five questions:

1. What is the descriptive knowledge base of the I.D model? This question addresses the theoretical background of the I.D. model. An exhaustive presentation of the descriptive knowledge base implies that all research fields and specific theories are enumerated.
2. What is the referent system of the model? Each I.D. model contains a specific referent system which defines the ecological scope (external validity) of the model. Elements of its specification are: level of instruction, types of goals, kinds of instructional materials, and characteristics of the target group. It is assumed that an I.D. model always has a restricted scope. The prescriptions pertain, for instance, to working adults with the capability to specify their learning goals and to monitor their learning process. Such prescriptions will clearly differ from those offered by an I.D. model for disabled six year-old children. Similar arguments can be made for the kind of instructional materials that are used. Prescriptions for designing printed self-study packages differ from those for designing interactive compact disc instruction, classroom teaching or broadcast television.
3. What parameters are taken into account by the model? The parameters of an I .D. model constitute the theoretical core of each model. In most cases parameters on the learning side are distinguished from parameters on the instruction side. Learning parameters identify the learner variables, whereas instructional parameters indicate what aspects of the instructional environment need to be changed in order to optimize the learning process.
4. How are these parameters instrumented, e.g. what are the concrete prescriptions offered by the model? As mentioned above, I.D. models offer prescriptions in the format of rules or

procedures. These prescriptions enable instructional designers to implement the parameters while designing instruction. The parameters selected for incorporation in the model or theory reflect the theoretical orientation of both the research fields and the referent system.

5. What developmental steps or tasks are identified? Traditionally, the developmental process often forms the core of I.D. model (Andrews & Goodson, 1981). It is argued here that, though being an integral part of any I.D. model, the developmental process is only part of it. The function of the developmental process offered by the model is to guarantee that the different parameters are looked in designing endeavors and that -- at the same time -- the use or application of prescriptions is facilitated.

These five questions reveal the structural components of I.D. models. The first two components, research fields and referent system, determine the constraints of the I.D. model. While decisions about research fields point to the theoretical orientation of the I.D. model at hand, the referent system identifies its ecological scope. Both structural components, however, are not always independent. Not every theoretical orientation allows the solution of specific practical problems, while for each practical problem the pertaining theories should be made explicit. Practical problems can, in a similar way, get various solutions depending upon the interpretation of the problem space within different theories.

The content of I.D. models is referred to by the three remaining questions. They constitute the core of the models. However, in order to adequately compare and interpret different models, information is needed about both the descriptive knowledge base and the referent system.

Transition Points

In this subsection the transition points from I.D. to C.I.D are discussed and instances of concrete examples provided. In order to do so, the structural components of I.D. are reviewed and for each of the components, the consequences of the cognitive shift are discussed.

Transitions in I.D. originate from changes in both the descriptive knowledge base and the referent system. Learning is viewed now to be an active, constructive, goal-directed and cumulative process (Shuell, 1986, 1988) that is continuously monitored and regulated (Simons, 1989). The processing capabilities of computers enable the design not only of programmed-instruction-like environments, but also of more open learning environments which function as resources for individual learners, like simulations, HyperCard stacks, and all kinds of tutoring systems. Changes in the descriptive knowledge base, new technological possibilities and societal demands (continuous learning, knowledge explosion) constitute the origins for the construction of a new cognitive oriented I.D.

Because decisions about research fields and referent system determine both the theoretical orientation and the scope of I.D. models and theories, they can be viewed as the starting points in building new C.I.D. models. Changing the theoretical orientation while the referent system remains unchanged, will alter the I.D. model as to its selected parameters, offered prescriptions and instrumentations and prescribed process. A modification of the referent system while keeping the theoretical orientation constant, will produce similar effects.

Design Parameters. In this section some examples are offered of changes in the selected parameters due to changes in the descriptive knowledge base of I.D. models. Next, the influence of parameters on the two remaining structural components are examined.

In traditional I.D. models, presentation variables are the most crucial ones. These are tuned essentially to the basic motivation and prior knowledge of the learner. C.I.D. models, on the contrary, not only have to take more learning variables into account, but they also are of a completely different quality. Variables on the learner side are not mediating variables, which enable a more precise explanation of learning outcomes, but are independent variables that more profoundly influence the learning process than do presentation or instructional variables. Jonassen (1985) has indicated this difference by contrasting 'mathemagenic learning' to 'generative learning'. This change in quality and quantity of learner variables also influences the possible impact and function of instructional variables. The function of instruction is no longer perceived to be the control of the learning process but rather the facilitation of the process building upon the learning capabilities of the learners.

An example of the implications of changes in these parameters is found in concept learning. Reif (1986), from a more traditional point of view, specifies a long list of information elements that should be made explicit in order to ensure concept learning. In contrast, researchers (e.g. Strike & Posner, 1985) who stress the importance of conceptual change, focus on instructional strategies that consider misconceptions and enable learners to experience and negotiate the consequences and limitations of their mental models. In reading research a similar shift has occurred. Whereas reading has been primarily viewed to be a decoding (bottom-up) process, it is currently perceived to be primarily a reconstructive (top-down) process (Spiro, 1980; Kintsch, 1986).

Instrumentation/Prescriptions. A second transition point is the need for instrumentation or translation of the descriptive knowledge base into concrete prescriptions, rules or procedures. It is this transition that constitutes the major I.D. problem. How can we make the descriptive knowledge base applicable. The parameters discussed above offer a start, but research is needed as to whether and how the descriptions can be made available for application in concrete design situations. As different parameters are regarded to be important, other instruments are necessary. Gardner (1985), for instance, argued that there is a need for cognitive task analysis. He still remains in the realm of a traditional I.D. framework by accepting the controlling nature of I.D. Other instruments are needed which more adequately indicate how content can be selected for enhancing and inducing constructive learning activities.

A clear cut example of the influence of a parameter shift on instrumentation is the discussion about the usability of 'readability formulas'. As reading is regarded to be not only a decoding but a constructive process, it is clear that prior knowledge should be taken into account and any text-base 'readability formula' will be of poor value (Baker, Atwood, & Duffy, 1988).

The importance not just of the amount of prior knowledge, but also of its quality and structure, was a serious impetus for constructing instruments and applying them to the analysis of cognitive structure and the changes in cognitive structure as instruction proceeds (Nelson, Magliaro, & Sherman, 1988; Shavelson, 1974).

Clark (1990b) illustrated the enormous difficulties of trying to construct adequate prescriptions. He looked for prescriptions which might enhance transfer of learning and took into account the various knowledge representation systems. Though all of these systems represent adequately one part of the problem, they had to get integrated in order to acheive the comprehensive account of transfer which is needed for the formulation of prescriptions. A deep theoretical understanding seems to be necessary in the construction of sound prescriptions.

Developmental Process. Taking a cognitive perspective implies that not only the learners but also the designers are regarded to be active and constructive thinkers. Winn (1989) argued that merely changing the parameters will not turn I.D. into a cognitive one. The procedures and processes of I.D. also have to be altered in order to accommodate the cognitive orientation to learning and instruction. He even questions whether the idea itself of designing instruction should not be abandoned.

A C.I.D. process should meet at least two requirements: enabling the implementation of cognitive parameters in instruction and allowing designers to follow their own path of thinking. Traditional processes with their rigid and inflexible sequence of steps and procedures, do not meet these requirements. Consequently, there is ample evidence that prescriptions are not followed by designers because their theoretical background is not well understood by designers (Duffy, 1990) and because they force them to work in a logical rather than in a psychological process (Lowyck, 1980). Designing instruction is not, as traditionally perceived, a well-structured problem, but an ill-structured problem. The developmental process, therefore, should not force the designers to act, but to enable them to constructively and elaboratively consider the cognitive parameters. Rather than offer rigid solutions, it should induce reflective thinking. Consequently, the process will be spiral rather than linear in nature.

A second issue concerns not the construction itself of I.D. models but their use in practice. I.D. models, either being behavioristic or cognitive, are related to instructional practice as concepts are to instances. They are based on scientific endeavors to represent and understand reality. An instructional designer, therefore, wanting to use a specific I.D. model has to translate it to the very concrete circumstances that are not, and cannot, be incorporated into such a model. I.D. models cannot be taken as the only base of design endeavors, but rather they have to be supplemented by experiential knowledge (Council of Europe, 1980; Lowyck, 1990).

An important, but too often neglected aspect of the construction of cognitive oriented I.D. models is the necessary transition that has to occur in the mind of the instructional designers. The shift in learning psychology urges not only for a reconceptualization of I.D. models but also the awareness that such models should be used reflectively. As purely procedural knowledge often leads to the unconscious application of prescriptions and instruments, it seems necessary that instructional designers possess a large amount of declarative knowledge (Clark & Voogel, 1985) and cognitive skills (Nelson, 1987). Moreover their perspective towards learning, and more globally their belief system (Richardson, 1990), should be compatible with the premises of cognitive psychology.

Conclusion

In this contribution the relationship between cognitive psychology and instructional design is discussed. The various positions taken toward the issue illustrate its complexity. The construction of new I.D. models will be a long-lasting effort because complexity must be considered and that complexity will impact all of the structural components of I.D. models.

Research endeavors that start from a clear theoretical conception of the learning process and aim at the formulation of theoretically sound and applicable prescriptions, will not only offer a valuable contribution to the field of I.D., but also to its theoretical foundations (Di Vesta & Rieber, 1987). The application of cognitive research outcomes might indeed question the ecological and prescriptive validity of empirical outcomes and theoretical constructs. I.D., therefore, offers a test-bed for cognitive psychology as it enables both falsification and validation of its findings.

Finally, given the necessarily general nature of I.D. models, even newly constructed C.I.D. models will never exhaustively model and guide design efforts in specific contexts. They are to be supplemented, therefore, with experiential knowledge in order to use them reflectively in constraining contexts. Consequently, in order to be really valuable to instructional practice, the discipline of I.D. should not only focus on the formulation of prescriptions, but should also consider and investigate the mental models and cognitive skills of instructional designers.

References

Andrews, D.H. & Goodson, L.A. (1981). A comparative analysis of models of instructional design. *Journal of Instructional Development, 3* (4), 2-16.

Baker, E.L., Atwood, N.K., & Duffy, T.M. (1988). Cognitive approaches to assessing the readability of text. In A. Davison, & G.M. Green (Eds.), *Linguistic complexity and text comprehension. Readability issues reconsidered.* Hillsdale, N.J.: Lawrence Erlbaum Associates, p. 55-83.

Bednar, A.K., Cunningham, D., Duffy, T.M., & Perry, J.D. (1992). Theory into practice: How do we link? In G.A. Anglin (Ed.). *Instructional technology: Past, present and future.* Denver, CO: Libraries Unlimited.

Bonner, J. (1988). *Implications of cognitive theory for instructional design: Revisited. Educational Communications and Technology journal, 36* (1), 3-14.

Briggs, L.J. (1982). Instructional design: Present strengths and limitations, and a view of the future. *Educational Technology, 22* (10), 18-23.

Calfee, R. (1984). Cognitive psychology and educational practice. *Review of Research in Education, 9*, p. 3-73.

Case, R. & Bereiter, C. (1984). From behaviorism to cognitive behaviorism to cognitive development: Steps in the evolution of instructional design. *Instructional Science, 13*, 141-158.

Clark, R.E. (1989). Current progress and future directions for research in instructional technology. *Educational Technology Research & Development, 37* (1), 57-66.

Clark, R.E. (1990a). *The contributions of cognitive psychology to the design of technology supported powerful learning environments. s.l.*: University of Southern California, 12 pp.

Clark, R.E. (1990b). *Domain-general transfer of problem solutions: Cognitive structures, processes and instructional methods.* California: University of Southern California, 41 pp.

Clark, R.E., & Voogel, A. (1985). Transfer of training principles for instructional design. *Educational Communication and Technology Journal, 33* (2), 113-125.

Cobb, P. (1990). A constructivist perspective on information-processing theories of mathematical activity. *International Journal of Educational Research, 14* (1), 67-92.

Collins, A. Brown, S.J., & Newman, S.E. (1989). Cognitive apprenticeship: Teaching the crafts of reading, writing, and mathematics. In: L.B. Resnick (Ed.), *Knowing, learning, and instruction: Essays in honor of Robert Glaser.* Hillsdale, N.J.: Lawrence Erlbaum Associates, 453-494.

Council of Europe (1980). *Educational technology for permanent education: A critical re-appraisal.* Strasbourg: Council of Europe.

Cziko, G.A. (1989). Unpredictability and indeterminism in human behavior: Arguments and implications for educational research. *Educational Researcher, 18* (3),17-25.

Di Vesta, F. & Rieber, L.P. (1987). Characteristics of cognitive engineering: The next generation of instructional systems. *Educational Communications and Technology Journal, 35* (4), 213-230.

Duffy, T.M. (1990). *Toward aiding the text design process.* Bloomington, In.: Indiana University, 9 pp. (Paper symposium 'Improving the quality of texts through rewriting', AERA, Boston).

Elen, J., & Lowyck, J. (1989). Een cognitief model voor de ontwikkeling van schriftelijk studiemateriaal. *Tijdschrift voor Hoger Onderwijs, 7* (3), 89-100.

Gagne , R.M., Merrill, M.D. (1989). Integrative goals for instructional design. *Educational Technology Research & Development, 38* (1), 23-30.

Gallini, J.K., & Fisk, A.D. (1986). An information-processing approach to instructional system design. *Educational Technology, 26* (4), 24-26.

Gardner, M.K. (1985). Cognitive approaches to instructional task analysis. *Review of Research in Education, 12,* 157-195.

Glaser, R. (1971). The design of instruction. In: M.D. Merrill (Ed.). *Instructional design: Readings.* Englewood Cliffs, NJ: Prentice Hall, p. 18-37.

Glaser, R. (1976). Components of a psychology of instruction: Toward a science of design. *Review of educational research, 46,* 1-24.

Greer, B. & Verschaffel, L. (1990). Introduction. In B. Greer & L. Verschaffel (Eds.). Mathematics education as a proving-ground for information-processing theories. *International Journal of Educational Research, 14* (1), 3-12.

Gropper, G.L. (1983). A meta-theory of instruction: A framework for analyzing and evaluating instructional theories and models. In C.M. Reigeluth (Ed.). *Instructional-design theories and models: An overview of their current status.* Hillsdale, N.J.: Lawrence Erlbaum Associates, p. 37-53.

Jonassen, D.H. (1984). The mediation of experience and educational technology. *Educational Communications and Technology Journal, 32* (3), 153-167.

Jonassen, D.H. (1985). Generative learning vs. mathemagenic control of text processing. In D.H. Jonassen (Ed.), The technology of text. Vol. 2. principles for structuring, designing, and displaying text. Englewood Cliffs, N.J.: Educational Technology Publications, p. 9-45.

Jonassen, D.H. (1990). Toward a constructivist view of instructional design. *Educational Technology, 30* (Sept.), 32-34.

Kintsch, W. (1986). Learning from text. *Cognition and Instruction, 3* (2), 87-108.

Landa, L.N. (1983). Descriptive and prescriptive theories of learning and instruction: An analysis of their relationships and interactions. In C.M. Reigeluth (Ed.). *Instructional design theories and models: An overview of their current status.* Hillsdale, NJ: Lawrence Erlbaum Associates, p. 55-69.

Lowyck, J. (1980). *A process analysis of teaching* (report number 21). Leuven: Leuven University.

Lowyck, J. (1988). Herorintatie in de cursusontwikkeling: een perspectief. In J. Lowyck, J. Elen, & J. Van den Branden (Eds.). *Actuele trends in cursusontwikkeling.* Leuven: K.U. Leuven, O.U. Eenheid, p. 3-8.

Lowyck, J. (1990) Teacher thinking studies: Bridges between description, prescription and application. In C. Day, M. Pope & P. Denicolo (Eds.). *Insights into teachers' thinking and practice.* London/New York: Falmer Press, 85-103.

Lowyck, J. & Elen, J. (1990). Self-study packages: vantage points for a new instructional design. *International Journal of Educational Research, 14* (6), 565-579.

Merrill, M.D. (1971). Fundamentals of instructional design. In M.D. Merrill (Ed.), *Instructional design: Readings.* Englewood Cliffs, N.J.: Prentice Hall, p.1-4.

Merrill, M.D., Kowallis, T. & Wilson, B.G. (1981). Instructional design in transition. In F.H. Farley & N.J. Gordon (Eds.). *Psychology and education: The State of the union.* Berkeley: McCutchan, p. 298-348.

Merrill, M.D., Li, Z., & Jones, M.K. (1990). Limitations of first generation instructional design. *Educational Technology, 30* (Jan.), 7-11.

Nelson, W.A. (1987). *Procedural differences and knowledge organization in expert and novice instructional designers.* Blacksburg, Virginia: Virginia Polytechnic Institute and State University, 17 pp. (Paper AERA, 1987, Washington D.C.).

Nelson, W.A., Magliaro, S. & Sherman, T.M. (1988). The intellectual content of instructional design. *Journal of Instructional Development, 11* (1), 29-35.

Palincsar, A.S. & Brown, A.L. (1984). Reciprocal teaching of comprehension-fostering and comprehension-monitoring activities.*Cognition and Instruction, 1,* 117-175.

Posner, G.S. (1978). Tools for curriculum research and development: Potential contributions from cognitive science. *Curriculum Inquiry, 8* (4), 311-340.

Pressey, S.L. (1960). A third and fourth contribution toward the coming 'industrial revolution' in education. In A.A. Lumsdaine, & R. Glaser (Eds.), *Teaching machines and programmed learning. A source book.* Washington, D.C.: National Education Association, p. 47-51.

Reif, F. (1985). Acquiring an effective understanding of scientific concepts. In L.H.T. West, & A.L. Pines (Eds.), *Cognitive structure and conceptual change.* Orlando/London: Academic Press, p. 133-156. (Educational Psychology Series)

Reigeluth, C.M. (1983). Instructional design: What is it and why is It ? In C.M. Reigeluth (Ed.). *Instructional design theories and models: An overview of their current status.* Hillsdale, NJ: Lawrence Erlbaum Associates, p. 3-36.

Reigeluth, C.M. (1989). Educational technology at the crossroads: New mindsets and new directions.*Educational Technology Research and Development,* 37 (1), 67-80.

Resnick, L.B. (1983). Toward a cognitive theory of instruction. In S.G. Paris, G.M. Olson, & H.W. Stevenson (Eds.). *Learning and motivation in the classroom.* Hillsdale, N.J.: Lawrence Erlbaum Associates, p. 5-38.

Richardson, V. (1990). Significant and worthwhile change in teaching practice. *Educational Researcher, 19* (7), 10-18.

Schmitt, M.C., & Newby, T.J. (1986). Metacognition: Relevance to instructional design. *Journal of Instructional Development, 9* (4), 29-33.

Shavelson, R.J. (1974). Methods for examining representations of a subject-matter structure in a student's memory. *Journal of Research in Science Teaching, 11* (3), 231-249.

Shuell, T.J. (1982). Developing a viable link between scientific psychology and educational practices. *Instructional Science, 11*, 155-167.

Shuell, T.J. (1986). Cognitive conceptions of learning. *Review of Educational Research, 56* (4), 411-436.

Shuell, T.J. (1988). The role of the student in learning from instruction. *Contemporary Educational Psychology, 13*, 276-295.

Simons, P.R.J. (1989). Learning to learn. In P. Span, E. De Corte, & B. Van Hout-Wolters (Eds.). *Onderwijsleerprocessen: Strategien voor verwerking van informatie.* Lisse: Swets & Zeitlinger, p. 15-25.

Skinner, B.F. (1954). The science of learning and the art of teaching. *Harvard Educational Review, 24*, 86-97.

Spencer, K. (1988). *The psychology of educational technology and instructional media.* London: Routledge.

Spiro, R.J. (1980). Constructive processes in prose comprehension and recall. In R.J. Spiro, B.C. Bruce, & W.F. Brewer. *Theoretical issues in reading comprehension.* Hillsdale, N.J., Lawrence Erlbaum Associates, 245-278.

Streibel, M.J. (1989). *Instructional design and situated learning: Is a marriage possible?* Madison: University of Wisconsin (Paper AERA, 1989, San Francisco).

Strike, K.A., & Posner, G.J. (1985). A conceptual change view of learning and understanding. In L.H.T. West, & A.L. Pines (Eds.). *Cognitive structure and conceptual change.* Orlando/London: Academic Press, p. 211-231. (Educational Psychology Series)

Taylor, R. & Doughty, P.L. (1988). Instructional development models: Analysis at the task and subtask level. *Journal of Instructional Development, 11*, 4, p. 19-28.

Tennyson, R.D., & Rasch, M. (1988). Linking cognitive learning theory to instructional prescriptions. *Instructional Science, 17*, 369-385.

Vermunt, J.D.H.M. (1989). *The interplay between internal and external regulation of learning, and the design of process-oriented instruction.* Tilburg: Tilburg University (Paper EARLI, 1989, Madrid).

Wildman, T.M. (1981). Cognitive theory and the design of instruction. *Educational Technology, 21*, 14-20.

Wildman, T.M., & Burton, J.K. (1981). Integrating learning theory with instructional design. *Journal of Instructional Development, 4*, 5-14.

Winn, W. (1987). Instructional design and intelligent systems: Shifts in designer's decision-making role. *Instructional Science, 16*, 59-77.

Winn, W. (1989). Toward a rationale and theoretical basis for educational technology. *Educational Technology Research and Development, 37* (1), 35-46.

Winn, W. (1990). Some implications of cognitive theory for instructional design. *Instructional Science, 19*, 53-69.

11 A Manifesto for a Constructivist Approach to Uses of Technology in Higher Education

David Jonassen*, Terry Mayes**, and Ray McAleese**

* Department of Instructional Technology, University of Colorado
** Heriot-Watt University, U.K.

In this book on designing constructivist learning environments, we offer a conception of why and how these environments should be used in higher education.

Context for Constructivism

Just as constructivistic learning is supported by rich contexts, designers and evaluators must consider the context in which constructivistic learning should take place. Otherwise, we risk falling into the academic pit that is filled with so many other panaceas for learning. We believe that constructivistic learning environments, although appropriate for stimulating thinking in younger, novice learners (Fosnot, 1989), most reliably support the advanced knowledge acquisition stage of learning. This stage of knowledge acquisition is most consistently required in university courses. Therefore, universities are among the most appropriate venues for implementing constructivistic learning environments.

Jonassen (in press) has described a continuum of knowledge acquisition that leads from ignorance to expertise. The learning phases that characterize this knowledge growth are introductory, advanced, and expert (see Figure 1). Introductory learning occurs when learners have very little directly transferable prior knowledge about a skill or content area. It represents the initial stages of schema assembly and integration. Since their schemata for content are not well developed, novice learners in the initial knowledge acquisition phase have little knowledge to use as foundations for building more personally meaningful knowledge representations. Therefore, initial schema development and knowledge acquisition normally must be guided more than advanced knowledge acquisition.

The second phase of knowledge building is advanced knowledge acquisition, which is the learning phase that follows introductory knowledge acquisition and precedes expertise (Spiro, Coulson, Feltovich, & Anderson, 1988). During this phase, learners acquire more advanced knowledge in order to solve more complex, domain- or context-dependent problems. Expertise is the final phase of knowledge acquisition. We know that experts have more internally coherent and more richly interconnected knowledge structures. They represent problems in a way that makes problem solutions more efficient. However, the richness of their representations and the automaticity of their performance is not necessarily a direct consequence of instruction. On the contrary, expertise usually results from extensive experience that requires broad transfer of the knowledge acquired during previous phases of learning.

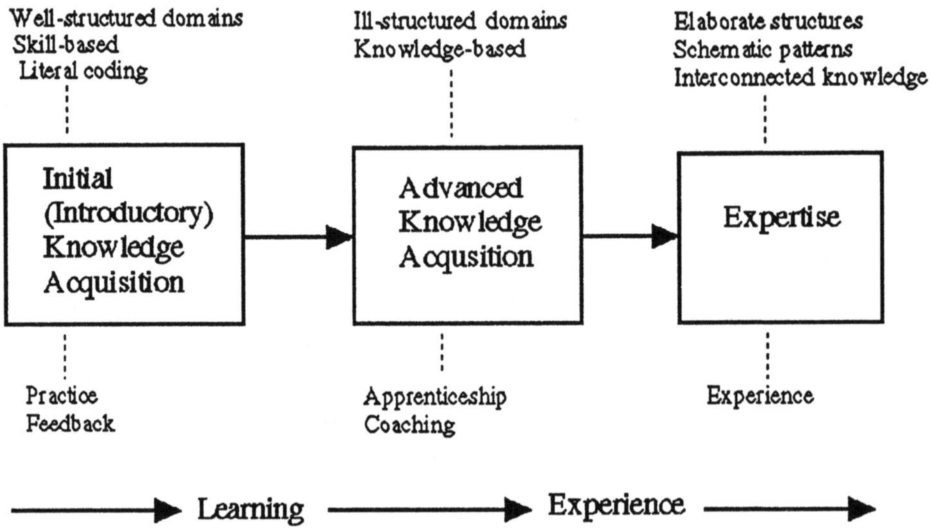

Figure 1

Figure 1 represents a continuum of knowledge acquisition (rather than distinct processes). Since each phase of knowledge acquisition entails different types of learning, each also suggests different approaches to learning. We believe that the initial knowledge acquisition phase is better served by instructional techniques that are based upon classical instructional design techniques. Classical instructional design is predicated upon predetermined learning outcomes, constrained and sequential instructional interactions, and criterion-referenced evaluation. We believe that constructivistic learning environments may be used during the latter stages of initial knowledge acquisition, and that they represent rich and meaningful environments for initial knowledge learners. However, constructivistic environments are more reliably and consistently applied to support the advanced knowledge acquisition phase. It is at this phase that misconceptions, such as reductive bias, are most likely to result from instruction classical instructionally designed materials that oversimplifies and pre-package knowledge (Spiro et al, 1988). So, more complex and constructivistic environments serve advanced knowledge learners better.

The final phase in the knowledge acquisition process is expertise. Since expertise results primarily from situated experience, its development will likely be enhanced by the rich level of instructional support provided by most constructivistic environments. The conclusion that can be drawn from this discussion is that it is important to consider the context (i. e. learning phase) before recommending any specific methodology, especially constructivistic approaches. That is, constructivistic learning approaches and environments are not equally suitable for all learning contexts.

Universities and tertiary education institutions exist to foster advanced knowledge acquisition. Initial knowledge is usually acquired during secondary education or early university preparation. Most university curricula, however, especially in the student's major area of study, purport to promote advanced knowledge acquisition. Therefore, we believe that universities are appropriate learning contexts for constructivistic learning processes and environments.

The remainder of this paper will describe our assumptions about advanced knowledge and skill acquisition in higher education and our assumptions about environments and tools that should support this phase of learning.

Assumptions About Learning

During the process of learning (coming to know), the knower constructs a reality or at least interprets it based upon his/her apperceptions. Traditional, objectivistic conceptions of learning focus on the object of our knowing rather than the process of coming to know or what is actually learned. Constructivists assume that learners construct knowledge by interpreting perceptual experiences in terms of prior knowledge, current mental structures, and existing beliefs. Some of these assumptions are considered in more detail, because these assumptions form the conceptual basis for a new domain of construction environments and tools.

Knowledge Construction

The most important epistemological assumption of constructivism is that meaning is a function of how the individual creates meaning from his/her experiences. What we know is internally generated by the individual rather than received from any external source. Radical constructivists, such as von Glasersfeld (1984), believe that there is no objective reality that is independent of human mental activity. Personal worlds are created by the mind, so no one 'world' is any more real than any other. Meaning-making does not rely on correspondence to the world but rather is dependent upon the understanding of the learner. All constructivists believe that the mind is instrumental and essential in interpreting events, objects, and perspectives on the external world, and that those interpretations comprise a knowledge base that is personal and individualistic (Jonassen, 1991).

Generative Processing and Active Learning. Knowledge construction relies on active mental processing of perceptions. It results in understanding, which results from generative processing. That is, knowledge construction is a generative learning process (Wittrock, 1974). Generative processing involves relating new information to prior knowledge in order to build more elaborate knowledge structures. These knowledge structures are necessary for interpreting new information, reasoning from what is known, and for solving problems.

Modern theory describes generative learning in terms of deeper levels of processing (Craik & Lockhart,1972). Normally only the results of the deeper analyses can be regarded as learning, the by-products of preliminary or 'surface' analysis are discarded. What is needed is meaning, and the extraction of meaning involves the deeper levels of processing. Depth of processing may be better thought of as the kind and number of elaborations generated by the learner (Eysenck & Keane, 1990). Indeed, the superior learning that results from material that has been acted upon, and the finding that material is better remembered if it is actually generated by the learner (rather than equivalent material merely presented to the learner) has been termed the generation effect (e.g., Gardiner, 1989).

Social Negotiation of Meaning

Individualistic experiences, perceptions, and constructions do not mean that it is impossible for individuals to construct essentially the same understanding for any object or event in the external world. Common understandings regularly result from social negotiation of meaning which is supported by collaborative construction of knowledge. Understandings and instructional outcomes can be negotiated between learners and teachers. Rather than imposing a prescribed and objective reality on learners, learning environment designers must accept that each learner will interpret the same object or event somewhat differently. That is, despite our intentions, the outcomes of learning will vary. Cognitive development occurs through the internalisation of cognitive activity originally experienced in social contexts (Glaser, 1990). This suggests an emphasis on cooperative learning in which the learner is exposed to alternative viewpoints that challenge initial understanding, that is, *reciprocal teaching* (Vygotsky, 1978).

Contextually Mediated Learning

Individual understandings are based upon interpretations of personal experiences. Hannabuss (1992) suggests that understandings are part of a *referential hierarchy* in which personal 'stories' subsume concepts which in turn subsume propositions. Constructivistic conceptions of learning claim that in the absence of a real-world, relevant context for learning information, the information is less meaningful. That is, it lacks a referential hierarchy. Individuals ascribe meaning to their world with regard to stories, events, etc.

Too often, learning materials or environments are stripped of contextual relevance. Learners are required to acquire facts and rules that have no direct relevance or meaning to them, because they are not related to anything the learner is interested in or needs to know. We believe that useful knowledge is that which can be transferred to new situations. The most effective learning contexts are those which are problem- or case-based, that immerse the learner in the situation requiring him or her to acquire skills or knowledge in order to solve the problem or manipulate the situation. So, instruction needs to provide contextually-based environments that are meaningful to the learners.

Reflective Thinkers

We believe that the goal of universities should be to produce reflective practitioners. It is possible to distinguish between two components of thinking - reasoning and reflection. Reasoning generally occurs as a conscious intentional and deliberate process. Learners, when they reason, use formalisms such as induction, and deduction. Other formalisms such as argumentation (Toulmin, 1983) may be part of professional activities or required to learn different perspectives. Reflection is a metacognitive strategy, that is, the process of thinking about thinking (e.g., thinking about how to approach a task). Schon (1983) distinguishes two different styles of professional thinking - thinking IN action and thinking ON action. "In his day to day practice (the professional) makes innumerable judgements of quality for which he cannot state adequate criteria, and he displays skills for which he cannot state rules and procedures. Even when he makes conscious use of research-based theories and techniques, he is dependent on tacit recognitions, judgements, and skill full performances" (Schon, 1983, p. 50).

Learners and professionals can think about their actions and feelings. This process of turning back thought on action is an executive action. Reflection IN action is a less formal approach that emphasizes thinking on ones feet. Schon argues that this process is the essence of professionalism. Such approaches are not always valued by traditional teaching. Technology used by learners can enhance the process. Computers can provide a conversational environment in which the learner can apply knowledge to problems and consider their actions as reusable events. Learners can control their learning, learn from others and develop reflection in action and reflection on actions as metacognitive skills.

Conclusion

Perhaps, the greatest limitation of many models of instructional design is the tendency to over-prescribe those models for all learners in all instructional contexts. A large range of individual difference variables interact with both learning outcomes and instructional techniques (Jonassen & Grabowski, in press). Most learners possess different aptitudes for learning different skills and knowledge. Learners also react quite differently to different instructional approaches based upon the information processing requirements of the instructional method as well as the social and contextual variables that describe the learning environment.

An important contextual variable to accommodate in learning environment design is the skill level or prior knowledge level of the learners. While it may appear intuitive that advanced learners be taught using different methods than novice learners, that intuition is not often reflected in instructional design models which prescribe the same approach to instruction for all learners. We believe that learners at an advanced level of knowledge acquisition be exposed to more open learning environments that reflect the complexities of the real world and require the learners to factor those complexities into their problem solutions. These environments should be case-based and situated in the realities of the external world. These environments should require learners to access prior knowledge and to assemble more elaborate schemata from it. These environments should require the learners to interact with the complexities of the external world and interact with other learners in a process of social negotiation. Ultimately these environments should require learners to reflect on the quality of the theories used, judgements and decisions made, and the skills and processes used to arrive at those decisions. These characteristics describe constructivistic environments. Instructional methods and environments for advanced learners, we believe, should reflect those characteristics.

Constructivist Roles of Technology in Education

Modern information technology can and should support advanced knowledge acquisition. It can best do that by providing environments and thinking tools that engage constructivistic conceptions of learning. Open learning environments are technology supported systems that are examples of open systems. Traditional computer-based learning environments are often driven by prescriptive programs that allow the learner to input information, however the responses to that input are prescribed and predetermined. In open systems, the goals of the system, its uses, activities and options are determined by sources both internal and external to the system. Open learning systems are those which are:

- need driven
- learner-initiated
- conceptually and intellectually engaging.

Technology-based learning environments should fulfill an information or knowledge construction need of the learner. Once a need is perceived, the learner will initiate a dialogue with the environment. To the degree that the environment is able to support the need, the learner's interactions will be engaging. That is, if the learner is seeking information to solve a problem or build a better understanding, then constructivistic environments, such as hypertext retrieval systems, should support that need and engage the learner. We believe that hypertext is among the best examples of constructivistic learning environments, because acquiring knowledge from hypertext requires the user to engage in constructivistic learning processes. Learning from hypertext is task driven. It depends largely on the purpose for using the hypertext, which in turn drives the level of processing (Jonassen & Wang, in press). Yet not all learning must be intentional (Mayes, 1992). Browsing may well result in learning, as will any engagement with information for which appropriate schemata already exist. For example, consider the almost universal popularity of magazines, a kind of text and graphics explicitly designed for browsing. Readers typically choose magazines in domains for which they already have well-developed knowledge structures. The act of browsing information which can be acquired without the need for the creation of new schemata is evidently a pleasing experience. Is such immersion in a familiar domain a matter of knowledge construction? It is perhaps more appropriately conceived of as the process that Rumelhart & Norman (1978) referred to as tuning. The point here is that browsing in a domain for which no properly developed schemata have yet been constructed is not likely to lead to satisfactory knowledge acquisition at all. Once someone has arrived at the point of enjoying the act of browsing in a domain, learning will be self-motivated. The challenge is to allow learners to get to that point. Construction tasks are needed first.

Technology-based environments can also support knowledge construction by providing thinking tools or *cognitive learning tools* (Kommers, Jonassen, & Mayes, 1992). Thinking tools are technology systems or applications that extend the intellectual functionality of the learner, that engage the leaner in tasks that facilitate knowledge construction. The application becomes a tool only if the learner uses it to represent his/her own understanding. Examples of these knowledge construction tools are semantic networking software, expert systems, databases, word processors, and microworlds.

In order to support the constructivistic conceptions of learning that are described above, we believe that technology-based learning environments and the tools that support those environments should possess the following characteristics.

Environments That Represent Multiple Realities

Designing instructional environments is difficult, among other reasons, because all too frequently the domain knowledge is ill-structured (Spiro at al, 1987, 1988). Ill-structured knowledge results from ill-defined categories of objects, which have variable attributes or ambiguous criteria. Ill-structured knowledge domains have few general rules or principles for class inclusion that describe most of the cases, no defining characteristics to determine appropriate action, and inconsistencies between cases.

Rationale. An effective approach to solving these problems is cognitive flexibility theory (Spiro et al, 1987, 1988). According to cognitive flexibility theory, technology environments, such as hypertexts, can represent the world to students in its natural complexity. Rather than simplifying interpretations of reality in order to make them more easily understandable, those interpretations of reality and the tasks that they engage need to embedded in some meaningful, real-world context that entails the natural complexity and ill- structuredness that the real world contains.

Example. In order to support learning of transfusion medicine problems, a case-based hypertext on transfusion medicine has been created that reflects the principles of flexibility theory (Jonassen, Ambruso, & Olesen, 1991). The program is oriented by seven primary cases. The student must determine the information needed to take any action (such as ordering tests, diagnosing the problem, or ordering treatment. She or he has the option of accessing information from a transfusion medicine textbook (a very common source of information in case resolution which represents a well- structured perspective of the knowledge domain), ask questions of important operatives in the case such as the attending physician, pathologist, resident, patient, phlebotomist or blood bank director (which provides conflicting perspectives), order tests (which provide evidence that may support or conflict with other perspectives), or compare the current case to a database of similar cases (accessed by type of similarity, e.g. symptomology, etiology, pathophysiology, or treatment). Each of these information sources provides a separate point of view that represents the case in a different way. These are the multiple perspectives that are normally available to a resident in solving a case. When the student takes an action, s/he is presented with feedback about the advisability of each action taken based upon these previous perspectives. The transfusion hypertext avoids oversimplifying instruction, provides multiple representations of the transfusion content, emphasizes case- based instruction and context dependent knowledge, supports complexity, and requires knowledge construction rather than transmission.

Real World, Case-Based Tasks and Environments

The most effective learning, that which is most meaningful and therefore transfers best, is case-based and involves meaningful real-world tasks. These are the experiences that contribute the most effective scripts to the development of expertise.

Rationale. An appropriate model for providing real-world experiences is cognitive apprenticeship (Collins, 1991). An important component of the apprenticeship model is situated learning, in which students learn the conditions for applying knowledge in situations that foster invention, focusing on the implications of knowledge. That is, the situated context structures knowledge appropriate to its uses. Apprenticeship uses different pedagogical tools than traditional instruction, such as modeling processes in the world and, of course, modeling expert performance. Modeling allows the student to see expert solutions to student generated problems, which makes visible the parts of a process not normally seen. This enables the student to integrate what happens with why it happens. The instructor is a coach who provides help directed at real difficulties at critical times. The students are required to reflect on their performance through imitation, reply, abstracted replay, and spatial reification. The object of instruction becomes the students comparing their performance to others while abstracting a set of strategies. Characteristics of cognitive apprenticeship include articulation (making tacit knowledge explicit) and exploration (learning how to form and test hypotheses).

Example. Perhaps the most common application of the apprenticeship model in professional education programs is the internship experience. Instructional design and technology degree programs, for example, make extensive use of internships for providing situated experiences for their students. The training and instructional requirements encountered in these experiences are real-world. Design students who have acquired introductory knowledge about design processes can apply those processes to the solution of real-world needs. They engage in needs analysis, content analysis, and designing learning environments to solve a variety of introductory and advanced knowledge requirements. Many of the design processes are modelled by the designers to whom they are assigned to work. Faculty members from the design programs function as coaches for the students. Our experiences indicate that students who are able to serve in different internships in a variety of situations gain a deeper understanding of the design process than those who can accommodate only a single experience. They in turn become more accomplished designers in a shorter period of time.

Collaborative Knowledge Construction Environments

The primary role of university lecturers and teachers throughout the world is purveyor of knowledge. We believe that learning environments should support collaborative construction of knowledge involving both teachers and student.

Rationale. Collaborative knowledge construction environments enable all members of a class or learning group the opportunity to contribute their interpretation. It is important for advanced knowledge acquisition that learners realize that there exist multiple interpretations for every event or object. Those interpretations may be dissonant or consonant, but they reflect the natural complexity that define most advanced knowledge domains. Collaborative environments enable learners to identify and reconcile those multiple perspectives in order to solve problems.

Example. Perhaps the most appropriate technology for facilitating and mediating collaborative environments is hypertext. Hypertext is non-sequential text that enables the interlinking of information chunks within a knowledge domain in a variety of meaningful ways. We have developed a hypertext shell to facilitate argumentation of issues within a advanced knowledge seminar (Jonassen, Dunlap & Wilson, 1992). The hypertext was inspired by the IBIS hypertext-based, collaborative problem solving environment (Conklin & Begeman, 1987) which provides an argument structure including issue, position, and argument nodes that can be added or edited remotely through a networked computer system. Our hypertext supports topic-oriented seminars by attaching issue links and nodes to content-related nodes, such as premises, assumptions, processes, and applications of the content. To each issue node, personal position and alternative model nodes and links can be automatically created. To each of these, argument nodes and links can be created. The purpose of this collaborative hypertext is to force learners into interrelating content within a domain and to take personal positions with regard to the issues.

The outcomes of imposing this type of formal argument structure onto the collaborative construction of a class text include more elaborate class discussions and better argued class papers. It is important that some sort of formal structure be imposed onto the hypertext (see for instance, McMahon & O'Neill, this volume) in order to avoid random connections. Collaborative hypertexts are among the best methods for communicating the complexities, multiple perspectives, and interconnectedness of knowledge.

Tools That Support Environments

Rather than representing the world to the learner, the computer should provide tool kits that enable the student to build more meaningful, personal interpretations and representations of the world. These tool kits must support the requisite intellectual functionality of the learning requirements of the course of study.

Tools for Active Learning

Cognitive learning tools (Kommers, Jonassen & Mayes, 1992) assist learners in representing their own knowledge or alternative representations of the external world. Computer-based application tools that can function as cognitive tools include database managers, semantic networking programs, hypertext, spread sheets, expert systems, and microworlds.

Rationale. These tools engage learners in meaningful, higher order information, specifically cognitive learning strategies that can be generalized to new problem spaces in new contexts. Cognitive learning strategies are mental operations that the learner may use to acquire, construct, retain and retrieve different kinds of knowledge or performance. Cognitive learning strategies are generative. They enable learners to take an active, constructive role in generating meaning for information by accessing and applying prior knowledge to new material. Generating meaning results from activating and altering existing knowledge structures or schemata in order to interpret what is presented. The application of cognitive learning strategies increases the number of links between presented information and existing knowledge which engages the learner in deeper levels of processing. The amended structures are then encoded into memory as distinctive features that may later be accessed to explain and interpret new information.

Example. An excellent example of a cognitive tool that engages learners in deeper level processing are expert systems. The process of analyzing domain knowledge in a manner necessary for building expert systems engages learners in a variety of higher order cognitive (concept, rule, principle and problem solving) and metacognitive (planning, assessing, estimating) activities (Jonassen & Grabinger, 1992). Expert systems can be used in a variety of ways to engage meaningful learning. The least engaging application of expert systems is to use an existing expert system advisor. An advisor is a rule base that a novice accesses in order to help make a decision. When used to provide advice, however, it is supplanting the thinking that should be learned. Advisors may support learning if used to guide a learner through an evaluation of their own products (Grabinger & Pollock, 1989), which can be informative and enlightening to the learner. Expert systems can also be used to build cognitive simulations of mental activities (Jonassen, Dallman,Wang & Hamilton, 1991), a process that requires a very deep level of process understanding. Finally, building expert systems is a cognitive tool that can be applied to a variety of knowledge domains (Trollip, Lippert, & Starfield, 1992). Rule-based expert systems are a formalism for representing knowledge. The intellectual processes that are engaged in building rule bases that represent a knowledge domain are especially deep and engaging.

Tools for Observational Learning

While the most meaningful learning is active, students acquire models or scripts for learning from observing others as they engage ideas and attempt to make meaning from them.

Rationale. Tools should also provide a venue for learning from peers as examples. This form of observational learning assumes that students may learn a lot from observing other students who are experiencing and resolving difficulties. This kind of learning has been curiously neglected. Much recent work has focussed on the benefits of collaborative problem solving, where the individual learner benefits from engaging in a group learning activity. (Howe et al.,1991). Yet, part of this benefit may simply derive from observing other learning events, rather than representing the direct effect of active interaction with other learners. Initially, the idea that a lot of learning is essentially "second-hand" is not consistent with a constructivistic philosophy. On the contrary, though, we argue that observing other learners asking questions, receiving answers, arguing, choosing paths through the knowledge, or constructing their own knowledge structures by using a mindtool, is a fundamental learning experience. Indeed, one of the dangers of using technology, or learning at a distance, is that less of this kind of experience is typically available. The exception may be the Open University (UK) where distance education students are encouraged to use local groups, study centers, tutors, and learning about learning. Engaging in other peoples' learning events, provided that they are sufficiently visible, and available at the right level and at the right time, may be as active and effective in producing deep learning as engaging in one's own. The critical point is probably that the engagement in these 'extra'- learning events should be triggered by a need or a hypothesis that is generated from the individual's own learning development.

Technologies provide us with the option of capturing and compiling learning events and making them available to other learners. Indeed, this may turn out to be the most effective use of computers in education. The learning events of succeeding generations of students can be stored and made accessible, as a kind of learning resource that has only previously been available as the expertise of an experienced teacher.

Example. We know of no currently existing tools which achieve the compilation of learning events in the way we envisage, but it seems certain that such systems will soon be developed. The development of centrally-managed campus-wide networks of workstations, such as MIT's Athena system (Champine, 1991), may achieve the goal of truly distributed learning resources and will provide effective environments for tutor-learner and learner- learner interactions to be registered as learning events. Thus, a database of learning events (i.e. questions from students and answers from tutors or from other students) can be compiled from computer conferencing and email associated with every course, and appropriate tools provided for allowing the learner "just-in-time" access to this database. Gradually, these learning events can be used to create a rationale for the design of courseware. It should be feasible to design courseware so that learning events are stored in a hyperbase along with the courseware.

Constructivistic Conceptions of Evaluation

If the goals of higher education support constructivistic learning, and if constructivist environments and methods are used to facilitate that level of knowledge acquisition, then the divergent types of processing entailed by those methods need to be evaluated as well as the convergent expectations normally associated with course evaluation.

Goals of Evaluation

Perhaps the most fundamental change in evaluation of constructivistic outcomes, as opposed to the more traditional criterion- or normative-referenced evaluations used in higher education, should be the goal of evaluation. Evaluation implies an appraisal or value judgement about a person or his/her performance relative to some criteria. If learning is the process of knowledge construction, should not that process provide the most appropriate goal? And who better can evaluate knowledge construction than the constructor? Evaluation from a constructivistic perspective should be less of a reinforcement and/or behavior control tool and more of a self-analysis and metacognitive tool. Constructivistic learning is not supposed to mirror reality, but rather to construct meaningful interpretations. Constructivistic evaluation is the mirror for viewing that construction process.

Goals of Learning

Perhaps the most common misinterpretation of constructivism is that it necessarily results in academic chaos. If all learners construct their own meaning from information, how can we share enough knowledge to even communicate. In fact, we do share the considerable meaning for objects, events and ideas through a long process of negotiation. However, individual differences in knowledge construction will always exist (e.g., try to get a group of people to agree on what are the critical attributes of a "chair"). That is, we will all develop a somewhat individualistic representation of any knowledge that we construct. However, we share enough meaning to communicate, to argue, to hypothesize, and so on.

If meaning is negotiated, why shouldn't we also negotiate the goals of learning or use the negotiation process, in the form of argumentation, as evidence of learning. Because learners interpret the world somewhat differently, the outcomes of learning will vary somewhat, and so objectives, if they are useful at all, can best be used as a negotiating tool for guiding learners during the learning process and for self-evaluation of learning outcomes. This prescription is especially problematic for training design, which is typically based upon the solution of specific, perceived problems. Most training is almost, by definition, convergent and objectivistic, because it supports explicit, company performance goals.

Evaluating Knowledge Construction

Constructivistic learning environments and tools are intended to engage learners in higher-order, more meaningful learning. If that is the case, then traditional measures of recall cannot be used to assess the outcomes of using these environments. Assessing knowledge acquisition will require a new set of assumptions about how learning is to be evaluated. Without making some of these assumptions, no efforts at integrating constructivistic principles in instruction should be attempted.

Higher-Order Thinking. Nearly every definition of constructivism refers to knowledge construction rather than reproduction, that is, learners actively engaging in building knowledge structures. If we accept that as a meaningful goal of learning, then as evaluators we need to assess the intellectual processes of knowledge construction, not repetition. We have stated that knowledge construction necessitates higher order thinking. So, outcomes of constructivistic environments should assess higher order thinking. This suggests new forms of assessment, emphasising process variables such as knowledge states, qualitative variables, such as learner interactions.

Process vs. Product. If we believe that learning emerges from processes that are grounded in perception and grow out of experience, then those are the conditions under which we should evaluate -- not behavior elicited by some arbitrary requirement. It is also important to evaluate how learners go about constructing knowledge. So, effective assessment should be integrated into the instructional process; as learners are acquiring knowledge in some meaningful context, we can evaluate what the learner is learning. Rather than establishing a criterion to reference learning, we should evaluate in case-based worlds what the learners are able to transfer. In the transfusion medicine hypertext, described earlier, the evaluation considers how the learners collect information, make hypotheses, and solve relevant problems.

Divergent Responses: Socially Negotiated Outcomes

If it is appropriate to present multiple perspectives in learning environments with the expectation that learners will meaningfully accommodate these different perspectives and draw their own more meaningful conclusions, then it is equally important to reflect and accept those multiple perspectives in the evaluation process. Why is it necessary to use a single set of products or criteria for assessing learning. Learning should be referenced by a domain of possible outcomes, each of which would provide acceptable evidence of learning.

Another implication of this multiple perspective criterion of constructivism is that, since evaluation is necessarily subjective to some degree, the assumption that a single evaluator is capable of providing an objective or a complete appraisal from their single perspective is impossible. Evaluation of constructivistic learning may suggest a panel of reviewers, each with a meaningful perspective from which to evaluate the outcomes and each with reasonable credentials for evaluating the learner. The panel may consist of novices as well as experts. It is likely that a novice could provide a much better evaluation that the expert, who frequently focuses on inappropriate criteria of learning.

Conclusion

We believe that constructivistic learning environments and methods are not appropriate for all learners. Universities are among the most appropriate venues for integrating constructivistic learning approaches because their goal is promote advanced knowledge acquisition. Constructivist environments facilitate the personal construction of knowledge about the external world. This process is facilitated by environments that represent multiple realities, that use real-world, case-based contexts for learning, and facilitate collaborative construction of knowledge. These environments should be supported by tools that engage learners meaningfully. All of these activities can be effectively supported by technology-based environments. Finally, constructivistic learning outcomes should be evaluated using evaluation methods that are sensitive to the goals of constructivistic learning. University environments, especially those supported by networked technologies, are the institutions best able to successfully implement the conceptions discussed in this chapter and those throughout this book.

References

Champine, G. A. (1991). *MIT Project Athena: A model for distributed campus computing.* Bedford, MA: Digital Press.

Collins (1991). Cognitive apprenticeship and instructional technology. In L. Idol & B. F. Jones (Eds.), *Educational values and cognitive instruction: Implications for reform.* Hillsdale, NJ: Lawrence Erlbaum Associates.

Conklin, J. & Begeman, M. (1987). IBIS: A hypertext tool for team design deliberation. In *Proceedings of Hypertext '87.* Chapel Hill, NC: University of North Carolina, Computer Science Department.

Craik, F. I. M. & Lockhart, R. S. (1972). Levels of processing: A framework for memory research. *Journal of Verbal Learning and Verbal Behaviour, 11,* 671-684.

Eysenck, M. W. & Keane, M. T. (1990). *Cognitive psychology: A student's handbook.* Hillsdale, NJ: Lawrence Erlbaum Associates.

Fosnot, C. T. (1989). *Enquiring teachers, enquiring learners: A constructivist approach for teachers.* New York: Teachers College Press.

Gardiner, J. M. (1989). A generation effect in memory without awareness. *British Journal of Psychology, 80,* 163-168.

Glaser, R. (1990). The reemergence of learning theory within instructional research. *American Psychologist, 45*, 1, 29-39

Grabinger, R. S. & Pollock, J (1989). The effectiveness of internally-generated feedback with an instructional expert system. *Journal of Educational Computing Research, 5* (3), 299-309.

Hannabuss S (1992). *The representation of effectiveness in management: An investigation into concepts and stories.* (Doctoral dissertation, Heriot Watt University). Edinburgh.

Howe, C. J. , Tolmie, A. & Mackenzie, M. (1991). Computer support for the collaborative learning of physics concepts. In C. O'Malley (Ed.). *Computer-supported collaborative learning.* (NATO/ASI Series F) Berlin: Springer-Verlag (in preparation).

Jonassen, D. H. (1991). Objectivism vs. constructivism: Do we need a philosophical paradigm shift? *Educational Technology: Research and Development, 39* (3), 5-14.

Jonassen, D. H. (1992). Cognitive flexibility theory and its implications for designing CBI. In S. Dijkstra, H.P.M. Krammer, J. van Merrienboer (Eds.), *Instructional models in computer-based learning environments.* (NATO/ASI Series F, Vol. 104.) Berlin: Springer-Verlag.

Jonassen, D. H., Ambruso, D. R. & Olesen, J. (1991). Designing a hypertext on transfusion medicine using cognitive flexibility theory. *Journal of Educational Multimedia and Hypermedia, 1* (2).

Jonassen, D. H. , Dunlap, J. & Wilson, B. G. (1992). *Supporting seminars with collaborative hypertext.* Paper presented at the annual meeting of the Association for the Development of Computer-based Instructional Systems, Norfolk, VA, November, 1992.

Jonassen, D. H. & Grabinger, R. S. (1992). Information processing analysis of building expert systems. In P.A.M. Kommers, D.H. Jonassen, & J.T. Mayes (Eds.), *Cognitive tools for learning.* (NATO/ASI Series F, Vol. 81) Berlin: Springer-Verlag.

Jonassen, D. H. & Grabowski, B. L. (in press). *Individual differences, learning and instruction.* New York: Allyn & Bacon.

Jonassen, D. H. , Dallman, B. , Wang, S. , & Hamilton, R. (1991). *A cognitive simulation of metacognitive processing using expert systems.* Paper presented at the annual meeting of the Association for the Development of Computer-based Instructional Systems, St. Louis, MO, November, 1991.

Jonassen, D. H. & Wang, S. (in press). Acquiring structural knowledge from hypertext. *Journal of Computer-Based Instruction.*

Kommers, P.A.M. , Jonassen, D.H. & Mayes, J.T. (Eds.) (1992). *Cognitive tools for learning.* (NATO/ASI Series F. Vol 81) Berlin: Springer-Verlag.

Mayes, J. T. (1992). Mindtools: A suitable case for learning. In Kommers, P.A.M., Jonassen, D.H. & Mayes, J.T. (Eds). *Cognitive tools for learning.* (NATO/ASI Series F, Vol. 81) Berlin: Springer-Verlag.

Rumelhart, D. E. & Norman, D. A. (1978). Accretion, tuning and restructuring: Three modes of learning. In J. W. Cotton & R. Klatzky (Eds.). *Semantic factors in cognition.* Hillsdale, NJ: Lawrence Erlbaum Associates.

Spiro, R. J. , Vispoel, W. , Schmitz, J. , Samarapungavan, A. , & Boerger, A. (1987). Knowledge acquisition for application: Cognitive flexibility and transfer in complex content domains. In B. C. Britton (Ed.), *Executive control processes*. Hillsdale, NJ: Lawrence Erlbaum Associates.

Spiro, R. J. , Coulson, R. L. , Feltovich, P. J. , & Anderson, D. K. (1988). *Cognitive flexibility theory: Advanced knowledge acquisition in ill-structured domains*. Tech Report No. 441. Champaign, IL: University of Illinois, Center for the Study of Reading.

Schon, D. A. (1983). *The reflective practitioner: How professionals think in action*. New York: Basic Books.

Toulmin (1983). *The uses of argument*. Cambridge: Cambridge University Press.

Trollip, S. R. , Lippert, R. , Starfield, A. , & Smith, K.A. (1992). Building knowledge bases: An environment for making cognitive connections. In Kommers, P.A.M. , Jonassen, D. & Mayes, T. (Eds.) (1992). *Cognitive tools for learning*. Heidelberg, FRG: Springer-Verlag.

von Glasersfeld, E. (1984). Radical constructivism. In P. Watzlawick (Ed.), *The invented reality*. Cambridge, MA: Harvard University Press.

Vygotsky, L. S. (1978). *Mind in society: The development of higher psychological processes*. Cambridge, MA: Harvard University Press.

Wittrock, M. C. (1974). Learning as a generative activity. *Educational Psychologist, 11*, 87-95.

12 Toward a Cognitive Ergonomics of Educational Technology

Cristina Zucchermaglio

Direzione Formazione - Italsiel s.p.a. Gruppo IRI-Finsiel, Rome, Italy

The unimportant and often negative results of the introduction of technology into various educational settings are mainly due to scarce consideration given to a realistic and cognitively based epistemology of learning and to an analysis of educative settings in which technology should be inserted and used. I will explain these points briefly.

Why Did Technologies Not Change Education?

The Success of a Technical Point of View

The traditional approach to the introduction of technologies into educational settings tends to emphasize the technical aspects of the technologies more than their cognitive, educative and cultural aspects[1]. Such a narrow approach has been the downfall of many projects. This is because the central issue involved in the problem of educational technology is human learning. A technical approach based only on computer science and engineering cannot provide the right solution for efficient learning and use of new technology in schools and the workplace. Educational technology often seems to be planned without the benefit of the best cognitive research knowledge. We should use the most recent results of the cognitive science of instruction (Resnick, 1988), not only to observe, in a critical way, the use of technology, but also to design cognitive based technology that really improves and sustains efficient social learning in schools and the workplace.

Technology Without a Context

Many software applications fail because designers are naive about the wider organizational context in which their technology is inserted. Context is an essential variable: differences in organizational structure and culture can explain different ways in which technology is used in organizational settings. Each organization can be expected to implement technology differently. It is not by chance that the organizational impact of computer support for adult work has recently become an important topic in the design of information technology and of computer systems for office settings (Tuschman & Anderson, 1988; Zuboff, 1988; Flores et al., 1988).

[1]The recent development of technology - not only educational - was mainly technical: the cognitive quality of interfaces and the system's usability (Suchman, 1987; Bagnara & Staiano, 1987) have not improved.

The fact that there is a domain of research concerned with the organization of computer-mediated work environments provides additional incentive to explore possible parallels with educational environments.

Training and school environments – as enterprises – are bearers of culture, values, goals and organization both previous to, and independent of, a technology's insertion and in spite of the technology designer's concerted efforts to create a different organizational structure and culture. Thus, it is necessary to pursue an organizational coherence between technologies and the educational contexts in which they should be used. Otherwise, their insertion could create confusing effects in the educational context itself. Designers ought to be sensitive to the socially organized settings in which technology might function. They should use the organizational change that technology produces as a *mediator* that can amplify the possibility of educative interaction. As Newman (1990) says:

> Our interest in the use of technology as a mediator of organizational changes derives from the theoretical approach that links the process of learning directly to the kinds of social interactions that constitute instruction" (p.10).

Technologies and Theories of Learning

Educational software developers always have a model – which is more or less explicit – in mind as they design their products. We can distinguish between the existing educational technology by analyzing both the nature and level of explicitness of these theories of learning.

In analyzing the existing educational technology, we can roughly distinguish between *empty* technology and *full* technology. The latter - which is the most common to date - was designed under the premise that learning is mainly a process of transferring "information" from a system into the head of the learner. All of the technology stemming from the development of the learning machine in the 1960s is included in this category. This includes courses implemented on authoring systems, the majority of CAI, CBT, and Intelligent Tutoring Systems. The common characteristic of these systems is the transfer of information from the machine to the learner via different paths which are totally, or for the most part, predefined. The learning model – never explicit – is the "pouring model": information exists objectively and correctly in the system and is transferred into the head of the learner.

Most educational software developers are still basically immured in the behavioristic paradigm that guided the earliest attempts at computer-aided instruction. They treat "knowledge as a fluid, which pours into the student-vessels" (Kaye, 1989), and thus use a learning theory that is not supported by recent developments in the cognitive psychology of instruction. The learning theories supporting most present educational technology do not correspond to the cognitive processes through which we learn. Traditional classroom procedures are simply transferred to technologies which are in danger of destroying, either deliberately or inadvertently, the learning potential present in any educational context. This rigid connotation of knowledge transmission causes a corresponding rigidness with regard to the educational uses of these technologies. In the best of contexts the uses are closed, of the "right or wrong" variety. They do not foresee the technology itself as an environment for constructive activity on the part of the user. They do not recognize the social uses of the technology. They simply reproduce the negative aspects of schools rather than contribute to change.

Empty and *open* technologies, on the contrary, are designed by taking into consideration a constructivist view of learning: a view that includes and implies situated cognition, metacognition and reflection, cognitive apprenticeship, cognitive complexity, functional context learning, and collaborative and social construction of cultural knowledge (Brown, 1989; Bruner, 1989; Resnick, in press; Cole, in press). These are innovative examples of educational technology and it is not by chance that the designers of these technologies are the only ones who address learning theory and design principles (see Wilson, 1991; Pea, 1991; Shank, 1991; Wenger, 1987).

From the design phase, these technologies are intended to be flexible, explorative and open to social uses and they are therefore able to best incorporate those principles which represent a "correct" or "realistic" theory of learning in addition to being able to substitute common sense learning theory which is utilized mostly by technical designers. Empty technologies are not really empty: their design - as we will analyze further - reify some important principles of human learning (Suchman, 1987). A good example of empty technology is Bubble Dialogue (see Mac Mahon and O'Neill, this volume). Bubble technology combines elements of role play, dialogue creation, and reflexive dialogue analysis. Users are required to play out the parts of characters on the screen, creating dialogue in the characters' private domain (their thoughts or "inner speech") as well as in the public domain (their public speech). The dialogue scripts which emerge can be used to stimulate reflexivity and the development of self awareness of the knowledge construction process. In addition, they are potentially rich sources of data about user's responses to the issues raised in the dialogue. The tool can be used in a wide variety of ways depending on how the characters are represented graphically, how the context of their exchange is introduced and how roles are allocated to users.

There is a third type of system which can be called *technology for doing*. Examples of this type of technology are the word processor, the data base, the spreadsheet, e-mail, etc. That is, they are those instruments first developed to support and ease certain work and communicative activities, and not to foster the learning process directly. Although, obviously, the design of this type of software can be greatly improved by taking into account our knowledge of the cognitive processes underlying the ability in question (for example cognitive and linguistic processes of text composition), the present structure of these instruments does not preclude a good educational use, even though it does not assure they will not be used badly in education. For this type of technology, the difference is more dependent on the level of educational use and the type of educational environment which they will be inserted into rather than on design only.

Technologies, including those related to education, are not *neutral.* Their different educative positions are defined by choices regarding the degree of student initiative, their transparency/visibility, their representation of the learner's knowledge, their representation of the tutored domain and, in general, the epistemology and learning theory they represent. The central issue concerns the learner's control of his own activities. Designing "full" and "closed" systems with a high level of directiveness will simply reproduce the effects of school learning and kill any chance of educational innovation. Technological learning environments have to break such models by promoting a social and active style of interaction which contradicts the passive habits that students acquire in most of traditional schools.

Supporting the notion of empty and open systems does not mean sacrificing beauty and utility for free exploration of the world (that is, without constraints). Using empty and open technology does not mean allowing users to lose themselves in the educational space offered by the system. On the contrary, empty and open systems should reify a conceptual and cognitive trajectory, toward which the user can actively contribute, while maintaining a task's complexity as an integral part of the activity of constructing meaning.

Therefore, there should be present constraints that sustain the user's knowledge construction and that prevent the user from getting lost in the educational space offered by the system. A structure, as well as some clues for exploration, should be included in the system. These should sustain and guide the learning process as it occurs in the best educational contexts, even those without technology. Real constructivist contexts are in fact those that seem empty, but in fact reify a great deal of analysis, organization and planning of possible educational interactions (Zucchermaglio, 1991).

A New Theory of the Learning Process

In the cognitive science of instruction there has recently been an important methodological shift. "Learning context" is used not only as the context in which results obtained out of research should be applied, but also as a specific research context in examining the cognitive processes of instruction. Cognitive science has paid increasingly more attention to educational contexts, considered social settings, in which it is possible to observe and understand those processes of individual cognitive growth that can be affected by social exchanges and by cultural transmission. This shift is directly connected to the recent interest of cognitive scientists in the study of so called "everyday cognition" (Rogoff and Lave, 1984). This includes the study of the cognitive, linguistic and thinking processes carried out in real and "ecological" contexts of life and work (Brown, Collins & Duguid, 1989; Gardner, 1985; Brown & Duguid, 1989; Latour & Wogar, 1986). These studies of the learning processes of children and adults who are embedded in real educational contexts highlight some important aspects of the learning process:

1. *Learning isn't a matter of transfer, but of construction.* The learning process should not be described with the metaphor of pouring knowledge into empty vessels. Information does not exist objectively and it is not sufficient to transmit information into the learner's head. Children and adults are always active knowledge constructors: the knowledge interacts with the physical and social context in which they live. The process of child language development is a good example of this constructive activity. It is not completely free and creative, but depends strictly on specific constraints and characteristics of the environment.

It is necessary not only to transfer information but to design significant learning contexts -- contexts in which the activities carried out are the most relevant for the process of knowledge construction and for socialization to the practices of the culture in which we live. As Resnick (1987) says:

> We need now to develop a psychology of instruction that places the learner's active mental construction at the heart of the instructional exchange. This theory must be capable of guiding the design of interventions that aim to place learners in situations where the constructions that they will inevitably make will be powerful and correct ones, *constrained* by the principles that govern a domain. (p. 47)

The keyword here is *constrained*, not allowing children or adults free to get lost in an educational environment, but giving them clues and pieces of information by which and through which they can construct new cultural knowledge.

2. *There are multiple intelligences, not just one.* Learning can be seen as a process of enculturation, of entry into a culture of practitioners. Given this view, it is necessary to evaluate how any symbolic system (oral and written language, music, mathematics) allows the development of different types of intelligence, that can be defined as "skills in a medium" (Bruner et al., 1986). This development presents great variability not only between individuals but also in the same individual (Gardner, 1983). This means that the content of thinking is an important variable and that the specific knowledge promoted by each symbolic system is more relevant than the development of general abilities and universal logical structures (Piaget, 1970).

3. *The importance of content and context of thinking and learning.* Recent developments of the cognitive psychology of instruction have completely modified the meaning of the word

"learning": from "learning" considered as a microphenomenon of which general laws, valid for all species, activities and contexts can be identified to "learning" intended as a cultural development. In this latter definition learning is regarded as a complex social action embedded in historically and culturally defined frames of activity (Vygotsky, 1966; Cole, 1989). We think and learn in ways that are directly connected to the instruments and the symbolic systems of the cultural context in which we live (that is, the cognitive artifacts of Norman (1989) and the cultural amplifiers of Bruner (1989)).

On the contrary, in traditional educational contexts the learning process is mainly considered as a decontextualized and solitary process is carried out without those supporting aspects (other persons, information, instruments, notes, books, etc) typical of the informal contexts of learning (Martin, 1982; Orr, 1990; Ajello, Pontecorvo, Zucchermaglio, 1991).

In this sense the distance between learning "in" educational contexts (intended as a specific ability) and learning "out" of educational contexts should be diminished (Resnick, 1987). In fact, the analysis of learning processes occurring in everyday contexts or among traditional populations that haven't "invented" a school system suggests that learning should be described as primarily a process of apprenticeship, that is, as a graded, contextually embedded practice inserted in a significant frame of activity (Lave, 1988; Childs & Greenfield, 1980; Collins, Brown & Newman, 1989). Learning about an activity depends on authentically participating in that activity - not in ersatz approximation to it. In this sense learning does not always involve abstract, decontextualized subject matter. In an apprenticeship practice, much crucial learning happens without teaching. Although there is very little "traditional teaching" (only occasional instructions or pointing out of errors by the masters) there is a great deal of learning through this graded, contextually embedded practice. Learners need to be able to establish an apprentice-like relationship with practitioners who model for learners, explicitly or implicitly, the practices of expertise.

Learners need to be allowed to begin on the periphery of authentic activity and to move progressively through increasingly full participation toward expertise (Greenfield, 1984). In this view learning is in part the process of socially constructing a communal understanding. Individual learning is not individual and receptive at all, but a collective, constructive social process. Knowledge after all is not a private substance. Learning is, therefore, not a competitive, individual, exclusionary practice, but a collaborative, collective, inclusionary one (Brown & Duguid, 1989).

An Applied Cognitive Science of Instruction for the Design of Technology

The problem of the relationship between technology and learning is embedded in the wider relationship between technology and cognition (Winograd & Flores, 1986). Technologies are cultural artifacts and amplifiers (both material and symbolic) that mediate our cognitive interactions with the environment. Their presence and use in life contexts change our way of working, doing, thinking and learning substantially[2].

Indeed, a cognitive artifact is an artificial device designed to maintain, display, or operate upon information in order to serve a representational function (Norman, 1989). The notion of artifact concerns the inseparability of individual human growth from the instruments of the culture in which it occurs (Cole, 1989). Developments in the cognitive science of instruction, also drawing on socio-historical theory (Leontiev, 1981; Luria, 1976), provide researchers with an appropriate theoretical approach, intended as cultural tools, to analyze technology. As Norman (1990) says, "By understanding the ways in which cognitive artifacts serve human cognition, we may be better able to design new ones and improve old ones" (p.28). Instructional design is compared with the need to take these cognitive research outcomes into account. This research aims to reach an ecological description of the cognitive processes by which humans think and learn.

This means that we need to construct a new perspective, which can be called ergonomics of educational technology, in order to allow a cognitive and educative based design of new technology and not only to suggest new educational uses of old technology. We should construct a "design science" of educational technology (Norman, 1988) or a "science of the artificial" as Simon (1981) defines it. Research on learning and instruction is always a science of the artificial, the study of how educational interactions work can never be far removed from the task of engineering them to work better. What is expected from the application of information and cognitive technologies to education would be radical changes in traditional ways of conceiving and realizing education.

Designers are forced to integrate the knowledge of learning processes consciously into their design effort, contributing to the creation of a new learning culture in educational contexts. The design of technology should be explicitly focussed on social interactions and communication. They are intended as cultural tools that mediate and support the social, distributed and situated construction of new knowledge. A technological system should not merely reveal itself to a user, but must be conceived as an instrument that helps the student to reflect on the learning

---

[2] For example, Simon (1988) highlights how the growth of managment technologies (decision support systems, etc) are changing the cognitive demands of working in the business workplace.

process and check it consciously. It supports communication and negotiation processes between members of a social community inserted in a rich learning context. If it should become the intellectual technology of a culture, efforts at designing artificially intelligent instructional systems will benefit from an analysis of the complexity of the teacher-child negotiation in the process of instruction (Pontecorvo, 1991). Technology should not attempt to replace the teacher but rather it should address the system as a tool that serves as a mediator between child, teacher and the object of knowledge. The amount of teaching performed by the adult teacher does not diminish; it simply changes. Indeed, one thing that has become clear is that far from making teachers unnecessary, the intelligent and cognitive based integration of technology requires them to rethink their roles and constitutes a major challenge to their flexibility and professionalism.

An objective of an ergonomics of educational technology is to develop specifications that are applicable to a wide range of educational systems and that are concerned with increasing the ability of the system to support higher order learning and thinking. An example of this is the work of Scardamalia and Bereiter (1987) in which they describe the principles of construction and the development of CSILE (Computer Supported Intentional Learning Environments). The objective of CSILE was that of increasing students' abilities toward the goal of learning to learn. In order to achieve this objective students were allowed to have access to more active processes of knowledge construction by being able to participate in activities that have been traditionally regarded as "teaching" rather than "learning" activities. Higher levels of knowledge that are associated with being able to teach what one has learned were promoted through CSILE.

Other projects (Woolf, Blegan, Jansen and Verloop, 1986; Pea, 1991; Wilson, 1991) are developing computer based simulation environment that reproduce several important features of good learning environment and that provide a "cognitive apprenticeship" in which learners engage in the central activities of a domain which is intended as a situated and social learning process.

To respect the constructive and social nature of the learning process it is necessary to build and use empty and open technologies rather than technologies which are already "full" of knowledge. These analyses suggest forecasting only in the design phase of social and open uses of technology, substituting the task of working with materials already given and completely organized by others with the task of constructing something (also in interaction with others), and selecting and finding more appropriate materials (apart from giving them a certain organization) to reach the objective of a learning task.

Cognitive Ergonomics of Educational Technology: Methodological Issues

The ergonomics of educational technology is an applied cognitive science aimed at designing and testing technological systems. There are three important aspects to take in account for further study:

1. *User knowledge:* This refers to analysis of the cognitive and personality characteristics of the user (child or adult), including taking into consideration prior and naive knowledge. In the technology design phase it is necessary to incorporate the results of basic cognitive research. Studies of the development of competence in people who are becoming experts in their field (Resnick, 1989) and those which address how people actually work, learn and function cognitively in their normal (in- and out-of-school) lives must be considered in the design of these technologies.

2. *Design and analysis of the context of use of technologies:* This includes analysis of the organizational and structural aspects of the context of use of technologies. Technology in general, and educational technology in particular, are bearers of their own "culture" transmitted by their designers. This "culture" is often incompatible with the "culture" of educational agencies (schools, enterprises, etc.) into which this technology would be inserted.

A learning organization reaches a high level of innovation and efficiency when structured in such a way that eases (and takes advantage of) the social, distributed, participative, situated processes of learning developed by its members and in interaction with the technological environment. The organizational structure, including the technology, should support and allow members to learn while the organization itself learns from its members. With this perspective, the design of educational technology should not be conceived only at the level of interaction with the human-system, but also at the organizational level.

3. *Constant assessment of the system's usability:* We should verify if technology is useful for learning, if we can learn better, in a more coherent way, and "adapt" to our learning processes. We should adopt a perspective of interactive design whereby the designer iteratively improves the product until it is successful in terms of effectiveness. This means paying particular attention to the use of technology in real contexts and on the part of specific users. We need ethnographic observations of what children and adults do in computer rich environments. Working in real educational contexts rather than laboratories is essential because of the focus on learning and its organizational impact. This particular example of study, analysis and contextualized assessment constitutes the necessary verification of the technology design phase and can also serve as a vehicle for feed-back to the organization in which it is used. Only through this cognitive ethnography will we be able to elucidate how different designs of educational technological environments contribute to success in terms of learning.

We should reach a cognitive, and not simply physical, compatibility between technology and the individual. Interfaces must *reify* implicit aspects of the learner's cognition in order to make them more available for reflection and learning.

The most important objective of an ergonomics of educational technology should be that of design and implementation tools that, permitting different and new communicative models, contribute (together with other traditional means) to the design of learning contexts which sustain an "efficient" knowledge construction. In doing so they must keep in mind that disciplines not only serve as information to transfer into the learner's head but also pieces of knowledge that the learner actively reconstructs.

It is necessary that the culture of people working in the area of educational technology change.[3] Technicians should abandon the idea that it is possible to solve design problems only by adopting a common sense theory of the learning process. Cognitive and educational psychologists should adopt an "ergonomic" perspective in order to design and implement educational contexts and cognitive technologies which sustaining learning as a socially situated activity.

References

Ajello, A.M., Pontecorvo, C., Zucchermaglio, C. (1991). *Discutendo si impara*, Roma: La Nuova Italia Scientifica.

Bagnara, S., Stajano, A. (1987). *Ergonomia del software*. Milano: Clup.

Brown, J.S. (1989). Towards a new epistemology for learning. In C. Frasson & J. Gauthiar (Eds.), *Intelligent tutoring systems at the crossroad of AI and education*. Norwood, NJ: Ablex.

Brown, J.S., Collins, A. Duguid P. (1989). Situated cognition and the culture of learning. *Education Researcher, 18*, 1, 32-42.

Brown,J.S., Duguid, P. (1989). *Innovation in the workplace. A perspective on organizational learning*. Paper presented at the CMU Conference on Organizational Learning, Pittsburgh, PA.

Bruner, J.S., Olver, R.R., Greenfield, P.M., et al. (1966). *Studies in cognitive growth*. Wiley & Sons: New York.

Bruner,J. (1983). *Child's talk. Learning to use language*. New York: W.W. Norton & Company.

Bruner, J. (1989). *Culture and human development: A new look*. Invited Address to Annual Meeting. Society for Research in Child Development. Kansas City, MS.

[3]My Department (Direzione Formazione Italsiel, Gruppo IRI-Finsiel) is supporting a group composed of professionals of different backgrounds. Technicians, educational and cognitive psychologists, experts in methodology and organizational analysis are working together to design and realize the adoption of a common methodological perspective, innovative educational contexts and technologies aimed at the training of different work competencies (managerial, medical, technical, etc.).

Childs, C.P., Greenfield, P.M., (1980). Informal modes of learning and teaching: the case of Zinanteco Weaving. In N.Warren (Ed.), *Studies in cross cultural psychology (2)*. New York: Academic Press.

Collins, A. Brown, J.S. & Newman, S.E. (1989). Cognitive apprenticeship: Teaching the crafts of reading, writing and mathematics. In L.B. Resnick (Ed.), *Knowing, learning and instruction: Essays in honor of Robert Glaser*. Hillsdale, NJ: Lawrence Erlbaum Associates.

Cole, M. (1989). Cultural psychology: A once and future discipline? In J. Berman (Ed.), *Nebraska symposium on motivation: Cross cultural perspectives*. Lincoln: University of Nebraska Press.

Cole, M. (in press). On socially shared cognition. In L.B. Resnick, J. Levine & S.D. Beherend, *Perspectives on socially shared cognition*. Washington, D.C.: American Psychological Association.

Flores, F., Graves, M. Hartfield, B. & Winograd, T. (1988). Computer systems and the design of organizational interaction. *ACM transactions on office information system* (6), 2, 153-172.

Gardner, H. (1983). *Frames of mind. The theory of multiple intelligences*. New York: Basic Books.

Gardner, H. (1985). *The mind's new science. A history of the cognitive revolution*. New York: Basic Books.

Greenfield. P.M. (1984). A theory of the teacher in the learning activities of everyday life. In B. Rogoff & J. Lave (1984). *Everyday cognition*. Cambridge MA: Harvard University Press.

Latour, B. Woolgar, S. (1986). *Laboratory life: The construction of scientific facts*. Princeton: Princeton University Press.

Lave, J. (1988). *Cognition in practice: Mind, mathematics and culture in everyday life*. New York: Cambridge University Press.

Leontiev, A.N. (1981). *Problems of the development of mind*. Moscow: Progress.

Kaye, A.R. (1989). Computers make slow progress in class. *Science*, vol. 244, pp. 906-909.

Luria, A.R. (1976). *Cognitive development: Its cultural and social foundations*. Cambridge,MA: Harvard University Press.

Martin, J. (1982). Stories and scripts in organizational settings. In A.H. Hastorf & A.M. Isen (Eds.), *Cognitive and social psychology*. Amsterdam: Elsevier.

Newman, D. (1990). Opportunities for research on the organizational impact of school computers, *Educational Researcher*, vol. 19, n. 3, pp.8-13.

Newman, D. Griffin, P. & Cole, M. (1989). *The construction zone: Working for cognitive change in school*. New York: Cambridge University Press.

Norman, D. (1988). *The psychology of everyday things*. New York: Basic Books.

Norman, D. (1989). Cognitive artifacts. *Workshop: Cognitive theory and design in human-computer interaction*, Kittle House Inn, Chappaqua, New York.

Orr, J. (1990). Sharing knowledge, celebrating identity: War stories and community memory among service technicians. In D.S. Middleton and D. Edwards, *Collective remembering: Memory in society*. Beverly Hills, CA: Sage publications.

Pea, R. (1991). Mediaworks: Students learning through design with multimedia tools for collaborative research. Golem Workshop *Multimedia Systems in Education*, Capri, Italy, 7-8 June.

Piaget, J. (1970). Piaget's theory. In P.H.Mussen (Ed.), *Charmachaels's manual of child psychology, Vol.1.* New York: Wiley.

Pontecorvo, C. (1991). Interazione sociale, mediazione culturale, interiorizzazione. In B.Vertecchi (Ed.), *Una scuola per tutta la vita.* Firenze: La Nuova Italia.

Resnick, L.B. (in press). Shared cognition: Thinking as social practice. In L.B. Resnick, J. Levine & Beherend, S.D. *Perspectives on socially shared cognition.* Washington, D.C:: American Psychological Association.

Resnick, L. B. (1987). Learning in School and Out, *Educational Researcher, 6* (9), 13-20

Resnick, L.B. (1989). *Knowing and learning.* Hillsdale, N.J.: Erlbaum.

Rogoff,B. & Lave,J.(1984). *Everyday cognition.* Cambridge, MA: Harvard University Press.

Scardamalia, M., Bereiter, C., McLean R., Swallow, J., Woodruff, E. (1987) Computer supported intentional learning environments. In A. Collins (chair) *Strategies for teaching thinking skills with interactive technologies.* Symposium conducted at the annual meeting of A.E.R.A., Washington.

Scribner, S. (1984). Studying working intelligence. In B. Rogoff & J. Lave (Eds.) 1984, *Everyday cognition.* Cambridge, MA: Harvard University Press.

Simon, H.A. (1988). *Informatica, direzione aziendale e organizzazione del lavoro.* Milano: Franco Angeli.

Simon, H.A. (1969). *The sciences of the artificial.* Cambridge, MA: MIT Press.

Shank, R. (1991). New perspectives on the design of teaching systems. *Golem Workshop Multimedia Systems in Education*, Capri, Italy, 7-8 June.

Suchman, L. (1987). *Plans and situated actions: The problem of human-machine communication.* Cambridge, U.K.: Cambridge University Press.

Tushman, M.L. & Anderson P. (1988). Technological discontinuities and organization environments. In A. M. Pettigrew (Ed.), *The managment of strategic change.* Oxford: Blackwell.

Vygotsky, L.S., (1966), *Pensiero e linguaggio.* Firenze: Giunti-Barbera.

Wenger E.(1987). *Glass box technology: Merging learning and doing.* Institute for Research and Learning, Palo Alto, CA: Research Abstract, I.

Wilson, K. (1991). Discovery-based learning. Experiences using multimedia: Two design examples. *Golem Workshop Multimedia Systems in Education*, Capri, Italy, 7-8 June.

Winograd, T. & Flores, F. (1986). *Understanding computers and cognition.* Norwood, NJ: Ablex.

Woolf, B. Blegan, D., Jansen, J. Verloop, A. (1986). *Teaching a complex industrial process. Proceedings of National Association of Artificial Intelligence.* Philadelphia, PA.

Wood, D., Bruner, J.S., Ross, G., (1976). The role of tutoring in problem solving. *Journal of Child Psychology and Psychiatry,* 17, 89 - 100.

Zuboff, S. (1988). *In the age of the smart machine: The future of work and power.* New York: Basic Books.

Zucchermaglio, C. (1991). *Gli apprendisti della lingua scritta.* Bologna: Il Mulino.

13 Varied Levels of Support for Constructive Activity in Hypermedia-Based Learning Environments

Brockenbrough S. Allen and Robert P. Hoffman

Department of Educational Technology, San Diego State University, San Diego, California, USA

There are very few human beings who receive the truth, complete and staggering, by instant illumination. Most of them acquire it fragment by fragment, on a small scale, by successive developments, cellularly, like a laborious mosaic.

Anais Nin

Although we are not confirmed constructivists, our experience as researchers, practitioners, and teachers of instructional design and hypermedia has made us very aware of the limitations of conventional instructional development paradigms for creating hypermedia-based educational products.

A *hypermedium* can be defined as a network in which information units, such as still and moving pictures, diagrams, animation, text, and audio are connected by relational links. A link may be unlabeled or may, through words, symbols, or icons, describe or characterize the relationship between two information units. Links may be anchored to an information unit as a whole or anchored to a sub-component such as a picture element, sound, or word. *Hypertext* (Nelson, 1978) is a more restrictive concept in which the information units that constitute the nodes of the network consist primarily of text displays. Complex hypertext and hypermedia systems require computers to manage the display of information units and the relational links. *Intermedia* is a a good example of a hypermedia system (see Knuth and Cunningham, this volume).

Hypermedia and Constructive Learning Activity

Hypermedia is often associated with *multimedia*, but we think the two can be distinguished by the relative degree of authority that is extended to users over the creation of links, paths, and networks. In multimedia, the authors of a particular product are generally responsible for determining the way in which information units will be sequenced or arrayed. It may be useful to think of multimedia and hypermedia as two ends of a continuum that is defined by the degree to which a user has authority and/or responsibility for establishing links, paths, or webs of relationships. This presents a new context for an ancient educational problem. How should the educational "system" and the user/learner share authority and responsibility for establishing relationships between information units. How should they use these relationships as a basis for communicating, knowing, and learning? Polya describes this problem of how to share responsibility and authority with admirable clarity:

> The student should acquire as much experience of independent work as possible. But if he is left alone with his problem without any help or with insufficient help, he may make no progress at all. If the teacher helps too much, nothing is left to the student. The teacher should help, but not too much and not too little, *so that the student shall have a reasonable share of the work* (emphasis added) (p. 6, 1957).

Polya's statement implies that educational "systems" should respond to a learner's increasing ability to understand or relate units of information or knowledge by gradually allocating a greater share of authority and responsibility to the learner, so that the learner's capacities will not be overloaded. We agree with Bednar, Cunningham, Duffy, and Perry (1991) in their criticism of models of learning that treat instruction merely as a process of systematic communication in which knowledge or skills are "instilled" or "acquired." Such models tend to degenerate into systems that reinforce authoritarian interpretation of meaning and passive patterns of learning. Based on its etymology, the word *instruction* (in + struere, Latin for "to build") can be interpreted to mean "to build within"— a reminder that all externalized methods and materials are only means for promoting or facilitating constructive mental activity that must ultimately be carried out by the learner. It might be useful to supplement the notion of *just-in-time learning* as proposed by various authors (Allen, 1991) with *just-enough teaching*. With this phrase we mean to capture thinking from the 1970s and 1980s which argued that unnecessary instructional "support" can actually interfere with the skills and abilities of successful learners. For a summary of the issues, see Allen and Merrill (1985).

The crux of the issue is not whether or how to "manage" the flow of information to the learner's "head," but how to manage negotiations between the learner and the educational system about the goals of the learning, the methods that will be employed to promote said goals, and yes, even the meaning of reality and systems for describing it.

Since much future learning will basically consist of interaction with large computer data bases containing a wide variety of mediated representations, a major challenge for constructivist designers will be to provide learners of varied ability and interests with means of support that are sufficient for achieving their learning goals but which do not impose unnecessary restrictions or constraints. Both hypermedia technology and the *zeitgeist* of its advocate community favor open, informational approaches that eschew explicit statement of learning outcomes or prescription of instructional strategies. For this reason, we suspect that hypermedia will first claim effectiveness with the motivated and educated—people with good learning skills, a self-directed approach to understanding, and an easy acquaintance with methods for organizing knowledge. The prospects for successful use of hypermedia by less able learners seems limited unless educational technologists can develop systems that provide advisement, coaching, and instruction appropriate to users who will otherwise find themselves rudderless in a sea of information — without a map or a first mate. In addition to differences in ability there are, as Noel Entwhistle describes (Entwhistle, this volume) important differences in the interest or need that users have for deep versus shallow approaches to a knowledge domain.

Cristina Zucchermaglio's notion (Zucchermaglio, this volume) of providing learners with "open" tools (such as microworlds and glassbox technologies) that do not unnecessarily force learners to subscribe to "objective" meanings is very helpful, but it must be recognized that no tool can be truly empty since, by structure and function, all tools restrict certain forms of expression and enable (or at least anticipate) others. A degrees-of-freedom metaphor is convenient here in which tools for constructing meaning are thought of as either more or less open. Our point throughout this article is that technology-based learning systems are generally more powerful, flexible, and fault-tolerant when the degrees of freedom or openness can be adjusted to the needs and capacities of learners and learning communities. Perhaps more important is that learning systems that are responsive to varying requirements for openness are more likely to degrade gracefully (rather than catastrophically) in less than optimal circumstances because they can be adjusted more easily to unforeseen goals or conditions.

Description of *SemNet*™

Our goal in this chapter is to share some of our reflections about *SemNet* (Faletti, Fisher, Lipson, Patterson, & Thornton, 1991), a Macintosh-based hypermedia program for creating and exploring semantic networks. We will examine some of the challenges and opportunities it presents to academics and professionals who are dissatisfied with conventional technology-based learning. *SemNet* has been described in a number of technical papers and articles (Fisher, Faletti, Patterson, Thornton, Lipson, & Spring, 1990; Fisher, Faletti & Quinn, 1990). Allen has worked with it during a four year "beta-test" period.

SemNet uses object-oriented programming and the Macintosh graphical interface to display labeled nodes (referred to as "concepts") and labeled arrow-links (called "relations"). Node-link-node sequences are called "instances." It can be used to represent a wide variety of domains to the extent that they can be represented as semantic networks or propositional networks. In typical browsing maneuvers, users see a central node connected to its immediate "satellites" (see Figure 1). Clicking on a satellite node "moves" the frame so that the satellite assumes the center position thus revealing its satellites. In the process, the visible label for asymetrical links will change. For example "bird—HASA—> wings" becomes "wing—is aspect of—>bird."

Moving through a sequence of alternating nodes and links generates a "path" which can be circuitous, that is, it may entail a single node several times. This results when the user visits the same concept repeatedly. Users can also move quickly and intuitively through large nets by selecting items in indexes, or by invoking utility commands such as "jump" and "replay path."

Easily-used commands afford several techniques for creating and modifying connections; experienced users can construct nets at rates exceeding several instances per minute if they are clear about how to organize their ideas. Users can assign graphics and short text passages to nodes and links (and in future versions will be able to assign video and audio segments to nodes). They can also export graphics and ASCII text representing indexes or net contents and subsets thereof.

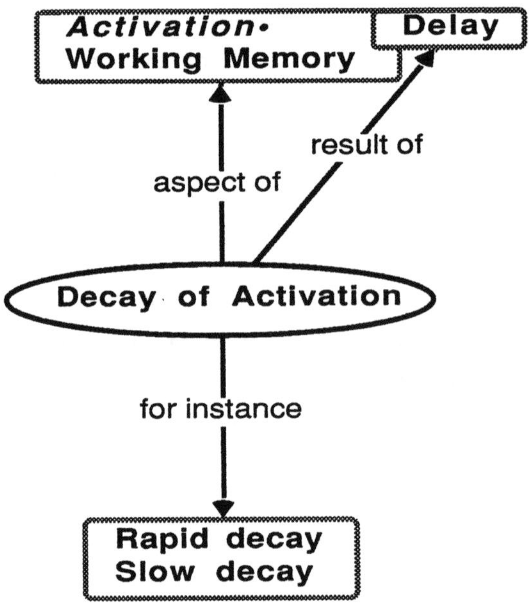

Figure 1a. SemNet uses object-oriented programming and the Macintosh™ graphical interface to display labeled nodes (referred to as "concepts") and labeled arrow-links (called "relations"). Node-link-node sequences are called "instances." In typical browsing maneuvers, users see a central node connected to its immediate "satellites" as in these figures. Multiple nodes having the same relation to the center are fitted into rectangular boxes. Clicking on a satellite node "moves" the frame so that the satellite assumes the center position thus revealing its satellites. In the process, the visible label for links that are asymmetrical will change. For example, "Decay of Activation —aspect of—> Working Memory" will become "Working Memory —HASA—> Decay of Activation." This display, from net developed by a student in an instructional psychology course taught by Allen, is based on Chapter 6, "Human Memory: Basic Concepts and Principles" from Cognitive Psychology and Its Implications by John R. Anderson (1990).

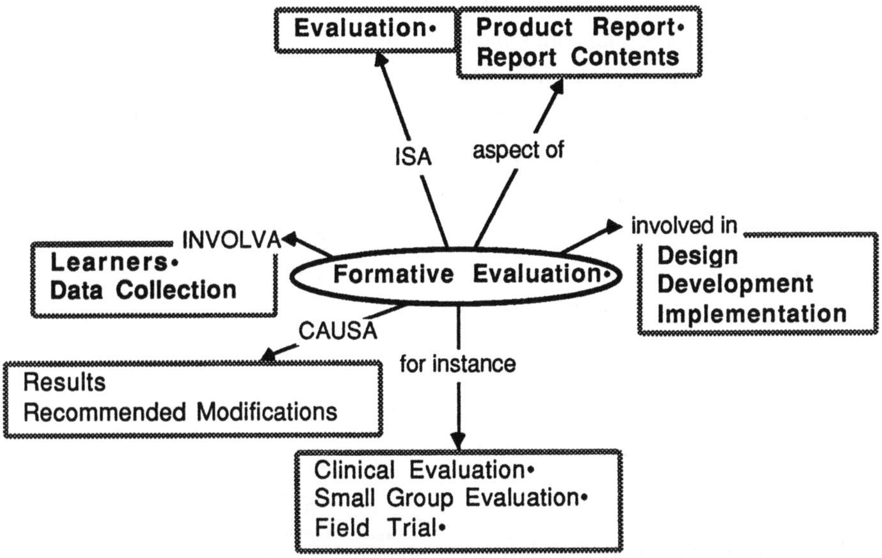

Figure 1b. Portion of a net with 500 plus nodes used to represent an intermediate instructional design course taught by Allen. Net developed by Alexandra Haag.

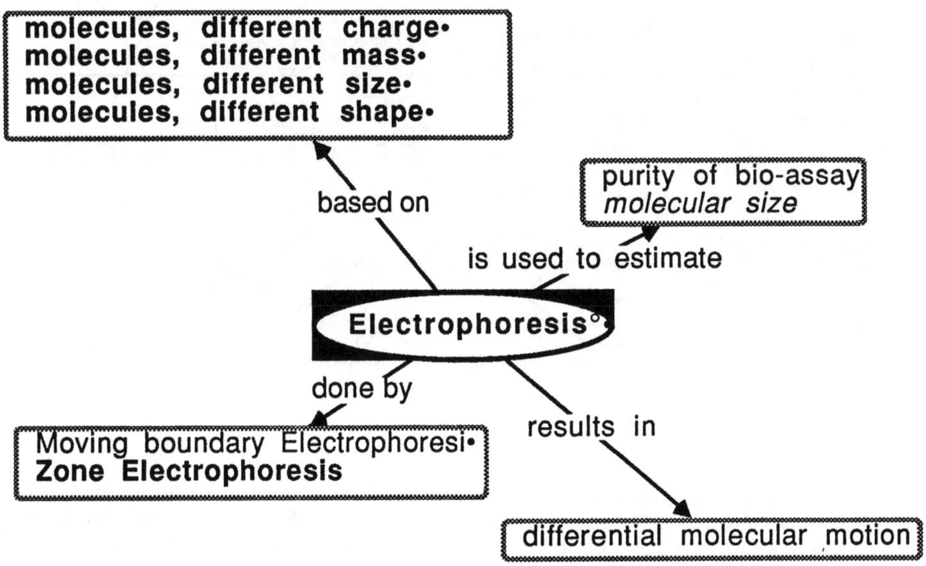

Figure 1c. Display from a net developed by Jacintha Kompella, a PhD physicist who was taking graduate seminar in instructional design. She developed the net as a subject matter analysis and later used it as a guide to development of flowcharts and storyboards for hypermedia-based lessons on biochemistry. "Tabs" attached to the central node indicate that "pictures," "text," and "synonyms" assigned to it by the net author can be accessed by mouse pointing.

The program provides a variety of metrics about the size and complexity of a net and uses these to assemble various types of summaries and overviews. Almost anyone who browses through a SemNet expresses interest in viewing "the whole net." This has proven problematical since semantic networks are n-dimensional structures that cannot easily be visualized in two dimensions. But the problem has been addressed by special displays. For example, measures of the "embeddedness" of concepts are used to generate a "knowledge core" in which the most embedded nodes are laid out in rows and connected by crisscrossed lines (see Figure 2). Other tools let users see the shortest path between two nodes, or traverse the net viewing only node-and-satellite frames that meet user-established criteria.

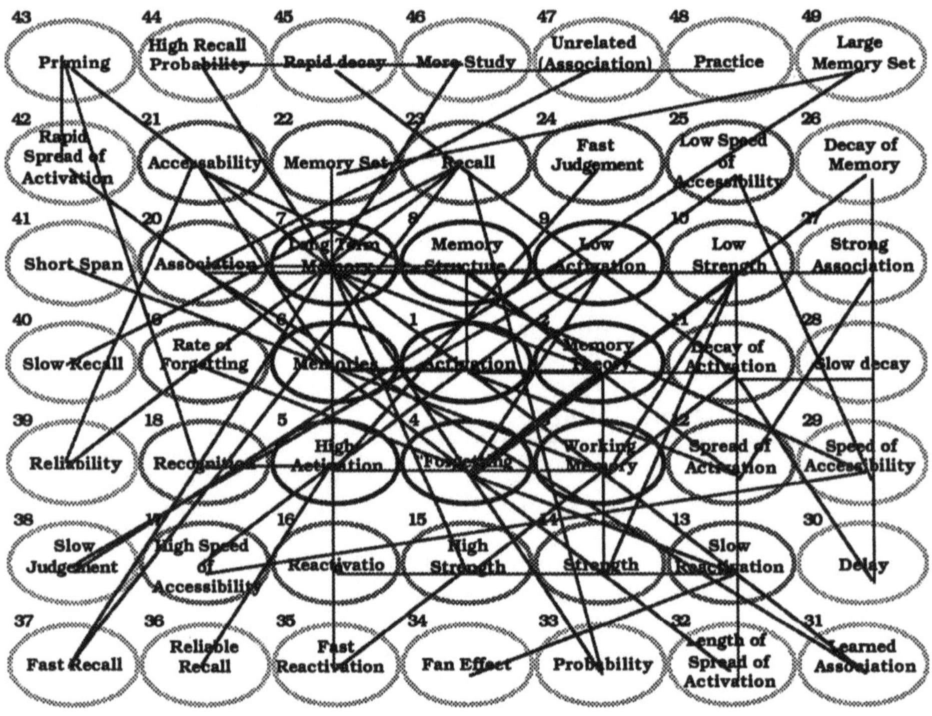

Figure 2. SemNets are n-dimensional structures that cannot easily be visualized in two dimensions. But the problem has been addressed by special displays. For example, measures of the "embeddedness" of concepts are used to generate a "knowledge core" in which the most embedded nodes are located in the center and connected to other nodes by connected by crisscrossed lines. This display was generated from the same net on memory represented in Figure 1a. The most embedded concepts are (in declining order) activation, memory theory, working memory, forgetting, high activation, memories, long-term memory, memory structure, and low activation.

We now provide graduate students with opportunities to use *SemNet* to make instructional design decisions and to map complex multimedia and hypermedia products. Our work may put us at odds with some advocates of constructivism because it emphasizes development of "subject matter" nets by instructional designers—nets that will be used to create technology-based learning products of various designs ranging from hypermedia-based surrogate travel programs to criterion-based mastery tests.

We intend to experiment with ways to use semantic nets to support conventional instructional development tasks such as specification of learning outcomes, development of test items, prescription of instructional strategies, allocation of strategies to media/delivery systems, and flowcharting of educational software. However, our long-range goals assume that many of these craft skills will change dramatically as hardware/software capabilities improve and as the pragmatic-empirical benefits of constructivist paradigms (and the advantages they offer for design of hypermedia products) become more widely understood. We certainly expect that product design skills for technology-based learning environments of the future will require a better understanding of learning in context; multiple, negotiable, and collaborative representations of meaning; cognitive complexity; situated cognition; metacognition; and other ideas favored by constructivists. However, we expect that for the foreseeable future much design will be conducted in settings that will require a blend of skills from conventional ID and constructivist methodologies.

SemNet as Hypermedia

SemNet looks and feels different from most hypermedia systems, yet we believe it epitomizes hypermedia because it emphasizes links as a source of meaning. Dynamic graphics, animation, random-access to user controllable video and audio, multiple windows,and other features commonly associated with hypermedia systems can also be found in multimedia, and even in film and television. However, without user-controllable links, paths, and webs, media are just not "hyper."

In many familiar hypermedia authoring systems such as *HyperCard*™, *SuperCard*™, *Plus*™, and *Toolbook*™, users navigate by activating links to move between information "blocks" represented by screens or windows. These blocks display narrative text or high-resolution images studded with "hot spots," "hot words," or icons that represent anchor points for links to other blocks. But controls for activating these links often bear only very general relational meanings such as "see something that's related," "go to," "next," or "return." Many block-oriented hypermedia designers emphasize so-called "seamless" transitions between blocks in an effort to make navigation correspond to the aesthetic of cinematographers and videographers (using, for example, dissolves or sliding cards). This approach favors a "look-

and-feel" that is continuous and film-like rather than text-like, easy to parse, and provocative of deeper reflection about the relationship between blocks. "Block-oriented" hypermedia systems frequently afford only limited maps or overviews of network connections. For example, Apple's *HyperCard* allows retracement through the last 40 "cards" visited by a user but does not have any inherent options for graphic presentation of all links between all cards.

SemNet, which can be classified as a "link-oriented" hypermedia system, affords navigation though a graphic but skeletal representation that encourages explicit text labels for the relationships between nodes. Text and graphic blocks are treated as secondary information accessible though nodes but not immediately visible. For all practical purposes, users must therefore forgo continuous navigation through information-dense media blocks and are forced to the skeletal level to take their bearings (where they must focus on links as the basis for organization). It is virtually impossible to navigate through SemNet's map-like primary graphical interface (Figure 1) without thinking about relationships. This effect is heightened when a SemNet user works with a parsimonious set of relational descriptors because use of a limited set of verbal labels inevitably results in juxtapositions of words such as "apple—HASA—>redness" that—while correct in terms of ideation—sound just unnatural enough to remind one that the real issue is deep-level meaning.

With developers in ever-accelerating pursuit of "user-friendly" hypermedia interfaces, there is a risk that in attempting to make navigation "seamless" or "effortless," the meaning that accompanies shifts of "place" in "hyperspace" will be lost. When buttons become bland, generic designators, one has to ask, Why use a spatial metaphor for organization of knowledge in the first place? If movement between information blocks is merely a matter of utility rather than meaning—of dividing up information so that it will fit on computer screens—then navigation gets reduced to a series of blind and uninformed leaps.

Representation of Relational Descriptors

The extent to which a hypermedia-based product can be considered link-oriented is a function of the salience of the links and the possibilities for visualizing paths and webs. We have also just argued that the extent to which links bear information about the meaning of a connection is also important. This introduces a theme which we will take up again later in more detail: the degree to which the system provides information about the meaning of a link is one means for controlling the level of system support for constructive mental activity.

Consider the conversion of a network represented in a link-oriented hypermedium such as *SemNet* to a block-oriented hypermedium such as *HyperCard*. One of the problems that must be resolved in such a transformation is how the relational information so readily apparent in the node-link-node graphics of *SemNet* will be displayed within blocks in *HyperCard*.

Brock Allen and Charles Hoscowitz have created *Wayfinder* as a program for converting any path through *SemNet* to a HyperCard stack. A path (sequences of alternating nodes and links) is first extracted from *SemNet* as an ASCII text file. Then the path is transformed to a HyperCard stack in which each node is represented as a "card" (single screen). The node-label is automatically placed in a slot that appears as a "title" text field for the card. (A HyperCard author can subsequently add detailed text and graphics to each card.) Wayfinder represents each link between nodes as a button ("hot spot").

But how should the relational descriptor for the link be represented as a label for the button? Descriptors are normally explicit in *SemNet*; when a node is located at the center of a screen, labeled links connect it with each satellite node. As *Wayfinder* converts a path to *HyperCard*, it affords three options for automatic labeling of buttons, providing three degrees of system support for learning activity:

1.) display only the relational label;
2.) display only the related concept label;
3.) display the relational label and the related concept label.

Our discussion will now consider two methods that appear to offer convenient means for varying the difficulty and complexity of "link-oriented" constructive activity so as to accommodate varying interests and abilities of learners. We will take up the first approach in some detail because it has many antecedents in the literature on semantic networks. It involves encouraging or requiring "relational parsimony" in net construction. The second approach, which we have dubbed "configuration management," extends and elaborates the three options described above for supplying information about links. It involves providing learners with various configurations of concept labels, relational labels and link connections. Using these configurations can reduce the difficulty of building networks while preserving in varying degrees the learner's responsibility and authority for constructing meaning.

Relational Parsimony in Semantic Networks

Since Quillian (1967) proposed semantic networks as a method for representing cognitive functions, numerous authors have proposed modifications, extensions, and alternatives. For the most part, these proposals have recognized the vital role of relational descriptors in the construction of semantic networks. While our literature review uncovered little empirical research on relational decriptors, various authors have given considerable thought to the way relations are represented in their systems.

Readers who prefer to skip this review may wish to refer to Table 1 for a summary and comparison of relational descriptors proposed by selected authors; a few authors with similar sets of descriptors are omitted. Our proposed descriptors, to be discussed later, are listed in the left-hand column of Table 1. In an effort to facilitate comparison among systems, we have ordered the sets and aligned them with our own descriptors (with apologies to the authors) based on rough similarities in meaning. In cases where an author does not name or describe a relational descriptor used in our system, the entry is left blank. Where an author's term spans more than one of our descriptors, it is repeated in the appropriate cells. Descriptors that do not seem to fit any of our categories are grouped under *INVOLVA*, which we use for undefined relationships.

Historical Notes

In their early work with semantic networks Rumelhart, Lindsay, and Norman (1972) recognized that within the universe of relations, some were more "general" than others. They specified a set of rules by which

> .....more concrete relations [may] be defined in terms of more abstract ones. In addition, we presume that there is a process of abstraction or generalization which derives more abstract relations from less abstract ones. (p. 216)

As examples of rules, they demonstrated how the verb *stroll* can be constructed of the more general term *walk* modified by the adjective *slowly*.

Kintsch (1974) also proposed a system of rules for classifying links.

> In principle any lexical entry may be used as a predicator of some proposition, and in actual fact there are in the semantic memory of a fluent speaker of English a very large number of lexical entries that are used, and usually in more ways than one. Can these predicators be organized, that is, classified in some way, so that one does not have to deal with an amorphous set of propositions, but with some orderly structure? For the application of any kind of rules, be it inference rules within semantic memory or grammatical rules to generate text from propositions, it would be of tremendous benefit if such a structure could be identified.... (p. 23)

Kintsch turned to linguistics case grammar, proposing *agent*, *experiencer, instrument, object, source,* and *goal* as major categories.

> Thus, *Mary* in "Mary opened the door with a key" is the instigator [agent] of an action, while *door* is the object of that action and *key* the instrument by means of which the action is performed. (Kintsch, p. 24)

Kintsch recognized "locative and times cases," and to deal with deductive reasoning within semantic memory, he suggested using "implications, parts, superconcepts, and contradictions" as relational operators. He noted that understanding of these operators is incomplete.

	Fisher	Armbruster & Anderson	Goetz	Long & Aldersley	Anderson & Bower	Holly & Dansereau	Lindsay & Norman	Frederickson
	1988	1984	1984	1984	1980	1984b	1977	1975
1. ISA	inclusion	A defines B A is instance of B	B is example of A	definition example	member subset	type (of) example (of)	class examples isa (is an instance)	classificatory
2. HASA	inclusion characteristic	A defines B	B is a property of A B is chrater isic of A	definition character-istic		part (of) character-istics	has-as-parts properties	part attributive
3. CAUSA	action process role	A causes B A enables B	A causes B	reason-result	agent	leads to	agent object recipient instrument	resultive actions
4. NEXTA	action process role temporal	A occurs before B	A occurs before B	sequence		leads to		processes
5. IDENTA		A is identical to B			fact			symbolic content
6. LOCATA	characteristic				location time		location time	locative temporal
7. INVOLVA	historical	A is similar to B A is not similar to B A or B A and B A but B Given a question Q, if A then do event A, if B then do event B	A is similar to B branches according to the answer to question Q	compare-contrast	generic object subject predicate context	analogy evidence	applies-to sensory image motor-control image	

Table 1. Systems of Relational Descriptors. In an effort to facilitate comparison, we have ordered the sets and aligned them with our own descriptors based on rough similarities in meaning. Descriptors that do not seem to fit any of our categories are grouped under *INVOLVA*, which we use for undefined relationships.

Woods (1975) also pursued the idea of using a few basic categories of relational descriptors. He reviews different types of links used in semantic network notation beginning with *intensions* and *extensions*. Intension refers to the characteristics of a concept, while extension refers to set membership. In Woods' scheme, concepts were further defined by what he termed a *property list*. The items in this list are related to their respective concepts as either *attributes* or *values*. For example, a person's height, hair color, and occupation can be called out by attributes and values relations. Other links do not stand for attributes of concepts, but rather serve as factual links, i.e, "arbitrary relations between the node and other nodes" (Woods, pp. 53-54). Woods also used case representation: a concept may be characterized by its links to other concepts as those links describe its roles, e.g., "agent," "recipient," and "object."

Norman and Rumelhart (1975) classified predicate links in terms of four primitives: *stative*, *change*, *causative*, and *actions*.

> .....The *stative* component of a verb conveys the fixed relationship that holds among its arguments for a specified period. The change component tells simply that a change of state has occurred. The *causative* component communicates the source of, or reason for, the change. The *actional* component describes the behavior involved in the performance of the action specified by the verb. All verbs seem to contain at least one of these primitive components and a single verb may contain all of them. (Norman and Rumelhart, p. 47)

The stative component includes *location* and *possession*. For example, a house is located in a street, or a baseball game *is located* at a particular time, and Joe *possesses* a Volkswagen. The *change* component indicates a change from one state to another, but with no cause implied. For example, the bus moved out of the station. *Cause* may be indicated by the primitive verb *do*, and denotes a change from one state to another for which the cause can be identified. For example, John drove the car into the gas station. Norman and Rumelhart (p. 53) noted that *actionals* are the "least well-developed" of their verb representations. Actionals modify predicates and have to do with *how* an action is performed.

Lindsay and Norman (1977) described semantic networks as consisting of *nodes* interrelated by pointers or *labeled relations*. They identified relations that are important to the way people think, including: *isa* (which can be read as *is an instance of*), *applies-to, sensory image, motor-control-image*, and *has-as-parts*. They also introduced case relations: *agent, object, recipient, time, instrument,* and location. They identified a small number of relationships that are useful in the construction of a dictionary definition of a concept: "the *class* of concepts to which it belongs, the *properties* which tend to make that concept unique, and *examples* of the concept" (Lindsay and Norman, p. 383).

We are reminded by Lindsay and Norman's sensory and motor-control-image relations that it may not be possible to represent important domains of human knowledge in the form of propositional or semantic networks.

> We *are* "rational *animals*," but we are also "*rational* animals," which means that our rationality is embodied.... Our reality is shaped by the patterns of our bodily movement, the contours of our spatial and temporal orientation, and the forms of our interaction with objects. It is never merely a matter of abstract conceptualization and propositional judgments. (Johnson, 1987, p. xix)

Johnson's a priori constraint on the scope and completeness of propositional networks is an important challenge to hypermedia design theorists and must be addressed if hypermedia is to be integrated with systems for representation of bodily knowledge such as "virtual reality" (see Allen, 1992).

The set of links which makes up propositions in Anderson and Bower's (1980) "deep grammar" includes *fact, context, predicate, object,* and *subject.* Further qualification is provided by using *time* and *location* links, and *member, subset,* and *generic* links.

Winston (1984), commenting on Schank's (1973) work suggested that the number of primitives required to represent acts denoted by English verbs

> ...may be a surprisingly small number. It seems that many ordinary verbs are used as a sort of shorthand for ideas that can be expressed as well by combinations of basic primitives together with default slot fillers (Winston, 1984, p. 271).

The links that qualify these primitive acts, according to Winston, are *cause, agent, object,* and *destination,* as well as *subacts.* Any of these acts or subacts may have their own qualifiers (Winston, pp. 272-275).

Disadvantages of Relational Parsimony

The effort to justify and achieve relational parsimony in knowledge representation systems is widespread, but by no means universal. Particularly in the field of artifical intelligence (AI), some authors have argued the disadvantages of relational parsimony. Hendrix (1979) proposed "knowledge representation networks" that he described as a collection of nodes each representing an object, situation, or set interconnected by "arcs" that are "restricted to the encoding of formal binary relationships, such as taxonomic (element and subset) relationships and deep case relationships" (Hendrix, p. 55).

In linguistics, "deep cases" refers to relationships between objects in the world, as opposed to relationships between syntactic elements. Hendrix argued that this set of deep case relationships is open-ended, and claims that "no fixed set such as {[agent, object], goal, theme} is especially known to the network system" (Hendrix, p. 55). He therefore favored an open-ended approach to labeling relational links noting that

> .....even our general-purpose routines that retrieve information from a network without special knowledge concerning the meanings of arc labels operate more efficiently when more case names are used, because an increase in the number of arc labels provides a finer index into the net. (Hendrix, p. 55)

Schubert, Goebel, and Cercone (1979) were also in favor of an open set of predicates for representing natural language in AI systems:

> The fundamental question is whether to admit a large number of highly specific predicates, comparable to the number of words in the language, or only a small number (perhaps dozens) of very general *primitive* predicates. Primitives would have to be chosen so as to allow *reconstruction* of all word senses. (p. 145)

Schubert and his associates assume that as the set of primitives is reduced, the computation of the resulting representations becomes more cumbersome and so they advocated the use of non-primitive predicates along with lists of frequently used properties of the predicates.

Educational Applications

Some educators view the categorizing and constraining of relational descriptors as a means for increasing ease of use by learners. This may be due in part to the character of educational discourse. Our experience in classrooms, our examination of many student nets, and our interviews with SemNet users suggest to us that the type of knowledge represented in educational domains is mainly public and informative, rather than expressive and idiosyncratic. We agree with Fisher (1990) that public knowledge is more easily represented with consistent vocabulary than idiosyncratic knowledge and is more amenable to parsimonious use of relational decriptors. Therefore, users who are constructing nets of a highly personal, expressive nature may not find relational parsimony to be convenient.

Dansereau (1978) and Holly and Dansereau (1984a; 1984b), whose work has focused on learning and study strategies, experimented with various ways to guide students as they constructed networks representing domains associated with college texts. As their work has evolved they found it useful to adjust the number of relational descriptors recommended to students. One of their sets is the most parsimonious we have seen. It includes only three relations: ISA, HASA, and TE (theme-evidence) (Holly & Dansereau, 1984b). Dansereau's early (1978) system offered a set

> ...composed of four relationships: *type* (e.g., "A dog is a type of animal"), *part* (e.g., "The hand is a part of the body"), *leads to* (e.g., "Reinforcement leads to repetition of

the reinforced behavior"), and *description* (e.g., "The male peacock can be described as colorful"). (Dansereau, p. 19)

Dansereau later substituted a set of 13 descriptors for this first set. For example, *leads to* was superseded by three more specific links: *cause*, *influence*, and *solve*; *description* was replaced by *similar* and *characteristic* (Dansereau cited in Feifer, 1989, p. 26).

In a review of approaches to net construction, Holly and Dansereau (1984a) argue that early approaches to net construction such as Quillian's were too simple to be useful to college students and that subsequent approaches such as Rumelhart, Lindsay, and Norman's (1972) were too complex. When they found their own set of 13 descriptors too difficult for students to remember and use, they considered schemes of consolidation. Reduced to just four links, the set wasn't specific enough to describe many of the relationships found in typical of college textbooks. But a set of six experimenter-provided links offered "an appropriate compromise between specificity and utility" (Holly and Dansereau, 1984b, p. 84). These six are: *part* (of), *type* (of), *leads to*, *analogy*, *characteristic*, and *evidence*.

Schallert, Ulerick, and Tierney (1984) assumed "that a relatively limited set of relationship types will be adequate in representing all of the ways in which two concepts can be related to each other in informative discourse" (p. 259).

The relationship types come from a rhetoric tradition and identify Concept B as defining Concept A, as being a property of Concept A, as being an example of Concept A, as being similar or not similar to Concept A, as being greater than or less than Concept A, as occurring before Concept A, or as causing Concept A. (Schallert et al., p. 259)

These types are further organized into four categories: *characteristics* (definitions and properties); *set membership* (example); *comparison* (similar, not similar, greater than, and less than); and *process* (temporal and causal).

Feifer (1989), who developed *Sherlock*, a computer semantic network construction tutorial, proposed a"primitive" set of relations that he adapted from Dansereau. For its own, internal semantic map, Sherlock uses *generalization* (set/subset), *equivalence* (identity), *has* (part/whole), and *inhibition* (mutual exclusivity). Two additional labels, internally constructed from combinations of the basic set of four relations, are provided for ease of use by the learner: *property* (characteristic) and *leads* (to).

Other authors who have proposed various sets of relational descriptors for student constructed networks include Goetz (1984), who described six relations in his process of using a spatial learning strategy for studying. While his system does not employ nodes and links per se, it uses an equivalent graphing system. Long and Aldersley (1984) described a text analysis procedure for hearing-impaired students that resorts to six links. Armbruster and Anderson (1984) developed a mapping system which assumes that text is structured hierarchically. Similar in graphic representation to Goetz' approach, theirs is one of the most extensive sets we have seen, consisting of 12 relationships.

Relational Parsimony in *SemNet*

Fisher (1988), a principal in the SemNet Research Group, the company that developed *SemNet*, reported on SemNets developed by nine students in a college biology class who were free to assign their own relational descriptors. She classified these relations into six broad categories. The largest category consisted of *Inclusion Relations*, which encompass both *part/whole* and *set/subset* relations, and *same as*. A second category, *Characteristic Relations* included both *attribute* and *has/function* links, as well *occurs at site*.

The third category, *Action Relations*, are, according to Fisher, "the least generalizable and most domain-specific of all relations" (p. 5). Collectively, students in this study used 26 action relations. Some of these, such as *caused by/causes*, and has *agent/agent in*, had been supplied to the students by the researchers for optional use. *Process Role Relations* comprise the fourth category and include object *of/has* object and overlap *Action Relations* in that both types include the relation *agent in/has agent*. Role Relations are "an alternative way to express the ideas contained in action verb relations" (p. 5). Because they

> .....can be used to describe virtually any process in the cell, their use can contribute to both the parsimony of relation types in a semantic network and perhaps also to the formation of a general template for reactions and processes in a student's mind. (Fisher, 1988, p. 5)

The categories*Temporal Relations* (follows/precedes) and *Historical Relations* (experimented with/researched by) were used infrequently by students in Fisher's study.

Fisher, Faletti, and Quinn (1990) noted that while variety is a desired feature of natural language production, consistency is more highly valued in knowledge representation.

> Using a small, finite number of relations helps promote consistency in the use of each relation and simplifies the process of systematic net construction.... A disadvantage of such parsimony, however, is that important discriminations may be lost. The most parsimonious set, for example, would have only one relation, *is related to*, and thus would be akin to using unnamed associations. . . . Alternatively, one can incorporate a wide array of relations into a net in order to capture many nuances of meaning. Proponents of this view argue that learning involves making finer and finer discriminations between things, and that such discriminations are achieved by using different (but similar) relations. (p. 9)

Justification for using a parsimonious set has often been coupled with some prescription for determining what should be included in that set. For example, Anderson and Bower (1980) recommended that

> ...it should make a minimum of *formal* (structural or syntactic) distinctions at the outset; more complex distinctions would be built up by the construction rules for concatenating primitive ideas. One motivation for minimizing the formal categories is for the sake of simplicity and elegance in the theory. Another motivation is that the fewer and simpler are the innate distinctions the mind must make, the more likely it is that the neural apparatus of a child can implement at least that much analysis of the input. (Anderson and Bower, p. 80)

In deciding whether to use a parsimonious or rich set of relations, the relative difficulty with which verbs are learned must be taken into account. Gentner (1981a) points out that verbs are more difficult to remember than nouns, and that it takes children longer to acquire verbs than nouns. Are specific verbs easier to remember than general verbs? Gentner (1981b) cites evidence favoring what she calls the "connectivity hypothesis" over the "complexity hypothesis." The complexity hypothesis states that the greater the number of semantic components in a word, the more difficult that word will be to process—leading to poorer, slower memory. The connectivity hypothesis predicts that a verb whose meaning structure sets up more semantic relationships between nouns should lead to stronger associations in memory; specific verbs contain more connective information than do general ones.

Ultimate Relational Parsimony

Perhaps the most parsimonious approach to relational descriptors is to leave links unlabeled. The result is generally known as the concept map. Nodes contain concepts but are linked only with lines indicating that the concepts are somehow related. None of the authors in our review who reported work with concept maps strongly opposed relational labels and their opinions actually seem to lie on the edge of advocacy.

Stewart's (1984) concept mapping system is a hierarchical spatial representation of knowledge which he found useful in the classroom. He noted, however, that "an obvious shortcoming of...concept maps is the lack of specifications concerning the nature of the relationships connecting concepts" (Stewart, p. 236). Vaughn's (1984) ConStruct procedure for spatial representation of concepts also omits relational descriptors. Although they "may provide a potential improvement to this procedure, [ConStruct] seems quite effective without such labeling and any benefits would have to be weighed against the increased complexity (as perceived by students)" (p. 130). Mirande's (1984) schematizing strategy also leaves links unlabeled, requiring that the relationship "either be remembered or inferred from the schematization....however, we have discovered in practice that in order to read back a schematization it is useful to add some other relationship symbols" (p. 152). These additional symbols serve to categorize the links as either static or dynamic, and further classify them as *classifications, characteristics, time-space, comparisons, conditional,* and *cause-and-result.* The individual user is free to modify the system of relations by further augmenting the relationship symbols in a personal way.

Anderson and Bower (1980) argue that, historically (though not without exception), descriptions of association are inadequate when they do not account for information about relations.

> The problem is that items that we know to be related in different ways are assumed to be connected in the mind by one and the same sort of association. For instance, in our mind a dining room is associated with eating, a glutton with eating, a fork with eating, and a steak with eating. How is it that we know that the relation expressed by the first association is one of location to act, the second is that of actor to act, the third of act to instrument, and the fourth of act to object? All are connected by the same one sort of associative link. (p. 24)

Problems and Potentials of Parsimony

SemNet is quite flexible for constructing subject-verb-object phrases, which as Lakoff (1988) points out are favored by most of the world's languages, possibly because they are so convenient for describing the flow of events from agents or causes to objects or consequents. But in our experience, this same flexibility confuses novice SemNet users and slows their understanding of possible strategies for representation. Since the number of relational descriptors accommodated by *SemNet* is essentially unlimited, it is possible to build nets in which many different labels are used to describe the same (or very similar) relationships. From this freedom flows several potential problems.

1. Idiosyncrasy. Relational descriptors (in *SemNet*) have a way of proliferating out of control and trimming them requires time. On the other hand, *SemNet* does make it possible to merge sets of relational descriptors, allowing skilled users to take a looser approach to initial analysis of a domain—working rapidly without worrying about consistency. Table 2 (left column) lists the relational descriptors generated by a physicist/instructional designer as she built a net on electrophoresis using a standard text as a source. The right column is from the same net after she merged, deleted, or renamed similar descriptors. This task—easily accomplished in this case because of the designer's familiarity with *SemNet,* her knowledge of the principles underlying the domain, and her experience in using textbooks—would have been difficult for most novices.

Before Merging

done by several techniques	is one of several techniques for
needs	is needed for
tracks sample components by	used to track samplcomponents
is made use of in	makes use of
analysed by	is used to analyse
works by	is the working principle
occurs when	basis for
can be done because	is the basis for
can be done by placing	results in
experience	experienced by
can be rewritten as	is derived from
is used to determine	is determined by
is done by placing	causes
done by 2 techniques	is one of 2 techniques
done in steps	part of
depends on the	affects the magnitude of
causes the molecule	is caused by
sets	due to
have a	is a property of
is caused due to	produces
is produced when	and produce
can be	is one type of
uses a	is used for
is made from	is used to make
has composed	is composed of
is limited to analysis of a	can be analysed by
is done with	is used in
has advantages over paper	is obtained by
has disadvantages	is provided by
use a	is used by
has advantages	is obtained from
is prepared by	is part of preparation of
pore size depends on	determines pore size
mobilty depends on	determines mobility
name in one direction	name in other direction
can be done with	can be used for
uses	is useful for
can be used in	can be done by

After Merging

based on	is basis for
depends on	determines
is used to estimate	is estimated by
uses format	is a format for
has disadvantage	is a disadvantage of
has properties	are properties of
has advantage	is an advantage of
types of	is a
is used in	uses
done by	technique for
results in	is a result of
experience	is experienced by
characterised by	characterises
opposed by	opposes
opposite and equal to	
preparation	to prepare

Table 2. Expansive and Parsimonious Sets of Relational Descriptors. Labels were extracted from net on electrophoresis (See Figure 1C). Those in the column on the left were assigned as the net author studied a basic text on electrophoresis. She used SemNet's "merge" and "delete" functions to create the shortened list on right.

2. Slowness in constructing representations. Net construction suffers when learners have to "invent" new descriptors each time they establish a relation. The mechanics of

specifying the label (such as determining the direction of the link or its screen position) take some time to work out. But more importantly, having to invent and evaluate a new descriptor takes more time (and cognitive overhead) than selecting one from a short list of proven alternatives.

3. Difficulty in making comparisons. Semantic nets contain many clusters of nodes representing taxonomies, structures (whole-part systems), causal webs, and so on which are difficult to recognize if the net has been built with undisciplined, uncategorized sets of relational descriptors. Consider taxonomic hierarchies which are probably the simplest clusters and which are easily recognizable when constructed with the ISA descriptor (mammal—ISA—>vertebrate). If multiple descriptors are used in place of ISA (e.g., "belongs to," "member of," "classified as," "type of," and so on) it will be harder for a net builder or reader to recognize the underlying taxonomic organization. Similarly, if multiple descriptors have been used to construct *several* kinds-of hierarchies within a net, users might never notice their structural similarity. Furthermore, inconsistent use of labels for what is in fact the same fundamental relationship interferes with an important SemNet utility that allows hierarchical clusters to be extracted as outlines that can be exported to other applications such as word processors.

   Perhaps the most serious problem with excessive proliferation of descriptors is the failure of insight that results when learners cannot see fundamental inconsistencies in reasoning and organization because these inconsistencies are obscured by trivial differences in labels for links. We suspect, for example, that users who employ multiple descriptors with similar meanings during extension of authoritative taxonomies will be more likely to establish links that are inconsistent with the original organizing principles–adding, say, a new cluster based on place of origin, or functional role, when the original principle of organization was based on physical attributes.

4. Disagreements on meaning. Lack of agreement on relational descriptors makes it difficult for users to interpret each other's nets even when they represent the same domain. Without some uniformity in the set of descriptors, it is difficult to determine whether dissimilar net structures result from a fundamental difference of understanding about the domain or are mere artifacts that result from differences in terminology.

   Many authors cited in the literature review have noted that the number of primitives needed to represent English verbs is relatively small. Perhaps this is fortunate since Genter's (1981a) work suggests that verbs (relations) are a more important source of ambiguity than nouns (concepts). Fisher (1990) notes that, in scientific domains at least, there is greater agreement among experts on the meaning of nouns (concepts) than on the meaning of verbs (relations). But she has also demonstrated that it is possible to build very large nets (with thousands of concepts) using a relatively small number of relations.

The point is that encouraging consistent use of relational descriptors reduces confusion without necessarily restricting the span of representation (size of the domain). It appears that the simplest way to facilitate communication about domains is to negotiate agreement on the meaning of relationships rather than to worry about differences in concepts. It also appears that while relational descriptors are a source of ambiguity, there is a relatively small number that need to be tamed.

A Starter Set of Relational Descriptors

The first strategy we propose in an effort to provide "just enough" support for learners constructing SemNets is to supply novice net builders with a parsimonious, generic set of relational descriptors. This set may be used exclusively or modified and expanded by the learners. It gives them a framework in which to begin net construction, but requires that they invent fewer elements "from scratch."

Our parsimonious set of descriptors (see Table 3) is generally consistent with frameworks produced by other authors (see Table 1). It evolved in the context of an intermediate-level course on instructional product design . The descriptors facilitate early student understanding of semantic networks. Later they serve as a simple, straightforward basis for eliciting knowledge from subject matter sources and for conducting subject matter analyses. This set of descriptors is also used because it is consistent with Merrill's (1983) taxonomy for classifying learning outcomes and prescribing instructional strategies, an important feature of this course. We have sometimes referred to these as "cardinal" descriptors, although we do not seriously argue that they are necessarily more useful or convenient than those proposed by other authors.

Ending each descriptor in an "a," in the manner proposed by Norman and Rumelhart (1975) for ISA and HASA, serves to remind net builders and readers alike that the descriptors are based on case grammar and should be thought of as "meta-verbs" that need not be conjugated. Ending each word in a vowel also makes node-link-node sequences sound more natural and blurs what might otherwise be perceived as disagreements in tense (for example "building—HASA—>door" in lieu of "buildings have doors" or "a building has a door"). For levity's sake, we sometimes read net "paths" with a pseudo-Italian accent. When students want to use additional relational descriptors, we encourage them to suffix an "a": INVENTA, INDICATA, ORGANIZA, FINDA, etc.

Relation with keywords	Reciprocals as keywords	Example	Typical Modifiers	Uses
ISA is a member of is a kind of is a type of is an example of belongs to the class	has a member includes	cat —ISA—> mammal	ISA (sometimes)	Indicates superordinate, coordinate, and subordinate relationships between concepts. Permits classification of concepts as belonging to groups of objects sharing similar characteristics.
HASA has an aspect has a part named has an attribute has a characteristic	aspect of part of attribute of characteristic of	apple —HASA—> seeds	HASA (part) (attribute) (capability) (function) (goal)	Indicates whole-part relationships, as well as concept attributes. Enables the user to identiry a concept as being a part of another concept, and to define/describe concepts.
CAUSA causes influences has the function of increase/decrease results in	results from is an effect of	NO_2 —CAUSA—> smog	CAUSA (if condition x) (probably) (influences) (corellation) (increase)	Describes cause-effect or action-reaction relationships. Includes partial causes, such as influences and correlations.
NEXTA precedes is followed by	is preceded by	buy —NEXTA —> eat	NEXTA (sometimes) (optional) (if condition x)	Describes sequences of decisions and operations, and indications required to solve a problem or achieve a goal. Used where one event follows another, but with no causality implied.
IDENTA specimen is named has the address assigned number	(no reciprocal)	621 —IDENTA—>widget	IDENTA (probably)	Conveys factual, historical links that are not described by above relations. Used to indicate substitution or equality. Used where relationship between concepts is arbitrary and must be learned by rote.
LOCATA is located occurred	is location of is date/time of	clock —LOCATA—>wall	LOCATA (in) (on) (under) (before)	Specifies relative spatial and temporal positions. Used to locate istorical or geographical location of concepts
INVOLVA is related to involves associate with entails	is related to is involved in associate with entailed in	sex —INVOLVA—>child	INVOLVA (probably)	Serves as a "placeholder" indicating an otherwise undefined relationship.

Table 3. Relational Descriptors for Introductory Work in Knowledge Elicitation and Subject Matter Analysis. This parsimonious set of relational descriptors is used by Allen to train novice instructional designers and is generally consistent with systems proposed by other authors (see Table 1).

These "cardinal" relations can be thought of as roots which may be modified to suit the needs of certain learners or knowledge domains. For example, an ecology net might utilize two distinct hasa relations, as in "stream—HASA (source)—>snowpack" and "city—HASA (policy)—>recycling." In these examples, the terms "source" and "policy" are appended to the HASA relation to create in effect two entirely distinct relations which each bear implications of functionality (causes and effects). But because both relations contain the root relation "HASA," learners may more easily be able to draw analogies and group relationships.

Configuration Management in Semantic Networks

Our second strategy for providing "just enough teaching," is to vary the SemNet user's authority and responsibility for constructive activity by constraining connections and labeling. The intent of our proposals is to suggest a natural and comprehensible means for regulating the demand that constructive activity in hypermedia places on the abilities of beginners and novices. Most importantly we want to argue the feasibility of "switches" for difficulty that can be controlled by teachers, mentors, authors, or learners themselves. First, we consider the value of constrained degrees of freedom in the use of tools and environments in general, and we consider constraints on language, since it also is a tool and perhaps an environment as well.

Constraints on the construction of built environments and devices ultimately flow from the nature of the physical world; constraints on the construction of representations of knowledge flow primarily from human biology, language, and culture. But in the context of systems of education and acculturation, constraints are often introduced during teaching so as to ensure that beginners and novices are faced with a limited set of meaningful components and limited ways of connecting these components. Tailoring the degrees of freedom in hypermedia to an appropriate number can promote success by increasing the frequency of useful, productive, or satisfying relationships between information units. Spiro and his associates (this volume) outline some of the risks that are inherent in efforts to reduce cognitive complexity in systems for advanced knowledge acquisition; some of his caveats may apply to our proposals.

SemNet is reminiscent of the hub-and-spoke kits such as *Tinker Toys* that allow novices to easily experiment with alternative organization of physical structures. The most important design feature of such childhood construction kits is that they constrain the number of ways in which components can be connected and so encourage useful connections without overloading a novice builder's schemata or memory. Norman (1988) notes that constraints are inherent in all devices that require assembly from components.

> What has to be remembered in order to put the parts together again in proper order? Not as much as might appear from an initial analysis. In the extreme case, if there are ten parts, there are...a little over 3.5 million alternatives....Some pieces are physically

> constrained from fitting into spots reserved for the others....There are even cultural constraints: we turn screws clockwise to tighten, counterclockwise to loosen.... The constraints by themselves are often not sufficient to determine the proper reassembly of the device—mistakes do get made—but the constraints reduce the amount that must be learned to a reasonable quantity. (Norman, pp. 61-62)

Norman argues that one of the most important techniques for making every day objects and built environments more "user friendly" is to carefully design constraints so as to shape optimal actions—helping users to avoid errors and reducing the requirement for "remembered" performance.

In the design of many electronic devices, there is a general trade-off between number of functions (greater degrees of freedom) on one hand and ease-of-use on the other hand. Van der Meij (1991) describes the dilemma well in the context of compact disc systems and he surveys specific techniques for constraining the degrees of freedom to suit the needs and preferences of various users. Noteworthy in his analysis is a comparison of "breadth" versus "depth" approaches to interface design. In the *breadth approach*, designers accommodate an expanded range of functions by increasing the number of, say, buttons while preserving a one-button-to-one-function correspondence. This makes it relatively difficult for users of a function-laden device to locate a desired button (since there will be many) but makes it easy to activate a function once the button has been found. In the *depth approach*, power to control the device is allocated to fewer buttons by assigning several functions to one button, or by requiring combined activation of several buttons. This makes it easier to locate an appropriate button, but harder to invoke a particular function, since the user must remember the required combination of buttons. Underlying both approaches is the principle that constrained degrees of freedom reduces memory burden and task complexity: one approach constrains the number of *functions* per button; the other constrains the number of *buttons*. (Where CD players are concerned, perhaps the easiest way to constrain degrees of freedom, der Meijis notes, is to hide controls for sophisticated features behind a panel until the owner is ready to use them.)

Language-based systems for constructing or representing knowledge can also benefit from constraints on degrees of freedom. As Norman points out, specially constrained language forms such as epic poems recited by village elders can make large amounts of information more memorable by using rhymes and rhythms to limit the number of possible words that can fit a particular structure. The phonics and cadences of nursery rhymes serve a similar function for younger minds—making it easier to learn rules of syntax, grammar, and semantics by constraining possible word combinations. Repetition and analogies in fairy tales such as those collected by the Brothers Grimm make story structures more easily remembered by constraining plot possibilities ("and then the *third* sister went into the cave and climbed down the rope.")

Activity	connections "instances"	labled links "relations"	filled nodes "concepts"
7. Establish and organize concepts. Learner assembles a coherent network representing a domain.	L	S	L
6. Establish and organize concepts using standard relations. System provides a set of labeled relations. Learner fills nodes and assembles a coherent network.	L	S	L
5. Establish and characterize relationships. System provides a set of filled nodes. Learner establishes appropriate relations and labels the relations using a) system-provided lists of labels or b) learner-provided lists of labels.	L	L	S
4. Establish relationships. System provides a set of filled nodes and a set of labeled relations. Learner assembles a coherent network by connecting the nodes.	L	S	S
3. Characterize relations. System provides a set of established but unlabeled relations between filled nodes. Learner labels the relations using a) system-provided lists of labels or b) learner-provided lists.	S	L	S
2. Label concepts in net clusters. System provides a set of established and labeled relations connecting empty nodes. Learner supplies "concepts" for the nodes.	S	S	L
1. Explore, critique, modify, or expand a system of related propositions. Learner examines an existing semantic network representing a domain.	S	S	S

Table 4. Configurations Supporting Constructive Mental Activity: System-Provided vs. Learner-Provided Components. Configurations range from a completed net which requires only study strategies (such as "pathing"), to building a net "from scratch." The list may be viewed as an ordered progression in which the learner is challenged to assume increasing responsibility and authority for net construction. However, other variables affect the difficulty of building a net including learner familiarity with the knowledge domain, the inherent complexity of the domain itself, the metacognitive skills of the learner, and the required or desired learning outcomes.

In searching for ways to constrain the number of possible combinations in SemNets, we have identified various configurations of linking and labeling in which the learner is expected to provide different types of input into a SemNet in response to other elements or structures supplied by the "system." Table 4 lists seven configurations ranging from a fully completed net which requires only study strategies (such as "pathing"), to a task constrained only by SemNet's inherent capabilities for representation: building a net "from scratch." Between these extremes, the learner can be provided or prompted with either connections (instances), labeled links (relations), filled nodes (concepts), or any combination of these.

The list of configurations may be viewed as an ordered progression in which the learner is challenged to assume increasing responsibility and authority for net construction. Variation in authority and responsibility is only one dimension that contributes to the total difficulty of a net building task. Other variables include learner familiarity with the knowledge domain, the inherent complexity of the domain itself, the metacognitive skills of the learner, and the required or desired learning outcomes.

Space does not permit a full examination of the specific techniques that a SemNet author would use to build these configurations, but two approaches merit comparison. The first technique invokes SemNet's built-in options for masking relations or concepts. Each option can be switched on or off at will and affects the entire net. Masking permits configurations that resemble our Configurations 2 and 3, but merely obscure names for nodes or links that have been supplied by an author. The learner simply clicks on the masked component to see an "answer." While useful in self-guided study of nets built by others, this technique provides no support for construction of nets.

The second technique is closer to what we have in mind. It involves the building of nets by knowledgeable net authors/designers who would assign numbers as "place-holders" for unlabeled links and nodes when omission of relational descriptors and concept names is called for in one of the configurations. In response the learner simply uses existing SemNet authoring capabilities to change a number to an appropriate label. (There are some minor technical limitations on this approach with current versions of *SemNet*, but we hope they will be removed in future modifications of the software.)

Variable Scaffolding

There may be a danger in over-use of a single configuration in that it might promote a narrow perspective on relationships. For example, if the learner works repeatedly with Configuration 2, he or she is only answering the question, "What concepts are linked by this relation?" and will never be challenged to consider appropriate relational descriptors. It is quite feasible to use several or all of the configurations in Table 4 within a single net, thus varying the components supplied to the learner across different portions of a knowledge domain. This approach might be thought of as a model of mental scaffolding in which sections are in various degrees of completion, thus providing learners with stable, foundational structures in some areas and much more tenuous (or no) support in others. For example, in a large domain, crucial concepts and instances that represent foundational content could be constructed using Configuration 1 in which concepts, links, and relational labels are all supplied. (Alternatively these might be set in Configuration 2 or 3 as a kind of pre-test or review.) As the learner moves out from this familiar core content into other portions of the domain, more or less demanding configurations (such as 5, 6, and 7) might be supplied depending on the author/designer's assessment of likely difficulty and learner needs. In some future version of *SemNet*, it might be possible to apply expert system technology to adjust these configurations diagnostically based on real-time empirical measures of learner success such as speed, consistency of constructions, or similarity to some "ideal" reference net. We believe that variable scaffolding is a means of supporting progressive development of individual knowledge that holds considerable promise as an alternative to conventional instructional analysis in the manner of Dick and Carey (1990).

One potential benefit of variable scaffolding that may not be obvious at first results from the n-dimensional structure of SemNets. Since nets are unconstrained by three-dimensional space, it is possible to locate "shaky" portions of the scaffolding that extend into "ill-structured" and unknown portions of the domain. Yet these same shaky portions can be within a few links of the core or other well-defined and stable portions of the net. Learners who become confused or overloaded can then trace tentative structures to immediately related and familiar ideas.

Rigorous constructivists might argue that the "core" of the net should be acknowledged as a socially constructed description or consensus description of the domain. We agree, and we think that a useful way for learning communities to work together on nets is to negotiate a common knowledge core that consists of stable, agreed-upon concepts and relations. Then individuals can contribute by extending salients into the unknown.

Conclusion

Most of the world's traditional knowledge systems teach that individual understanding of reality is limited. For example, the Vedic scriptures of ancient India pay homage to the God-head as possessing complete and simultaneous knowledge. Individual consciousness is characterized by the ability to know everything as well, but only one thing at a time. The guru is the teacher who points the student's attention in a useful direction at a given time.

Research on cognition has yet to delineate the capacity of human long-term memory. There would seem to be no practical limits to the amount of knowledge a person can develop. Yet it is clear that there are profound temporal and quantitative limitations on human perception and working memory.

We walk the paths of knowledge step by step, gradually assembling our understanding of the whole from serial experience of its parts. We are beginning to realize that the role of teaching is to guide the learner through critical junctures and to coach students as they develop a confident stride and the skills to map their own way.

References

Allen, B. S. & Merrill, M. D. (1985). System-assigned strategies and CBI. *Journal of Educational Computing Research, 1*(1), 2-21.

Allen, B. S. (1990). Just in time. *DID dialogue, 1*(1), p. 1.

Allen, B.S. (1990). Virtualities. In B. Branyan-Broadbent & R.K. Wood (Eds.), *Educational media & technology yearbook, Volume 16*. Englewood, CO: Libraries Unlimited.

Anderson, J.R. & Bower, G.H. (1980). *Human associative memory: A brief edition*. Hillsdale, NJ: Lawrence Erlbaum Associates.

Anderson, J.R. (1990). *Cognitive psychology and its implications*. New York: W.H. Freeman.

Armbruster, B., & Anderson, T. (1984). Mapping: Representing informative text diagrammatically. In C.D. Holly & D.F. Dansereau (Eds.), *Spatial learning strategies*. Orlando, FL: Academic Press, Inc.

Bednar, A.K., Cunningham, D.J., Duffy, T.M., & Perry, J.D. (1991). Theory into practice: How do we link? In G.J. Anglin (Ed.), *Instructional technology: Past, present, and future*. Enlewood, CO: Libraries Unlimited.

Dansereau, D. (1978). The development of a learning strategies curriculum. In H.F. O'Neil, (Ed.), *Learning strategies*. Orlando, FL: Academic Press, Inc.

Dick, W., & Carey, L. (1990). *The systematic design of instruction*. Glenview, Illinois: Scott, Foresman and Company.

Faletti, J., Fisher, K., Lipson, J., Patterson, P., & Thornton, R. (1986). *SemNet*™ [Computer program]. 1600 Johnson Avenue, San Diego, CA: SemNet Research Group

Feifer, R.G. (1989). *An intelligent tutoring system for graphic mapping strategies* (Tech. Rep. UCLA-AI-89-04). Los Angeles: University of California at Los Angeles, Computer Science Department, Artificial Intelligence Laboratory.

Fisher, K.M. (1988). *Relations used in student-generated knowledge representations*. Paper presented at the AERA Symposium on Student Understanding in Science: Issues of Cognition & Curriculum.

Fisher, K.M. Faletti, J., Patterson, H., Thornton, R., Lipson, J., & Spring, C. (1990). Computer-based concept mapping. *Journal of Science Teaching, 19* (6), 347-352.

Fisher, K.M., Faletti, J., & Quinn, C.N. (1990). *Exploring cognitive structure with semantic networks*. Unpublished paper. (Available from Kathleen M. Fisher, Center for Research in Mathematics & Science Education & Department of Natural Science, San Diego State University, San Diego, CA 92182)

Frederickson, C.H. (1975). Representing logical and semantic structure of knowledge acquired from discourse. *Cognitive Psychology, 7,* 378-386.

Gentner, D. (1981a). Some interesting differences between verbs and nouns. *Cognition and Brain Theory, 4,* 161-178.

Gentner, D. (1981b). Verb semantic structures in memory for sentences: Evidence for componential representation. *Cognitive Psychology, 13,* 56-83.

Goetz, E. (1984). The role of spatial strategies in processing and remembering text: A cognitive—information-processing analysis. In C.D. Holly & D.F. Dansereau (Eds.), *Spatial learning strategies.* Orlando, FL: Academic Press, Inc.

Hendrix, G.G. (1979). Encoding knowledge in partitioned networks. In N.V. Findler (Ed.), *Associative networks.* Orlando, FL: Academic Press, Inc.

Holly, C.D. & Dansereau, D.F. (1984a). The development of spatial learning strategies. In C.D. Holly & D.F. Dansereau (Eds.), *Spatial learning strategies.* Orlando, FL: Academic Press, Inc.

Holly, C.D. & Dansereau, D.F. (1984b). Networking: Technique and empirical evidence. In C.D. Holly & D.F. Dansereau (Eds.), *Spatial learning strategies.* Orlando, FL: Academic Press, Inc.

Johnson, M. (1987). *The body and the mind: The bodily basis of meaning, imagination, and reason.* Chicago: University of Chicago Press.

Kintsch, W. (1974). *The representation of meaning in memory.* New York: John Wiley & Sons.

Lakoff, G. (1987). *Women, fire, and dangerous things: What categories reveal about the mind.* Chicago, IL: University of Chicago Press.

Lindsay, P.H. & Norman, D. (1977). *An introduction to psychology.* New York: Academic Press, Inc.

Long, G. & Aldersley, S. (1984). Networking: Application with hearing impaired students. In C.D. Holly & D.F. Dansereau (Eds.), *Spatial learning strategies.* Orlando, FL: Academic Press, Inc.

Merrill, M.D. (1983). Component display theory. In C.M. Reigeluth (Ed.), *Instructional-design theories and models: An overview of their current status.* Hillsdale, NJ: Lawrence Erlbaum Associates.

Mirande, J. (1984). Schematizing: Technique and applications. In C.D. Holly & D.F. Dansereau (Eds.), *Spatial learning strategies.* Orlando, FL: Academic Press, Inc.

Nelson, T. H. (1978). Electron publishing and electronic literature. In E. C. DeLand (Ed.), *Information technology in health science education.* New York: Plenum Press.

Norman, D. A. (1988). *The psychology of everyday things.* New York: Basic Books.

Norman, D.A. & Rumelhart, D.E. (1975). *Explorations in cognition.* San Francisco: W.H. Freeman and Company.

Polya, G. (1957). *How to solve it: A new aspect of mathematical method.* New York: Doubleday.

Quillian, M.R. (1967). Word concepts: A theory and simulation of some basic semantic capabilities. *Behavioral Sciences, 12,* 410-430.

Rumelhart, D.E., Lindsay, P.H., & Norman, DA. (1972). A process model for long-term memory. In E. Tulving & W. Donaldson (Eds.), *Organization of memory.* New York: Academic Press, Inc.

Schallert, D., Ulerick, S., & Tierney, R.J. (1984). Evolving a description of text through mapping. In C.D. Holly & D.F. Dansereau (Eds.), *Spatial learning strategies.* Orlando, FL: Academic Press, Inc.

Schank, R.C. (1973). Identification of conceptualization underlying natural language. In R.C. Schank & K.M. Colby (Eds.), *Computer models of thought and language.* San Francisco: W.H. Freeman and Company.

Schubert, L.K., Goebel, R.G., & Cercone, N.J. (1979). The structure and organization of a semantic net for comprehension and inference. In N.V. Findler (Ed.), *Associative networks.* New York: Academic Press, Inc.

Stewart, J. (1984). The representation of knowledge: Curricular and instructional implications for science teaching. In C.D. Holly & D.F. Dansereau (Eds.), *Spatial learning strategies.* Orlando, FL: Academic Press, Inc.

Van der Meij, H. (1991). *Instructing users to know it all in seconds.* Paper presented at NATO Workshop: The Design of Constructive Learning Environments: Implications for Instructional Design and the Use of Technology. Leuven, Belgium.

Vaughan, J. (1984). Concept structuring: The technique and empirical evidence. In C.D. Holly & D.F. Dansereau (Eds.), *Spatial learning strategies.* Orlando, FL: Academic Press, Inc.

Winston, P.H. (1984). *Artificial intelligence.* Reading, MA: Addison-Wesley Publishing Company.

Woods, W.A. (1975). What's in a link: Foundations for semantic networks. In D.G. Bobrow, & A. Collins (Eds.), *Representation and understanding, Studies in cognitive science.* New York: Academic Press, Inc.

14 Constructive Learning: The Role of the Learner

P. Robert-Jan Simons

University of Nijmegen, Nijmegen, The Netherlands

In long term memory there are, we think, three kinds of memory representations: semantic, episodic and action representations (see Boekaerts, 1987). Semantic representations refer to concepts and principles with their defining characteristics (like a bird is an animal with feathers). Episodic representations are based on personal, situated and affective experiences with instances of the concepts and principles (like I love my little bird). Action representations refer to the things one can do with the semantic and episodic information: solving certain kinds of problems, using the knowledge (like birds can bring over messages).

In our definition, constructive learning has to do with attempts of learners to build rich and complex memory representations showing a high degree of connectedness (see Prawat, 1989) and having strong relations between semantic, episodic and action knowledge. Ideally, the connections both within these three kinds of representations and between them are rich and strong. Furthermore connections with the three kinds of knowledge representations in other domains are also thought to be important. Constructive learning is learning striving for these kinds of connected representations.

Characteristics of Constructive Learning

Six Core Characteristics of Constructive Learning

The main characteristics of constructive learning were formulated by Shuell(1988):

> ....(constructive) learning is an active, constructive, cumulative and goal directed process.... It is **active** in that the student must do certain things while processing incoming information in order to learn the material in a meaningful manner. It is **constructive** in that new information must be elaborated and related to other information in order for the student to retain simple information and to understand complex material. It is **cumulative** in that all new learning builds upon and/or utilizes the learner's prior knowledge in ways that determine what and how much is learned. It is **goal oriented** in that learning is most likely to be successful if the learner is aware of the goal (at least in a general sense) toward which he or she is working and possesses expectations that are appropriate for attaining the desired outcome. (p. 277-278)

Two additional characteristics of constructive learning are, in our view, that it is diagnostic and reflective. This means that learners should undertake activities like monitoring, self-testing and checking that help them diagnose and judge whether they are still pursuing the goal they had set. Moreover, it means that learners should be or become aware of their way of learning.

Though these six characteristics form the core of constructive learning, this does not mean that all constructive learning is proceeding or should proceed according to all of these lines at the same time. Sometimes constructive learning is very active indeed, but at other times the amount and quality of activity drops to lower levels. Nobody can stay active all the time: activity levels should vary. Perhaps very active learning periods and more passive ones should follow each other for learners to hold on for longer periods of time. In a similar way constructive learning cannot be cumulative all the time. Some times prior learning confuses new learning so much that it is better to build a wall between the two. Moreover if you do not have much prior knowledge in a certain domain it is impossible to learn cumulatively. Of course you may then use prior knowledge of a general nature or from other domains (analogies).

Thus, the amount of cumulativity possible and desirable should and will also vary across learning situations. Furthermore, learners cannot learn constructively (in the sense meant by Shuell) all the time. Sometimes you have to concentrate on the specific subject matter that you have to learn without elaborating and integrating too much. As shown by Pask (1976) some learners act as globe-trotters, who go everywhere without finding a place to rest or stay: they relate everything with everything else and end in total chaos and confusion because they do not focus on details and procedures. Also, learning cannot and should not be goal-directed all the time. Sometimes one should be satisfied with a global, general learning goal and let the learning environment guide discoveries. Sometimes it is even impossible to have clear learning goals: if there is no teacher to help formulate goals reachable in a certain amount of time, learners can only know what goals are possible when they have become an expert in the field. Of course learning cannot be diagnostic all the time either. If a learner spends all the time diagnosing his own learning he has no time to learn. Focusing too much on the state of your mind may even hinder learning, as Kuhl (1983) has shown. Finally, the argument also holds for our last characteristic reflectivity. In learning, reflective periods should occur, but not continuously.

The six characteristics of constructive learning thus do not form necessary conditions that have to be fulfilled in all instances of constructive learning. Instead they should be seen as prototypical in the sense that when they are all there it is clear that learning is constructive. But if one or more fail to occur, learning still can be constructive. Still in our approach they are considered to be so important that they belong to the six core characteristics.

Six Secondary Characteristics of Constructive Learning

Some other characteristics of constructive learning, though showing up in some instances of constructive learning and in its descriptions by others, do, in our view, not belong to its prototypical core. We do not believe that constructive learning in its essence should be discovery oriented, contextual, problem oriented, case-based, social, or intrinsically motivated. Thus, these six other characteristics, although they may have to do with some forms of constructive learning, are in our approach not as central as the prior mentioned six.

Although discovery learning can be very powerful and constructive, the research and debates in the educational psychology of the sixties, has clearly shown that we should not confine learning to discovery learning alone. It is too time-consuming and inefficient. Discovery learning can have an important place in a sequence of learning processes (especially in the beginning phases to motivate and in the final stages when application is the goal of learning), but it should not be the only learning model.

Probably the most controversial part of our view of constructive learning is that we do not believe that contextualization belongs in the key characteristics. Of course, many instances of school learning are too decontextualized and many improvements can and should be made as to the contextualization of school learning. Contextualizing knowledge representations with episodic and action representations are, however, only two of many instances of constructive learning. Building strong connections within semantic, episodic or action representations form equally important instances of constructive learning. Furthermore, forming connections between different domains of (semantic) knowledge also are important examples of constructive learning. Experience with learning environments that have hagh context (e.g. job training, discovery learning, simulation) has shown that decontextualization, rather than contextualization, is the main problem. Under these circumstances learning is often not constructive because there is no decontextualization. Learning remains bound to the context of the simulation, or some job contexts. The consequence is that the resulting memory representations are inflexibly related to one or a few contexts only. The key problem is that there should be a balance between contextualization and decontextualization. Not the question whether there is contextualization and decontextualization, but their interrelations and their timing are the important issues in learning. Finally, we have serious doubts whether the sequence of contextualizing first and decontextualizing afterwards is the optimal sequence for all kinds of subject matter (see higher mathematics) and is the optimal one for all kinds of students (see also Prawat, 1989).

We also question the position taken by some others that constructive learning should be problem-oriented and case-based. Problem orientation and organizing learning around cases clearly is good for contextualization and motivation. Problem orientation strengthens the connections between semantic and action representations. Cases connect episodic and semantic representations. As stated before, these are important indeed, but not the only ones to be considered in constructive learning (see above).

The position that constructive learning is social or even that only social constructions of reality are possible, is strongly defended. Most of the time in this connection, in one way or another, Vygotsky shows up. In the Netherlands, already in the seventies, when we had our "Russian revolution" in educational psychology, many of the debates concentrated on this social issue. Learning together with other learners can be a very powerful form of learning, in which learners help each other's construction processes. Many studies show how powerful social learning environments can be (see Palincsar and Brown, 1984). In our view, however, and according to our experience, social learning can also be very ineffective and inefficient (see also Salomon, 1988b). Some teams do not function the way they ought to. Some learners (for instance the author of this paper) prefer to learn without social support. Some contents and domains do not lend themselves to social learning (see for instance Biemans and Simons, 1991). Besides, people can also discuss and interact with themselves and be social in this way. Finally, social aspects of learning can also be built into teaching materials and computers.

The last characteristic to be considered is intrinsic motivation. Constructive learning can have some connections with intrinsic motivation, but many times it will not. Convincing arguments were put forward by Brophy (1988). It is not the kind of motivation that comes out of the materials and the environment that is the most important, but the motivation to learn. This means being motivated to find out certain things, to have a desire for knowledge, to like learning and to keep on learning even if its relevance is not immediately clear or when it gets boring.

Constructive Learning is Self-Regulated Learning

The points discussed before can be summarized as follows. Constructive learning is learning striving for rich and varied memory representations within the three kinds of memory representations discerned, as well as between them and between different domains. Six characteristics are believed to be of primary importance without them being present necessarily all the time: that constructive learning is active, cumulative, constructive, goal-directed, diagnostic and reflective. Six other characteristics, being stressed in other theories are considered to be of secondary importance only: that constructive learning is discovery oriented, contextual, problem oriented, case based, social and intrinsically motivated.

Because constructive learning relates so closely to the building up of certain kinds of memory representations by learners themselves, a very important role for the learner himself cannot be missed or denied. Only learners themselves can be the active participants in the learning process. Only they know the prior knowledge that should be used cumulatively. Only the learner himself can be constructive (in the narrow sense meant by Shuell). Only the learners can be the diagnostics of their own learning. An outsider (like a teacher) can never have access to the inside of the learner that the learner himself can have. Only a goal that a learner himself strives for counts. One can never force people to have goals they don't want to have. Finally, reflectivity also demands an active role of the learner. Constructive learning presupposes, it is our conviction, self-regulated learning. In part three of this paper therefore we elaborate on the subject of self-regulated learning. First, however, some of our experiences with constructive learning are discussed in part two.

Students View Learning Differently: Some Experiences With Constructive Learning

We have experience with constructive and self-regulated learning in several research projects in our laboratory. One study, for instance, was about learning conceptions and learning styles of Open University students who are learning out of self-instructional packages (Vermunt & Van Rijswijk, 1988). Another studied self-regulated learning of students from secondary education (De Jong & Simons, 1988; 1991; Simons & De Jong, 1991). A third research project was on self-regulated learning of a word-processing package, WordPerfect, (see Biemans & Simons, 1991; Teurlings & Simons, 1991). A fourth research project was on the activation of prior knowledge (De Klerk, Ali & Simons, 1991). Innovative projects concerned on the one hand introducing open learning in an industrial context, implementing so called Leittexts and problem oriented learning environments in industrial and school contexts (see below) and on the other hand trying to implement learning to learn approaches in schools. Currently we are involved in a large scale innovative project in the city of Rotterdam. Here, schools are stimulated to introduce integrated learning to learn approaches in all of their lessons and to stress constructive learning by students themselves. One very powerful strategy introduced here is that teachers should divide instructional and learning time equally over knowledge, integration and application. This means that if there is, for instance, one hour time, maximally 20 minutes are devoted to knowledge transfer by the teacher. The other 40 minutes are to be used for integration activities by the students (for instance finding relations with episodic knowledge, increasing connectedness) and for applications. It proved very difficult for teachers to hand over control to the students. Those who succeeded, however, improved the learning of the students considerably.

A general conclusion from our research and innovations is that both in students from secondary education and in adult learners there are different views about learning. Some see learning as the reproduction of facts and ideas, whereas others see the essence of learning as construction of knowledge representations. Some of these constructive learners emphasized semantic and episodic kinds of knowledge. Others stressed action knowledge and were oriented to the possible use and application of the information they encounter. Thus there were three kinds of views: reproduction, construction and use-oriented. These different views on learning correlated closely with different learning styles and strategies: surface learning, deep learning and concrete learning. Against our expectations, we failed to find evidence for some expected correlations between the different learning styles and learning outcomes. We had expected that reproductive surface learners would reach better results on recall questions, constructive, deep learners on insight questions and concrete use-oriented learners on application and problem solving kinds of questions. Instead, constructive learners performed the best on all three kinds of outcomes and reproductive learners the worst.

One important thing we learned is that constructive learning is, for reproduction-oriented learners, not an easy approach to learn. There are many obstacles in real life impeding the development of constructive learning abilities and tendencies (see Simons, 1989). Reproductive learners do not believe in the possibility to learn without their secure "learning by heart procedure". They have fears of constructive learning activities. They tend to distort assignments in a reproductive direction (for instance by learning the answers to questions that were meant to stimulate constructive learning by heart instead of thinking about it). They avoid learning situations that call upon constructive learning abilities. They interpret exam demands as calling for extreme reproductive abilities (even though they may be directed at higher level skills). They lack the skills to use their prior knowledge and to monitor and check their own construction processes.

Learning is an ability that is deeply rooted in personality, that develops over years and years and that cannot be changed easily. Furthermore, there are all kinds of interactive patterns between learners and teachers that impede the development of constructive learning abilities and tendencies in learners. Teachers tend to believe in active, constructive learning by students themselves. Eighty percent of teachers agreed with the statement that independent learning is very important. If and when they try to call upon independent learning abilities, however, they discover that many students are not able or willing to reach an adequate level of independent learning on their own. Therefore, they decide to take back control over the learning processes by providing structure and informing students intensively. In this way, however, students do not learn how to control their own learning processes. Many even come to believe that it is the teacher who should organize learning. It is our belief that this interactive pattern of teachers and learners, showing up in all kinds of learning situations and with learners of all kinds of ages and ability levels (see Larsson, 1983), forms the main obstacle for constructive learning. Because of its circularity and because it reinforces all kinds of needs of both teachers and learners it is very difficult to break the circle. If we want to have constructive learners, however, we should find a way out. Below we will come back on this interactive pattern and illustrate it.

Toward a Theory of Self-Regulation in Learning

Self-Regulated Learning

In this section we discuss our theory of self-regulated learning. What are important abilities of self-regulated learners? Self-regulated learning, in our opinion pertains to: being able to prepare one's own learning, taking the necessary steps to learn, regulating learning, providing for one's own feedback and judgement and keeping one's concentration and motivation high. The five tasks underlying these abilities can also be executed by teachers. This happens in many highly structured forms of teaching. Teachers then prepare the learning of the students, let them make learning steps (through assignments or the presentation of information), regulate the learning of the students through testings, questions observations (etc.), judge the learning progress and provide feedback and try to keep students motivated and students' concentration levels high. One may also say a self-regulated learner is able to be his own teacher. Following Shuell (1988), the underlying psychological functions to be fulfilled either by learners themselves or by teachers will be called learning functions.

Below follows our view of the various skills that comprise self-regulated learning or, in other words, of the various learning functions to be fulfilled:

Self-regulated preparation on learning consists of:

- An adequate orientation on learning goals and learning activities.
- An adequate planning of learning activities tuned to the goals set.
- An adequate choice of learning goals tuned to your ability and knowledge.
- Knowing what learning goals you strive for and why they are relevant.
- Self-motivation: intrinsic motivation for the goals or motivation to learn (Brophy, 1988).
- Being able to find relevant prior knowledge and skills that can be used in the new learning.
- Attentional, volitional and emotional strategies (i.e. getting started, getting attention, self-esteem, attribution (Corno,1988).

Self-regulated learning itself consist of the use of adequate learning activities and strategies (tuned to the goals set). A self-regulated learner is able to shift flexibly between different learning activities, depending on the goals and task constraints. He is able to execute learning activities that lead to knowledge, to comprehension, to integration and to problem solving. Several authors studied the learning activities that lead to these four kinds of goals (for instance Biggs, 1984; Entwistle & Ramsden, 1983; Janssen & Deneve, 1987; Marton & SÑljî,

1984; Ng, 1988). Vermunt (1987) integrated many previous attempts in his description of learning activities used by Dutch Open University students. He discerned the following: memorizing, repeating, analyzing, structurizing, relating, selecting, concretizing, personalizing and criticizing. Like previous investigators, Vermunt found individual differences in the extent to which students were able and ready to use these learning activities. Three kinds of processing of study texts showed up: deep processing (using the activities relating, structurizing, criticizing and selecting of relations, views, conclusions, structure and aim of the author), surface processing (using the activities analyzing, memorizing, repeating and selecting factual information) and concrete processing (using the activities concretizing, personalizing and selecting applicable content). Some students only used one kind of processing, others switched between two or three approaches, depending on conditions like exam demands, task characteristics (i.e. interestingness) and time constraints.

Self-regulation processes in learning consist of monitoring, testing and questioning, revision and evaluation. Monitoring refers to constant observation and interpretation of the learning processes in light of the goals. Thus, learners should observe and interpret their own behavior and thinking and control whether they are still on their way to the goals and whether the information is recalled, understood, integrated or applied (consulting their feeling of knowing). Testing has to do with more explicit attempts to check whether one is still progressing towards the learning goals through paraphrasing, trying to think of new examples, schematizing, searching an analogy (etc.). Also by answering self-made or supplied questions self-regulated learners can test their state of knowledge and understanding. One important result from studies done in our laboratory is that especially the extent to which students tune their self-testings to the learning goals is a powerful predictor of performance (Simons & Lodewijks, 1987; de Jong, 1988). Revision mechanisms refer to decisions one has to take when problems or blocks occur. One then can try another strategy, think of the possible causes of the comprehension failure, shift to a different goal (etc.). There is growing evidence that especially a reflective way of processing forms an important aspect of self-regulated learning (Nelissen, 1987; Vermunt, 1987; Salomon, 1988a). Evaluation of the process of learning forms the last regulation mechanism leading to changes in future processing and metacognitive knowledge of learning.

The fourth aspect of self-regulation, **performance judgement and feedback,** is of special significance in learning situations. Teachers have very dominating roles as to performance judgment (grading) and feedback. Self-regulated students, however, have to be able to judge their performance on their own. In addition, they will not receive feedback from the outside. Self-regulated learners should use opportunities for obtaining feedback optimally. When there is a possibility to get feedback (for instance because the correct answers are given at the end of a book), a self-regulated learner should resist the temptation to cheat himself by looking up answers he does not know immediately.

The final aspect of self-regulated learning, self-motivation and concentration management, concerns for instance keeping oneself motivated to learn by looking back at the learning goals and their relevance, or by thinking of future rewards. Concentration management refers to questions like: when and how long should one take a break, what should one do when concentration fails, how can one exclude internal and external distractions, etc.

Self-Regulation Versus Regulation by Others

The most extreme form of self-regulation in learning occurs when people have ample opportunity to perform all five of the task aspects themselves: making their own preparations, executing the actions independently, regulating themselves, making their own performance judgments, feeding back to themselves and maintaining high motivation and concentration. Most of the time, however, third persons (teachers, or their substitutes, books or computers) take care of at least part of these tasks. In essence, there always seems to be a division of tasks and responsibilities. Hardly anyone learns completely independent of others. On the other hand in almost every situation there is some opportunity for self-regulation, be it only decisions as to speed of working or effort expenditure.

Extension of the responsibility of people for their own learning may in some cases improve performance. Lodewijks (1981) for instance showed that students learning science concepts in a self-chosen sequence performed better than students learning these concepts in a predetermined sequence. Likewise, Van der Sanden (1986) showed that some people (especially the better performing ones) performed better on a practical construction task without instructions than with detailed and explicit advice.

According to these and other studies improvement of performance might be reached by giving people more opportunities to regulate their own activities and to bear responsibility. This, however, is often problematic in practice. Apart from the people who might profit from these opportunities, there are also who will perform (even) worse when left free (Lodewijks,1981; Van der Sanden, 1986). People who are not used to freedom and responsibility may not (yet) have the capabilities needed for independence. People may not believe that they are capable of self-regulation. People may dislike responsibility. Responsible persons may hesitate to hand over power to their subordinates. Larsson (1983) discussed these kinds of conceptions, circularities and paradoxes: Some teachers would like to give students more freedom to learn, but do not believe that students are able to handle this freedom. Some students believe that only the teachers should make decisions on learning and seem to hand over all responsibility to the teachers. An important lesson to be learned from all of this, is that there is needed much more than just giving opportunities for independent work: there is (metacognitive) knowledge to be acquired, there are conceptions to be changed and there are activities and regulation processes to be learned.

On Becoming a Self-Regulated Learner

In our opinion there is only one way out of the paradoxes and circularities discussed and this is by training people in self-regulation. We propose a kind of paradoxical solution. We can only expect teachers to hand over control to students when they believe that they can bear the responsibility. Therefore we need to convince students that it is important to become a self-regulated learners. Moreover we need to teach them certain basic self-regulatory skills and habits. Following that, the teacher should withdraw gradually and hand over control to the students more and more. One main goal of training programs should thus be to convince students that they have their own responsibility and that they can become able to regulate their learning.

Instructional systems differ in the extent to which they provide for explicit help, structure or advise for the various learning functions. Some systems take care of almost all of the functions, leaving only few possibilities for the student. Other systems let students fulfill many of the functions themselves. We think that there are three ways instructional systems can have an influence on the learning functions of students: taking over, activation or stimulation (cf. Wittrock, 1979). Taking over a learning function means that the system initiates and fills the learning function. This happens for instance when students are obliged to answer multiple choice questions provided by the teacher, or when a teacher presents information. Activating a certain function pertains to forcing students to use certain functions in a specified way, for instance by assigning that they should make a scheme of the concepts discussed in a text book. Stimulating students to use certain functions concerns either general advise to execute certain learning activities and leave out some other, or training students in the learning functions. Stimulation occurs for instance when a teacher advises students to learn in a meaningful way, or when he teaches them to use certain learning strategies or self-regulation skills.

There are advantages and disadvantages connected to the three ways to cope with learning functions. **Taking over learning activities** that students could perform themselves decreases the active participation by students (sometimes even interference effects may occur, see Simons, 1980; 1984). A consequence may be that students learn below their qualitative level: their prior knowledge and intellectual abilities are not exploited as much as they might have been. Furthermore, when this "taking over" happens all the time, students will not develop their learning skills any further. On the other hand, when students are not able to execute and regulate learning activities themselves, taking over forms the only feasible short-term solution.

The **activation of learning activities and regulations** has the following advantages and disadvantages. Activating regulations and or activities mostly increases the effort expenditure by students themselves. They have to execute the assigned learning activities and regulations. This way they may learn how to do it and develop their learning and regulation skills somewhat better than in cases where the teacher "takes over". However, they do not learn when to use which activities and regulation processes (for instance choosing and controlling their own learning goals and activities). Furthermore, they may often fail to exploit all the possibilities of integrating pre-conceptions and advance knowledge with new knowledge and skills. Perhaps self-chosen activities and regulation processes might lead to better results than the activated ones.

Stimulating students to use certain ways of learning and regulation, or teaching them how to learn, will in our view, lead to the best learning processes eventually. On the short term, however, this may result in lower performance, frustration and resistance.

Thus, when teachers present a summarizing scheme students cannot and will not create their own structure. When teachers activate structurizing activities by giving them the assignment to create a scheme of relations, students cannot and perhaps will not use their other structurizing abilities. Finally, when teachers stimulate students to structurize text information in a way that is too general, students who are unable to do so may acheive lower results than they would have given other methods.

What happens in many instructional situations is that teachers feel obliged to take over learning activities because they observe that students are not able to execute them when activated. For instance teachers expect their students to make their own notes using their schematizing and structurizing abilities. Soon, however, they discover that many of the students are not able to make adequate notes. Then they feel obliged to take over by literally dictating the notes. Because of this these students never learn how to take notes independently and the circle closes.

When one wants to teach students how to learn independently, one is usually forced to take over important learning activities as a first step. Gradually then the learning activities and regulation processes, once they have been learned, can be activated. Thus while taking over learning activities, a teacher should teach the students how to execute and regulate the learning activities on their own. When different learning activities and regulation processes have been practiced and activated, gradually the teacher should replace his activations with stimulations, depending on the developing learning and regulation skills. An important question is whether such learning to learn approaches can be given in separate courses or can only be successful in integrated domain-specific courses. General learning to learn courses until now have failed to succeed. Overall there was a complete lack of transfer to regular learning situations. Domain-specific approaches, however, seem to be more promising (see below). Perhaps a combined general and domain specific approach might form an acceptable compromise.

In the next section three new instructional systems will be discussed in light of the concepts introduced in the present section.

Analyzing Three Learning Environments that Aim to Induce Constructive Learning

The Leittext Method

In the West-German industrial sector, as a reply to new demands on flexibility and independence of workers, a new method was developed to teach practical working skills, like constructing a machine. Later this method was broadened and became applied to other kinds of skills and subject matter, for instance machine repair, selling strategies and text processing. In this method one structures the learning by the workers in six phases: informing, planning, deciding, executing, controlling and evaluating. Thus workers are informed (or inform themselves) about the kind of product they have to make, how it looks, what principles to use, what is important, etc. (informing). Then they plan for the way they want to proceed. This plan is discussed with the teacher or counsellor (deciding). Then the plan is executed. Next, the product is controlled by the workers themselves (controlling). Finally, together with the teacher, the whole process of learning is evaluated.

When the method is used for the first time the steps are structured in a detailed way. Later the role of the teacher can be reduced and workers take over more and more, using the same six steps on their own. This method was developed out of dissatisfaction with independent learning projects that were used often in German industrial training. The projects often failed. In seeking ways to give more structure to the approach, the Leittext method arose.

Four specific kinds of learning aids were developed: steering questions, information questions, planning aids and control lists. Steering and information questions are used in the first phase (informing), directing students towards an analysis of the end product, both with reference to skills and knowledge to be used and to regulation processes. Different kinds of planning aids are used: a) planning cards on which the different steps to be taken were ordered randomly (to be put in the right sequence by the workers); b) planning cards where certain steps were filled in already, while others had to added by the workers themselves and c) empty planning cards. Control lists consisting of the criteria to be used in judging the product when ready. These can be ready made, or filled in by the workers themselves.

The Leittext method explicitly aims at allowing one to work independently and to solve problems on one's own. It does so by creating a structure in which workers can work independently without encountering too many problems or straying too far away from the intentions of the teachers. The preparatory phase of the work planning and problem solving are especially highly structured. At first, the method takes over the orientation on goals and activities, the choice of goals and their relevance (through steering questions and informative questions), the planning of activities and their sequence (planning and deciding) and the evaluation afterwards. The recall of prior learning is activated through questions. The control of the work, when it is finished, is activated through control-lists and the evaluation, judgment and feedback is taken over in the evaluation phase. When workers get used to the method, taking over of the orientation and planning is replaced by activation or perhaps even stimulation and the activation of control is replaced by stimulation of control.

It remains unclear, however, how and when the gradual shift toward activation or stimulation takes place. Also, it remains unclear whether the other aspects of self-regulation play any systematic role at all, for instance: Is self-confidence stimulated? Are students helped with other noncognitive aspects of self-regulation (getting started, getting attention, staying motivated, concentration management). Is there any systematic help during the execution phase (monitoring, testing, revision, reflection)?

One remarkable tendency we noted, is that most of the published applications of the Leittext method apply it in rather distal situations. For instance students develop a hobby machine in a school-like setting having hardly anything to do with the kinds of machine they have to construct or use later on. Few applications use real life simulations or even on-the-job settings.

The Leittext method does not explicitly aim at learning to work independently and learning to learn since its main purpose is to guarantee that independent work leads to satisfactory results. Perhaps, however, the system as a whole has some influence on the way students tackle other problems and on how they proceed when learning independently.

Typically in the Leittext method one tries to create conditions that permit students to work independently without doing too much harm. This is accomplished by placing heavy emphasis on the orientation and planning phase: "Think before you do. Collect all the information you might need; think of criteria your product should meet; make an explicit work plan; start only when your teacher says your planning and list of criteria is complete (etc.)". For some products (like constructing a machine) this seems to be the only way to do it. In other cases (for instance in learning to work with a text processing program) there might be solutions that place less emphasis on the orientation and planning phase. In our experience, as is the finding of Carroll (1987), many people hate to think before they start doing. Carroll's subjects for instance "jumped the gun" and wanted to start working as soon as possible. Also, in many Dutch training studies applying Galpe´rin's theory on the stepwise building of mental activities, similar problems occurred (Van Parreren, 1983). Students did not like to become oriented completely beforehand, they wanted to start as soon as possible. Furthermore, in many situations (according to Van Parreren) it is impossible to plan everything before you get started: only during the working or learning event itself can complete control develop.

Therefore, in our opinion, adaptations of the Leittext method should be developed which incorporate possibilities for orientation and planning during or even after the completion of construction activities. Moreover, perhaps "on-the-job" applications or real life simulations like "lernburos (office simulations)" of the Leittext method should be preferred in the future. Finally, there is, in our view, need for a more systematic approach in the Leittext method toward the gradual withdrawal of the external regulation of the orientation, planning and control phases, incorporating notions about learning to work independently and learning to learn. The theory described might offer some help in this respect.

The main experiences we had with the Leittext method show that in general learners are very enthusiastic about it. However, they sometimes think it is cumbersome to find out everything on their own. They prefer to have simple information told to them instead of having to discover it themselves. Moreover, it became clear that the method takes a lot of time. This time-investment may perhaps have long-term effects. Since we are not able to measures these kinds of effects adequately, it is difficult to prove that they are real and not only existing in the minds of teachers and learners. Finally, it also became clear that it takes some time to convince teachers and learners that the method really works and to teach them the relevant teaching and learning skills.

Problem-Oriented Learning

In the Netherlands another new system of instruction was developed. Originally it was used in professional medical education. Later on, applications in other domains like law, social science industrial training and teacher education were used successfully. This method consists of fixed phases: problem discussion, analysis, hypothesis generation, finding knowledge gaps, deciding on individual learning goals, individual study and synthesis. At first the students get a written problem description (for instance about a patient coming to his doctor with certain symptoms like coughing, breathing problems, blood spitting,etc). This description is as realistic as possible. The students' task (as a group) is not to solve the problem, but to analyze it and to generate as many hypotheses as possible about explanations of the symptoms. Moreover, they have to find out what they already know about these explanations and what their knowledge gaps are.

Following this they decide on group or individual learning goals: what do we (or do I) want to learn relating to this problem and its possible explanations. Then follows individual study in the library or at home, using lists of books and articles supplied by the department. A tutor is available for any help the group or individuals might find useful. Finally, individual learning results are brought together in the group. The students inform each other about what they found and learned. They look one more time at the problem description that started the whole learning process and try to formulate conclusions. At regular times there are exams where the subject matter knowledge and skills to be learned are tested. Every year of study the students should be better able to answer the exam questions. At the end they should be able to know the answer to 80 % of the questions.

In the Problem Oriented method, like in the Leittext method, an emphasis lies on the preparatory phase. Through the problem description that is provided, students are activated to orient themselves on possible learning goals. The problems are written in such a way that there is a close link to the later professional practice. In this way the motivating to learn function is taken over by the system. Either as a group, or individually, students are activated to choose certain learning goals which automatically have relevance for them (through the connection with their later professional practice). Also, the recall of prior learning is taken care of explicitly: students are activated to think of everything they know in relation to the problem and its explanations.

The actual learning steps and their regulation are unguided however. Students are expected to be able to take the necessary steps to learn in order to reach their agreed upon learning goals. The way they should monitor and test their learning, or revise their strategy when confronted with problems, is unguided. They have, however, ample opportunities to "practice" independent learning. Furthermore, the tutors may provide help to those students asking for it. Some structuring of the judgment, feedback and evaluation occurs in the synthesis phase where students integrate and discuss their individual learning. Finally, there is no help in staying motivated and concentrated.

The Problem Oriented method does not aim at the improvement of problem solving or thinking skills in a direct way. Students do not learn how to solve the problems presented, nor do they learn a problem solving strategy. Because of the direct connection of the learning goals to the problem descriptions, however, some effects on problem solving skill may perhaps be expected. In most of the Problem Oriented systems of education separate skills courses supplement the theoretical study.

Finally, the Problem Oriented method can teach students how to learn to a certain extent. They learn how to prepare themselves for learning (orientation on possible learning goals;

choice of goals, recall of prior learning, motivating oneself to learn). It depends on coincidence however whether the actual skill of learning and regulation of it will develop or not.

What one could and, in our view, should learn from the experiences with Problem Oriented learning is that it is very important to focus on real professional problems (for instance through problem descriptions) and help students connect their learning to professional practice in a direct and clear way (promoting the relevance of learning goals). Furthermore, the great success of the Problem Oriented method, from our experience, lies mainly in the possibility for students to pursue their own learning goals. However, these are restricted to the domain of professional practice through the connection with the problem descriptions. This not only motivates students to learn, it also takes care of an optimal connection between existing knowledge and gaps in it and the knowledge and skills to be learned (stressing the cumulative nature of learning as discussed by Shuell). A final important aspect of the Problem Oriented method is its emphasis on integration at the end. Students have to inform their fellows students, discover what they learned, and address how it relates to the central problem.

Experience with the Problem-oriented learning approach in different Dutch Universities shows two kinds of results. On the one hand, about one-third of the students do not like the problem-oriented method. They prefer to learn in traditional ways where less activity is demanded of them. Furthermore, some students tended to get back to more traditional forms of learning (going over the problem descriptions very quickly and learning a text book by heart). On the other hand, the results of experiments show that the learning performance of students learning through a problem-oriented method was as good as or better than that of students learning through traditional university teaching on traditional tests. However, there were effects on less traditional tests measuring general skills of problem diagnosis and problem solving that are not reached by the traditional system.

From Apprenticeship to Cognitive Apprenticeship

In earlier days, apprenticeship formed one of the most frequently used systems of education. According to this system, one became a tailor, for instance, by starting to cooperate with a master tailor, most of the time together with one or more fellow youngsters. In the United States and in the Netherlands this out of school system disappeared (recently, Achtenhagen showed that the German history on this point differs greatly from the American and Dutch; we will not go into this discussion here). According to Resnick (1987), this system of "on-the-job training", in contrast to the school system, typically employed: (1) group learning instead of individual learning (2) learning with tools instead of tool-less learning, (3) domain-specific learning instead of widely usable knowledge and skills and, (4) object-manipulation instead of symbol-manipulation. Learning took place in a real-life context. The master-tailor appointed certain tasks to the pupils. At first the tasks were rather simple, but they gradually became more difficult and complex. In the beginning the pupils had only a few responsibilities, but later on they became more and more responsible for their own work. They learned by doing, by observing and by imitating the expert and by getting feedback from him as well as from their fellow-pupils.

Nowadays, the apprenticeship-system has been replaced by the school-system, which stresses symbol-manipulation and knowledge. Even in skill-training and industrial and military training, we prefer to use the school-system. Typically we send our trainees (for instance in management, medical, professional and military training) to school-like settings to learn and understand the concepts and theories to be applied later on in practice. Then we let them practice in real settings, without adequate structuring of the level of difficulty of the tasks, the feedback, or the cooperation opportunities. Resnick refers to American studies showing that the results of these kinds of training are rather disappointing in general. People fail to apply in practice what they learn in theory. According to Resnick, therefore, it may be fruitful to go back to the apprenticeship system. Especially when we want to teach our students how to learn, how to think and how to solve problems, the principles of the old apprenticeship systems should be rehabilitated: this is cognitive apprenticeship. The cognitive apprenticeship approach may also be used in computer-aided instruction, and more in particular in interactive videodisc systems (see below). First we shall discuss the cognitive apprenticeship system in more detail.

In American instructional psychology there is a revived pedagogical optimism: many researchers now believe that it is possible to improve abilities of the self-regulation of learning, thinking, intelligence and problem solving. This optimism stems mainly from the remarkable results of training studies by Palincsar and Brown (1984) on reading comprehension, by Schoenfeld (1985) on mathematical reasoning and by Scardamalia, Bereiter & Steinbeck (1984) on writing processes. In these three studies and their later replications, durable, generalizable and transferable results of training were realized.

Palincsar and Brown (1984) devised a teaching procedure, which they named "reciprocal teaching". Learning disabled children learned how to comprehend texts by discussing text interpretations and text processing strategies in groups. The teacher and the students read text passages together and tried to make sense of them cooperatively. The students had to verbalize their interpretations and their way of thinking and understanding as explicitly as possible. Teaching and student roles were executed both by the students and the teacher (that is why the procedure was called reciprocal). In that way the teacher could demonstrate her own explicit thinking processes (acting as an expert model), at the same time forcing students to make their processes explicit. An important principle used in Palincsar's training was "scaffolding". Gradually, the students were made more responsible for their own reading comprehension.

According to Paris (1988) the following characteristics are fundamental in reciprocal teaching: 1) model strategies explicitly; 2) model strategies in their usual context; 3) inform students of the need to use strategies and their utility; 4) make students realize that the strategies work for them; 5) transfer responsibility gradually; 6) gradually challenge internalization of strategies; 7) tailor feedback and encouragement.

Schoenfeld (1985) taught mathematical reasoning processes. He also used forms of cooperative learning. Students solved mathematical problems in small groups. Through all kinds of questions posed by the teacher, their thinking processes were made explicit and communicated to the teacher and fellow pupils. In cognitive coaching, the following is emphasized (see Paris, 1988): 1) shared goals and affect; 2) linked assessment and instruction; 3) demonstration and explanation provided; 4) responsibility shifted to students; 5) progress is personal and continuous.

Scardamalia and Bereiter (1984) used a direct explanation method to teach children how to write texts. Through a series of questions they posed themselves during writing they were forced to plan and regulate their writings explicitly and publicly. The most important ingredients of the approach were: 1) direct modelling of strategies and regulations; 2) explanation of strategies and their utility; 3) emphasis on student's beliefs.

Resnick (1987) in her analysis of the apprenticeship system, found the following to be characteristic of programs proving successful for acquiring school learning skills:

> 1. They involve socially shared intellectual work. 2. They are organized around mutual accomplishment of tasks so that elements of the skill take on meaning in the context of the whole. Second many of the programs also shared elements of apprenticeship: 1. They make usually hidden processes overt, subject to observation and commentary. 2. They allow skill to build up bit by bit, yet permit participation even for the relatively unskilled. This is often enabled by the social sharing of tasks. Finally, the most successful programs were organized around particular bodies of knowledge and interpretation (subject matters if you will) rather than "general" abilities. They thereby engaged students in processes of meaning construction and interpretation which seem to have the effect of blocking the kind of symbol-detached-from-sense thinking that I have noted as a major problem in school but not in out-of-school-activity. It is just this kind of self-conscious meaning construction and interpretation that is likely to be needed in conditions of breakdown and transition out of school when it is necessary (probably) to use ones powers of reflection and analysis to craft sensible responses to new and as yet ill-understood-situations. (p. 20-21)

The cognitive apprenticeship systems, though they form by no means a uniform system, all focus on the learning functions and stages that the other two systems discussed neglect: these are taking the necessary steps to learn and regulating learning. They teach students how to remember, comprehend, integrate and apply and how to monitor and test whether they do so. Also, revision mechanisms (what to do when you fail to understand, how to proceed in case of trouble) get attention, as do reflection and evaluation. Furthermore, (external) feedback by the teacher and by the fellow pupils plays an important role. In these systems there is an explicit transition from taking over (modelling and explanation by the teacher) to activation and stimulation.

From the descriptions in the literature, however, it is unclear whether the preparatory phases of learning also are stressed. Some cognitive apprenticeship systems pay more attention to affective aspects of learning than others (Paris, 1988).

The cognitive apprenticeship approach focuses both on learning to think and solve problems independently and on learning to learn, depending on the particular program chosen. What one can learn from the experiences with cognitive apprenticeship systems is that learning to learn and learning to solve problems is possible, but it should be guided more closely and explicitly than was done before and a direct connection and integration of attempts to teach students how to learn and solve problems with domain specific normal instruction seems to be of vital importance.

The Three Systems Compared

The Leittext method was described as a method that accentuates the preparatory phase of independent work. The system does not provide for explicit means to teach learning to work independently or learning to learn. Furthermore there is hardly any attention paid to the executive stages of working and problem solving, nor to affective components of self-regulation. The Problem-Oriented method also focuses on the preparatory phase of independent learning. It is more a method that motivates students to learn independently and provides a way to proceed in choosing learning goals than it is a method to teach problem solving skills or other learning to learn skills. In this method, there is also no attention to the executive phases, nor to affective aspects. When students learn to learn through these two systems it is more or less coincidental and dependent on the ingenuity of individual counsellors and tutors instead of built-in approaches. The cognitive apprenticeship system on the other hand neglects the preparatory phase of learning and problem solving, but accentuates the executive phase and (more or less) affective aspects, stressing learning to think and learning to learn.

The three systems, though having much in common, differ greatly when analyzed in terms of our theory. Perhaps an integration is possible and useful. The Leittext method can then be used to structure the orientation and planning phases, using steering and informative questions, planning aids and control criteria. The Problem-Oriented method can be used for guiding the process of goal selection, recall of prior knowledge and promoting awareness of goal relevance, using problem descriptions to be analyzed by the students. The principles of the Cognitive

Apprenticeship system can especially be used in the executive phase of learning and problem solving, incorporating an explicit learning to think and learning to learn approach.

However, such an ideally integrated learning to think and learning to learn approach is difficult for human teachers. Perhaps we will be able to realize it through computer aided instruction. The possibilities of computer tools can be used to shape human thinking and learning (see Salomon, 1988a).

Conclusions

The main argument we would like to put forward in this paper is that constructive learning can not be expected to result from constructive learning environments automatically. Learners, in their long history of experiences with learning, develop persistent beliefs, habits and styles related to learning activities that will make it difficult for some of them to work and learn in constructive learning environments. Learners, from our research experience, interpret learning environments in their own way, depending among other things on their learning conceptions. Thus, we need to teach learners how to behave in constructive learning environments. If we do not, effective systems will be distorted and used in ways we would not want or expect. The tendency is very strong for learners to learn by heart, to stick to the surface, to refrain from thinking and to hand over responsibility for learning to others (such as teachers). We need learning to learn approaches embedded or immersed (see Prawat, 1991) in constructive learning environments.

A second point is that we must educate teachers. As we discovered in studying and implementing Leittext methods, it is not easy for teachers to change a traditional approach into one that stresses learner activities that they cannot control or influence. Strong tendencies which are developed through years of experience make it hard to believe that learners can learn constructively if you give them adequate opportunities combined with a learning to learn approach. Thus, we have to convince teachers, show them how to do it, and teach them the necessary skills.

Finally, we believe it is very important to plan constructive learning thoroughly and to embed it into the total instructional design. We cannot expect learners and teachers to learn constructively during a part of their school days and to return to their habitual way of learning during the rest of the time. This means that we have to offer the following principles for instructional design of constructive learning environments:

- Embed constructive learning environments in the total instructional system.
- Teach learners how they can learn in a constructive way, embedding or immersing this learning to learn into the environment.

- Teach self-regulatory skills. Learning to learn constructively presupposes and encompasses self-regulated learning. Therefore, in instructional design the teaching of self-regulatory skills should be planned.
- Teach teachers how to use constructive learning environments.
- Find a balance between contextualization and decontextualization.
- Develop learning environments that explicitly organize the five aspects of self-regulated learning: preparation, learning skills, self-regulation, judgement and feedback and motivation and concentration.

References

Biemans, H., & Simons, P.R.J. (1991). *Regulation support in computer aided learning to use Wordperfect.* Paper presented at the Annual Meeting of the German Educational Psychology Association, Koln, September 25-27.

Biggs, J.B. (1984). Learning strategies, student motivation patterns, and subjectively perceived success. In J.R. Kirby (Ed.), *Cognitive strategies and educational performance.* New York: Academic Press.

Boekaerts, M. (1987). *Psychologie van de leerling en het leerproces (Psychology of the pupil and the learning process).* Nijmegen: Dekker & Van de Vegt.

Brophy, J.J. (1988). *The teacher's role in stimulating student motivation to learn.* Paper presented at the Annual Meeting of the American Educational Research Association, New Orleans, April.

Carroll, J.M. (1987). *The minimal manual. Human Computer Interaction, 3,* 123-153.

Corno, L. (1988). *Volitional strategies in classroom tasks.* Paper presented at the Annual Meeting of the American Educational Research Association, New Orleans, April.

De Jong, F.P.C.M. (1988). *Computer gestuurd leren leren. (Computer aided learning to learn).* Paper presented at the meeting of the Dutch Psychological Association (NIP). Tilburg, 20-21 October

De Jong, F.P.C.M., & Simons, P.R.J. (1988). Self-regulation in text-processing. *European Journal of Psychology of Education, 3,* 177-190.

De Jong, F.C.M., Simons, P.R.J. (1991). Training metacognitive processes of self-regulated learning. In B. Wong (Ed.), *Intervention research with students with learning disabilities.* New York: Springer-Verlag.

De Klerk, L.F.W., Ali, K.S., & Simons, P.R.J. (1991). *Activating preconceptions through a computer assisted strategy.* Paper presented at the fourth Meeting of the European Association for Research on Learning and Instruction. Turku, August 23-29.

Entwistle, N.J., & Ramsden, P. (1983). *Understanding student learning.* London: Croom Helm.

Janssen, P.J., & De Neve, H. (1987). *Studeren en doceren aan het hoger onderwijs. (Studying and lecturing in higher education).* Acco: Leuven, Amersfoort.

Kuhl, J. (1983). *Motivation, konflikt und handlungskontrolle (Motivation, conflict and action control).* Berlin: Springer-Verlag.

Larsson, S. (1983). Paradoxes in teaching. *Instructional Science, 12*, 355-365.

Lodewijks, J.G.L.C. (1981). *Leerstofsequenties: Van conceptueel netwerk naar cognitieve structuur.(Subject matter sequences: from conceptual network to cognitive structure).* Dissertation, Lisse: Swets & Zeitlinger.

Marton, F., & SÑljî, R. (1984). Approaches to learning. In F. Marton, D. Hounsell, & N. Entwistle (Eds.), *The experience of learning*. Edinburgh: Scottish Academic Press.

Nelissen, J.M.C. (1987). *Kinderen leren wiskunde (Children learning mathematics).* Gorinchem: Dissertation.

Ng, E. (1988). *Three levels of goal-directedness in learning*. Paper presented at the Annual Meeting of the American Educational Research Association, New Orleans, April 5-9.

Palincsar, A.S. en Brown, A.L. (1984). Reciprocal teaching of comprehension-fostering and comprehension-monitoring activities. *Cognition and Instruction, 1*, 117-175.

Paris, S. (1988). *Fusing skill and will: The integration of cognitive and motivational psychology.* Paper presented to the Annual Meeting of the American Educational Research Association, New Orleans, April 5-9.

Pask, G. (1976). *Conversation theory: Applications in education and epistemology.* Amsterdam: Elsevier.

Prawat, R.S. (1989). Promoting access to knowledge, strategy, and dispositions in students: A research synthesis. *Review of Educational Research, 59*, 1-41.

Prawat, R.S. (1991). The value of ideas: The immersion approach to the development of thinking. *Educational Researcher, 20*, 3-10.

Resnick, L.B. (1987). *Relationship between learning at school and what we do in the rest of our lives.* Presidential address at the Annual Meeting of the American Educational Research Association, Washington.

Salomon, G. (1988a). *Artificial intelligence in reverse: Computer tools that become cognitive.* Paper presented at the Annual Meeting of the American Educational Research Association, New Orleans, April 5-9.

Salomon, G. (1988b). *When teams do not function the way they ought to.* Paper presented at the Annual Meeting of the American Educational Research Association, New Orleans, April 5-9.

Scardamalia, M., Bereiter C. & Steinbeck, R. (1984). Teachability of reflective processes in written composition. *Cognitive Science, 8*, 173-190.

Schoenfeld, A.H. (1985). *Mathematical problem solving*. New York: Academic Press.

Shuell, T.J. (1988). The role of the student in learning from instruction. *Contemporary Educational Psychology, 13*, 276-295.

Simons, P.R.J. (1980). *Vergelijkenderwijs: Onderzoek naar de invloed van metaforen op het leren (Influences of concrete analogies on learning).* Tilburg University: Dissertation.

Simons, P.R.J. (1984). Instructing with analogies. *Journal of Educational Psychology, 76*, 513-527.

Simons, P.R.J. (1989). Learning to learn. In P. Span, E. de Corte, & B. van Hout-Wolters (Eds.). *Onderwijsleerprocessen* (pp. 15-25). Lisse: Swets en Zeitlinger.

Simons, P.R.J., & De Jong, F.P.C.M. (1991). Metacognitive skills and computer aided instruction. *Applied psychology: An international review.*

Simons, P.R.J., & Lodewijks, J.G.L.C. (1987). Regulatory cognitions during learning from texts. In E. de Corte, H. Lodewijks, & R. Parmentier en P. Span (Eds.), *Learning and instruction.* Leuven: Pergamon.

Teurlings, C., & Simons, P.R.J. (1991). *De Leittextmethode toegepast bij tekstverwerking (The Leittext method applied in the domain of text processing).* Paper presented at the Annual meeting of the Dutch Educational Research Association. Amsterdam: May.

Van der Sanden, J.M.M. (1986). *Het leren van technische vaardigheden: Individuele verschillen bij het uitvoeren van praktijkopdrachten in het lager technisch onderwijs (The learning of technical skills: Individual differences in executing practical assignments in lower vocational education).* Den Haag: SVOSelecta.

Van Parreren, C.F. (1983). *Leren door handelen (Learning through acting).* Apeldoorn: Walraven.

Vermunt, J.D.H.M. (1987). *Learning styles and self-regulation.* Paper presented to the Annual meeting of the American Educational Research Association, Washington, April.

Vermunt, J.D.H.M., & Van Rijswijk, F. (1988). Analysis and development of students' skill in self-regulated learning. *Higher Education, 17*, 647-682.

Wittrock, M.C. (1979). Learning as a generative process. *Educational Psychologist, 11*, 87-95.

15 Transfer of Learning from a Constructivist Perspective

Manfred Prenzel and Heinz Mandl

Institut für Empirische Pädagogik und Pädagogische Psychologie, Universität München, München, Germany

According to Resnick (1989, p. 8) transfer of learning is the holy grail of educators – everyone is in search of it, but researchers hoping to find it have been dissappointed after every new experiment or reform program to date. In her research survey, Resnick (Resnick, 1991) is obviously sceptical of the idea that traditional transfer research will be able to solve the educational, or rather, instructional problem of teaching widely applicable knowledge and skills. A major feature of the grail's myth is, in Resnick's opinion, the commonly held conception among educators and cognitive scientists that skills and knowledge are represented in a person independent of the contexts in which they have been acquired, thus enabling the person to apply acquired knowledge regardless of the situation.

This conception is being challenged by Resnick and other authors (e.g., Bednar, Cunningham, Duffy & Perry, 1991; Lave, 1988; Pea, 1991) who support a constructivist position. Their approach focuses on the idea of situated or contextualized cognition. Constructivists demand other theoretical and instructional research approaches to the problem of the applicability of knowledge and skills. However, they refer to the term "transfer" only occasionally, and on these rare occasions primarily according to a commonplace everyday understanding which emphasizes the instructional problems of conveying applicable knowledge. The central concepts of constructivist theories are now *contextualization* and *decontextualization* and their implications for the *applicability* of knowledge and skills.

At this point, the most challenging question is whether and to what extent the constructivist position has dashed, demystified or merely reformulated the hope to find what Resnick called the holy grail of educators – transfer. In view of the necessity to improve our knowledge of the conditions in which flexibly applicable knowledge and skills can be constructed, it is high time to approach this subject under a less general perspective. After almost 100 years of research on the transfer of learning, the question arises whether the concept of transfer is in principle incompatible with the constructivist approach. It may be more practical to regard the concept of transfer under a constructivist perspective and find a feasible definition.

In the first section, we translate the traditional concept of transfer into constructivist terminology. The second section deals with implications of a contextualistic position necessary for a constructivist understanding of transfer. In this section, we discuss different views of how "context" is understood. In addition, we address conceptions of contextualized representations. In the third section, we propose a concept of representation which integrates contextualized and abstract knowledge, and thus could serve as a basis for constructivist transfer research. In the final section, we outline some implications of this concept for instruction which aims to support transfer.

A Constructivist Transfer Concept

Research on the transfer of learning deals with the way in which knowledge that has been acquired in performing a certain task (Voss, 1987), within a certain situation (Singley & Anderson, 1989) or setting (Sternberg & French, 1990) can be applied to another task or to another situation or setting. From a general viewpoint, the object of transfer research is identical to the object of constructivist approaches that deal with the problem of flexible applicability of knowledge (e.g., Resnick, 1989).

The fact that transfer research strictly distinguishes between learning on the one hand and application on the other allows experimental approaches. In this context, the crucial question is whether such a distinction fits the constructivist perspective. In principle, it seems justified to distinguish analytically between the situation or phase in which knowledge and skills are constructed and the situation or phase in which knowledge is subsequently applied. However, difficulties may arise due to differing concepts of "construction". According to the constructivist position, construction occurs within both the learning and application situations. The construction processes in turn affects learning processes within both situations.

Messner (1978) presented a way out of this dilemma some time ago by developing a constructivist transfer concept in the tradition of Piaget and Aebli. Messner defines learning as the *construction* of a (cognitive) structure. He defines application (transfer) as the *reconstruction* of a structure. He distinguishes between reconstruction under *familiar* versus *novel* conditions, and in *unchanged* versus *changed* form, thus obtaining a simple categorization schema (Table 1).

The reconstruction of a structure is effected:

	under familiar conditions	under novel conditions
in unchanged form	reproduction	application (transfer)
in changed form	transformation	application (transfer)

Table 1: Categorization schema for transfer (according to Messner, 1978, p. 53)

Messner's suggestion opens up practical ways of formulating a constructivist definition of transfer that distinguishes between learning and application. In addition, the notion of transfer as reconstruction under novel conditions is granted special status. These distinctions provide a basis for discussing the theoretical aspects of the constructivist approach as far as transfer of learning is concerned.

Problems With a Constructivist Transfer Concept

Certain theoretical conceptions about the nature of the learning process, the representation of knowledge, and the application process characterize the current constructivist position (e.g., Bednar, Cunningham, Duffy & Perry, 1991; Duffy & Jonassen, 1991; Spiro, Feltovich, Jacobson, & Coulson, 1991, Cognition and Technology Group, 1991). Special emphasis is placed on "context", which decisively affects the way in which the learner constructs and represents experiences. Furthermore, context also affects new application situations. Thus, transfer – in it's reconstructing function – depends in various ways on context. The critical characteristic of a constructivist transfer concept is the importance of taking contextual effects into consideration.

Different Concepts of Context

Before we investigate the significance of context for transfer it is important to point out what constitutes "con-text" within the learning and application environments respectively, and to differentiate between "con-text" and "text". From a constructivist perspective, the "context" which a learner constructs is of major importance, of course, within the constraints of the specific situation.

However, it is not easy to identify a clear definition of the expressions "context" and "contextualization" in the constructivist literature. Lave (1988, p. 39 ff) accuses traditional transfer research of neglecting context to a large extent and of drawing no distinction between context and the content of the problem to be solved in either learning or application situations. She continues that when the expression "context" is referred to, it is interpreted in different ways, such as in the sense of the social situation or the institutional or cultural context.

While Lave's reproach of traditional transfer research is justified, it also applies to constructivist authors. When using the term "context", Bednar and coworkers (1991, p. 95) emphasize real-life connections; Pea (1991, p. 9) speaks of a context of "authentic activities"; the Cognition and Technology Group (1991) refers to "meaningful problem solving contexts" (p. 34), to "familiar text structures as presentation context" (p. 35), to video-adventures which create different contexts (p. 36); Bransford, Goldman, and Vye (1991) mention a social context (p. 12), a "familiar task-context" (p. 13), and a context of "meaningful objectives"(p. 32).

The fact that the term "context" is used in various ways becomes problematic when central theoretical importance is assigned to it. In its broadest sense, "context" stands for the "ecology" in its entirety, including the material/content-related and social aspects of the learning or application environment. The constructivist perspective is, of course, not interested in objective-ecological features, but in subjective perceptions and interpretations of the learning and application environments.

Constructivist approaches focus primarily on a particular aspect of context which is, by the way, addressed by all authors; namely the "context of meaning" in the sense of a "context of use". Emphasizing this aspect as the core of the constructivist position and neglecting other usages of the term "context" found in commonplace formulations considerably augments the constructivist position. Within any learning environment, not only is knowledge constructed, but simultaneously the significance of the knowledge is being constructed in terms of its applicability with regard to a specific purpose. To a certain extent, the constructivist position advocates Wittgenstein's (1971) opinion that the meaning of a concept (or of knowledge) is best understood by looking at the use of the concept. Thus, in the course of construction, knowledge and application (context) are inseparably connected to each other. In other words, knowledge is "contextualized".

Contextualized Knowledge

The next step toward a constructivist approach to transfer is to address the problem of developing conceptions of how contextualized knowledge is represented in the learner. In this section we look at some constructivist approaches and their suggestions for solving the above-mentioned problem.

Bransford, Franks, Vye & Sherwood (1989) and Bransford, Sherwood, Hasselbring, Kinzer & Williams (1990), refer to the concept of "*conditionalized knowledge*" in which knowledge itself includes information about the conditions and constraints in its application. Bransford and coworkers refer to Simon (1980) and Anderson (1983, 1987) in their attempt to put this notion into concrete form. They refer to it as knowledge organized "in form of condition-action pairs mediated by appropriate goal-oriented hierarchies" (Bransford et al., 1991, p. 120). In accordance with the ACT* approach, the condition-part specifies conditions of application in procedural knowledge. The combination of productions leads to more specific application conditions. For the time being, this model's conception of "conditionalized knowledge" originating from the ACT* approach applies exclusively to procedural knowledge. Thus, it is limited to a very restricted "range of application".

Although the ACT* approach provides for the possibility of retrieving declarative knowledge in a concrete problem solving situation, interpretative procedures have to be added. Declarative knowledge per se is not (specifically) conditioned. A different conceptualization can be found in Anderson, Greeno, Kline & Neves (1981). They consider schemata as elaborated structures of knowledge which also contain schematizing productions. These schematizing productions allow a direct subsumption of a problem under a schema. The schematizing productions define a range of applications for that schema (Fortmüller, 1991). Another conception of "conditionalized knowledge", which may be more compatible with the constructivist position, is that of Schoenfeld (1983, 1985) who emphasizes the necessity of learning not only individual strategies, but also of acquiring the specific application conditions for each strategy.

Collins, Brown & Newman (1989) also refer to Schoenfeld's concept of application conditions. However, they include an additional conception, claiming that knowledge might be, at least partly, represented in an "*indexed*" manner (indexical knowledge):

> That is, our representations might not be abstract and self-sufficient; rather, they might be constructed from the context, social and physical, in which they are formed. (Brown, Collins & Duguid, 1989, p. 12).

Duffy and Jonassen (1991) interpret this statement in such a way that meaning and understanding are indexed by experience. They state that, "Each experience with an idea – and the environment of which that idea is a part – becomes part of that idea (p. 8)." Collins (1990) specifies the idea of indexed knowledge by referring to Agre & Chapman (1987). Indices (like an index-finger pointing the way) immediately indicate what has to be done within a certain context (with regard to a subject's current position and his or her goals). Agre demonstrates the functioning of indexed representations in a navigation-program for a robot. In order to understand that notion, it is important to consider indices as a separate class of signs which have to be distinguished from icons or symbols – as is common practice in semiotics (e.g., Eco, 1977). If we do so, it becomes clear that constructivist approaches have been taking up hitherto largely unconsidered representational models.

Greeno's approach (1989) focuses on this fundamental problem. In his opinion, considerable limitations of cognitive science are due to the fact that cognitive scientists have been restricting themselves to models of symbolic computation. Empirical evidence has prompted Greeno to rethink the issue. This evidence includes findings on everyday cognition (e.g., Scribner, 1984; Lave, 1988) which frequently refer directly to resources in the situation and come to solutions without making use of symbolic computation. It also includes findings on school learning, which function on a symbolic level, but cannot be related to real-life situations (e.g., Caramazza, McCloskey, & Green, 1981). In this respect, Greeno's basic assumption is closely related to the transfer issue. According to Greeno, knowledge represents the relation between a person and a social or physical situation.

Within this relational structure, Greeno distinguishes four main levels (i.e., object, abstract, symbol, and model) with each level again being subdivided into a structure level and a unit level. The levels, in turn, are connected by relations. This relational structure allows Greeno to map different ways of thinking, ranging from situated thinking (or indexical thinking, in the sense of Agre's) to thinking in terms of mental models. The quality of the relations determines whether or not symbolic knowledge remains "isolated" (i.e., in the sense of Whitehead "inert knowledge") and thus only applicable to symbolic units, but not to realistic situations. In this way, Greeno expands traditional models of knowledge representation and reformulates them in the form of a relational concept which is supposed to contribute to the explanation of "generative thinking". The quality of the relational structure determines whether processing on the model level can be effected on symbolic, abstracted, or object levels, thus facilitating the application of knowledge in differing as well as novel situations. From an instructional point of view, Greeno is, in this context, interested in the relevance of different types of information (e.g., linguistic or graphical information, or simulations) in order to establish relations across the different levels.

With reference to Greeno's suggestions, Kintsch (1991) also deals with the problem of correspondence between symbol processing and real-world events by advocating a similar model. According to his theory, knowledge is only "decontextualized", if the "problem model" does not correspond with the "world" – that is, if there is no one-to-one mapping between real-world events and the symbol representation in the problem model. In contrast to Greeno's model, Kintsch distinguishes fewer levels and relations. He introduces the "situation model" as a mediator, "But the situation model represents already a significant abstraction from the real world, so that the mapping from the situation model to the formal problem model is more straightforward than the direct mapping from the problem model to the real world (Kintsch, 1991, p. 239)." According to Kintsch, since learners already have powerful situation models at their disposal, the mapping between the situation model and the problem model has to be supported. For example, in the case of mathematical problems, animations can elucidate the relations between algebraic schemata and problem situations.

This brief survey makes it clear that although the constructivist claim for taking contextualized knowledge into account has stimulated fresh reflection on representation models, there has not yet been a systematic elaboration of a constructivist representation model. Greeno comes closest to designing an integrative model which connects knowledge with varying degrees of abstractness to differing representation modi by means of relations. However,

Greeno, as well as Kintsch, focuses the mappings between different types of representation and on the possible ways of transducing one type of representation into another. This issue is akin to the past issue of "representational competence" (e.g., Sigel, 1970) in developmental psychology, which was raised in connection with Bruner's (1964) distinction between enactive, iconic, and symbolic representations.

At this point, the problem of transfer has been addressed. However, there is still no answer to the question of how a contextualized representation system should be conceptualized. This issue has been addressed by Duffy and Jonassen (1991) in their interpretation of "indexical knowledge". In contrast to Duffy and Jonassen, the concept of indexed knowledge, which Collins (1990) refers to, is narrower. It illustrates a type of knowledge which remains unconsidered in traditional symbolic representation models. However, the question arises as to which types of indices, apart from the standard example of the pointers, mentioned already by Wittgenstein (1971), are important with regard to human knowledge. In everyday language we often come across indexical expressions (e.g., "she brought that over to me yesterday") which gain their meaning only from the context. However, there are no hints to further important indices. Thus, constructivists still must take up the challenge of developing a feasible model of contextualized representation which contrasts with the concept of context-independent knowledge.

Contextualized Knowledge by Means of Range of Application

In this section, a model conception for contextualized knowledge representation will be developed which can serve as a basis for a constructivist theory of transfer. The above-mentioned ideas addressing the connection of knowledge with application conditions (Anderson, 1983; Anderson, Greeno, Kline & Neves 1981; Schoenfeld, 1983) form the basis for the following discussion. Similar considerations are also found in Messner's (1978, p. 114 ff) constructivist transfer conception which interprets schemata in the Piagetian sense. He interprets the range of application of a schema to be its "*extension*" and the schema's "content" to be its "*intension*" according to the distinction drawn by Carnap (1956). Logically speaking, the intension of a schema determines its extension (the potential range of application). In this context, the following rule applies: the more abstract a schema is and the more it lacks meaning, the broader is the logical extension.

We take up Messner's ideas and develop them a bit further. In this context, we are not only interested in the extension and intension in their logical sense, but also with regard to their *psycho-logical* sense. The intension (content) of a schema (of knowledge) determines the potential range of application (frequently this is an open set). However, the schema's subjective and psychological range of application can be much narrower than its logical extension. Thus, a set of all possible logical applications, may contain only one psycho-logical application (a single "context of use").

To illustrate, we present a typical example of transfer research (Gick & Holyoak, 1980). During the learning phase of this experiment, subjects were acquainted with the problem of a fortress which should be taken by means of distributing forces directed toward a focal point. In this example, the principle of the schema or knowledge, "strong effects and weak detrimental effects by means of converging weak forces", can be understood as its intension. From a logical point of view, the intension implies a large extension (range of application). However, from a psychological point of view the extension encompasses only one application context, namely "taking a fortress".

From a constructivist perspective, the subjects had constructed knowledge *and* a range of application during the learning phase of the experiment. During the subsequent transfer phase, subjects were confronted with a Radiation Problem (Duncker,1935). This problem – to treat an ulcer with rays – did not fit into the range of application that had been constructed so far (the psychological extension). Many subjects were able to find the solution to the "transfer problem" only when given the hint that the fortress-problem might be related to the Duncker problem (same range of application).

This example shows that it is possible to operate quite effectively under the principle of distinguishing intension, potential extension, and psychological extension. The construction of knowledge occurs parallel to the construction of a range of application. The "context of use" with regard to the learning situation becomes part of the range of application. Applying knowledge beyond the application context is, at first, very difficult. In order to achieve this, a person must generate further applications starting from the knowledge construction process (or intension). But why should someone attempt this? If the range of application of knowledge is exclusively determined by the learning context, considerable difficulties arise when the person is confronted with a different or novel type of problem which does not belong to any of the present ranges of application. The person then has to generate new extensions starting from the intensions of his or her knowledge resources. There are many possible ways to reach this end, but they involve a great deal of effort. Knowledge becomes more flexible if the set of applications contains more elements and is determined more accurately. Instructional support for this could include describing or modeling potential applications.

Furthermore, the distinction between intension, potential extension, and psychological extension contributes to a better understanding of the basic problem of abstract knowledge. On the one hand, the rule applies that the more abstract the knowledge, the broader the potential extension (Messner, 1978). On the other hand, the potential extension serves the subject only inasmuch as the psychological applications are linked to the knowledge. If abstract knowledge is conveyed within a certain learning context, then at first, only this learning context is present in the range of application of that knowledge – the knowledge is "inert" (Whitehead, 1929). Adams' (1989) distinction between "abstract" and "abstracted" knowledge makes this fundamental difference more obvious. If knowledge is abstracted through many and varying applications, multiple applications are discovered. The knowledge can be flexibly applied. Knowledge with only a few elements in the application range is rigid.

In order present a solution to the constructivist problem of "contextualized knowledge", we propose a representation model which connects knowledge with range of application. Knowledge can be of varying quality. In simple words, it may range from "concrete" to "abstract". The more abstract the knowledge, the greater the potential range of application (the logical extension). If the psychological range of application is not specified, even abstract knowledge has only a limited scope of application. In the extreme case, this would be only the context wherein the abstract knowledge was constructed. In sum, the quality of knowledge *and* the quality of the psychological range of application together determine the flexibility of knowledge application.

Knowledge and Range of Application: Instructional Implications for a Constructivist Transfer Concept

Traditional cognitive research has mainly analyzed knowledge structures, focusing on knowledge acquisition and how it is conveyed. Recently, constructivist approaches are stressing context and emphasizing the situated character of the construction processes. The notion of relating knowledge to a range of application necessitates an investigation of both concepts. From this perspective, cognitive development can occur in various domains:

- Knowledge concerning a range of application can become more extensive, more differentiated, more integrated, or more abstract.
- The range of application concerning knowledge can be enlarged by other application contexts.
- Modifications in the range of application can occur in parallel with a specification or abstraction of knowledge. Conversely, through the modification of knowledge, alternative applications can be defined.
- Finally, different knowledge domains and ranges of application can be combined and integrated.

Concerning the issue of transfer of learning, the question arises as to how the development of both knowledge and range of application can be supported so that a knowledge application (reconstruction), which is as flexible as possible, occurs. Some instructional approaches to the facilitation of transfer which are in line with the constructivist position will be discussed in the following section. These are based on the notion of combining knowledge and range of application. The primary question is: Which instructional measures support the construction of ranges of knowledge application and their enlargement?

A suggestion can be extracted from the conceptions of Greeno (1989) and Kintsch (1991). They address the problem that, quite often, symbolic computation cannot be made to relate more to reality. The range of application of knowledge remains on the symbolic level. Understanding that symbols stand for world domains, onto which knowledge can also be applied, lies beyond the scope of the individual. However, the range of application of knowledge can be enlarged if the learner receives support in establishing links from the symbol-level to reality. Greeno and Kintsch reveal the possibilities of simulations which clarify the connections which prevail between the symbolic level and reality.

A second, more general constructivist conception has been developed by Bransford, et al. (e.g., Bransford, Goldman, & Vye. 1990; Bransford, Vye, Kinzer, & Risko, 1990; Cognition and Technology Group, 1990, 1991). This approach emphasizes the relevance of "conditionalized knowledge". This conception resembles the notion of range of application developed above. According to these researchers, the transfer problem is one of inert knowledge. Instructional strategies for the development of flexibly applicable knowledge would include the following:

- Situating learning in order to relate knowledge to action, to create a significant and problem-oriented context, to initiate active engagements, and to support understanding;
- Emphasizing application contexts in order to define both potential and non-potential application contexts;
- Examining the subject matter from multiple points of view in order to effect more flexible knowledge and knowledge access;
- Decontextualizing in order to include different examples, to bridge domains, and to foster abstraction.

The concept of "anchored instruction" presents the learner with authentic problem contexts which define a range of application. Videodisc technology provides the anchors to reality. Knowledge which is necessary for solving problems can be retrieved within the video-based learning environment (even if the knowledge is, in part, implicit and hidden) and can be included in the learner's construction process. This supports reconstruction (transfer) in real situations. Multiple perspectives serve the purpose of enlarging the range of application to which the learner is exposed. Additionally, pairwise learning environments permit application of knowledge beyond the limits of a respective domain. Multiple perspectives and multiple contexts systematically enlarge the range of application of the knowledge.

Some of these principles are also evident in the third instructional approach, "cognitive apprenticeship" (Collins, Brown, & Newman, 1989). Studies on expert practice comprise the core of the theoretical foundation for cognitive apprenticeship. They reveal that experts, in their activities, always apply situated (or "contextualized") thinking strategies (Brown, 1990). In order for learners to develop applicable knowledge, Collins and his coworkers consider it necessary to learn in a situated contexts which incorporate the explicit cognitive processes (especially strategies and heuristics) externalized by experts with authentic application situations. First, the individual is offered applicable knowledge within specific situation. However, the objective of cognitive apprenticeship goes beyond the application of knowledge in one learning context. Situated learning takes place in successively sequenced learning environments of increasing complexity and diversity. The teacher or the expert models knowledge application cognitively (explicitly) within the respective situations. Another important feature is that the individual is encouraged to develop a global framework in which he or she can integrate situated experiences (Collins, 1990). The emphasis is on the applicability of knowledge to authentic problems in expert practice. In addition, the multiple applicability of knowledge for diverse application and problem situations is disclosed.

In addition to emphasizing different application contexts, the approach also varies the observational perspectives within learning situations. In this way it addresses, on the one hand, different views of problem aspects, and on the other hand, varying social perspectives through cooperation among experts and students. Similarly to the work of Bransford and his colleagues, cognitive apprenticeship enlarges the range of application of knowledge through multiple contexts and multiple perspectives. A difference between these approaches is that, in the Apprenticeship approach, the expert is assigned an important role of modeling further application relations. In this way, the expert defines and demonstrates examples for knowledge application.

The final approach, that of Spiro and coworkers, reveals important aspects of the development of flexibly applicable competence (Spiro, Feltovich, Coulson, & Anderson, 1989; Spiro & Jehng, 1990; Spiro, Feltovich, Jacobson, & Coulson, 1991). This approach is especially concerned with the advanced construction of knowledge within ill-structured knowledge domains. The problem addressed is that of learners who construct knowledge which they cannot apply to new problems. Additionally, learners develop oversimplified concepts which necessarily lead to incorrect applications. Spiro and coworkers emphasize the significance of complex problem contexts for fostering comprehension in the sense of construction. Central to the transfer aspect is the principle of "multiple juxtapositions of instructional content... revisiting the same material, at different times, in rearranged contexts, for different purposes, and from different conceptual perspectives" (Spiro et al., 1991, p. 28).

This principle systematically enlarges and specifies the range of application of knowledge in combination with the construction of knowledge structures.

To Sum Up

The instructional approaches discussed above all address the construction of knowledge that students can flexibly apply. Learning environments which assist the learner in developing widely applicable knowledge depend on situated learning, where the "context of use" of knowledge is obvious for the student. These constructivist approaches allows individuals to first learn how to handle problems in specific contexts. The second goal in these approaches is to overcome narrow contextualization. This goal corresponds to the issue of transfer.

The notion proposed here – that of transfer as reconstruction – leads to a definition of contextualized knowledge which relates knowledge to a range of application. The crucial point for the flexible application of knowledge from this position is the psychological extension of the range of application. Learning implies the construction of knowledge connected with a range of application. On the basis of this theoretical position we have discussed recent instructional approaches in the constructivist framework. Constructivist principles for the design of learning environments which foster the development of flexibly applicable knowledge can be interpreted in terms of a theory of application range. More important, however, are the theoretical implications of the concept of application range. It suggests that we reflect on, and reformulate, our theoretical ideas of the constructive learning process and of contextualized representation systems.

References

Adams, M. J. (1989). Thinking skills curricula: Their promise and progress. *Educational Psychologist, 24,* 25-77.

Agre, P. E. & Chapman, D. (1987). Pengi: An implementation of a theory of activity. *American Association for Artificial Intelligence.*

Anderson, J. R. (1983). *The architecture of cognition.* Cambridge, MA: Harvard University Press.

Anderson, J. R. (1987). Skill acquisition: Compilation of weak-method problem solutions. *Psychological Review, 94*, 192-210.

Anderson, J. R., Greeno, J. G., Kline, P. J. & Neves, D. N. (1981). Acquisition of problem-solving skill. In J. R. Anderson (Ed.), *Cognitive skills and their acquisition.* Hillsdale, NJ: Lawrence Erlbaum Associates.

Bednar, A. K., Cunningham, D., Duffy, T. M. & Perry, J. D. (1991). Theory into praxis -- how do we link? In G. J. Anglin (Ed.), *Instructional technology: Past, present and future.* Englewood: Libraries Unlimited.

Bransford, J. D., Arbitman-Smith, R., Stein, B. S. & Vye, N. J. (1985). Improving, thinking and learning skills. In S. F. Chipman & R. Glaser (Eds.), *Thinking and learning skills. Vol. 1: Relating Instruction to research.* Hillsdale, N J: Lawrence Erlbaum Associates.

Bransford, J. D., Franks, J. D., Vye, N. J. & Sherwood, R. D. (1989). New approaches to learning and instruction: Because wisdom can't be told. In S. Vosniadou & A. Ortony (Eds.), *Similarity and analogical reasoning.* Cambridge: Cambridge University Press.

Bransford, J. D., Goldman, S. R. & Vye, N. J. (in press). Making a difference in people's abilities to think: Reflections on a decade of work and some hopes for the future. In R. J. Sternberg & L. Okagaki (Eds.), *Influences on children.*

Bransford, J. D., Sherwood, R. D., Hasselbring, T. S., Kinzer. C. K. & Williams, S. M. (1990). Anchored instruction: Why we need it and how technology can help. In D. Nix & R. Spiro (Eds.), *Cognition, education, and multimedia: Exploring ideas in high technology.* Hillsdale, NJ: Lawrence Erlbaum Associates.

Bransford, J. D., Vye, N. J., Adams, L. T., & Perfetto, G. A. (1989). Learning skills and the acquisition of knowledge. In A. M. Lesgold & R. Glaser (Eds.), *Foundations for a psychology of education.* Hillsdale, NJ: Lawrence Erlbaum Associates.

Bransford, J. D., Vye, N., Kinzer, C., & Risko, V. (1990). Teaching thinking and content knowledge: Toward an integrated approach. In B. F. Jones & L. Idol (Eds.), *Dimensions of thinking and cognitive instruction.* Hillsdale, NJ: Erlbaum.

Brown, J. S. (1990). Toward a new epistemology for learning. In C. Frasson & J. Gauthier (Eds.), *Intelligent tutoring systems: At the crossroad of AI and education.* Norwood, NJ: Ablex.

Brown, J. S., Collins, A. & Duguid, P. (1989). Situated cognition and the culture of learning. *Educational Researcher, 18,* 32-42.

Bruner, J. S. (1964). The course of cognitive growth. *American Psychologist, 19,* 1-15.

Caramazza, A., McCloskey, M., & Green, B. (1981). Naive beliefs in "sophisticated" subjects: Misconceptions about trajectories of objects. *Cognition, 2,* 117-123.

Carnap, R.(1956). *Meaning and necessity.* Chicago: Phoenix.

Cognition and Technology Group at Vanderbilt (1990). Anchored instruction and its relationship to situated cognition. *Educational Researcher, 19,* 2-10.

Cognition and Technology Group at Vanderbilt (1991). Technology and the design of generative learning environments. *Educational Technology, 31,* 34-40.

Collins, A., Brown, J. S. & Newman, S. E. (1989). Cognitive apprenticeship: Teaching the crafts of reading, writing, and mathematics. In L. B. Resnick (Ed.), *Knowing, learning, and instruction.* Hillsdale, NJ: Lawrence Erlbaum Associates.

Collins, A. (1990). *Generalizing from situated knowledge to robust understanding.* Paper presented at the Annual Meeting of the American Educational Research Association, Boston, April 16-20.

Duffy, T. M. & Jonassen, D. H. (1991). Constructivism: New implications for instructional technology? *Educational Technology, 31*, (5), 7-12.

Duncker, K. (1935). *Zur Psychologie des produktiven Denkens.* Berlin: Springer-Verlag.

Eco, U. (1977). *Zeichen. Einführung in einen Begriff und seine Geschichte.* Frankfurt: Suhrkamp.

Fortmüller, R. (1991). *Der Einfluß des Lernens auf die Bewältigung von Problemen. Eine kognitionspsychologische Analyse des Problembereichs "Lerntransfer".* Wien: Manz.

Gick, M. L, & Holyoak, K. J. (1980). Analogical problem solving. *Cognitive Psychology, 12*, 306-355.

Greeno, J. G.(1989). Situations, mental models, and generative knowledge. In D. Klahr & K. Kotovsky (Eds.), *Complex information processing. The impact of H. A. Simon.* Hillsdale, NJ: Lawrence Erlbaum Associates.

Kintsch, W. (1991). A theory of discourse comprehension: Implications for a tutor for word algebra problems. In M. Carretero, M. Pope, R. J. Simons & J. I. Pozo (Eds.), *Learning and instruction. European research in an international context. Vol. 3.* Oxford: Pergamon Press.

Lave, J. (1988). *Cognition in practice: Mind, mathematics and culture in everyday life.* Cambridge, U.K.: Cambridge University Press.

Messner, H. (1978). *Wissen und Anwenden. Zur Problematik des Transfers im Unterricht.* Stuttgart: Klett-Cotta.

Pea, R. D. (1991). Augmenting the discourse of learning with computer-based learning environments. In E. De Corte, M.C. Linn, H. Mandl & L. Verschaffel (Eds.), *Computer-based learning environments and problem solving.* (NATO/ASI Series F, Vol. 84) Berlin: Springer-Verlag.

Resnick, L. B. (1989). Introduction. In L. B. Resnick (Ed.), *Knowing, learning, and instruction.* Hillsdale, NJ: Lawrence Erlbaum Associates.

Resnick, L. B. (1991). *Award for distinguished contributions to educational research 1990.* Recipient address (cassette recording). Washington, D. C.: American Educational Research Association.

Schoenfeld, A. H. (1983). Problem solving in the mathematics curriculum: A report, recommendations and an annotated bibliography. *The Mathematical Association of America,* MAA Notes, No. 1.

Schoenfeld, A. H. (1985). *Mathematical problem solving.* New York: Academic Press.

Scribner, S. (1984). Studying working intelligence. In B. Rogoff & J. Lave (Eds.), *Everyday cognition.* Cambridge, MA: Harvard University Press.

Sigel, I. (1970). The distancing hypothesis: A causal hypothesis for the acquisition of representational thought. In M. R. Jones (Ed.), *Effects of early experience.* Coral Gables: University of Miami Press.

Simon, H. A. (1980).Problem solving and education. In D. T. Tuma & R. Reif (Eds.), *Problem solving and education: Issues in teaching and research.* Hillsdale, NJ: Lawrence Erlbaum Associates.

Singley, M. K. & Anderson, J. R. (1989). *The transfer of cognitive skill.* Cambridge, U.K.: Cambridge University Press.

Spiro, R. J., Feltovich, P. J., Coulson, R. L. & Anderson, D. K. (1989). Multiple analogies for complex concepts: Antidotes for analogy-induced misconceptions in advanced knowledge acquisition. In S. Vosniadou & A. Ortony (Eds.), *Similarity and analogical reasoning.* Cambridge, U.K.: Cambridge University Press.

Spiro, R. J., Feltovich, P. J., Jacobson, M. J. & Coulson, R. L. (1991). Cognitive flexibility, constructivism and hypertext: Random access instruction for advanced knowledge acquisition in ill-structured domains. *Educational Technology, 31,* 24-33.

Spiro, R. J. & Jehng, J. C. (1990). Cognitive flexibility theory and hypertext: Theory and technology for the nonlinear and multidimensional traversal of complex subject matter. In D. Nix & R. Spiro (Eds.), *Cognition, education and multimedia.* Hillsdale, NJ: Lawrence Erlbaum Associates.

Sternberg, R. J. & Frensch, P. A. (1990). Mechanisms of transfer. In D. K. Detterman & R. J. Sternberg (Eds.), *Transfer critical: Intelligence, cognition, and instruction.* Norwood, NJ: Ablex.

Voss, J. F. (1987). Learning and transfer in subject-matter learning: A problem solving model. *International Journal of Educational Research, 11,* 607-622.

Whitehead, A.N. (1929). *The aims of education.* New York: Macmillan.

Wittgenstein, L. (1971). *Philosophische Untersuchungen.* Frankfurt: Suhrkamp.

16 Academic Understanding and Contexts to Enhance It: A Perspective from Research on Student Learning

Noel Entwistle, Abigail Entwistle, and Hilary Tait

Centre for Research on Learning and Instruction, University of Edinburgh, Scotland

The theme of this volume is *The Design of Constructivist Learning Environments*. To begin, we need to explore why we might need such environments in education, and then to identify research findings which might guide the establishment of such environments. Nancy Cole (1990) has recently criticized schooling in the USA for overemphasizing the acquistion of knowledge and basic skills to the detriment of higher-order skills and advanced knowledge. She comments:

> *Students can repeat science facts and principles, but in explanations of events, they fail to use them. They also fail to use them in new, relevant, problem situations. ... Conceptions of educational achievement - how we view and characterize achievement - affect what teachers teach and how they teach it. ... Present conceptions of educational achievement as basic skills and facts tend to focus attention on the short-term goals of schooling. ... We must have conceptions ... that help us attend to the long-term goals (with) some flavour of the higher-order skills and advanced knowledge. ... We have under-emphasized (both) the associative uses of schooling (increasing the web of associations students have) and the interpretive uses (translation of ideas, giving meanings). (pp. 2, 4, 6)*

The idea of a *constructivist* learning environment has been taken from a growing body of literature which emphasizes that knowledge and understanding has to be reconstructed within the cognitive structure of the individual learner. The concept has been further extended to introduce the idea of *situated cognition* (Greeno, 1988; Brown, Collins & Duguid, 1989) in which the components of the mental construction are drawn from the social environment, as well from the knowledge and prior experience of the learner. An allied idea from artificial intelligence is that of *connectionism*, which has been introduced to provide a model of the learner which moves away from the rule-bound image of most current work in AI, to envisage knowledge residing in the web of interconnections which make up cognitive structure (Bereiter, 1991). These new ideas both imply that instructional methods designed simply to pass on knowledge as separate, decontextualized pieces of information miss the whole essence of the ways in which knowledge is constructed and understanding developed.

However, it is important not to locate implications for instructional design solely within this new generation of cognitive theory. It is essential to keep an appropriate historical perspective, which sees a continuing tradition from both philosophers and psychologists to avoid the narrow mechanistic view of human learning espoused by another powerful tradition of theorists. In psychology, an early view of constructivism in problem-solving can be seen in the work of Kohler (1925) with apes, while aspects of Piaget's work were clearly constructivist. Take, for example, the following extract from *Genetic Epsistemology* .

> *To my way of thinking, knowing an object does not mean copying it - it means acting upon it. ... It means constructing systems of transformations that correspond, more or less adequately, to reality... The transformational structures of which knowledge consists are not copies of the transformations in reality ; they are simply possible isomorphic models among which experience can enable us to choose. Knowledge, then, is a system of transformations that become progressively (more) adequate (Piaget, 1971, p.15)*

Barlett's (1932) work on the way narratives are reconstructed in memory, and George Kelly's (1955) theory of personal constructs show the continuing strength of the constructivist tradition. Applications of constructivism in education can be seen most clearly in the work of Bruner (1974) and Ausubel (Ausubel, Novak & Hanesian, 1978). Philosophical ideas stressing the need to provide for the holistic education of the individual stem at least from Rousseau, and the child-centred pedagogies (Friedlander, 1975) all suggest teaching methods which are consonant with suggestions now being derived from current constructivist ideas. Current ideas on constructivism should not be located just in the most recent formulations from cognitive psychology, but should be considered alongside the theories and implications coming from a family of related theories which will serve to establish the essential meaning of constructivism, and its implications for education, in a truly constructivist way.

This chapter presents a form of constructivism which has been developed within a specific research area - student learning in higher education. Although the original concepts emerged from interview and questionnnaire surveys in universities, they have subsequently informed thinking about school education as well (Entwistle, 1987a). The influential ideas of Ference Marton in Gothenburg underpin this research area (Marton & Saljo, 1976, 1984). It was his research team in the mid-1970's which challenged the incrementalist view of knowledge widely accepted in cognitive psychology at that time. He pointed out that academic learning could be understood only in terms of the student developing understanding through relating new ideas to previous knowledge in an active process which depended crucially on both the specific content being learned and on the context in which that learning took place. Since Marton's pioneering work, a whole series of concepts and relationships has been described which has led to implications for teaching and learning in higher education (Marton, Hounsell & Entwistle, 1984). This research has a particular strength in that the concepts derive directly from students' descriptions of their own learning experiences, and so tend to be expressed within a set of concepts and categories immediately communicable to teachers and students alike. It has also identified contextual influences on the quality of learning outcomes, and so can be used to suggest ways of designing learning environments to enhance one form of constructivism - conceptual understanding - within academic courses. By considering these ideas and their implications, alongside those derived more directly from the emerging forms of constructivism within cognitive psychology, more firmly based conclusions should be possible.

Descriptions of Student Learning

Methodology

Before presenting a survey of the concepts and findings emerging from research on student learning, the research methodology on which it is based needs to be introduced. This is necessary because the methodology does not conform to the tradition of experimental work so commonly used within cognitive psychology. Although some of the studies have investigated the effects of interventions on student learning, it is rare to find research designs which fully conform to the 'experimental paradigm'. The research designs more commonly found in this research area are surveys using Likert-type inventories and, increasingly, qualitative studies based on interviews with students and staff. The reasons for the use of surveys can be found in the origins of the researchers who did most of the early work on student learning: they came from education departments and drew from the psychology of individual differences. The more recent work has concentrated more on interviews, drawing from the experiential and phenomenological traditions. In Gothenburg, innovative methodological work led to the development of rigorous analytic techniques to identify concepts and categories within interview transcripts (Marton, 1981; Marton & Saljo, 1984). The essence of this work has been to use either naturalistic experiments (Marton & Saljo, 1984) or interviews concerned with the everyday context of teaching and learning in higher education (Entwistle & Ramsden, 1983). There has been some interplay between the survey and interview methodologies, with concepts from the qualitative studies being operationalized within inventories (Entwistle, Hanley & Hounsell, 1979), and the findings from multivariate analyses being explored further within interviews (Ramsden, 1981; Meyer, 1991).

Concepts Describing Student Learning

The application of these alternating methodologies has led to distinctive concepts and categories which have now become widely used in the literature of higher education in Europe and Australasia. These may be best presented, not in historical order, but in order of generality. The concepts tend to be broader than those typically used by cognitive psychologists, and so lack precision. Yet they are strongly situated within a social context, and so present a 'recognisable reality' (Parlett & Hamilton, 1972) to those involved in higher education. They gain in communicability, acceptability and 'pedagogical fertility' (Entwistle, 1991b) what they lack in precision. The idea of intentionality in academic learning runs through most of these concepts, and it is coupled with a recognition that intention has to be seen in relation to the full social and educational setting within which learning takes place.

Intention can be seen most broadly within the reasons students give for taking a particular course. This has been described as their *educational orientation.* From interviews with students, Taylor (1983) distinguished between three main orientations (*vocational, academic,* and *personal)* each of which showed a distinctive type of interest in the course (*extrinsic* or *intrinsic*). These categories are shown in Table 1. The different educational orientations describe the aims students report as they embark on higher education courses, and they also help to explain not only the *amount* of effort they subequently put into the course, but also the *kind* of effort, as we shall see.

Orientation	*Aims*
Vocational	
Extrinsic	Obtaining a qualification of recognized worth
Intrinsic	Effective and relevant training for career
Academic	
Extrinsic	Progressing further up the academic ladder
Intrinsic	Pursuing the subject for its own sake
Personal	
Extrinsic	Compensating for past failures
Intrinsic	Broadening horizons and providing challenges

Table 1: Categories of Educational Orientations (adapted from Taylor, 1983)

Students also come into higher education with different beliefs about what learning itself actually involves. In an interview study by Saljo (1979), adults from a wide range of ages and educational backgrounds were asked to explain what they meant by 'learning'. Their descriptions showed a hierarchy of *conceptions of learning* with a systematic progression in both sophistication and complexity (Saljo, 1979). A revised and extended form of the hierarchy (Marton, Dall'Alba & Beaty, 1992) is shown in Table 2.

Saljo found that many people who had attended school only to the minimum leaving age saw learning in incremental terms, as indeed many psychologists have done. Learning, to

A. Increasing one's knowledge B. Memorizing and reproducing C. Applying facts and procedures	*Reproducing*
D. Understanding E. Seeing something in a different way F. Changing as a person	*Transforming*

Table 2: Conceptions of Learning (from Beaty, Dall'Alba, & Marton, 1990)

them, involved a process of accumulating bits of knowledge, like bricks in a wall. This view seems to be reinforced by traditional forms of education which overemphasize the acquisition of facts and procedures, as Cole (1990) has been arguing, and also by the quiz shows on television which publicize and reward the same kind of incremental, decontextualized knowledge. Closely allied to this simplest conception, is the idea that learning depends on memorizing what has to be learned. But to be useful, information eventually has to be applied in some way, and this recognition leads to a third conception. However, this simple application of incremental knowledge must be carefully distinguished from the more complex applications of knowledge which become possible on the basis of conceptual understanding.

All these first three conceptions imply that information is presented to learners whose task is seen as *reproducing* information on demand, effectively in the same form as it was originally learned. This is not unreasonable when facts are being learned, but understanding depends on *transforming* the knowledge presented, by relating it to what is already known and making sense of it in personal terms. The more sophisticated conceptions stress that learners have to be active in making sense of the material and, in the process, the cognitive structure may change in ways which not only transform understanding, but may also cause fundamental shifts in values, which imply changing as a person. The three conceptions of learning as transforming knowledge can be seen to be at the heart of constructivist and humanistic psychologies as applied to education.

Implicit in the hierarchy of conceptions of learning is developmental change. Acceptance of the idea of learning as tranforming knowledge was more likely to be found among adults who had experienced higher education. Perry (1970) described an explicitly developmental sequence for students at Harvard, which showed how they progressed from *dualism* - the belief that 'right' and 'wrong' answers exist and are taught - to *relativistic reasoning* . Towards the end of their degree course, Perry found that students had begun to appreciate the uncertainities involved in describing aspects of everyday reality and then gradually developed a commitment to individually constructed interpretations based on evidence and analytic thinking. Perry's work also reminds us that the construction of relativistic conceptions of the world is not something which even students entering Harvard are able to do without considerable intellectual effort and occasional emotional blocks.

These initial broadly based concepts have identified major differences among individual students which affect their learning. When students are asked to carry out an academic task, like preparing for a tutorial or writing an essay, the way in which they tackle that task depends on why they are taking the course (their orientation to education) and on what they believe learning requires of them (their conception of learning). This means that when they think about how to tackle the task, different students may have very different *intentions* and *perceptions of the task requirements*. And those intentions and perceptions have proved to be closely related both to learning processes and strategies and to the quality of the learning outcomes achieved.

Research on this topic was carried out initially by Ference Marton and his colleagues in Gothenburg (Marton & Saljo, 1976, 1984; Svensson, 1984). From interviews with students who had been asked to read an academic article and to be " ready to answers questions on it afterwards", they distinguished between *deep* and *surface approaches to learning* which depended on the students' intention when tackling the task. Some students intended simply to spot facts likely to form questions, and then to memorize them; in other words they focused on the suface level of the text. Other students intended to understand what the author was saying, and so looked more deeply for the underlying meaning, and sought to integrate the components. The characteristics of these contrasting approaches are summarized below in Table 3.

It has been established that the adoption of a deep approach is a critical influence on the level of understanding reached (Marton & Saljo, 1976; Entwistle, Hanley & Ratcliffe, 1979). And in a recent study of first-year students taking a physics course, Prosser and Millar (1989) showed that only students who had used a deep approach in their learning developed the more sophisticated, technical conceptions required by the lecturers. Students relying on surface approaches were left with inadequate conceptions, which would create increasing problems for them as they progressed through the course. Conceptual understanding was traditionally emphasized as one of the main aims of higher education, as the outcome of the critical, analytic thinking which academics require of their students (Entwistle, 1984). Nowadays, it would be endorsed by cognitive theorists as well, because of the greater flexibility it allows in applying the knowledge to novel contexts or to problem-solving (Greeno & Riley, 1987). In terms of current constructivist theory, the deep approach can be seen as a necessary, but not sufficient, condition for the type of learning now being encouraged. The deep approach describes what a student has to do in order to achieve a thorough conceptual understanding, while constructivist learning environments emphasize the importance of 'real world' examples and applications. Nevertheless, encouraging a deep approach is an important first step.

Deep Approach Intention to understand material for oneself Interacting vigorously and critically with content Relating ideas to previous knowledge / experience Organizing ideas within integrating frameworks Relating evidence to conclusions Examining the logic of the argument
Surface Approach Intention simply to reproduce parts of the content Accepting ideas and information passively Concentrating only on assessment requirements Not reflecting on purpose or strategies in learning Memorizing facts and procedures routinely Failing to recognize guiding principles or patterns

Table 3: Defining features of approaches to learning (adapted from Marton et al., 1984, and Entwistle & Ramsden, 1983)

When the research on approaches to learning was extended from the naturalistic experiment to everyday studying, it became clear that the influence of assessment requirements had also to be taken into account in describing how students learn and study. In the everyday context, an additional approach was identified which related to studying (Entwistle & Ramsden, 1983) - *strategic* - and also a more loosely defined set of *study pathologies* covering a general lack of motivation and purpose related to studying, associated with disorganized study methods, ease of distraction, inability to concentrate, and negative attitudes towards the courses taken. The strategic approach describes well-organized and conscientious study methods linked to achievement motivation, and the determination to do really well in the courses taken (Entwistle, 1988). Another important aspect of the strategic approach is the way the student relates studying to the assessment requirements in a manipulative, even cynical, manner. As a politics student explained:

> *I play the examination game. The examiners play it too. ... The technique involves knowing what is going to be in the exam and how it's going to be marked. You can acquire these techniques from sitting in the lecturer's class, getting ideas from his point of view, the form of the notes, and the books he has written - and this is separate to picking up the actual work content. (Miller & Parlett, 1974)*

It is important to note, in this extract, the existence of what seem to be two separate focuses of attention - one on the content and the other on what is likely to pay off in assessment terms. This suggests a tension in the student's mind between learning the subject and passing the examination, with rather different strategies being used for each.

The operationalization of the concepts describing approaches to learning and studying through the development of self-report inventories (Biggs, 1978; Entwistle, Hanley & Hounsell, 1979) confirmed the existence of three separable factors which could be identified as deep, surface and strategic approaches. These studies went on to show that each approach was associated with a distinctive form of motivation (Biggs, 1987; Entwistle, 1988). The surface approach was associated with anxiety and fear of failure, and to some extent with vocational motives, while a deep approach was consistently linked with academic interest in the subject for its own sake, and with self-confidence.

Although these forms of motivation are characteristics of the learner, interest and self-confidence, or boredom and anxiety, are also the products of experiences within higher education. Increasingly, the main thrust of this research has turned towards the effects of the learning environment on learning processes and outcomes.

Influences of the Learning Environment on Approaches to Learning

To lead on to a more general review of the influences of the learning environment on the quality of learning outcomes, a useful starting point is an inventory survey which looked at both approaches to studying and perceptions of courses across some 60 departments in British higher education (Entwistle & Ramsden, 1983). It was found that, irrespective of discipline and entry requirements, departments rated more highly by students in terms of 'good teaching' and allowing 'freedom in learning' contained a higher proportion of students with a deep approach to learning. In contrast, where the workload was perceived as 'heavy', more students were likely to adopt a surface approach. Subsequent interviews with students confirmed these effects and indicated which aspects of lecturing fostered the deep approach. The level at which the lectures are pitched has been shown to be particularly important for first-year students (Wall *et al., 1*991). At all stages, students have commented on the importance of the pace of presentation (to obtain good notes), and of the lecture structure. But perhaps the most influential in encouraging a deep approach in students has been a set of characteristics which reflect lecturing style - the quality of the explanations provided (striking examples and concrete illustrations), interest and enthusiasm shown for the material taught, and empathy with the students (being friendly and anticipating potential difficulties) (Entwistle & Ramsden, 1983; Hodgson, 1984).

Interviews, and experiments using inventories, have demonstrated the very strong influence on students' learning strategies of the assessment procedures encountered (Entwistle & Ramsden, 1983). Short-answer or multiple-choice questions, requiring mainly factual recall, tend to push students towards a surface approach, while essay questions are more likely to encourage a deep approach (Thomas, 1986). And more recently, over-loaded curricula and lack of perceived relevance have been shown to induce surface approaches (Entwistle *et al.*, 1989). Moreover, handouts which 'spoon-feed' predigested information may inhibit deep approaches (Mahmoud, 1989).

Besides the influence of teaching methods and assessment procedures, it is important not to lose sight of the importance of the student's own study skills in influencing the quality of learning. In the past, most higher education institutions have assumed that obtaining the necessary entry qualifications will guarantee adequate study skills. In both the USA and Europe, this expectation has proved false for at least some entering students, and attempts are being made to provide additional training, particularly for students with weak entry qualifications and for minority students (Meyer, 1991). The provision of appropriate, and timely, study skills advice depends on identifying students at risk. The use of inventories linked to specific forms of study skills support has proved effective, where the advice encourages the students to become more active in monitoring their own strategies (Weinstein, 1988), and also more aware of the opportunities for effective learning provided within their learning environment (Meyer, 1991). But for all students the balance between self-regulation and course regulation has a profound influence on the extent to which students are likely to adopt deep, active approaches to learning, as Robert-Jan Simons explains (this volume).

Table 4 summarizes these findings and also indicates the student characteristics which also influence the approach to learning adopted. It is important to recognize that the approach adopted depends on an *interaction* between the student and the learning environment.

Perceptions of the Learning Environment

There is an apparent paradox within the relationship between approach and context. The use of inventory methods of assessing approaches to learning implies a stability in the dimensions identified, and yet the influences of the instructional environment suggest variability. The study by Thomas (1986) helped to resolve that paradox. While the changes in the assessment procedures affected the balance between deep and surface approaches for all students, the *relative* strength of these approaches remained consistent. Thus, relative stability of approach can be maintained, while accepting the clear effects of the learning environment.

Student Characteristics	*Departmental Influences*
	Deep Approach
Previous knowledge of topics	Matching content to previous knowledge
Perceived relevance of subject matter	Good teaching (seen in lectures as) - level, pace, structure, explanation, enthusiasm and empathy
Intrinsic interest in the subject	Opportunities for individual choice
Study skills	Study skills training and support
	Surface Approach
Fear of failure	Short-answer and multiple-choice questions
Anxiety	Heavy workload and overloaded curricula
Reliance on memorizing	Spoon-feeding through handouts
Extrinsic motivation	Lack of relevance or choice

Table 4: Influences on approaches to learning. (adapted from Entwistle, 1987b, 1991a,b)

Although this consistent effect of context on approach was reported in relation to assessment procedures, other aspects of the learning environment seem to have much less general effects. They are mediated by the students' own characteristics - in particular, their previous educational experience, their ability, and their expectations and intentions in relation to the courses they are taking. The use of a course perceptions questionnaire indicated that there were relationships with approaches to learning, as we have seen. But Meyer (1988) pointed out that close relationships should not be expected if students perceived their environment in ways which depended on their own individual characteristics. Subsequent research has strongly confirmed the existence of what Meyer (1991) has termed *study orchestrations* - that is characteristic patterns of response on inventories which link together approaches to learning with perceptions of the learning environment.

An example of these associations comes from another recent study in Edinburgh in which 153 first-year psychology students completed an inventory which contained questions about their orientations to education (Taylor, 1983), approaches to learning and studying, and their preferences for differing types of teaching, assessment, and courses. These preferences described aspects of the learning environment expected to encourage either deep or surface approaches. Maximum likelihood factor analysis was used to explore the patterns of relationship between the scores on the dimensions covered by the inventory. The most interpretable solution involved the extraction of four factors which explained 50% of the variance. After oblique rotation, the factor structure produced the loadings shown in Table 5, with intercorrelations between factors being all less than 0.2.

The patterns establish very clearly the connections between approaches to learning and, on the one hand, intrinsic orientations to education and, on the other, preferences for differing learning environments. Students indicating that they were adopting a deep approach without associated strategic study practices (Factor III) had entered higher education with intrinsic orientations, had positive attitudes, and preferred teaching which challenged them to develop their own ideas independently. In contrast, students who had a surface approach to learning (Factor II), showed associated fear of failure and study pathologies. They also indicated that they preferred methods of teaching which would allow them to carry out rote learning with a minimum of effort. Such methods of teaching are, in fact, ones which would be criticized by educationists intent on designing more effective instructional environments, and so imply a potential problem in creating situations which might prove too demanding for many students. It must be kept in mind that students vary considerably in the extent to which they are ready to put in the intense intellectual effort required to develop the broader and deeper forms of understanding. The findings also serve to warn administrators against the too ready acceptance of student ratings of teaching in higher education. Students seem to be using quite different criteria of effectiveness when filling in feedback questionnaires (Entwistle & Tait, 1990).

Besides the link between surface approaches and preferences for what might be summarized as 'spoon-feeding', recent studies have also shown that the study orchestrations of many of the students who fail their first-year examinations can be described as 'disorganized'. Whereas the whole year group of students show the expected patterns linking approaches to learning and perceptions of, or preferences for, equivalent learning environments, failing students produce factor structures which are incoherent and, on occasions, virtually uninterpretable (Meyer, 1991; Meyer & Dunne, 1991; Entwistle, Meyer & Tait, 1991). Another form of analysis - unfolding analysis - has been used to demonstrate, in three-dimensional space, the way in which the pattern of relationships among these variables disappears among failing students (Meyer, Parsons & Dunne, 1990). Such 'disintegrated' patterns may indicate that some students are unable within their learning environment to recognize, let alone use in an effective way, the resources they need to carry out their preferred approaches to learning. There is now accumulating evidence, however, that such students may be helped to see the necessary connections, and so alter their study orchestrations, by individual counselling (Parsons & Meyer, 1990; Meyer, 1991).

The Experience of Understanding

To understand more fully how the everyday learning environment in higher education comes to affect the quality of student learning, it is worth looking in some detail at a recent exploratory study carried out in Edinburgh. One of the declared aims of higher education is the development of conceptual understanding (see Entwistle, 1984), and in the British system that understanding has been tested at the end of the degree course by requiring students to sit a series of some six three hour examinations over a period of some ten days.

Inventory Scale *Factor*	*Factor Loadings* I	II	III	IV
Approaches to Learning and Studying				
Deep approach	44		42	
Strategic approach	86			
Surface approach		83		
Study pathologies		45		
Effort put into studying	89			
Time spent on studying	76			
Fear of failure		59		
Negative attitudes			- 45	
Preferences for Learning Environment				
Deep approach encouraged in				
- lectures			33	
- examinations		- 34	52	
- courses			69	
Surface approach encouraged in				
- lectures		38		
- examinations		53		
- courses		56		
Orientations to Education				
Intrinsic - Vocational		47		
- Academic			68	
- Personal			47	
Extrinsic - Vocational				46
- Academic				71
- Personal				53
Drifted into higher education			53	
Percentage of variance explained by factor	13	12	9	6

Table 5: Factor structure matrix for orientations to education, approaches to learning, and preferences for contrasting learning environments

Traditionally, each examination requires students to write three one-hour essays designed to assess the conceptual understanding of the course or discipline, and performance on those examinations, together with course-work and dissertation marks, will determine the class of degree awarded. Usually, students in their final year finish classes in March, and use the following ten weeks or so to revise their notes in preparation for 'finals'. The period immediately after those examinations thus offers an ideal opportunity to ask students to reflect on their experiences of revision, and in so doing to explore the influences of the examination on the quality of the conceptual understanding developed. That was the purpose of this recent exploratory study (Entwistle & Entwistle, 1991), which also provides an illustration of the type of qualitative research used to derive descriptive categories in research on student learning.

Method

Students who had recently completed their final examinations in two British universities (mainly in psychology, but also in zoology and medicine) were invited to take part in interviews to discuss their revision strategies. The semi-structured interviews began by asking the students to describe how they had revised for these examinations, but then went on to explore other aspects of the experience of developing understanding. Interviews with 13 students, most lasting an hour or more, were transcribed in full, and these data were supplemented by written responses from a further 11 students. Analyses concentrated on identifying categories which described the main areas of comment by students within each theme included in the interviews. Transcripts were read and reread repeatedly to identify the types of comment which recurred across the sample. Provisional categories were then revised iteratively until the minimum number of distinct categories needed to cover the most salient issues was established (see Marton & Saljo, 1984). After identifying the main categories which described the experience of understanding, the development of understanding, and the individual forms of understanding developed, the influences of teaching and assessment were also explored. Here only the last two areas are described.

Forms of Understanding

The categories identified in the analyses of the interview transcripts, and which were considered to be relevant to the purposes of the volume, are listed in Table 6 below. In the full report (Entwistle & Entwistle, 1991, 1992), each category is defined partly by a descriptive summary covering the whole range of comments made by students, and partly by a set of extracts from the interview transcripts, chosen to bring out the meaning of the category within the specific academic context to which they apply. Here, only a few extracts from the interviews can be used as illustrations of the type of comments from which the categories were derived.

When asked about their experiences of understanding, students talked about feeling confident both to provide a convincing explanation and to adapt ideas flexibly for use in varying and in novel contexts. It was these characteristics which students believed, most

General Aspects of Understanding
Active engagement with the task
Relating to previous knowledge and experience
Using or developing a structure
Confidence about explaining
Flexibility in adapting and applying
Individual Differences in Understanding
Breadth of understanding
Depth of understanding
Source and nature of structures
- from lectures or books
- through own structure in revision notes
- from theories
- from an individual conception of the discipline

Table 6: Aspects of understanding (adapted from Entwistle & Entwistle, 1991)

clearly distinguished 'understanding' from 'knowledge'. A constructivist view of understanding was particularly apparent in many of their comments on the nature of understanding - for example.:

> *If I don't understand, it's just everything floating about and you can't quite get everything into place - like jigsaw pieces, you know, suddenly connect and you can see the whole picture... But there is always the feeling you can add more and more and more. ... It is as though one's mind has finally 'locked in' to the pattern. Concepts seem to fit together in a meaningful way, when before the connections did not seem clear, or appropriate, or complete.*

The feeling of confidence which came with understanding was repeatedly mentioned. Students felt ready to explain what they had understood to someone else. In general terms, an explanation can be seen as a reconstruction of understanding to serve a particular purpose. It seems unlikely that 'understanding', as such, is represented in memory. Rather, information and ideas have come to be related, and there is also some memory of the way in which those elements have been brought together in the past, perhaps acting in a similar way to a 'script' (Schank & Abelson, 1977). In constructing an explanation, we should not expect understanding to be demonstrated the same way on each occasion, although a 'family resemblance' would be expected through the control of the 'script'. The explanation is ultimately context specific: it depends on who asks the question, the social context in which it is asked, and what is thought to be required for a convincing answer.

In developing their understanding, students described an *active engagement* with the material being learned, involving internal debates about the new material and its meaning, or discussions with friends. The internal debates took the form of *relating to previous knowledge or personal experience*, and using that familar knowledge or experience to make sense of the new information. Difficulty in understanding was attributed to a lack of recognisable structure in what was being learned. Where this problem arose, students relied on *working out a structure* for themselves through which they could then make sense of the material. To do this, students talked about going back to first principles, or looking over notes from a previous year which they had understood and then extending the structure to encompass the new material.

When it came to describing how they went about their own studying and revision, however, substantial differences emerged in what different students meant by, or accepted as, 'understanding'. The first distinction was in terms of *breadth*. Several students recognized that the word 'understanding' was being used in different ways. It might refer to recognizing the meaning of a technical term, following a lecturer's explanation, a research article, or a textbook chapter, grasping what lies behind an essay title and how to tackle it, seeing how different lectures or different courses fit together, or appreciating the philosophical and methodological traditions underlying the discipline as a whole.

These different usages of the term seem to represent a hierarchy which indicates increasing complexity and inclusiveness, with the progression from one level to the next placing additional demands on students. The different usages also imply different experiences and processes involved in understanding. The narrower forms of understanding often required no conscious effort; they were simply 'absorbed' while reading or attending lectures - perhaps 'comprehension' is a better term to describe this process. Tackling, and eventually understanding a difficult new topic, required an active process of analysing and relating, which culminated in an 'aha' experience. Understanding the discipline was perhaps never consciously sought, and came only slowly after long periods of reflection about various aspects of the subject. It certainly led to feelings of pleasure, but these were less sure or definite than those associated with mastering difficult topics. No students relied on just comprehension, but there were wide differences in the extent to which students were prepared to extend their understanding to the point where they were able to make connections across courses in mapping out the discipline as a whole.

Understanding was recognized as being a temporary achievement - 'provisional wholeness'. Understanding was thus judged in terms of what was needed at a particular time and for a particular purpose - which led to the idea of *depth of understanding*, which can be seen to involve both the amount of relevant detail brought together and the strength of the interconnectedness among the component parts. Students generally recognized the importance of increasing the depth of their understanding, but differed in the extent to which they were ready to do this, or felt that it was required of them for the purposes of the examination.

Students generally used, or developed, structures within which knowledge became meaningful, but *the source and nature of the structure* was variable. Some students relied heavily on the 'external' structures provided in lectures or books. Others were more active in discovering organizing principles for themselves. The ability to construct appropriate frameworks for personal understanding is what Svensson (1977, 1984) has referred to as 'skill in learning', and seems to be essential for the development of broad conceptual understanding. It was the structures used by students which differentiated most clearly between students, but the form of these structures also depended on both the breadth and the depth of the understanding being sought.

The contrasting intentions underlying the 'approaches to learning' identified in the Gothenburg research (Marton & Saljo, 1984) could be seen clearly, but the dichotomous distinction between intentions to understand (deep approach), or to reproduce (surface approach), was too limited to cover the range of comments found in our interviews. As with 'conceptions of learning' (Saljo, 1979), a hierarchy of variations was found in the extent to which students engaged in a transformation of knowledge, through the process of creating personally meaningful structures of ideas and evidence. The variations depended not just on the individual, but also on the particular circumstances under which understanding was required. In the present interviews, the anticipated examination requirements had a substantial influence on the type of understanding being sought by a student.

The patterns identified in the students' responses have been described as *forms of understanding*. They represent distinctive combinations of breadth, depth and structure used by the students in developing their understanding, both in the original learning process and during revision (Entwistle & Entwistle, 1992). It must be stressed that the way these forms of understanding have been described here is specific to the particular context within which understanding was being sought - *preparing to meet the perceived examination requirements*. It is also important to recognize that the descriptions are used as *analytic categories* only. They do not describe individuals; rather they indicate the form of understanding reached on a particular occasion, or for a specific topic. Different forms of understanding of topics coexist in the same student. Five analytic categories, shown in Table 7, proved adequate to cover the range of comments made by students, although the first of these, which is close to the original description of a 'surface' approach, was found only in retrospective comments on work carried out at earlier stages of the course.

In the first two of these categories, understanding is largely limited to grasping the material presented directly by the lecturer and through required reading. Students in these categories

A.	Reproducing content from lecture notes without a clear structure
B.	Reproducing content and logical framework from lecture notes
C.	Using own structure for individual topics, mainly from lecture notes
D.	Adjusting structures from strategic reading to meet exam requirements
E.	Developing an individual conception of the discipline from wide reading

Table 7: Forms of Understanding

(medical students in particular) were concerned with remembering facts, procedures, and details.

One thing I do is, at the beginning of every course, I read the past papers on the day I start the course, and ... get orientated towards the exams... Well, medicine is different, I think, from other subjects in that because it's not contentious, the facts you have to learn, there's no debates, you just have to learn them... Sometimes, I would ... get up at 5 am and read a few subjects the morning before and use (that, and pass), which is a scandal considering some people will have been working on it for weeks. But then I would forget it very quickly after the exam, which isn't much good for the patients in the future, but ...

The second category introduces the use of a structure, but only an *external* one readily available in lecture notes or in books. In revision, this form of understanding involves a concentration on rote learning parts of the notes in two ways - firstly, by remembering the structure of the lecturer's explanation, which could then be used as the structure for their own examination answer and, secondly, by rote learning the details to fill out the answer. Of course, all students used the lecturer's structure and the rote learning of details to some extent, but here it is a more dominant activity.

The third form of understanding showed a reduced reliance on memorizing, and introduced an element of reorganization of the material by creating an individual framework of understanding to structure answers to past examination questions. These predetermined structures were intended to be used in the final examinations, but they created inflexibility in answering the questions set.

Sometimes I was lucky, when the question said (in) effect "Re-write your mind map in prose". ... But other times I had to make connections which weren't there in the first place, by extending them (as I went). ... By and large, those were worse essays than ... I would have written, had the question been more favourable.

The remaining two categories describe much broader and deeper forms of understanding. Students had sought additional information from a wide range of materials and were interested in developing a broad understanding not just of individual topics but of the course or discipline as a whole. Within the third category, students' comments described active attempts to develop their own understanding, and to represent that understanding within the structures of their revision notes. But they reflected a very strategic approach, both in revision strategies and in writing examination answers. As mentioned earlier, the strategic approach involves a focus of attention not just on the content, but also on the purposes for which that content is to be used within assessments. And in the examination itself, strategic students were aware of monitoring their process of writing to satisfy the examiner.

When you're revizing ... you're trying to convince yourself that you can convince the examiner. ... In an exam, ... you try and explain your ideas... You can't use all the information for a particular line of argument, and you don't need to; you only need to use what you think is going to convince the examiner. ... The more I have done exams, the more I'd liken them to a performance, like being on a stage; ... having not so much to present the fact that you know a vast amount, but having to perform well with what you do know. ... Sort of, playing to the gallery. ... I was very conscious of being outside what I was writing.

Comments from students in the final category again showed depth and breadth. There was an emphasis on trying to expand understanding of the subject by progressively broadening the links being established - from topic to course, and then to the discipline as a whole. Depth was added to breadth by active contructivist processes - reading widely, asking questions, and seeking to make sense of evidence and theories across different contexts. In this way, a personal conception of the discipline might also be developed. In this category, there was a less powerful controlling influence from the perceived requirements of the examination: it was even suggested that being strategic in revision would be a form of cheating. Revision usually involved the creation of condensed notes both to check understanding and to learn details, but the emphasis on the broad form of understanding meant that facts were learned within a personal interpretative framework. Being less bound by the structure originally provided by the lecturer, much greater flexibility was possible in tailoring examination answers to the precise question set. But the strength of feeling about demonstrating understanding fully, also led to difficulties in the examination itself.

Well, there were cases where I knew too much ... and I would spend half the essay giving the background and showing what I understood... I had to go through all the stages of working through (the topic) and showing that I had understood it. I couldn't gloss over the surface. And once I started writing, it all just 'welled up'. I felt that I couldn't interrupt the argument half-way as it was developing.

I: Why did you feel you had to do that?

Basically, the way it ties together as a whole - it's very difficult to pick something like that apart, when you understand the theory like that. Half an understanding doesn't make sense!

I: Are you saying that you have to explain it in the way you understand it for yourself?

Yes... It's essential to demonstrate your understanding of the whole, and its implications and limitations.

I: Might that insistence affect your exam marks?

You could say I shouldn't be (doing) that in an exam, but basically I have to do it that way, because that's me.

In these contrasting forms of understanding can be seen direct parallels with the hierarchy of conceptions of learning described earlier (Marton *et al.*, 1992) and with the developmental sequence identified by Perry (1970). It is also clear that, to some extent, the particular forms of understanding that an individual student chooses to rely on is a function of their intentions as a student, in other words their educational orientation (Taylor, 1983). But the relative prevalence of the different forms is also a product of the assessment procedures.

Influences of Examinations

Perhaps the most worrying features of the findings were, firstly, the way in which the examination distorted the efforts of the students to achieve personal understanding and, secondly, the limited extent to which some types of examination question actually tapped conceptual understanding. Moreover, students who had been developing a broadly based personal understanding of the discipline were forced into rather trivial learning activities for several weeks before they felt confident about being able to provide satisfactory examination answers. As one student said:

After I'd been reading all the books for three or four weeks after the Easter holidays, I understood things perfectly well... But I knew that understanding (like that) wouldn't help me in the exam. When you're under pressure, you've got to remember things quickly and get the facts down. ... I could discuss books with people, but if it actually came to an exam and writing an essay, I would have been hopeless. So, I took my lecture notes and actually memorized them, not verbatim, but memorized the themes and the questions that were brought up at each point.

The influence of question structure and format on examination answers has been demonstrated already (Pollitt *et al.*, 1985). It is possible to adapt the difficulty level of a question by controlling the balance between openness and inbuilt support within it. Here, we see how the questions not only affected the ability of students to answer them effectively, but also how, in anticipation, they influenced the form of understanding which students were seeking. Some of the questions set in the final examinations did seem to demand, and so to encourage, no more than a fairly narrow form of understanding. Where questions were also presented in a way which matched the original structure of the lecture notes, they could be answered perfectly well by students who had revised simply by learning the structures in their original lecture notes. Broader questions, or those where the wording required answers to be individually adapted to them, could be answered effectively only by the students who had developed a broader form of understanding. As many students look at previous years' papers quite early in the course, the type of questions set influence the form of understanding which students seek to develop. It might be said that students were, to varying degrees, developing understanding which was situated in the perceived requirements of the examination questions, rather than in the discipline or profession, thus restricting the likelihood of ready knowledge transfer into the world outside.

Influences of Teaching

There seemed to be a general appreciation of lectures which provided a clear structure to guide further reading, and some students found that, without the lecture and its overview, they found difficulty in coping with the books. The importance of well-structured lectures does seem to present a potential paradox, however. Lecturers who give clear, well-structured lectures provide students with sets of notes which can be used directly in that form, for revision and in answering examination questions. Students may not need to work on them, in order to transform them into a personally intelligible form. Where the lectures were disorganized, on the other hand, students talked about having to reorganize them in order to make sense of what the lecturer was saying. It might be thought, therefore, that disorganized lectures would encourage deeper understanding. In practice, although students were content to leave well-structured notes in their original form, the students adopting a fully deep approach used them as a platform for doing their own reading and thinking, which led them towards broader and deeper forms of personal understanding.

There was also evidence that some structures provided by lecturers interfered with the type of structure which students were trying to develop for themselves. For example, pre-clinical courses were presented within a logical structure determined by a scientific analysis of the individual disciplines, while students might be more concerned with situating their understanding within a framework required by the doctor in a clinical, professional setting.

> *I found it very difficult to actually study something like 'head injury' without relating it to my own personal knowledge of clinical situations, and to have that real life basis to it. ... I tackle it from what would happen if somebody came into hospital with head injury. What would you do? What scans would you give ? ... Ask a series of questions, and through that then we could build up an argument. And we talked to people who were doing houseman jobs in head injury wards. I think it is ludicrous to teach something like 'head injury' ... without having that clinical basis, because (then)*

you (remember) what you are learning as a series of disconnected facts ... (just) a very efficient way to pass an exam.

This extract is particularly interesting in extending the idea of the form of understanding being situated in the academic context rather than in the professional setting towards which the training is directed. The form of understanding evoked by a convention pre-clinical lecture course can be contrasted with the form of understanding encouraged by the hypertext environment described by Rand Spiro. There, repeated passes through case studies linked to relevant conceptual descriptions firmly situate understanding in the clinical setting.

The analyses of the interviews, as a whole, have highlighted both the constructivist nature of understanding itself, and the influence that the context has on the forms of understanding which students seek. If we are to encourage in students the active and deep approaches to learning which facilitate conceptual understanding, it will be necessary to map out more fully how the learning environment affects approaches to learning.

A Systems Approach to Teaching and Learning

This chapter has described the contribution of research on student learning in higher education to defining constructivist instructional environments. It has shown how deep, active approaches to learning lead to the conceptual understanding required for the effective transfer of knowledge to other contexts. It has also shown that the form of understanding developed is not just a product of the student's ability or intention, but is an interaction with aspects of the learning environment. Above all the type of teaching encountered together with the nature of the assessment procedure will affect the approach to, and the outcome of, learning. But other factors have been shown to be influential. It now seems essential to begin to examine learning environments as *systems,* each component of which may affect both approach and outcome (Entwistle, 1987b, 1991a,b; Biggs, 1991). Figure 1 presents a conceptual map of those components of the learning environment in higher education which have been shown to influence the quality of learning. It is used here to draw attention to the interaction between student characteristics, previous educational experience, and teacher and institutional characteristics.

The model places at the centre the active, deep approach to learning required for personal conceptual understanding and the ability to apply knowledge effectively. The top half of the diagram shows some of the main characteristics of the students which will affect the quality of their learning. Between the top and bottom halves, the dotted lines indicate the indirect effects which the learning environment has on students. The effects, as we have seen, depend on how students *perceive* the environment, and those perceptions derive from personal goals and motives, and how well prepared they are for the chosen course.

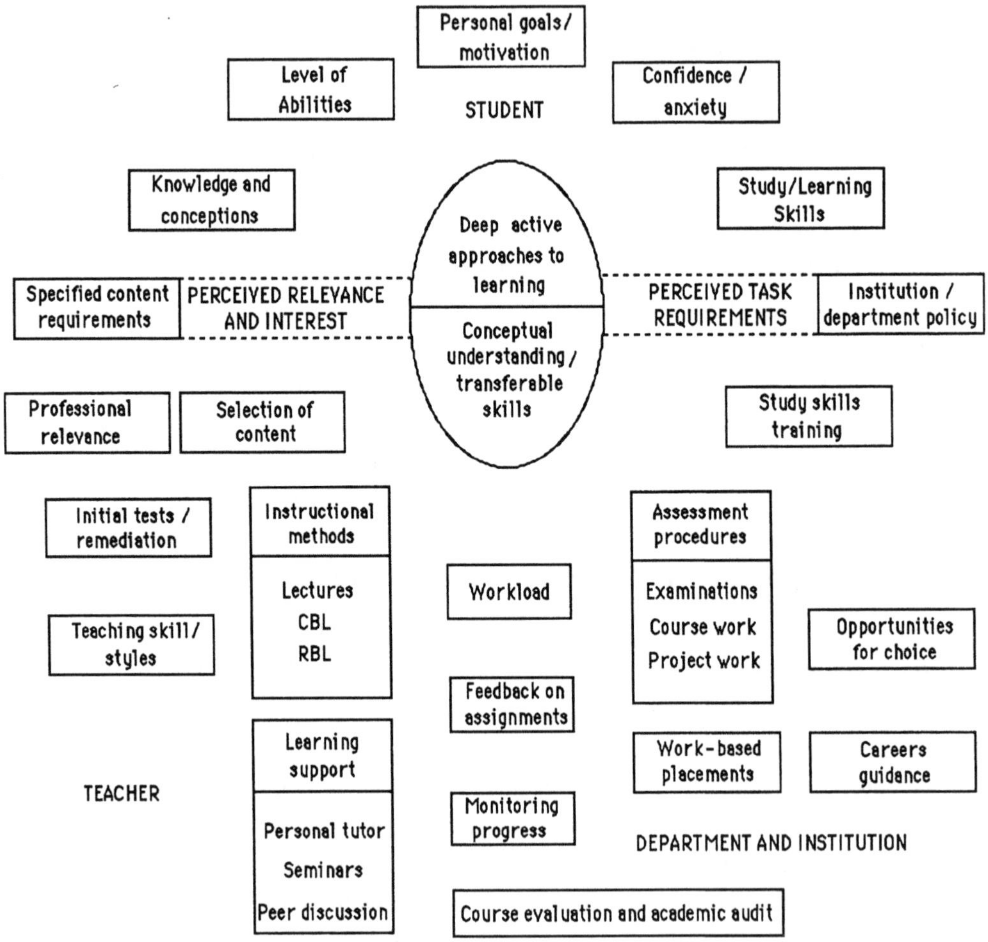

Figure 1: A conceptual model of a teaching-learning system in higher education

What an individual department can achieve is constrained by the institutional policies and also, to a varying extent, by the content requirements imposed by professional bodies or disciplinary conventions. These two broad restraining frameworks are indicated as boxes at either side of the model. The lower half of the model is divided into two, indicating, on the left, responsibility which lies more with the individual lecturer and, on the right, responsibility resting more with the department or the institution. The boxes represent a selection of the components which have been shown to influence the effectiveness of teaching and the quality of learning outcomes. As far as possible, the positioning of the boxes is intended to imply relationships both with adjacent boxes, and with those vertically above within the top half of the model. Thus, the selection of content, and the remedial materials which may be necessary, depend on the range of knowledge, conceptions, and ability of the entrants. Similarly, the assessment procedures are known to have a major effect on the level of confidence or anxiety of students, while the type of study skills training required depends on how well those skills are already developed. Other connections between adjacent boxes are self-evident, such as those between 'personal tutor' and 'monitoring progress'.

Presenting all these components together in this diagrammatic scheme is intended to remind departments that learning depends on the complementary interaction of many components. The model can be viewed as a heuristic device which would allow them to review their teaching provision against a background of research findings. An example of how such an appraisal might be carried out has been provided in a recent report from an Australian anatomy department. A thorough review of their learning environment, against criteria drawn from the research literature on student learning led to fundamental changes being introduced in lecturing, assessment, textbooks, and indeed the whole ethos of the department (Eizenburg, 1988).

Only through a greater awareness of the complex ways in which students and staff interact within the whole learning environment will it be possible to design instructional contexts which will fully support high quality learning. If this is true in conventional teaching and learning contexts, similar principles will also have to be considered wherever the newer techniques made possible by instructional technology are introduced into the teaching-learning system. While it may be possible to demonstrate the effectiveness of particular uses of IT within a controlled experimental setting, the only valid test of effectiveness will be where it has been integrated into an established curriculum. There is a tendency for innovations of any kind within higher education to create 'backwash effects' as students may, for example, spend more time on innovative learning materials and so create an imbalance in their studying, not to mention annoyance among colleagues (Mahmoud, 1989).

It will also be crucial to recognize two other conclusions which can be drawn from the research into student learning. The first conclusion is that assessment procedures have a profound effect on the way in which students learn. Providing a constructivist teaching environment will have little effect on the quality of learning while conventional assessment procedures remain in place. To encourage constructivism through imaginative learning material while retaining tests which demand factual recall would be absurd, as indeed would be the retention of conventional, objectivist evaluation techniques in judging the effectiveness of constructivist interventions. The principles of constructivism will have to be applied to the design of new forms of assessment, perhaps relying much more on self- and peer-assessment than in the past (Boud & Falchikov, 1989).

However, there are good reasons for believing that learning environments should not be entirely constructivist. The second conclusion from the research on student learning is that different students react quite differently to the same learning context. Therefore, uniform effects from the introduction of constructivist learning envionments should not be expected. Students who are content with accepting information will find the challenges of constructivism uncomfortable. The development of understanding may will require an *alternation* of complementary modes of thinking - the *holistic* and the *serialistic* (Pask, 1988). Information presented in a objectivist way by direct instruction can be restructured subsequently, if appropriate encouragement is provided within the learning environment. Roy Heath (1964) introduced the idea of a student who was a *reasonable adventurer*, whose thinking showed the alternation between two mental attitudes - the critical and the curious. Overemphasis on providing constructivist environments - at least in their extreme forms - might well deflect students from adopting an appropriate emphasis on logic and detail. At least, we shall have to recognize that constructivist techniques can run in parallel with more conventional approaches, and that for some purposes more direct instruction may still be the most effective.

It is interesting to see in the oppostion between objectivist and constructivist theorists the same polarity that is found in cognitive styles - the proponents of the strict 'scientific' approach and those who favour a more holist and intuitive approach to both teaching and research. In the same way that the *corpus callosum* links the cerebral hemispheres of the brain, so our instructional environments should encourage the versatile linking of both rigorous and imaginative thinking. Students and teachers alike have strong preferences for their own ways of thinking, but teachers have a professional responsibility to avoid teaching in too extreme a way.

> *It is argued that (there are) fundamental differences in ... our preferred ways of thinking. And that our approaches to teaching reflect previous experiences with learning. We teach as we prefer to learn. ... The creative tension between these opposite (ways of thinking and teaching) should not be destroyed by too readily accepting one extreme or the other. ... The alternation and tension between fundamental opposites is an essential part of education, as of life itself. ... It provides a challenge to teachers and students alike to ... create a new, and necessarily individual, synthesis of opposite styles of learning - the critical and the curious, the precise and the speculative, the logical and the imaginative...* (Entwistle, 1988b, pp.4, 272)

References

Ausubel, D.P., Novak, J.S., & Hanesian, H. (1978). *Educational psychology: A cognitive view*, New York: Holt, Rinehart, & Winston.

Bartlett, F.C. (1932). *Remembering: A study in experimental and social psychology.* Cambridge, England: The University Press.

Bereiter, C. (1991). Implications of connectionism for thinking about rules. *Educational Researcher, 20*, (3), 10-16

Biggs, J.B. (1978). Individual and group processes in study processes. *British Journal of Educational Psychology, 48*, 266-279.

Biggs, J.B. (1987). *Student approaches to learning and studying*. Melbourne: Australian Council for Educational Research.

Biggs, J.B. (in press). Teaching: Design for learning. *Higher Education Research and Development.*

Boud, D., & Falchikov, J.N. (1989). Quantitative studies of student self-assessment in higher education: a critical analysis of findings. *Higher Education, 18*, 529-549.

Brown, J.S., Collins, A., & Duguid, P. (1989). Situated cognition and the culture of learning. *Educational Researcher, 18*, 1, 32-42.

Bruner, J.S. (1974). *Beyond the information given.* London: George Allen & Unwin.

Cole, N. (1990). Conceptions of educational achievement. *Educational Researcher, 19*, 2-7.

Eizenburg, N. (1988). Approaches to learning anatomy: Developing a programme for preclinical medical students. In P. Ramsden (Ed.), *Improving learning: New perspectives.* London: Kogan Page.

Entwistle, A.C., & Entwistle, N.J. (in press). Experiences of understanding in revising for degree examinations. *Learning and Instruction, 2.*

Entwistle, N.J. (1984). Contrasting perspectives on learning. In F. Marton, D.J. Hounsell & N.J. Entwistle (Eds.), *The experience of learning*. Edinburgh: Scottish Academic Press.

Entwistle, N.J. (1987a). *Understanding classroom learning.* London: Hodder & Stoughton.

Entwistle, N.J. (1987b). A model of the teaching-learning process. In J.T.E. Richardson, M.W. Eysenck, & D. Warren Piper (Eds.), *Student learning: Research in education and cognitive psychology.* London: S.R.H.E./Open University Press.

Entwistle, N.J. (1988a). Motivational factors in students' approaches to learning. In R.R. Schmeck (Ed.), *Learning strategies and learning styles.* New York: Plenum.

Entwistle, N.J. (1988b). *Styles of learning and teaching.* London: David Fulton.

Entwistle, N.J. (1991a). How students learn and why they fail. In J. Radford (Ed.), *Talent, teaching and achievement.* London: Jessica Kingsley.

Entwistle, N.J. (1991b). *The impact of teaching on learning outcomes in higher education.* Literature review prepared for the Employment Department, Moorfoot, Sheffield.

Entwistle, N.J., & Entwistle, A.C. (in press). Developing, revising, and examining conceptual understanding: The student experience and its implications. *Higher education.*

Entwistle, N.J., Hanley, M., & Hounsell, D.J. (1979). Identifying distinctive approaches to studying, *Higher Education, 8*, 365-380.

Entwistle, N.J., Hanley, M., & Ratcliffe, G. (1979). Approaches to learning and levels of understanding. *British Educational Research Journal, 5*, 99-114.

Entwistle, N.J., Macaulay, C., Situnayake, G., &Tait, H. (1989). *The performance of electrical engineers in Scottish higher education.* University of Edinburgh: Centre for Research on Learning and Instruction.

Entwistle, N.J., Meyer, J.H.E., & Tait, H. (1991). Student failure: Disintegrated patterns of study strategies and perceptions of the learning environment. *Higher Education, 21,* 249-261.

Entwistle, N.J. & Ramsden, P. (1983). *Understanding student learning.* London: Croom Helm.

Entwistle, N.J. & Tait, H. (1990). Approaches to learning, evaluations of teaching, and preferences for contrasting academic environments. *Higher Education, 19,* 169-194.

Friedlander, B.Z. (1975). Some remarks on open education. *American Educational Research Journal, 12,* 465-468.

Greeno, J.G. (1988). *Situations, mental models, and generative knowledge.* IRL Report 88-0005. Palo Alto, Ca.: Insitute for Research on Learning.

Greeno, J.G., & Riley, M.S. (1987). Processes and development of understanding. In F.E.Weinert & R.H. Kluwe (Eds.), *Metacognition, motivation, and understanding.* Hillsdale, NJ: Lawrence Erlbaum Associates.

Heath, R. (1964). *The reasonable adventurer.* Pittsburgh: University of Pittsburgh Press.

Hodgson, V. (1984). Learning from lectures. In F. Marton, D.J. Hounsell & N.J. Entwistle (Eds.), *The experience of learning.* Edinburgh. Scottish Academic Press.

Kelly, G.A. (1955). *The psychology of personal constructs.* New York: W.W. Norton.

Kohler, W. (1925). *The mentality of apes.* New York: Harcourt Brace.

Mahmoud, M. (1989). Contrasting perceptions of an innovation in engineering education. *European Journal of the Psychology of Education, IV,* 453-468.

Marton, F. (1981). Phenomenography. *Instructional Science, 10,* 177-200.

Marton, F., Dall'Alba, G., & Beaty, E. (in press). Conceptions of learning. *International Journal of Educational Research.*

Marton, F., Hounsell, D.J. & Entwistle, N.J. (1984). (Eds.), *The experience of learning.* Edinburgh: Scottish Academic Press.

Marton, F., & Saljo, R. (1976). On qualitative differences in learning. I - Outcome and process. *British Journal of Educational Psychology, 46,* 4-11.

Marton, F., & Saljo, R. (1984). Approaches to learning. In F. Marton, D.J. Hounsell & N.J. Entwistle (Eds.), *The experience of learning.* Edinburgh: Scottish Academic Press.

Marton, F., & Svensson, L. (1979). Conceptions of research on student learning. *Higher Education, 8,* 471-486.

Meyer, J.H.E. (1988). Student perceptions of learning context and approaches to learning. *South African Journal of Higher Education, 2,* 73-82.

Meyer, J.H.E. (1991). Study orchestration: The manifestation, interpretation and consequences of contextualized approaches to studying. *Higher Education, 22,* 297-316.

Meyer, J.H.E., & Dunne, F.F. (in press). The study orchestration of nursing students: Effects of an extended clinical context. *Medical Education.*

Meyer, J.H.E, Parsons, P, & Dunne, F.F. (1990). Individual study orchestrations and their association with learning outcome. *Higher Education, 20,* 67-89.

Miller, C.M.L., & Parlett, M.R. (1974). *Up to the mark: A study of the examination game.* Guildford: Society for Research into Higher education.

Parlett, M.R., & Hamilton, D. (1972). Evaluation as illumination: A new approach to the study of innovatory programmes. Unpublished research report. (Reprinted in D. Hamilton *et al.* (1977) *Beyond the numbers game.* London: Macmillan)

Parsons, P., & Meyer, J.H.E. (1990). The academically 'at risk' student: A pilot intervention programme and its observed effects. *Higher Education, 20,* 323-334.

Pask, G. (1988). Learning strategies, teaching strategies and conceptual or learning style. In R.R. Schmeck (Ed.), *Learning styles and strategies.* New York: Plenum Press.

Perry, W.G. (1970). *Forms of intellectual and ethical development in the college years: A scheme.* New York: Holt, Rinehart & Winston.

Piaget, J. (1971). *Genetic epistemology.* New York: W.W. Norton.

Pollitt, A.B., Hutchinson, C., Entwistle, N.J., & de Luca, C. (1985). *What makes exam questions difficult?* Edinburgh: Scottish Academic Press.

Prosser, M., & Millar, R. (1989). The 'how' and 'what' of learning physics. *European Journal of the Psychology of Education, 4,* 513-528.

Ramsden, P. (1981). *A study of the relationship between student learning and its academic context.* Unpublished Ph.D. thesis, University of Lancaster.

Saljo, R. (1979). Learning in the learner's perspective. I - Some common-sense conceptions. *Reports from the Department of Education, University of Gothenburg.*

Schank, R.C. & Abelson, R.P. (1977). *Scripts, plans, goals, and understanding: Human 31 knowledge structures.* Hillsdale, NJ: Lawrence Erlbaum Associates.

Svensson, L. (1977). On qualitative differences in learning. III - Study skill and learning. *British Journal of Educational Psychology, 47,* 233-243.

Svensson, L. (1984). Skill in learning. In F. Marton, D.J. Hounsell, & N.J. Entwistle (Eds.), *The experience of learning.* Edinburgh: Scottish Academic Press.

Taylor, E. (1983). *Orientations to study: A longitudinal interview investigation of students in two human studies degree courses at Surrey University.* Unpublished Ph.D. thesis, University of Surrey.

Thomas, P. (1986). *The structures and stability of learning approaches.* Unpublished Ph.D. Thesis, University of Queensland, Australia.

Wall, D., Macaulay, C., Tait, H., Entwistle, D., & Entwistle, N.J. (1991). *The transition from school to higher education in Scotland.* University of Edinburgh: Centre for Research on Learning and Instruction.

Weinstein, C.E. (1988). Assessment and training of student learning strategies. In R.R. Schmeck (Ed.), *Learning strategies and learning styles.* New York: Plenum.

Subject and Author Index

NATO ASI Series F

Including Special Programmes on Sensory Systems for Robotic Control (ROB) and on Advanced Educational Technology (AET)

Vol. 1: Issues in Acoustic Signal - Image Processing and Recognition. Edited by C. H. Chen. VIII, 333 pages. 1983.

Vol. 2: Image Sequence Processing and Dynamic Scene Analysis. Edited by T. S. Huang. IX, 749 pages. 1983.

Vol. 3: Electronic Systems Effectiveness and Life Cycle Costing. Edited by J. K. Skwirzynski. XVII, 732 pages. 1983.

Vol. 4: Pictorial Data Analysis. Edited by R. M. Haralick. VIII, 468 pages. 1983.

Vol. 5: International Calibration Study of Traffic Conflict Techniques. Edited by E. Asmussen. VII, 229 pages. 1984.

Vol. 6: Information Technology and the Computer Network. Edited by K. G. Beauchamp. VIII, 271 pages. 1984.

Vol. 7: High-Speed Computation. Edited by J. S. Kowalik. IX, 441 pages. 1984.

Vol. 8: Program Transformation and Programming Environments. Report on a Workshop directed by F. L. Bauer and H. Remus. Edited by P. Pepper. XIV, 378 pages. 1984.

Vol. 9: Computer Aided Analysis and Optimization of Mechanical System Dynamics. Edited by E. J. Haug. XXII, 700 pages. 1984.

Vol. 10: Simulation and Model-Based Methodologies: An Integrative View. Edited by T. I. Ören. B. P. Zeigler, M. S. Elzas. XIII, 651 pages. 1984.

Vol. 11: Robotics and Artificial Intelligence. Edited by M. Brady. L. A. Gerhardt, H. F. Davidson. XVII, 693 pages. 1984.

Vol. 12: Combinatorial Algorithms on Words. Edited by A. Apostolico, Z. Galil. VIII, 361 pages. 1985.

Vol. 13: Logics and Models of Concurrent Systems. Edited by K. R. Apt. VIII, 498 pages. 1985.

Vol. 14: Control Flow and Data Flow: Concepts of Distributed Programming. Edited by M. Broy. VIII, 525 pages. 1985.

Vol. 15: Computational Mathematical Programming. Edited by K. Schittkowski. VIII, 451 pages. 1985.

Vol. 16: New Systems and Architectures for Automatic Speech Recognition and Synthesis. Edited by R. De Mori, C.Y. Suen. XIII, 630 pages. 1985.

Vol. 17: Fundamental Algorithms for Computer Graphics. Edited by R. A. Earnshaw. XVI, 1042 pages. 1985.

Vol. 18: Computer Architectures for Spatially Distributed Data. Edited by H. Freeman and G. G. Pieroni. VIII, 391 pages. 1985.

Vol. 19: Pictorial Information Systems in Medicine. Edited by K. H. Höhne. XII, 525 pages. 1986.

Vol. 20: Disordered Systems and Biological Organization. Edited by E. Bienenstock, F. Fogelman Soulié, G. Weisbuch. XXI, 405 pages.1986

Vol. 21: Intelligent Decision Support in Process Environments. Edited by E. Hollnagel, G. Mancini, D. D. Woods. XV, 524 pages. 1986.

NATO ASI Series F

Including Special Programmes on Sensory Systems for Robotic Control (ROB) and on Advanced Educational Technology (AET)

Vol. 22: Software System Design Methods. The Challenge of Advanced Computing Technology. Edited by J. K. Skwirzynski. XIII, 747 pages. 1986.

Vol. 23: Designing Computer-Based Learning Materials. Edited by H. Weinstock and A. Bork. IX, 285 pages. 1986.

Vol. 24: Database Machines. Modern Trends and Applications. Edited by A. K. Sood and A. H. Qureshi. VIII, 570 pages. 1986.

Vol. 25: Pyramidal Systems for Computer Vision. Edited by V. Cantoni and S. Levialdi. VIII, 392 pages. 1986. *(ROB)*

Vol. 26: Modelling and Analysis in Arms Control. Edited by R. Avenhaus, R. K. Huber and J. D. Kettelle. VIII, 488 pages. 1986.

Vol. 27: Computer Aided Optimal Design: Structural and Mechanical Systems. Edited by C. A. Mota Soares. XIII, 1029 pages. 1987.

Vol. 28: Distributed Operating Systems. Theory und Practice. Edited by Y. Paker, J.-P. Banatre and M. Bozyiğit. X, 379 pages. 1987.

Vol. 29: Languages for Sensor-Based Control in Robotics. Edited by U. Rembold and K. Hörmann. IX, 625 pages. 1987. *(ROB)*

Vol. 30: Pattern Recognition Theory and Applications. Edited by P. A. Devijver and J. Kittler. XI, 543 pages. 1987.

Vol. 31: Decision Support Systems: Theory and Application. Edited bv C. W. Holsapple and A. B. Whinston. X, 500 pages. 1987.

Vol. 32: Information Systems: Failure Analysis. Edited by J. A. Wise and A. Debons. XV, 338 pages. 1987.

Vol. 33: Machine Intelligence and Knowledge Engineering for Robotic Applications. Edited by A. K. C. Wong and A. Pugh. XIV, 486 pages. 1987. *(ROB)*

Vol. 34: Modelling, Robustness and Sensitivity Reduction in Control Systems. Edited by R.F. Curtain. IX, 492 pages. 1987.

Vol. 35: Expert Judgment and Expert Systems. Edited by J. L. Mumpower, L. D. Phillips, O. Renn and V. R. R. Uppuluri. VIII, 361 pages. 1987.

Vol. 36: Logic of Programming and Calculi of Discrete Design. Edited by M. Broy. VII, 415 pages. 1987.

Vol. 37: Dynamics of Infinite Dimensional Systems. Edited by S.-N. Chow and J. K. Hale. IX. 514 pages. 1987.

Vol. 38: Flow Control of Congested Networks. Edited by A. R. Odoni, L. Bianco and G. Szegö. XII, 355 pages. 1987.

Vol. 39: Mathematics and Computer Science in Medical Imaging. Edited by M. A. Viergever and A. Todd-Pokropek. VIII, 546 pages. 1988.

Vol. 40: Theoretical Foundations of Computer Graphics and CAD. Edited by R. A. Earnshaw. XX, 1246 pages. 1988.

Vol. 41: Neural Computers. Edited by R. Eckmiller and Ch. v. d. Malsburg. XIII, 566 pages. 1988.

NATO ASI Series F

Including Special Programmes on Sensory Systems for Robotic Control (ROB) and on Advanced Educational Technology (AET)

Vol. 42: Real-Time Object Measurement and Classification. Edited by A. K. Jain. VIII, 407 pages. 1988. *(ROB)*

Vol. 43: Sensors and Sensory Systems for Advanced Robots. Edited by P. Dario. XI, 597 pages. 1988. *(ROB)*

Vol. 44: Signal Processing and Pattern Recognition in Nondestructive Evaluation of Materials. Edited by C. H. Chen. VIII, 344 pages. 1988. *(ROB)*

Vol. 45: Syntactic and Structural Pattern Recognition. Edited by G. Ferraté, T. Pavlidis, A. Sanfeliu and H. Bunke. XVI, 467 pages. 1988. *(ROB)*

Vol. 46: Recent Advances in Speech Understanding and Dialog Systems. Edited by H. Niemann, M. Lang and G. Sagerer. X, 521 pages. 1988.

Vol. 47: Advanced Computing Concepts and Techniques in Control Engineering. Edited by M. J. Denham and A. J. Laub. XI, 518 pages. 1988.

Vol. 48: Mathematical Models for Decision Support. Edited by G. Mitra. IX, 762 pages. 1988.

Vol. 49: Computer Integrated Manufacturing. Edited by I. B. Turksen. VIII, 568 pages. 1988.

Vol. 50: CAD Based Programming for Sensory Robots. Edited by B. Ravani. IX, 565 pages. 1988. *(ROB)*

Vol. 51: Algorithms and Model Formulations in Mathematical Programming. Edited by S. W. Wallace. IX, 190 pages. 1989.

Vol. 52: Sensor Devices and Systems for Robotics. Edited by A. Casals. IX, 362 pages. 1989. *(ROB)*

Vol. 53: Advanced Information Technologies for Industrial Material Flow Systems. Edited by S. Y. Nof and C. L. Moodie. IX, 710 pages. 1989.

Vol. 54: A Reappraisal of the Efficiency of Financial Markets. Edited by R. M. C. Guimarães, B. G. Kingsman and S. J. Taylor. X, 804 pages. 1989.

Vol. 55: Constructive Methods in Computing Science. Edited by M. Broy. VII, 478 pages. 1989.

Vol. 56: Multiple Criteria Decision Making and Risk Analysis Using Microcomputers. Edited by B. Karpak and S. Zionts. VII, 399 pages. 1989.

Vol. 57: Kinematics and Dynamic Issues in Sensor Based Control. Edited by G. E. Taylor. XI, 456 pages. 1990. *(ROB)*

Vol. 58: Highly Redundant Sensing in Robotic Systems. Edited by J. T. Tou and J. G. Balchen. X, 322 pages. 1990. *(ROB)*

Vol. 59: Superconducting Electronics. Edited by H. Weinstock and M. Nisenoff. X, 441 pages. 1989.

Vol. 60: 3D Imaging in Medicine. Algorithms, Systems, Applications. Edited by K. H. Höhne, H. Fuchs and S. M. Pizer. IX, 460 pages. 1990.

Vol. 61: Knowledge, Data and Computer-Assisted Decisions. Edited by M. Schader and W. Gaul. VIII, 421 pages. 1990.

Vol. 62: Supercomputing. Edited by J. S. Kowalik. X, 425 pages. 1990.

Vol. 63: Traditional and Non-Traditional Robotic Sensors. Edited by T. C. Henderson. VIII, 468 pages. 1990. *(ROB)*

NATO ASI Series F

Including Special Programmes on Sensory Systems for Robotic Control (ROB) and on Advanced Educational Technology (AET)

Vol. 64: Sensory Robotics for the Handling of Limp Materials. Edited by P. M. Taylor. IX, 343 pages. 1990. *(ROB)*

Vol. 65: Mapping and Spatial Modelling for Navigation. Edited by L. F. Pau. VIII, 357 pages. 1990. *(ROB)*

Vol. 66: Sensor-Based Robots: Algorithms and Architectures. Edited by C. S. G. Lee. X, 285 pages. 1991. *(ROB)*

Vol. 67: Designing Hypermedia for Learning. Edited by D. H. Jonassen and H. Mandl. XXV, 457 pages. 1990. *(AET)*

Vol. 68: Neurocomputing. Algorithms, Architectures and Applications. Edited by F. Fogelman Soulié and J. Hérault. XI, 455 pages. 1990.

Vol. 69: Real-Time Integration Methods for Mechanical System Simulation. Edited by E. J. Haug and R. C. Deyo. VIII, 352 pages. 1991.

Vol. 70: Numerical Linear Algebra, Digital Signal Processing and Parallel Algorithms. Edited by G. H. Golub and P. Van Dooren. XIII, 729 pages. 1991.

Vol. 71: Expert Systems and Robotics. Edited by T. Jordanides and B.Torby. XII, 744 pages. 1991.

Vol. 72: High-Capacity Local and Metropolitan Area Networks. Architecture and Performance Issues. Edited by G. Pujolle. X, 536 pages. 1991.

Vol. 73: Automation and Systems Issues in Air Traffic Control. Edited by J. A. Wise, V. D. Hopkin and M. L. Smith. XIX, 594 pages. 1991.

Vol. 74: Picture Archiving and Communication Systems (PACS) in Medicine. Edited by H. K. Huang, O. Ratib, A. R. Bakker and G. Witte. XI, 438 pages. 1991.

Vol. 75: Speech Recognition and Understanding. Recent Advances, Trends and Applications. Edited by P. Laface and Renato De Mori. XI, 559 pages. 1991.

Vol. 76: Multimedia Interface Design in Education. Edited by A. D. N. Edwards and S. Holland. XIV, 216 pages. 1992. *(AET)*

Vol. 77: Computer Algorithms for Solving Linear Algebraic Equations. The State of the Art. Edited by E. Spedicato. VIII, 352 pages. 1991.

Vol. 78: Integrating Advanced Technology into Technology Education. Edited by M. Hacker, A. Gordon and M. de Vries. VIII, 185 pages. 1991. *(AET)*

Vol. 79: Logic, Algebra, and Computation. Edited by F. L. Bauer. VII, 485 pages. 1991.

Vol. 80: Intelligent Tutoring Systems for Foreign Language Learning. Edited by M. L. Swartz and M. Yazdani. IX, 347 pages. 1992. *(AET)*

Vol. 81: Cognitive Tools for Learning. Edited by P. A. M. Kommers, D. H. Jonassen and J. T. Mayes. X, 278 pages. 1992. *(AET)*

Vol. 82: Combinatorial Optimization. New Frontiers in Theory and Practice. Edited by M. Akgül, H. W. Hamacher and S. Tüfekçi. XI, 334 pages. 1992.

Vol. 83: Active Perception and Robot Vision. Edited by A. K. Sood and H. Wechsler. IX, 756 pages. 1992.

NATO ASI Series F

Including Special Programmes on Sensory Systems for Robotic Control (ROB) and on Advanced Educational Technology (AET)

Vol. 84: Computer-Based Learning Environments and Problem Solving. Edited by E. De Corte, M. C. Linn, H. Mandl and L. Verschaffel. XVI, 488 pages. 1992. *(AET)*

Vol. 85: Adaptive Learning Environments. Foundations and Frontiers. Edited by M. Jones and P. H. Winne. VIII, 408 pages. 1992. *(AET)*

Vol. 86: Intelligent Learning Environments and Knowledge Acquisition in Physics. Edited by A. Tiberghien and H. Mandl. VIII, 285 pages. 1992. *(AET)*

Vol. 87: Cognitive Modelling and Interactive Environments. With demo diskettes (Apple and IBM compatible). Edited by F. L. Engel, D. G. Bouwhuis, T. Bösser and G. d'Ydewalle. IX, 311 pages. 1992. *(AET)*

Vol. 88: Programming and Mathematical Method. Edited by M. Broy. VIII, 428 pages. 1992.

Vol. 89: Mathematical Problem Solving and New Information Technologies. Edited by J. P. Ponte, J. F. Matos, J. M. Matos and D. Fernandes. XV, 346 pages. 1992. *(AET)*

Vol. 90: Collaborative Learning Through Computer Conferencing. Edited by A. R. Kaye. X, 260 pages. 1992. *(AET)*

Vol. 91: New Directions for Intelligent Tutoring Systems. Edited by E. Costa. X, 296 pages. 1992. *(AET)*

Vol. 92: Hypermedia Courseware: Structures of Communication and Intelligent Help. Edited by A. Oliveira. X, 241 pages. 1992. *(AET)*

Vol. 93: Interactive Multimedia Learning Environments. Human Factors and Technical Considerations on Design Issues. Edited by M. Giardina. VIII, 254 pages. 1992. *(AET)*

Vol. 94: Logic and Algebra of Specification. Edited by F. L. Bauer, W. Brauer and H. Schwichtenberg. 1993.

Vol. 95: Comprehensive Systems Design: A New Educational Technology. Edited by C. M. Reigeluth, B. H. Banathy and J. R. Olson. 1993. *(AET)*

Vol. 96: New Directions in Educational Technology. Edited by E. Scanlon and T. O'Shea. VIII, 251 pages. 1992. *(AET)*

Vol. 97: Advanced Models of Cognition for Medical Training and Practice. Edited by D. A. Evans and V. L. Patel. XI, 372 pages. 1992. *(AET)*

Vol. 98: Medical Images: Formation, Handling and Evaluation. Edited by A. E. Todd-Pokropek and M. A. Viergever. IX, 700 pages. 1992.

Vol. 99: Multisensor Fusion for Computer Vision. Edited by J. K. Aggarwal. XI, 456 pages. 1993. *(ROB)*

Vol. 100: Communication from an Artificial Intelligence Perspective. Theoretical and Applied Issues. Edited by A. Ortony, J. Slack and O. Stock. XII, 260 pages. 1992.

Vol. 101: Recent Developments in Decision Support Systems. Edited by C. W. Holsapple and A. B. Whinston. XI, 618 pages. 1993.

Vol. 102: Robots and Biological Systems: Towards a New Bionics? Edited by P. Dario, G. Sandini and P. Aebischer. XII, 786 pages. 1993.

NATO ASI Series F

Including Special Programmes on Sensory Systems for Robotic Control (ROB) and on Advanced Educational Technology (AET)

Vol. 103: Parallel Computing on Distributed Memory Multiprocessors. Edited by F. Özgüner, F. Erçal. VIII, 332 pages. 1993.

Vol. 104: Instructional Models in Computer-Based Learning Environments. Edited by S. Dijkstra, H. P. M. Krammer, and J. J. G. van Merriënboer. X, 510 pages. 1993. *(AET)*

Vol. 105: Designing Environments for Constructive Learning. Edited by T. M. Duffy, J. Lowyck, and D. H. Jonassen. VIII, 374 pages. 1993. *(AET)*